Lecture Notes in Computer Science 2441

Edited by G. Goos, J. Hartmanis, and J. van Leeuwen

Springer

Berlin
Heidelberg
New York
Barcelona
Hong Kong
London
Milan
Paris
Tokyo

Zhenjiang Hu   Mario Rodríguez-Artalejo (Eds.)

Functional and Logic Programming

6th International Symposium, FLOPS 2002
Aizu, Japan, September 15-17, 2002
Proceedings

 Springer

Series Editors

Gerhard Goos, Karlsruhe University, Germany
Juris Hartmanis, Cornell University, NY, USA
Jan van Leeuwen, Utrecht University, The Netherlands

Volume Editors

Zhenjiang Hu
University of Tokyo
Department of Mathematical Informatics
Hongo 7-3-1, Bunkyo-Ku, Tokyo 113-8656, Japan
E-mail: hu@ipl.t.u-tokyo.ac.jp

Mario Rodríguez-Artalejo
Universidad Complutense de Madrid
Department of Informatic Languages and Systems
Av. Complutense s/n, 28040 Madrid, Spain
E-mail: mario@sip.ucm.es

Cataloging-in-Publication Data applied for

Die Deutsche Bibliothek - CIP-Einheitsaufnahme

Functional and logic programming : 6th international symposium ; proceedings
/ FLOPS 2002, Aizu, Japan, September 15 - 17, 2002. Zhenjiang Hu ; Mario
Rodríguez-Artalejo (ed.). - Berlin ; Heidelberg ; New York ; Barcelona ;
Hong Kong ; London ; Milan ; Paris ; Tokyo : Springer, 2002
  (Lecture notes in computer science ; Vol. 2441)
  ISBN 3-540-44233-2

CR Subject Classification (1998): D.1., D.1,6, D3, F.3, I.2.3

ISSN 0302-9743
ISBN 3-540-44233-2 Springer-Verlag Berlin Heidelberg New York

Springer-Verlag Berlin Heidelberg New York
a member of BertelsmannSpringer Science+Business Media GmbH

http://www.springer.de

© Springer-Verlag Berlin Heidelberg 2002
Printed in Germany

Typesetting: Camera-ready by author, data conversion by DA-TEX Gerd Blumenstein
Printed on acid-free paper   SPIN 10870960   06/3142   5 4 3 2 1 0

Preface

This volume contains the proceedings of the *Sixth Fuji International Symposium on Functional and Logic Programming* (FLOPS 2002), held in Aizu, Japan, September 15–17, 2002, hosted by the University of Aizu, and colocated with the First Asian Symposium on Partial Evaluation Semantics-Based Program Manipulation (ASIA-PEPM 2002), which was held on September 12–14.

FLOPS is a forum for research on all issues concerning functional programming and logic programming. In particular, it aims to stimulate the cross-fertilization as well as the integration of the two paradigms. The previous FLOPS meetings took place in Fuji-Susono (1995), Shonan (1996), Kyoto (1998), Tsukuba (1999), and Tokyo (2001). The proceedings of FLOPS '99 and FLOPS 2001 were published by Springer-Verlag as Lecture Notes in Computer Science, Vols. 1722 and 2024, respectively.

There were 27 submissions, and these came from Australia (1), Brazil (1), China (1), Denmark (2), Germany ($1\frac{1}{2}$), Italy (1), Japan (6), Korea (1), Portugal (2), Russia ($\frac{2}{3}$), Spain (6), Sweden (1), the UK ($2\frac{1}{3}$), and the USA ($\frac{1}{2}$). Each paper was reviewed by four reviewers. The program committee meeting was conducted electronically for a period of two weeks in May 2002. As a result of active discussions, 15 papers (55.55%) were selected for presentation, one of them to be delivered as a one-hour tutorial. In addition to the selected papers, this volume contains full papers by the three invited speakers, namely Kokichi Futatsugi, Peter Stuckey, and Philip Wadler.

On behalf of the program committee, the program chairs would like to thank the invited speakers who agreed to give talks and contribute papers, all those who submitted papers, and all the referees for their careful work in the reviewing and selection process. The support of our sponsors is also gratefully acknowledged. In addition to the University of Aizu and Universidad Complutense de Madrid, we are indebted to the Japan Society for Software Science and Technology (JSSST), Special Interest Group on Programming, and the Association for Logic Programming (ALP). Finally, we would like to thank the members of the local arrangements committee, notably Mizuhito Ogawa and Taro Suzuki, for their invaluable support throughout the preparation and organization of the symposium.

July 2002

Zhenjiang Hu
Mario Rodríguez-Artalejo

Symposium Organization

Program Chairs

Zhenjiang Hu   University of Tokyo, Japan
Mario Rodríguez-Artalejo   Universidad Complutense de Madrid, Spain

Program Committee

María Alpuente	Technical University of Valencia, Spain
Wei-Ngan Chin	National University of Singapore
Pierre Deransart	INRIA-Rocquencourt, France
Moreno Falaschi	University of Udine, Italy
Michael Hanus	University of Kiel, Germany
Jan Maluszynski	University of Linköping, Sweden
Aart Middeldorp	University of Tsukuba, Japan
Gopalan Nadathur	University of Minnesota, USA
Susumu Nishimura	Kyoto University, Japan
Catuscia Palamidessi	Pennsylvania State University, USA
Francesca Rossi	University of Padova, Italy
Harald Sondergaard	University of Melbourne, Australia
Kwangkeun Yi	KAIST, Korea
Kazunori Ueda	Waseda University, Japan

Local Arrangements Chair

Taro Suzuki   University of Aizu, Japan

List of Referees

The following referees helped the program committee in evaluating the papers. Their assistance is gratefully acknowledged.

Elvira Albert
Ola Angelsmark
Sergio Antoy
Guillaume Arnaud
Demis Ballis
Woongsik Choi
Manuel Clavel
Marco Comini
Bart Demoen
Wlodek Drabent
Hyun-joon Eo
Santiago Escobar
Gérard Ferrand
Robert Glück
Frédéric Goualard
Masahito Hasegawa
Hideya Iwasaki
Peter Jonsson
Pascual Julián
Hyun-goo Kang
Naoki Kobayashi
Ludovic Langevine
Francisco J. López-Fraguas
Salvador Lucas
Mircea Marin
Narciso Martí-Oliet
Frédéric Mesnard

Dale Miller
Yasuhiko Minamide
Claudio Mirolo
Eugenio Moggi
Angelo Montanari
Lee Naish
Susana Nieva
Ulf Nilsson
Mizuhito Ogawa
Fernando Orejas
Salvatore Orlando
Ricardo Peña
Carla Piazza
John Power
Femke van Raamsdonk
María José Ramírez
Chiaki Sakama
Tom Schrijvers
Clara Segura
Peter J. Stuckey
Kenjiro Taura
Germán Vidal
Marie-Catherine Vilarem
Fer-Jan de Vries
David Wolfram
Hongseok Yang
Y. L. Zhang

Table of Contents

Formal Methods in CafeOBJ

Kokichi Futatsugi

Chair of Language Design
Graduate School of Information Science
Japan Advanced Institute of Science and Technology
1-1 Asahidai, Tatsunokuchi, Ishikawa 923-1292, JAPAN
kokichi@jaist.ac.jp
www.jaist.ac.jp/~kokichi

Abstract. Formal methods are still expected to improve the practice of software engineering. The areas in which formal methods will play important roles include at least: (1) distributed component software, (2) network/system security, (3) embedded systems. Formal methods are better supported by formal specification languages equipped with formal verification capability.

CafeOBJ is a formal specification language equipped with verification methodologies based on algebraic specification technique. CafeOBJ is an executable wide spectrum language based on multiple logical foundations; mainly based on initial and hidden algebras. Static aspects of systems are specified in terms of initial algebras, and dynamic aspects of systems are specified in terms of hidden algebras.

CafeOBJ is the first algebraic specification language which incorporates observational (or behavioral) specifications based on hidden algebras in a serious way. Observational specifications in CafeOBJ can be seen as a nice combination of static and dynamic specifications, and facilitate natural and transparent specification and verification of complex systems.

This paper gives an overview of CafeOBJ language system and formal methods based on the language. Some parts of this paper are updated and modified versions of the parts of already published book or papers such as [10, 18, 3, 7].

1 Introduction

In almost every area of system/software development, we can find many kinds of notations, diagrams, and sort of languages which are used to write specifications. One of the most typical drawbacks of them is lack of semantics, and it is difficult or even impossible to reason about the specifications written in them. Formal specfication techniques are expected to improve this situation.

Algebraic specification technique is one of the most promising system modeling and specification techniques for a wide area of applications. Algebraic specification technique was introduced around 1975 as a method for modeling and specifying so called **abstract data types**[26, 27, 29]. The substantial research efforts were invested to the wide range of area from the basic algebraic semantics theory to many areas of applications[1, 8, 13, 10, 39, 12, 19].

Z. Hu and M. Rodríguez-Artalejo (Eds.): FLOPS 2002, LNCS 2441, pp. 1–20, 2002.

CafeOBJ is an **executable** algebraic specification language which is a modern successor of OBJ[9, 11, 28] and incorporating several most recent algebraic specification paradigms. Its definition is given in [3]. CafeOBJ is intended to be mainly used for system specifications, formal verification of the specifications, rapid prototyping. This section gives a brief presentation of its most important features.

1.1   Design Considerations for Formal Specification Language Systems

The basic design principles of any formal specification language systems should be as follows:

- Make the system which can be used by not only by researchers but also by motivated practitioners.
- Minimize the number of ideas which underlie the language system to make users have a transparent view.
- Modularize the components of environment as much as possible to increase flexibility, mainenability, and extensibility.

The following are a list of actions which should be taken following the above principles.

- Adopt a simple but powerful underlining logic.
- Provide languages which are powerful enough to write complex and big specificatios, and simple enough to have clear semantics based of the underlining logic.
- Provide effective methodologies which can guide users to construct specifications in well structured and easy to understand style.
- Provide libraries of specifications for each important application domains which can be used by users as collections of building blocks for constructing larger specifications.
- Provide checkers and/or provers which can be used to check and/or proof meaningful and necessary properties of specifications.
- Provide the clear interface protocols so that new tools can be incooperated into the environment in a consistent way. This not only makes it possible to coordinate tools in a unified fashion, but also makes it easy to incorporate newer tools into the environment.

The design of CafeOBJ language system is one answer for the design considerations listed above.

1.2   A Brief History of CafeOBJ Language

CafeOBJ is a direct successor of OBJ; one of the most famous formal specification languages.

The origins of OBJ can be traced back to Goguen's gradual realization, around 1970, that Lawvere's characterization of the natural numbers as a certain initial algebra [32] could be extended to other data structures of interest for Computing Science. The influence of Saunders Mac Lane was also important during that period, leading to the beginning of the famous ADJ group led by Goguen. During the ADJ group period, a mathematical theory of abstract data types as initial algebras was developed. Together with considering term rewriting as the computational side of abstract data types, this constitutes the pillar of the OBJ basic specifications level. It is important to mention that from the very beginning the design of OBJ had been emerging directly from clean and elegant mathematical theories, this process being (rather subtle) reflected as one of the main strength of the language.

Another major step in the development of OBJ was the relativization of algebraic specification over any logic due to Goguen and Burstall's **institutions** (categorical abstract model theory for specification and programming). This pushed the theory of algebraic specification into a modern age. At the beginning institutions provided support for developing advanced structuring specification techniques (i.e., module composition systems) independently of the actual formalism, as emerging from the research on Clear [1]. However, today, after nearly two decades, their significance has been widely expanded. For example, institutions support in an essential way the design of multi-paradigm (declarative) systems.

Following the vitally important idea of module composition of Clear, several attempts of implementing modularized algebraic specification languages were done including the early pioneering design and implementation of HISP language [8, 16, 17]. After these experiences, the stabilization of the OBJ design (and its most prominent implementation at SRI) started after the design and prototype implementation of OBJ2 at SRI in 1984 [9, 11]. It coincides with several attempts to extend OBJ towards other paradigms, most notably constraint logic programming [23], object-oriented programming [25], and generic theorem proving [40]. Although, all these attempts were successful, the interest of the OBJ community has been recently shifting towards a new generation of OBJ focusing more on the recent internal developments in algebraic specification rather than in integrating powerful paradigms from the outside world. Two such examples are CafeOBJ [18, 3, 14] and Maude [33, 34].

Many methodological works were done around OBJ and CafeOBJ . We refer here to [10] for a general account for understanding the potentiality of algebraic techniques in software engineering, to [13] for parameterized programming, to [37, 36] for communication protocol specifications, to [6, 15] for distributed system and/or object-oriented specifications. These works can be seen as a sort of precursor for the design and definition of CafeOBJ .

1.3 Important Features of CafeOBJ Language

The following are the most important features of the CafeOBJ language.

Equational Specification and Programming: This is inherited from OBJ [9, 11, 28] and constitutes the basis of the language, the other features being somehow built on top of it. As with OBJ, CafeOBJ is **executable** (by term rewriting), which gives an elegant declarative way of functional programming, often referred as **algebraic programming**.[1] As with OBJ, CafeOBJ also permits equational specification modulo several equational theories such as associativity, commutativity, identity, idempotence, and combinations between all these. This feature is reflected at the execution level by term rewriting **modulo** such equational theories.

Behavioral Specification: Behavioral specification [22, 4] provides a novel generalisation of ordinary algebraic specification. Behavioral specification characterises how objects (and systems) **behave**, not how they are implemented. This new form of abstraction can be very powerful in the specification and verification of software systems since it naturally embeds other useful paradigms such as concurrency, object-orientation, constraints, nondeterminism, etc. (see [22, 4] for details). Behavioral abstraction is achieved by using specification with hidden sorts and a behavioral concept of satisfaction based on the idea of indistinguishability of states that are observationally the same, which also generalises process algebra and transition systems.

CafeOBJ directly supports behavioral specification and its proof theory through special language constructs, such as

- hidden sorts (for states of systems),
- behavioral operations (for direct "actions" and "observations" on states of systems),
- behavioral coherence declarations for (non-behavioral) operations (which may be either derived (indirect) "observations" or "constructors" on states of systems), and
- behavioral axioms (stating behavioral satisfaction).

The advanced coinduction proof method receives support in CafeOBJ via a default (candidate) coinduction relation (denoted =*=). In CafeOBJ , coinduction can be used either in the classical HSA sense [22] for proving behavioral equivalence of states of objects, or for proving behavioral transitions (which appear when applying behavioral abstraction to RWL).

Besides language constructs, CafeOBJ supports behavioral specification and verification by several methodologies. CafeOBJ currently highlights a methodology for concurrent object composition which features high reusability not only of specification code but also of verifications [3, 30]. Behavioral specification in CafeOBJ may also be effectively used as an object-oriented (state-oriented) alternative for traditional data-oriented specifications. Experiments seem to indicate that an object-oriented style of specification even of basic data types (such as

---

[1] Although this paradigm may be used as programming, this aspect is still secondary to its specification side.

sets, lists, etc.) may lead to higher simplicity of code and drastic simplification of verification process [3].

Behavioral specification is reflected at the execution level by the concept of **behavioral rewriting** [3, 4] which refines ordinary rewriting with a condition ensuring the correctness of the use of behavioral equations in proving strict equalities.

Rewriting Logic Specification: Rewriting logic specification in CafeOBJ is based on a simplified version of Meseguer's **rewriting logic** [34] specification framework for concurrent systems which gives a non-trivial extension of traditional algebraic specification towards concurrency. RWL incorporates many different models of concurrency in a natural, simple, and elegant way, thus giving CafeOBJ a wide range of applications. Unlike Maude [33, 34], the current CafeOBJ design does not fully support **labelled** RWL which permits full reasoning about multiple transitions between states (or system configurations), but provides proof support for reasoning about the **existence** of transitions between states (or configurations) of concurrent systems via a built-in predicate (denoted ==>) with dynamic definition encoding both the proof theory of RWL and the user defined transitions (rules) into equational logic.

From a methodological perspective, CafeOBJ develops the use of RWL transitions for specifying and verifying the properties of **declarative encoding of algorithms** (see [3]) as well as for specifying and verifying transition systems.

Module System: The principles of the CafeOBJ module system are inherited from OBJ which builds on ideas first realized in the language Clear [1], most notably institutions [20]. CafeOBJ module system features

- several kinds of imports,
- sharing for multiple imports,
- parameterised programming allowing
  - multiple parameters,
  - views for parameter instantiation,
  - integration of CafeOBJ specifications with executable code in a lower level language
- module expressions.

However, the theory supporting the CafeOBJ module system represents an updating of the original Clear/OBJ concepts to the more sophisticated situation of multi-paradigm systems involving theory morphisms across institution embeddings [2], and the concrete design of the language revise the OBJ view on importation modes and parameters [3].

Type System and Partiality: CafeOBJ has a type system that allows subtypes based on **order sorted algebra** (abbreviated **OSA**) [24, 21]. This provides a mathematically rigorous form of runtime type checking and error handling, giving CafeOBJ a syntactic flexibility comparable to that of untyped languages, while preserving all the advantages of strong typing.

We decided to keep the concrete order sortedness formalism open at least at the level of the language definition. Instead we formulate some basic simple conditions which any concrete CafeOBJ order sorted formalism should obey. These conditions come close to Meseguer's OSA^R [35] which is a revised version of other versions of order sortedness existing in the literature, most notably Goguen's OSA [21].

CafeOBJ does not directly do partial operations but rather handles them by using error sorts and a sort membership predicate in the style of **membership equational logic** (abbreviated **MEL**) [35]. The semantics of specifications with partial operations is given by MEL.

Logical Semantics: CafeOBJ is a declarative language with firm mathematical and logical foundations in the same way as other OBJ-family languages (OBJ, Eqlog [23], FOOPS[25], Maude [33, 34]) are. The reference paper for the CafeOBJ mathematical foundations is [5], while the book [3] gives a somehow less mathematical easy-to-read (including many examples) presentation of the semantics of CafeOBJ . In this section we give a very brief overview of the CafeOBJ logical and mathematical foundations, for a full understanding of this aspect of CafeOBJ the reader is referred to [5] and [3].

The mathematical semantics of CafeOBJ is based on state-of-the-art algebraic specification concepts and results, and is strongly based on category theory and the theory of institutions [20, 2]. The following are the principles governing the logical and mathematical foundations of CafeOBJ :

P1: There is an underlying logic[2] in which all basic constructs and features of the language can be rigorously explained.
P2: Provide an integrated, cohesive, and unitary approach to the semantics of specification in-the-small and in-the-large.
P3: Develop all ingredients (concepts, results, etc.) at the highest appropriate level of abstraction.

The CafeOBJ Cube: CafeOBJ is a multi-paradigm language. Each of the main paradigms implemented in CafeOBJ is rigorously based on some underlying logic; the paradigms resulting from various combinations are based on the combination of logics. You can find the details in [5]

1.4   Basic Constructs of CafeOBJ Language

This section explains basic constructs of CafeOBJ by using simple examples.

---

[2] Here "logic" should be understood in the modern relativistic sense of "institution" which provides a mathematical definition for a logic (see [20]) rather than in the more classical sense.

Module and Its Constructs In CafeOBJ , everything is modeled as a algebra, that is an aggregation of several kind of objects and operations defined among them. These objects and operations are grouped into a module, which is a basic building block of the problem description. A module denotes order-sorted algebra in mathematical sense [24, 38]; we call a set of objects with some common properties a **sort** following the terminology of algebraic specification. The most simplest module is:

```
module* TRIV { [ Elt ] }
```

This defines a module named TRIV, and specifies that there is a sort of objects, and we call it Elt. No property of Elt is mentioned. This module should be interpreted loosely which is indicated by the * symbol at the end of module. That is, it denotes a class of algebras which have at least one carrier set.

Operators To describe the properties of sorts, we define the operations among them.

```
module! NAT {
 [ Nat ]
 op 0 : -> Nat
 op s_ : Nat -> Nat
}
```

This is a module which models a set of natural numbers as the sort Nat. This module shoud be interpreted tightly (initially) which is indicated by the ! symbol at the end of module. That is, it denotes the initial algebra which has one sort Nat with a constant 0 and a successor function s_.

Sort Inclusion One of the most important features of the object-oriented modeling is the concept of subclasses which enable us to declare that one class of objects is included in another class of objects. In CafeOBJ , the concept of class just corresponds to sort, we can specify the subclass relations by a declaration:

```
[ A < B ]
```

This says that a set (class) of objects of sort A is included in a set (class) of objects of sort B. This implies that sort A inherits all properties, i.e., operators which has sort B as the one of its arguments. To make terminology simple, we call "a class (or set) of objects of sort A" just "class A" or "sort A". It is said that sort A is a subsort of sort B, or sort B is a supper sort of sort A if the declaration of [A < B] exists. Also notice we don't distinguish the word "class", "set" and "sort".

One of the simplest examples of subsort declaration is given as follows.

```
[ Nat ]                       -- Natural number
op 0 : -> Nat
op s_ : Nat -> Nat
[ Nat < Int ]                 -- Integer, Nat is included in Int
|_| : Int -> Nat              -- absolute value of Int
```

In this example, since sort Nat is declared to be a subsort of sort Int, the operator |_| is also applicable to the object of sort Nat. Hence the term | s s s 0 | is well-formed.

A set of declarations of sorts of objects, operations , or subsorts are called signature. Signatures defines the fundamental structure of what to be modeled. The algebraic models with sort inclusions are order-sorted algebras. In this sense, the signature which is available in CafeOBJ is order-sorted signature.

Equations The meaning of operators are specified by **equations**. Equations declare the equivalence of two terms. Equations are simple but very powerful for describing meaning of operations. In CafeOBJ , equations are primary constructs to specify the requirements, behaviors, and functions of systems.

The next example module NAT+ extends the module NAT by introducing new operator + with its meaning specified by an equation.

```
module! NAT+ {
  extending(NAT)
  op _+_ : Nat Nat -> Nat { assoc comm id: 0 }
  var N1 N2 : Nat
  eq N1 + s N2 = s(N1 + N2) .
}
```

The meaning of + is described by an equation (the line preceded by keyword eq in above code). Keyword var is used to introduce variables; in above example, N1 and N2 are both declared as variables of sort Nat.

In mathematical sense, this module represents an equational theory, or an algebra. Equations can be understood operationally by considering them as rewrite rules from left to right; then, a term s s 0 + s 0 is rewritten to s s s 0. "Computation" in CafeOBJ is done like this; a term is rewritten to another term by applying possible equations until no more rewrite rule can be applied.

Parameterized Modules A module can be parameterized. This enable us to prepare and composite of generic reusable modules. The following example represents a generic list whose element is parameterized. [X::TRIV] specifies that the actual parameter must be a member of class of algebras which the module TRIV represents. In this case, it only requires a designated sort corresponding to Elt from an actual module.

```
module! LIST[ X :: TRIV ] {
  -- the object which is substituted for X must be
```

```
  -- a instance of module(theory) TRIV.
  [ Elt < List ]          -- elements are also lists.
  op nil : -> List        -- empty list
  op __ : List List -> List { assoc id: nil }
  -- associative concatenation operation of List
}
```

We can make a list of natural numbers by instantiating the module LIST by giving NAT as an actual parameter which satisfies the requirement specified by TRIV as follows:

```
make NAT-LIST (LIST[NAT])
```

2   An Example of Verification in Initial Models: Equivalence of Two Definitions of Factorial

This section gives one of the most simplest example of CafeOBJ code for verifying that the two different definitions of factorial are equivalent.

First comes the definition of the natural number in unary form, and two operations of plus (_+_) and times (_*_)over them.

```
mod! NAT* { [ Nat ]
  op 0 : -> Nat
  op s_ : Nat -> Nat {prec 1}

  op _+_ : Nat Nat -> Nat {assoc comm} -- should be proved
  eq M:Nat + 0 = M .
  eq M:Nat + s N:Nat = s(M + N) .

  op _*_ : Nat Nat -> Nat {assoc comm} -- should be proved
  eq M:Nat * 0 = 0 .
  eq M:Nat * s N:Nat = (M * N) + M .
}
```

The following CafeOBJ module specifies that times (_*_) operation distributes over a term composed of plus (_+_) operators.

```
mod! NAT*dist { protecting(NAT*)
  -- distributive law: should be proved
  eq L:Nat * (M:Nat + N:Nat) = (L * M) + (L * N) .
}
```

The following FACT module gives the first definition of factorial function.

```
mod! FACT { protecting(NAT*)
  op fact : Nat -> Nat
  eq fact(0) = s 0 .
  eq fact(s N:Nat) = (s N) * fact(N) .
}
```

The following `FACT2` module gives the second definition of factorial function.

```
mod! FACT2 { protecting(NAT*)
  op fact2 : Nat Nat -> Nat
  eq fact2(0, A:Nat) = A .
  eq fact2((s N:Nat), A:Nat) = fact2(N, (s N) * A) .
}
```

Based on given specifications, the following "proof script" gives a script for verifing that the first and the second definitions of factorial function give the same result. This script can be executed by CafeOBJ reducer/interpreter, and gives the proof of what we want to prove.

```
open (FACT + FACT2 + NAT*dist)
ops i j k : -> Nat .
--> Proof of:
--> (for-all I:Nat, J:Nat) fact2(I, J)  = J * fact(I)
--> by induction of I:Nat
--> induction base  = 0
red fact2(0,j) == j * fact(0) .
--> induction hypothesis
**> eq fact2(i,J:Nat) = J * fact(i) .
eq fact2(i,J:Nat) = J * fact(i) .
--> induction step

--> left hand side
red fact2(s i, j) .
-->   right hand side
red j * fact(s i) .

red fact2(s i, j) == j * fact(s i) .
--> QED (quod erat demonstrandum: which was to be demonstrated)
close
```

3   An Example of Verification in Behavioral Specification: Simple Bank Account

In this section, one of the simplest example of verification in observational specification is shown.

In this example, we will consider a bank acount with the following behavioral specification.

In behavioral specifications, observational behaviors of systems are modeled as follows:

- A behavior of a system is modeled as actions and observations.
- Actions model the operations which change the state of the system.

- Obeservations model the operations which oberve the current state of the system. Observations do not change the state of the system.
- States of the system are modeled as a hidden (or behavioral) sort.
- A state of the system is characterized by the data of visible (or data) sorts the observations returns.

```
mod* ACCOUNT {
  protecting(INT)
  *[ Account ]*
  -- an observation
  bop balance : Account -> Nat
  -- actions
  ops deposit withdraw : Account Nat -> Account {coherent}

  op init-account : -> Account
  eq balance(init-account) = 0 .

  var N : Nat
  var A : Account
  eq balance(deposit(A,N)) = balance(A) + N .
  cq balance(withdraw(A,N)) = balance(A) - N if N <= balance(A) .
  cq balance(withdraw(A,N)) = balance(A)      if balance(A) < N .
}
```

With this specification, we want to prove that for any a : Account which is reachable from init-accout, the predicate 0 <= balance (a) always holds. The following CafeOBJ code gives the proof score for this.

```
open ACCOUNT

-- base
red 0 <= balance(init-account) .

op a : -> Account .
ops n n' : -> Nat .

-- hypothesis
eq (0 <= balance(a)) = true .

-- proving that deposit preserves observational equivalence
red 0 <= balance(deposit(a, n)) .

-- proving that withdraw preserves observational equivalence
-- hypotheses
eq n <= balance(a) = true .
eq 0 <= balance(a) + (- n) = true .
```

```
eq n' <= balance(a) = false .
eq N1:Nat < N2:Nat = not(N2 <= N1) .

red 0 <= balance(withdraw(a, n))  .
red 0 <= balance(withdraw(a, n')) .

close
```

4   An Example of Verification in Behavioral Concurrent Object Composition: Compositional Bank Account

The object-oriented method in CafeOBJ [3, 6, 30] supports concurrent object composition within the behavioral specification approach by using the so-called **projection operations** [3, 6, 30] from the hidden sort of the compound object to the hidden sorts of the components. We distinguish two kinds of objects: **static** and **dynamic**. Dynamic objects can be created or deleted during the runs of

the system, while the static objects cannot. By using some object-oriented terminology, we may say that dynamic objects form a class, while the static objects represent the particular case in which the class contains only one object.

As example, consider a bank accounts system consisting of several individual accounts. In UML notation this may be represented by the the following figure.

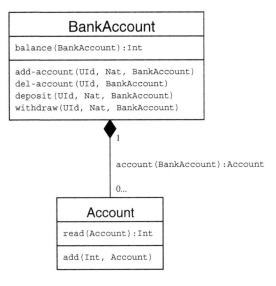

The specification of personal accounts can be considered as a dynamic system of counters of integers. The following specifies the class of the counters, with the counter identifiers parameterized by X.

```
mod* COUNTER(X :: TRIV) {
  protecting(INT)

  *[ Counter ]*

  op init-counter : Elt -> Counter  -- initial state
  op no-counter : -> Counter        -- error
  bop add : Int Counter -> Counter
  bop amount_ : Counter -> Nat

  var ID : Elt
  var I : Int
  var C : Counter

  beq add(I, no-counter) = no-counter .
  eq amount init-counter(ID) = 0 .
  ceq amount add(I, C) = I + amount(C) if I + amount(C) >= 0 .
  ceq amount add(I, C) = amount(C) if I + amount(C) < 0 .
}
```

The space of the states of a counter is represented by the hidden sort Counter. The action add counts up or down (if a negative number is passed as argument) and we can observe the state of a counter by using the observation amount_. This counter allows the application of the action add only when the observation of the resulting state is positive. This means that no substraction which would result in a negative result is allowed.

The counter is represented as a dynamic object and we require an identifier for specifying an individual counter. The operation no-counter is used for error situations, i.e. when some other objects specify a wrong identifier (meaning the object does not exist).

Accounts are just a renaming of the COUNTER instantiated by USER-ID (for identifiers).

```
mod* USER-ID {
  [ UId ]
}
```

```
mod* ACCOUNT {
  protecting(COUNTER(X <= view to USER-ID { sort Elt -> UId })
                  *{ hsort Counter -> Account,
                     op init-counter -> init-account,
                     op no-counter -> no-account })
```

Now we can compose the account objects to form a dynamic system of bank accounts:

```
mod* ACCOUNT-SYS {
```

```
protecting(ACCOUNT)

*[ AccountSys ]*

op init-account-sys : -> AccountSys
bop add-account : UId Nat AccountSys -> AccountSys
bop del-account : UId AccountSys -> AccountSys
bop deposit : UId Nat AccountSys -> AccountSys
bop withdraw : UId Nat AccountSys -> AccountSys
bop balance : UId AccountSys -> Nat
bop account : UId AccountSys -> Account

vars U U' : UId
var A : AccountSys
var N : Nat

eq account(U, init-account-sys) = no-account .
ceq account(U, add-account(U', N, A)) = add(N, init-account(U))
    if U == U' .
ceq account(U, add-account(U', N, A)) = account(U, A)
    if U =/= U' .
ceq account(U, del-account(U', A)) = no-account
    if U == U' .
ceq account(U, del-account(U', A)) = account(U, A)
    if U =/= U' .
ceq account(U, deposit(U', N, A)) = add(N, account(U, A))
    if U == U' .
ceq account(U, deposit(U', N, A)) = account(U, A)
    if U =/= U' .
ceq account(U, withdraw(U', N, A)) = add(-(N), account(U, A))
    if U == U' .
ceq account(U, withdraw(U', N, A)) = account(U, A)
    if U =/= U' .

eq balance(U, A) = amount account(U, A) .
}
```

Notice the following steps involved in specifying a compound object:

1. import the component objects (ACCOUNT),
2. define a new hidden sort for the compund object and a (behavioral) projection operation to the hidden sort of each of the components (account),
3. define actions on the compound object (withdraw, deposit) corresponding to the component objects actions and express the relationship between compound object actions and components objects actions by (strict) equations, and

4. (eventually) define some observations on the compound objects as abbreviations for component objects observations (`balance`).

In the initial state (`init-account-sys`), the system of bank accounts does not contain any individual account. The operation `add-acount` add individual accounts and `del-account` deletes individual accounts.

The projection operations are subject to several precise technical conditions which are mathematically formulated in [3, 6, 30].

4.1   Proving Behavioral Properties for the Composed Object

One of the advantages of this methodology for composing objects is not only the high reusability of the specification code, but also of verification proofs. This is supported by the follwing:

Theorem 1. *[30] The behavioral equivalence of the compound object is the conjunction via the projection operations of the behavioral equivalences of the component objects.*

This means that the behavioral equivalence for the compound object is obtained directly without having to do any proofs about it (it is enough to establish the behavioral equivalence at the level of the composing objects). In the case of a hierarchical object composition process (involving several levels of composition), this may prove very effective in practice.

Coming back to our example, let us first look at the behavioral equivalence of ACCOUNT. This is exactly the default coinduction relation =*=, but due to the lack of automatic bulit-in case analysis the CafeOBJ system fails to prove it. So, let us do it by ourselves:

```
mod BEQ-ACCOUNT {
  protecting(ACCOUNT)

  op _=*=_ : Account Account -> Bool {coherent}

  vars A1 A2 : Account

  eq A1 =*= A2 = amount(A1) == amount(A2) .
}

open BEQ-ACCOUNT .
  ops a1 a2 : -> Account .
  op i : -> Int .

  -- The hypothesis for the first case:
  eq i + amount(a2) >= 0 = true .
  eq amount(a1) = amount(a2) .
```

```
  -- Here is the proof:
  red add(i, a1) =*= add(i, a2) .
close
```

The second case is very similar:

```
open BEQ-ACCOUNT
  ops a1 a2 : -> Account .
  op i : -> Int .

  -- The hypothesis for the second case:
  eq i + amount(a2) < 0 = true .
  eq amount(a1) = amount(a2) .

  -- the proof:
  red add(i, a1) =*= add(i, a2) .
close
```

Now, we obtain the behavioral equivalence of ACCOUNT-SYS by reusing the behavioral equivalence =*= of ACCOUNT:

```
mod BEQ-ACCOUNT-SYS {
  protecting(BEQ-ACCOUNT)
  protecting(ACCOUNT-SYS)

  op _R[_]_ : AccountSys UId AccountSys -> Bool {coherent}

  vars BA1 BA2 : AccountSys
  var U : UId

  eq BA1 R[ U ] BA2 = account(U, BA1) =*= account(U, BA2) .
}
```

Notice that the behavioral equivalence of ACCOUNT-SYS is parameterized by UId; this is because it is an infinite conjunction of the behavioral equivalences for the individual accounts:

$$ba1 \sim_{\text{ACCOUNT-SYS}} ba2 \text{ iff } \text{account}(u, ba1) \sim_{\text{ACCOUNT}} \text{account}(u, ba2)$$

for all user identifies u, where $\sim_{\text{ACCOUNT-SYS}}$ and $\sim_{\text{ACCOUNT}}$ are the behavioral equivalences of ACCOUNT and ACCOUNT-SYS, respectively.

Consider the following very simple behavioral property:

$$\text{withdraw}(u, n, ba) \sim ba$$

if there is no account corresponding to the user identifier u, where n is a natural value and ba is any state of the acounts system, meaning basically the protection of the individual accounts of the bank account system from outsiders.

The following is a proof script in CafeOBJ for verifying the above behavioral property.

```
open BEQ-ACCOUNT-SYS
  op ba : -> AccountSys .
  ops u u' : -> UId .
  op n : -> Nat .

  -- This is the working hypothesis:
  eq account(u, ba) = no-account .

  -- This is the proof by very simple case analysis;
  -- that is,

  -- whether the parameter is the same,
  red withdraw(u, n, ba) R[ u ] ba .
  -- expected to return {\tt true}

  -- or not with the user identifier
  red withdraw(u, n, ba) R[ u' ] ba .
  -- expected to return {\tt true}

  --> QED (quod erat demonstrandum: which was to be demonstrated)

close
```

5 Conclusion

Investigations of modeling, specification, and verification in CafeOBJ can be largely classified into the following three categories.

Abstract Data Types Abstract data types are considered to capture the most fundamental structure of wide variety of systems [1, 8, 10].

Abstract Machines/Objects/Agents It is also widely recognized that many important systems are naturally modeled by state transition machines. State transition machines can be considered to be a special kind of abstract data types, i.e. *abstract machines*, and algebraic specification techniques are effective to describe them too [10].

At the same time, the importance of object-oriented paradigm in system modeling/specification is widely recognized recently. There are several approaches for supporting object-oriented paradigm based on algebraic specification techniques. CafeOBJ provides a powerful way to achieve object-oriented modeling/specification based on two different formalizes: hidden algebra and rewriting logic[34, 3]

The term agent is used to mean adaptable or situated object. There are several attempts to apply algebraic techniques for specifying agents [31].

Generic Reusable Modules The most promising and important application of algebraic specification is to prepare *generic reusable modules* and to compose them for specific requirement [8, 16, 17, 39]. Parameterized programming already realized in **OBJ** is powerful programming method for preparation and composition of generic reusable modules [13, 28]. CafeOBJ inherits the power of OBJ's parameterized programming completely. Besides, CafeOBJ provides more powerful style which results from the combination of parameterized programming and object-orientation. This combination will provide a promising semantic framework for component based software constructions.

CafeOBJ has multiple specification and verification methodologies based on a single algebraic and logical foundation which is cohesive and transparent. This is a quite unique and strong characteristic of CafeOBJ which can support a wide variaties of applications in many areas.

Information about CafeOBJ can be found at:

http://www.ldl.jaist.ac.jp/cafeobj

References

[1] Burstall,R. and Goguen,J. A., "Putting Theories Together to Make Specifications", In Reddy,R. editor, Proc. of 5th IJCAI, 1977, pp. 1045-1058.   1, 3, 5, 17

[2] Diaconescu,R., Extra Theory Morphisms for Institutions: logical semantics for multi-paradigm languages, Jour. of Applied Categorical Structures, 1998, a preliminary version appeared as JAIST Technical Report IS-RR-97-0032F in 1997. 5, 6

[3] Diaconescu,R. and Futatsugi,K., *CafeOBJ report*. AMAST Series in Computing, 6. World Scientific, Singapore, 1998.   1, 2, 3, 4, 5, 6, 12, 15, 17

[4] Diaconescu,R. and Futatsugi,K., Behavioural Coherence in Object-Oriented Algebraic Specification. *Journal of Universal Computer Science*, 6(1):74–96, 2000. 4, 5

[5] Diaconescu,R. and Futatsugi,K., Logical Foundations of CafeOBJ , *Theoretical Comuputer Science*, to appear.   6

[6] Diaconescu,R., Futatsugi,K., and Iida,S., Component-based Algebraic Specification and Verification in CafeOBJ, Lecture Notes in Computer Science, 1708, pp.1644-1663, 1999.   3, 12, 15

[7] Diaconescu,R., Futatsugi,K., and Iida,S., CafeOBJ Jewels, in Futatsugi,K., Nakagawa, A. T., and Tamai,T., editors, *CAFE: An Industiral-Strength Algebraic Formal Method*, Elsevier, pp.33-60, 2000.   1

[8] Futatsugi,K., Hierarchical Software Development in HISP, in *Computer Science and Technologies 1982*, ed. Kitagawa,T., Japan Annual Review in Electronics, Computers and Telecommunications Series, OHMSHA/North-Holland, pp.151–174, 1982.   1, 3, 17, 18

[9] Futatsugi,K., An Overview of OBJ2", Proc. of Franco-Japanese Symp. on Programming of Future Generation Computers, Tokyo, Oct. 1986, published as *Programming of Future Generation Computers*, ed. Fuchi,K. and Nivat,M., North-Holland, pp.139–160, 1988.   2, 3, 4

[10] Futatsugi,K., Trends in Formal Specification Methods based on Algebraic Specification Techniques – from Abstract Data Types to Software Processes: A Personal Perspective –, Proceedings of the International Conference of Information Technology to Commemorating the 30th Anniversary of the Information Processing Society of Japan (InfoJapan'90), pp.59-66, October 1990, (invited talk). 1, 3, 17

[11] Futatsugi,K., Goguen,J. A., Jouannaud,J.-P., and Meseguer,J., Principles of OBJ2, Proceedings of the 12th ACM Symposium on Principles of Programming Languages, ACM, pp.55-66, 1985. 2, 3, 4

[12] Futatsugi,K., Goguen,J., Meseguer,J., editors, *OBJ/CafeOBJ/Maude at Formal Methods '99*, The Theta Foundation, Bucharest, Romania, (ISBN 973-99097-1-X), 1999. 1

[13] Futatsugi,K., Goguen,J. A., Meseguer,J., and Okada,K., Parameterized Programming in OBJ2, Proc. of the 9th ICSE, IEEE, pp.51–60, 1987. 1, 3, 18

[14] Futatsugi,K. and Nakagawa,A., An Overview of CAFE Specification Environment – an algebraic approach for creating, verifying, and maintaining formal specifications over networks –, Proc. 1st Intl. Conf. of Formal Engineering Methods, IEEE Press, pp.170–181, 1997. 3

[15] Futatsugi,K. and Ogata,K., Rewriting Can Verify Distributed Real-time Systems, Proc. of International Symposium on Rewriting, Proof, and Computation, PRC'01, pp.60-79, Oct. 2001, (invited talk). 3

[16] Futatsugi,K. and Okada,K., Specification Writing as Construction of hierarchically Structured Clusters of Operators, Proc. of IFIP Congress 80, Tokyo, pp. 287–292, Oct.1980. 3, 18

[17] Futatsugi,K. and Okada,K., A Hierarchical Structuring Method for Functional Software Systems, Proc. of the 6th ICSE, pp.393–402, 1982. 3, 18

[18] Futatsugi,K. and Sawada,T., Design Considerations for Cafe Specification Environment, in *Proc. OBJ2 10th Anniversary Workshop*, Numazu, Japan, Oct.1995. 1, 3

[19] Futatsugi,K., Nakagawa,A., and Tamai,T., editors, *CAFE: An Industrial-Strength Algebraic Formal Method*, Elsevier Science B. V., Amsterdam, The Netherlands, (ISBN 0-444-50556-3), 2000. 1

[20] Goguen,J. and Burstall,R., Institutions: Abstract Model Theory for Specification and Programming, Journal of the Association for Computing Machinery, 39 (1), pp.95–146, 1992. 5, 6

[21] Goguen,J. and Diaconescu,R., An Oxford Survey of Order Sorted Algebra, Mathematical Structures in Computer Science, 4 (4), pp.363–392, 1994. 5, 6

[22] Goguen,J. and Malcolm,G., A hidden agenda. *Theoret. Comput. Sci.*, 245:55–101, 2000. 4

[23] Goguen,J. and Meseguer,J., Eqlog: Equality, Types, and Generic Modules for Logic Programming, in *Logic Programming: Functions, Relations and Equations*, DeGroot,D. and Lindstrom,G. editors, Prentice-Hall, pp.295–363, 1986. 3, 6

[24] Goguen,J. A. and Meseguer,J., Order-Sorted Algebra I: Equational Deduction for Multiple Inheritance, Overloading, Exceptions and Partial Operations, *Theoretical Computer Science*, 105 (2), pp.217–273, 1992. 5, 7

[25] Goguen,J. and Meseguer,J., Unifying Functional, Object-Oriented and Relational Programming with Logical Semantics, in *Research Directions in Object-Oriented Programming*, Shriver,B. and Wegner,P. editors, MIT Press, pp.417–477, 1987. 3, 6

[26] Goguen,J. A., Thatcher,J. W., and Wagner,E. G., An Initial Algebra Approach to the Specification, Correctness, and Implementation of Abstract Data Types,

IBM Research Report RC-6487, 1976; also in *Current Trends in Programming Methodology, Vol.4: Data Structuring*, ed. Yeh,R. T., Prentice-Hall, pp.80–149, 1978. 1

[27] Goguen,J. A., Thatcher,J. W., Wagner,E. G., and Wright,J. B., Abstract Data Types as Initial Algebras and the Correctness of Data Representation, *Computer Graphics, Pattern Recognition and Data Structure*, IEEE, pp.89–93, 1975. 1

[28] Goguen,J., Winkler,T., Meseguer,J., Futatsugi,K., and Jouannaud,J. P., Introducing OBJ, in Joseph Goguen and Grant Malcolm, editors, *Software Engineering with OBJ*, pp.3 -167 , Kluwer Academic Publishers, 2000. 2, 4, 18

[29] Guttag,J. V. and Horning,J. J., The Algebraic Specification of Abstract Data Types, *Acta Infomatica*, 10, pp.27–52, 1978. 1

[30] Iida,S., Diaconescu,R., Futatsugi,K., Component-Based Algebraic Specification - Behavioural Specification for Component-based Software Engineering -, in *Behavioral Specifications of Bussiness and Systems*, Kluwer Academic Publishers, pp.105-121, 1999. 4, 12, 15

[31] Ishikawa,H., Futatsugi,K., and Watanabe,T., Concurrent Reflective Computations in Rewriting Logic (Extended Abstract), in Proc. of TRS Sympo. at RIMS, Kyoto, June, 1995. 17

[32] Lawvere,F. W., Functorial Semantics of Algebraic Theories (Summary of Ph.D. Thesis, Columbia University), Proceedings, National Academy of Sciences, U. S. A., 50, pp.869–872, 1963. 3

[33] Meseguer,J., A logical theory of cuncurrent objects, In *ECOOP-OOPSLA'90 Conference on Object-Oriented Programming*, ACM, Oct.1990, pp.101-115. 3, 5, 6

[34] Meseguer,J., Conditional rewriting logic as a unified model of concurrency, *Theoretical Computer Science*, 96 (1), pp73-155, 1992. 3, 5, 6, 17

[35] Meseguer,J., Membership algebra as a logical framework for equational specification, in Parisi-Presicce,F. ed., Proc. WADT'97, Springer LNCS 1376, pp.18-61, 1998. 6

[36] Okada,K. and Futatsugi,K., Supporting the Formal Description Process for Communication Protocols by an Algebraic Specification Language OBJ2, Proc. of Second International Symposium on Interoperable Information System (ISIIS'88), Tokyo, pp.127-134, 1988. 3

[37] Ohmaki,K., Futatsugi,K., and Takahashi,K., A Basic LOTOS Simulator in OBJ, Proceedings of InfoJapan'90 Computer Conference, Part 1, IPSJ, pp.497–504, 1990. 3

[38] Smolka,G., Nutt,W. Goguen,J., and Meseguer,J., Order-Sorted Equational Computation, in *Resolution of Equations in Algebraic Structures, Vol 2., Rewriting Techniques*, eds Aït-Kaci,H. and Nivat,M., Academic Press, Inc., pp.297–368, 1989. 7

[39] Srinivas,Y. V., Jülling,R., SPECWARE: Formal Support for Composing Software, Tech. Reprot KES. U.94.5, Kestrel Institute, 1994. 1, 18

[40] Stevens,A. and Goguen,J., Mechanised theorem proving with 2OBJ: A tutorial introduction, Programming Research Group, University of Oxford, 1993. 3

The Essence of XML
(Preliminary Version)

Jérôme Siméon[1] and Philip Wadler[2]

[1] Bell Laboratories, Murray Hill, NJ 07974, USA
simeon@research.bell-labs.com
[2] Avaya Labs Research, Basking Ridge, NJ 07920, USA
wadler@avaya.com

Abstract. The World-Wide Web Consortium (W3C) promotes XML and related standards, including XML Schema, XQuery, and XPath. This paper describes a formalization XML Schema. A formal semantics based on these ideas is part of the official XQuery and XPath specification, one of the first uses of formal methods by a standards body. XML Schema features both named and structural types, with structure based on tree grammars. While structural types and matching have been studied in other work (notably XDuce, Relax NG, and previous formalizations of XML Schema), this is the first work to study the relation between named types and structural types, and the relation between matching and validation.

1 Introduction

There are a number of type systems for XML, including: DTDs, part of the original W3C recommendation defining XML [1]; XML Schema, a W3C recommendation which supersedes DTDs [13]; Relax NG, an Oasis standard [5]; Relax [10] and TREX [4], two ancestors of Relax NG; and the type systems of XDuce [8] and YATL [6]. All of these take a structural approach to typing, with the exception of XML Schema, which takes a named approach. (Another possible exception is DTDs, which are so restricted that the named and structural approaches might be considered to coincide.)

The W3C is responsible for three programming languages connected with XML: XSLT, a language for stylesheets [3, 9]; XQuery, an analogue of SQL for XML data [15]; and XPath, the common core of XSLT and XQuery, which is jointly managed by the working groups responsible for the other two languages [14]. All three of these are functional languages. XSLT 1.0 and XPath 1.0 became recommendations in November 1999 — they are untyped. XML Schema 1.0 became a recommendation in May 2001. XSLT 2.0, XQuery 1.0, and XPath 2.0 are currently being designed — they have type systems based on XML Schema.

This paper presents a formalization of XML Schema, developed in conjunction with the XQuery and XPath working groups. The paper presents a simplified version, treating the essential constructs. The full version is being developed as

Z. Hu and M. Rodríguez-Artalejo (Eds.): FLOPS 2002, LNCS 2441, pp. 21–46, 2002.

part of the XQuery and XPath Formal Semantics [16], one of the first industrial specifications to exploit formal methods. The full version treats not just XML Schema, but also the dynamic and static semantics of the XQuery and XPath.

Formal methods are particularly helpful for typing — the only complete description of the static type system of XQuery and XPath is in the formal specification. However, keeping two specifications in sync has not always been easy.

An earlier formal specification of XML Schema [2] was influenced by XDuce [8]; it ignored the named aspects of Schema and took a purely structural approach. The specification of Relax NG [5] also uses formal methods, and also is purely structural; it was influenced by the earlier work on XML Schema [2].

Matching and validation.   Types in XML differ in some ways from types as used elsewhere in computing. Traditionally, a value *matches* a type — given a value and a type, either the value belongs to the type or it does not. In XML, a value *validates* against a type — given an (external) value and a type, validation produces an (internal) value or it fails.

For instance, consider the following XML Schema.

```
<xs:simpleType name="feet">
  <xs:restriction base="xs:float"/>
</xs:simpleType>
<xs:element name="height" type="feet"/>
```

In our type system, this is written as follows.

```
define type feet restricts xs:float
define element height of type feet
```

Now consider the following XML document.

```
<height>10023</height>
```

In our model, before validation this is represented as follows.

```
  <height>10023</height>
=>
  element height { "10023" }
```

And after validation it is represent as follows.

```
  validate as element height { <height>10023</height> }
=>
  element height of type feet { 10023.0 }
```

Validation has annotated the element with its type, and converted the text "10023" into the corresponding floating point number 10023.0.

Our model provides both validation and matching. Validation attaches types to XML data. Unvalidated data may not match against a type. The following *does not* hold.

```
   element height { "10023" }
matches
   element height
```

After validation, matching succeeds. The following *does* hold.

```
   element height of type feet { 10023.0 }
matches
   element height
```

The inverse of validation is type erasure.

```
   element height of type feet { 10023.0 }
erases to
   element height { "10023" }
```

The following theorem characterizes validation in terms of matching and erasure.

Theorem 1. *We have that*
   validate as *Type* { *UntypedValue* } => *Value*
if and only if
   Value matches *Type*
and
   Value erases to *UntypedValue*

Perhaps this theorem looks obvious, but if so let us assure you that it was not obvious to us when we began. It took some time to come to this formulation, and some tricky adjustments were required to ensure that holds.

One trick is that we model validation and erasure by relations, not functions. Naively, one might expect validation to be a partial function and erasure to be a function. That is, for a given type each untyped value validates to yield at most one typed value, and each typed values erases to one untyped value. One subtlety of the system presented here is that validation and erasure are modeled by relations. For example, the strings "10023" and "10023.0" both validate to yield the float 10023.0, and hence we also have that the float erases to yield either string.

Shortcomings of XML and Schema. Our aim is to model XML and Schema as they exist — we do not claim that these are the best possible designs. Indeed, we would argue that XML and Schema have several shortcomings.

First, we would argue that a data representation should explicitly distinguish, say, integers from strings, rather than to infer which is which by validation against a Schema. (This is one of the many ways in which Lisp S-expressions are superior to XML.)

Second, while derivation by extension in Schema superficially resembles sub-classing in object-oriented programming, in fact there are profound differences. One can typecheck code for a class without knowing all subclasses of that class (this supports separate compilation), but one cannot typecheck against a Schema type without knowing all types that derive by extension from that class (and hence separate compilation is problematic).

Nonetheless, XML and Schema are widely used standards, and there is value in modeling these standards. In particular, such models may: (i) improve our understanding of exactly what is mandated by the standard, (ii) help implementors create conforming implementations, and (iii) suggest how to improve the standards.

Relation of our model to Schema.   Schema is a large and complex standard. In this paper, we attempt to model only the most essential features. These include: simple types and complex types; named and anonymous types; global and local elements; atomic, list, and union simple types; derivation by restriction; and derivation by extension. We model only two primitive datatypes, `xs:float` and `xs:string`, while Schema has nineteen primitive datatypes.

Many features of Schema that are omitted here are dealt with in the formal semantics for XQuery [16]. These include: namespaces; attributes; all groups (interleaving); text nodes; mixed content; substitution groups; `xsi:nil` attributes; and `xsi:type` attributes. There are other features of Schema that are not yet dealt with in the full formal semantics, but which we hope to model in future. These include: abstract types; default and fixed values; skip, lax, and strict wildcards; and facets of simple types.

Schema is normally written in an XML notation, but here we use a notation that is more readable and compact. The mapping of XML notation into our notation is described in the XQuery formal semantics.

There are a few aspects in which our treatment diverges from Schema. First, we permit ambiguous content models, while Schema does not. We do this because it makes our model simpler, and because ambiguity is important to support type checking, as discussed in Section 9. Second, we permit one type to be a restriction of another whenever the set of values belonging to the first type is included in the set of values belonging to the second, while Schema imposes ad hoc syntactic constraints. Again, we do this because it makes our model simpler, and because our more general model better supports type checking. Third, we only support the occurrence operators ?, +, and *, while Schema supports arbitrary counts for minimum and maximum occurrences. This is because arbitrary counts may lead to a blow-up in the size of the finite-state automata we use to check when one type is included in another.

2   XML Schema by Example

XML Schema supports a wide range of features. These include simple types and complex types, anonymous types, global and local declarations, derivation by restriction, and derivation by extension.

Simple and complex types.   Here are declarations for two elements of simple type, one element with a complex type, and one complex type.

```
define element title of type xs:string
define element author of type xs:string
define element paper of type paperType
define type paperType {
  element title ,
  element author +
}
```

Schema specifies nineteen primitive simple type types, including `xs:string` and `xs:float`.

A type declaration associates a name and a structure. The structure of a complex type is a regular expression over elements. As usual, , denotes sequence, | denotes alternation, ? denotes an optional occurrence, + denotes one or more occurrences, and * denotes zero or more occurrences.

Validating annotates each element with its type.

```
validate as paper {
  <paper>
    <title>The Essence of Algol</title>
    <author>John Reynolds</author>
  <paper>
}
=>
  element paper of type paperType {
    element title of type string { "The Essence of Algol" },
    element author of type string { "John Reynolds" }
  }
```

Anonymous types. Instead of naming a type, it can defined in place without a name. Here is the **paper** element with its type expanded in place.

```
define element paper {
  element title , element author +
}
```

Validating now yields the following result.

```
validate as paper {
  <paper>
    <title>The Essence of ML</title>
    <author>Robert Harper</author>
    <author>John Mitchell</author>
  </paper>
}
=>
  element paper {
    element title of type xs:string { "The Essence of ML" },
    element author of type xs:string { "Robert Harper" },
```

```
    element author of type xs:string { "John Mitchell" }
}
```

Now the **paper** element has no type annotation, because there is no type name to annotate it with. The other elements still have type annotations.

Global and local declarations. Similarly, one may include an element declaration in place. Here is the **paper** element with the nested elements expanded in place.

```
define element paper {
    element title of type xs:string ,
    element author of type xs:string +
}
```

Here the **paper** is declared globally, while `title` and `author` are declared locally. In this case, validation proceeds exactly as before.

Allowing local declarations increases expressiveness, because now it is possible for elements with the same name to be assigned different types in different places; see [11, 7]. An example of such a definition appears later.

Atomic, list, and union types. Every simple type is an atomic type, a list type, or a union type. The atomic types are the nineteen primitive types of Schema, such as `xs:string` and `xs:float`, and the types derived from them. List types are formed using the occurrence operators ?, +, and *, taken from regular expressions. Union types are formed using the alternation operator |, also taken from regular expressions.

Here is an example of a list type.

```
element floats { xs:float + }
```

In XML notation, lists are written space-separated.

```
validate as floats { <floats>1.0 2.0 3.0</floats> }
=>
    element floats { 1.0, 2.0, 3.0 }
```

Some types may be ambiguous. XML Schema specifies how to resolve this ambiguity: every space is taken as a list separator, and in case of a union the first alternative that works is chosen.

```
element trouble { ( xs:float | xs:string )* }
```

```
validate as trouble { <trouble>this is not 1 string</trouble> }
=>
    element trouble {"this", "is", "not", 1, "string" }
```

Ambiguous types can be problematic; this will be further discussed in Section 9.

Derivation by restriction on simple types. New simple types may be derived by restriction.

```
define type miles restricts xs:float
define type feet restricts xs:float
```

Here is an example, with two `height` elements have different types.

```
define element configuration {
  element shuttle { element height of type miles },
  element observatory { element height of type feet }
}
```

We have the `miles` and `feet` are both subtypes of `xs:float`, but neither is a subtype of the other. The following function definition is legal.

```
define function observatory_height (element configuration $c)
returns element height of type feet {
  $c/observatory/height
}
```

It would still be legal if `feet` were replaced by `xs:float`, but not if it were replaced by `miles`. In this example, `element configuration` is the type of the formal parameter `$c`, the XPath expression `$c/observatory/height` extracts the `observatory` child of the `configuration` element, and then extracts the `height` child of the `observatory` element.

Derivation by restriction on complex types. New complex types may also be derived by restriction. The following example is a simplified form of the information that may occur in a bibliographic database, such as that used by Bib-TeX.

```
define element bibliography {
  element of type publicationType *
}
define type publicationType {
  element author *,
  element title ?,
  element journal ?,
  element year ?
}
define type articleType restricts publicationType {
  element author +,
  element title,
  element journal,
  element year
}
define type bookType restricts publicationType {
  element author +,
```

```
    element title,
    element year
}
define element book of type bookType
define element article of type articleType
```

Here a publication may have any number of authors, a mandatory title, and a optional journal, and year. An article must have at least one author, and a mandatory title, journal, and year. A book must have at least one author, a mandatory title and year, and no journal.

Derivation by restriction declares a relationship between two types. This relation depends on both names and structures, in the sense that one name may be derived by restriction from another name only if every value that matches the structure of the first also matches the structure of the second.

When one type is derived from another by restriction, it is fine to pass the restricted type where the base type is expected. For example, consider the following function.

```
define function getTitle ( element of type publicationType $p )
returns element title {
  $p/title
}
```

Here it is acceptable to pass either an article or book element to the function getTitle().

There is a type xs:anyType at the root of the type hierarchy. If a type definition does not specify otherwise, it is considered a restriction of xs:anyType.

Derivation by extension. New complex types may also be derived by extension.

```
define type color restricts xs:string
define type pointType {
  element x of type xs:float ,
  element y of type xs:float
}
define type colorPointType extends pointType {
  element c of type color
}
define element point of type pointType
define element colorPoint of type colorPointType
```

When one type restricts another, one must check that the proper relation holds between the types. When one type extends another, the relation holds automatically, since values of the new type are defined to consist of the concatenation of values of the base type with values of the extension.

Again, when one type is derived from another by extension, it is fine to pass the extended type where the base type is expected. Unlike with restriction, this can lead to surprising consequences. Consider the following.

```
define function countChildren (element of type pointType $p)
returns xs:integer {
  count($p/*)
}
```

This function counts the number of children of the element $p, which will be 2 or 3, depending on whether $p is an element of type `point` or `colorPoint`.

In XQuery, type checking requires that one knows all the types that can be derived from a given type — the type is then treated as the union of all types that can be derived from it. Types derived by restriction add nothing new to this union, but types derived by extension do. This "closed world" approach — that type checking requires knowing all the types derived from a type — is quite different from the "open world" approach used in many object-oriented languages — where one can type-check a class without knowing all its subclasses.

In an object-oriented language, one might expect that if an element of type `colorPoint` is passed to this function, then the x and y elements would be visible but the c element would not be visible. Could the XQuery design adhere better to the object-oriented expectation? It is not obvious how to do so. For instance, consider the above function when `pointType` is replaced by `xs:anyType`.

```
define function countChildren (element of type xs:anyType $x)
  returns xs:integer {
    count($x/*)
  }
```

Here it seems natural to count all the children, while an object-oriented interpretation might suggest counting none of the children, since `xs:anyType` is the root of the type hierarchy.

3   Values and Types

This section describes values and types. For brevity, we consider only 2 atomic types: *String* and *Float*.

3.1   Values

A value is a sequence of zero or more items. An item is either an element or an atomic value. An atomic value is a string or a float. Elements are optionally annotated with their type. An element with no type annotation is the same as an element with the type annotation `xs:anyType`.

Value	::=	*()*
	|	*Item*(, *Item*)*
Item	::=	**element** *ElementName Annotation?* { *Value* }
	|	*AtomicValue*
AtomicValue	::=	*String* | *Float*
Annotation	::=	**of type** *TypeName*

We also write $Value_1$, $Value_2$ for the concatenation of two values.

An untyped value is a sequence of zero or more untyped items. An untyped item is either an element without type annotation or a string. Untyped values are used to described XML documents before validation. Every untyped value is a value.

$$
\begin{array}{lcl}
UntypedValue & ::= & () \\
& | & UntypedItem(\,,UntypedItem)* \\
UntypedItem & ::= & \texttt{element}\ ElementName\ \{\ UntypedValue\ \} \\
& | & String
\end{array}
$$

A simple value consists of a sequence of zero or more atomic values. Every simple value is a value.

$$
\begin{array}{lcl}
SimpleValue & ::= & () \\
& | & AtomicValue(\,,AtomicValue)*
\end{array}
$$

Here are some examples of values.

```
element paper of type paperType {
  element title of type string { "The Essence of Algol" },
  element author of type string { "John Reynolds" }
}
element title of type string { "The Essence of Algol" },
element author of type string { "John Reynolds" }
```

Here are some examples of untyped values.

```
element paper {
  element title { "The Essence of Algol" },
  element author { "John Reynolds" }
}
element latitude { "20.0" },
```

Here are some examples of simple values.

```
"John Reynolds"
10023
1.0, 2.0, 3.0
```

3.2 Types

Types are modeled on regular tree grammars [12, 7]. A type is either an item type, the empty sequence (()), or composed by sequence (,), choice (|), or multiple occurrence – either optional (?), one or more (+), or zero or more (*).

$$
\begin{array}{rcl}
\textit{Type} & ::= & ()\\
& | & \textit{ItemType}\\
& | & \textit{Type , Type}\\
& | & \textit{Type} \mid \textit{Type}\\
& | & \textit{Type Occurrence}\\
\textit{Occurrence} & ::= & \texttt{?} \mid \texttt{+} \mid \texttt{*}
\end{array}
$$

An item type is an element type or an atomic type. Atomic types are specified by name; these names include `xs:string` and `xs:float`.

$$
\begin{array}{rcl}
\textit{ItemType} & ::= & \textit{ElementType}\\
& | & \textit{AtomicTypeName}\\
\textit{AtomicTypeName} & ::= & \textit{TypeName}
\end{array}
$$

An element type gives an optional name and an optional type specifier. A name alone refers to a global declaration. A name with a type specifier is a local declaration. A type specifier alone is a local declaration that matches any name. The word "element" alone refers to any element.

$$
\textit{ElementType} \quad ::= \quad \texttt{element } \textit{ElementName}? \ \textit{TypeSpecifier}?
$$

A type specifier either references a global type, or defines a type by derivation. A type derivation either restricts an atomic type, or restricts a named type to a given type, or extends a named type by a given type.

$$
\begin{array}{rcl}
\textit{ItemType} & ::= & \textit{TypeReference}\\
& | & \textit{TypeDerivation}\\
\textit{TypeReference} & | & \texttt{of type } \textit{TypeName}\\
\textit{TypeDerivation} & | & \texttt{restricts } \textit{AtomicTypeName}\\
& | & \texttt{restricts } \textit{TypeName} \ \{ \ \textit{Type} \ \}\\
& | & \texttt{extends } \textit{TypeName} \ \{ \ \textit{Type} \ \}
\end{array}
$$

A simple type is composed from atomic types by choice or occurrence. Every simple type is a type.

$$
\begin{array}{rcl}
\textit{SimpleType} & ::= & \textit{AtomicTypeName}\\
& | & \textit{SimpleType} \mid \textit{SimpleType}\\
& | & \textit{SimpleType Occurrence}
\end{array}
$$

We saw many examples of types and simple types in Section 2.

3.3   Top Level Definitions

At the top level, one can define elements, and types.

$$
\begin{array}{rcl}
\textit{Definition} & ::= & \texttt{define element } \textit{ElementName} \ \textit{TypeSpecifier}\\
& | & \texttt{define type } \textit{TypeName} \ \textit{TypeDerivation}
\end{array}
$$

Global element declarations, like local element declarations, consist of a name and a type specifier. A global type declaration specifies both the derivation and the declared type. We saw many examples of definitions in Section 2.

3.4 Built-In Type Declarations

The two XML Schema built-in types `xs:anyType` and `xs:anySimpleType` are defined as follows.

```
define type xs:anyType restricts xs:anyType {
  xs:anySimpleType | element*
}
define type xs:anySimpleType restricts xs:anyType {
  ( xs:float | xs:string )*
}
```

4 Relationships between Names

We need auxiliary judgments to describe relationships between element names and between type names.

4.1 Element Name Sets

An element name set is either a singleton consisting of just the given element name, or the wildcard * describing the set of all element names.

$$ElementNameSet \quad ::= \quad ElementName \mid *$$

The judgment

$$ElementName \ \textbf{within} \ ElementNameSet$$

holds when the element name is within the specified element name set. For example:

```
paper within paper
paper within *
```

An element name is within the set consisting of just that element name.

$$\overline{ElementName \ \textbf{within} \ ElementName}$$

An element name is within the set consisting of all element names.

$$\overline{ElementName \ \textbf{within} \ *}$$

4.2 Derives

The judgment

$$TypeName_1 \text{ derives from } TypeName_2$$

holds when the first type name derives from the second type name. For example,

```
bookType derives from publicationType
bookType derives from xs:anyType
colorPointType derives from xs:anyType
feet derives from xs:float
feet derives from xs:anySimpleType
feet derives from xs:anyType
```

This relation is a partial order: it is reflexive and transitive by the rules below, and it is asymmetric because no cycles are allowed in derivation by restriction or extension.

Derivation is reflexive and transitive.

$$\frac{}{TypeName \text{ derives from } TypeName}$$

$$\frac{TypeName_1 \text{ derives from } TypeName_2 \quad TypeName_2 \text{ derives from } TypeName_3}{TypeName_1 \text{ derives from } TypeName_3}$$

Every type name derives from the type it is declared to derive from by restriction or extension.

$$\frac{\text{define type } TypeName \text{ restricts } BaseTypeName}{TypeName \text{ derives from } BaseTypeName}$$

$$\frac{\text{define type } TypeName \text{ restricts } BaseTypeName \{ \ Type \ \}}{TypeName \text{ derives from } BaseTypeName}$$

$$\frac{\text{define type } TypeName \text{ extends } BaseTypeName \{ \ Type \ \}}{TypeName \text{ derives from } BaseTypeName}$$

5 Auxiliary Judgments

We now define two auxiliary judgments that are used in matching and validation. Here is the rule from matching that uses these judgments.

$$\frac{\begin{array}{c} ElementType \text{ yields } ElementNameSet \ TypeSpecifier \\ TypeSpecifier \text{ resolves to } BaseTypeName \{ \ Type \ \} \\ ElementName \text{ within } ElementNameSet \\ TypeName \text{ derives from } BaseTypeName \\ Value \text{ matches } Type \end{array}}{\text{element } ElementName \text{ of type } TypeName \{ Value \} \text{ matches } ElementType}$$

The element type yields an element name set and a type specifier, and the type specifier resolves to a base type name and a type. Then the given element matches the element type if three things hold: the element name must be within the element name set, the type name must derive from the base type name, and the value must match the type.

5.1   Yields

The judgment

$$ElementType \text{ yields } ElementNameSet \; TypeSpecifier$$

takes an element type and yields an element name set and a type specifier. For example,

```
element author yields author xs:string
element height of type feet yields height of type feet
element of type feet yields * of type feet
element yields * of type xs:anyType
```

If the element type is a reference to a global element, then it yields the the name of the element and the type specifier from the element declaration.

$$\frac{\texttt{define element } ElementName \; TypeSpecifier}{\texttt{element } ElementName \texttt{ yields } ElementName \; TypeSpecifier}$$

If the element type contains an element name and a type specifier, then it yields the given element name and type specifier.

$$\overline{\texttt{element } ElementName \; \{ \; TypeSpecifier \} \texttt{ yields } ElementName \; TypeSpecifier}$$

If the element type contains only a type specifier, then it yields the wildcard name and the type specifier.

$$\overline{\texttt{element } \{ \; TypeSpecifier \; \} \texttt{ yields } * \; TypeSpecifier}$$

If the element type has no element name and no type specifier, then it yields the wildcard name and the type xs:anyType.

$$\overline{\texttt{element yields } * \; \texttt{xs:anyType}}$$

5.2   Resolution

The judgment

$$\textit{TypeSpecifier} \text{ resolves to } \textit{TypeName} \;\{\; \textit{Type} \;\}$$

resolves a type specifier to a type name and a type. For example,

```
    of type colorPoint
  resolves to
    colorPoint {
      element x of type xs:float ,
      element y of type xs:float
      element c of type color
    }
```

and

```
    restricts xs:float   resolves to   xs:float { xs:float }
```

and

```
    restricts publicationType {
        element author +,
        element title,
        element year
    }
  resolves to
    publicationType {
        element author +,
        element title,
        element year
    }
```

and

```
    extends pointType {
      element c of type color
    }
  resolves to
    colorPoint {
      element x of type xs:float ,
      element y of type xs:float
      element c of type color
    }
```

If the type specifier references a global type, then resolve the type derivation in its definition, yielding a base type name and a type. Resolution returns the type name and the type (the base type name is discarded).

$$\frac{\textnormal{\texttt{define type}} \; \textit{TypeName} \; \textit{TypeDerivation}}{\textnormal{\texttt{of type}} \; \textit{TypeName} \; \texttt{resolves to} \; \textit{TypeName} \; \{ \; \textit{Type} \; \}}$$

If the type specifier restricts an atomic type, then return the atomic type as both the type name and the type.

$$\frac{}{\texttt{restricts} \; \textit{AtomicTypeName}}$$
$$\texttt{resolves to} \; \textit{AtomicTypeName} \; \{\textit{AtomicTypeName}\}$$

If the type specifier is a restriction of a non-atomic type, then return the given type name and the given type.

$$\overline{\texttt{restricts} \; \textit{TypeName} \; \{ \; \textit{Type} \; \} \; \texttt{resolves to} \; \textit{TypeName} \; \{ \; \textit{Type} \; \}}$$

If the type specifier is an extension, then resolve the name to get the base type, and return the given type name, and the result of concatenating the base type and the given type.

$$\frac{\texttt{of type} \; \textit{TypeName} \; \texttt{resolves to} \; \textit{TypeName} \; \{ \; \textit{BaseType} \; \}}{\texttt{extends} \; \textit{TypeName} \; \{ \; \textit{Type} \} \; \texttt{resolves to} \; \textit{TypeName} \; \{ \; \textit{BaseType} \, , \; \textit{Type} \; \}}$$

6   Matches

The judgment

$$\textit{Value} \; \texttt{matches} \; \textit{Type}$$

holds when the given value matches the given type. For example,

```
element author of type xs:string { "Robert Harper" },
element author of type xs:string { "John Mitchell" }
matches
element author of type xs:string +
```

and

```
10023 matches feet
```

and

```
element colorPoint of type colorPointType {
  element x of type xs:float { 1.0 }
  element y of type xs:float { 2.0 }
  element c of type color { "blue" }
}
matches
element colorPoint
```

The empty sequence matches the empty sequence type.

$$\frac{}{\text{() matches ()}}$$

If two values match two types, then their sequence matches the corresponding sequence type.

$$\frac{Value_1 \text{ matches } Type_1 \qquad Value_2 \text{ matches } Type_2}{Value_1 \text{ , } Value_2 \text{ matches } Type_1 \text{ , } Type_2}$$

If a value matches a type, then it also matches a choice type where that type is one of the choices.

$$\frac{Value \text{ matches } Type_1}{Value \text{ matches } Type_1 \text{ | } Type_2}$$

$$\frac{Value \text{ matches } Type_2}{Value \text{ matches } Type_1 \text{ | } Type_2}$$

A value matches an optional occurrence of a type if it matches either the empty sequence or the type.

$$\frac{Value \text{ matches () | } Type}{Value \text{ matches } Type?}$$

A value matches one or more occurrences of a type if it matches a sequence of the type followed by zero or more occurrences of the type.

$$\frac{Value \text{ matches } Type \text{ , } Type*}{Value \text{ matches } Type+}$$

A value matches zero or more occurrences of a type if it matches an optional one or more occurrences of the type.

$$\frac{Value \text{ matches } Type+?}{Value \text{ matches } Type*}$$

A string matches an atomic type name if the atomic type name derives from xs:string. Similarly for floats.

$$\frac{AtomicTypeName \text{ derives from xs:string}}{String \text{ matches } AtomicTypeName}$$

$$\frac{AtomicTypeName \text{ derives from } \texttt{xs:float}}{Float \texttt{ matches } AtomicTypeName}$$

The rule for matching elements was explained at the beginning of Section 5.

$$\frac{\begin{array}{c} ElementType \texttt{ yields } ElementNameSet \; TypeSpecifier \\ TypeSpecifier \texttt{ resolves to } BaseTypeName \; \{ \; Type \; \} \\ ElementName \texttt{ within } ElementNameSet \\ TypeName \texttt{ derives from } BaseTypeName \\ Value \texttt{ matches } Type \end{array}}{\texttt{element } ElementName \texttt{of type } TypeName \; \{ \; Value \; \} \texttt{ matches } ElementType}$$

7   Erasure

7.1   Simply Erases

To define erasure, we need an ancillary judgment. The judgment

$$SimpleValue \texttt{ simply erases to } String$$

holds when *SimpleValue* erases to the string *String*. For example,

```
10023.0 erases to "10023.0"
"10023.0" erases to "10023.0"
"John Reynolds" erases to "John Reynolds"
(1.0, 2.0, 3.0) erases to "1.0 2.0 3.0"
```

The empty sequence erases to the empty string.

$$\overline{\texttt{() simply erases to } \texttt{""}}$$

The concatenation of two non-empty sequences of values erases to the concatenation of their erasures with a separating space.

$$\frac{\begin{array}{cc} SimpleValue_1 \texttt{ simply erases to } String_1 & SimpleValue_1 \neq \texttt{()} \\ SimpleValue_2 \texttt{ simply erases to } String_2 & SimpleValue_2 \neq \texttt{()} \end{array}}{SimpleValue_1, SimpleValue_2 \texttt{ simply erases to } \texttt{concat}(String_1, \texttt{" "}, String_2)}$$

A string erases to itself.

$$\overline{String \texttt{ simply erases to } String}$$

A float erases to any string that represents it.

$$\overline{\texttt{float-of-string}(String) \texttt{ simply erases to } String}$$

7.2   Erases

The judgment

$$Value \ \textsf{erases to} \ \ UntypedValue$$

holds when the given value erases to the untyped value. For example,

```
    element author of type xs:string { "John Reynolds" }
  erases to
    element author { "John Reynolds" }
```

and

```
    element shuttle of type SpaceLocation {
      element latitude of type degrees { 20.0 },
      element longitude of type degrees { -155.5 },
      element height of type miles { 5.7 }
    }
  erases to
    element shuttle {
      element latitude { "20.0" },
      element longitude { "-155.5" },
      element height { "5.7" }
    }
```

The empty sequence erases to itself.

$$\frac{}{\textsf{() erases to ()}}$$

The erasure of the concatenation of two values is the concatenation of their erasure, so long as neither of the two original values is simple.

$$\frac{Value_1 \ \textsf{erases to} \ UntypedValue_1 \qquad Value_1 \ \textsf{not a simple value}}{Value_1 \ , \ Value_2 \ \textsf{erases to} \ UntypedValue_1 \ , \ UntypedValue_2}$$
$$Value_2 \ \textsf{erases to} \ UntypedValue_2 \qquad Value_2 \ \textsf{not a simple value}$$

The erasure of a simple value is the corresponding string content using simpler erasure.

$$\frac{SimpleValue \ \textsf{simply erases to} \ String}{SimpleValue \ \textsf{erases to} \ String}$$

The erasure of an element is an element that has the same name and the erasure of the given content.

$$\frac{Value \ \textsf{erases to} \ UntypedValue}{\textsf{element} \ ElementName \ \textsf{of type} \ TypeName \ \{ \ Value \ \} \\ \textsf{erases to} \\ \textsf{element} \ ElementName \ \{ \ UntypedValue \ \}}$$

8   Validation

8.1   Simply Validate

The judgment

> simply validate as *SimpleType* { *String* } => *SimpleValue*

holds if validating the string against the simple type succeeds and returns the simple value. For example,

```
simply validate as xs:float { "10023.0" } => 10023.0
simply validate as xs:string { "10023.0" } => "10023.0"
simply validate as xs:string {"John Reynolds"} => "John Reynolds"
simply validate as xs:float* { "1.0 2.0 3.0" } => (1.0, 2.0, 3.0)
```

Simply validating a string against a choice type yields the result of simply validating the string against either the first or second type in the choice.

$$\frac{\text{simply validate as } SimpleType_1 \; \{ \; String \; \} \; \Rightarrow \; SimpleValue}{\text{simply validate as } SimpleType_1 \; | \; SimpleType_2 \; \{ \; String \; \} \; \Rightarrow \; SimpleValue}$$

The rules for occurrences look slightly different from those in matching, because the simple types do not include the empty sequence or sequencing. Validating one or more occurrences breaks into two cases. In the first there is exactly one occurrence; in the second there is one occurrence followed by one or more occurrences, where the strings are separated by a space.

$$\frac{}{\text{simply validate as } SimpleType? \; \{ \; "" \; \} \; \Rightarrow \; ()}$$

$$\frac{\text{simply validate as } SimpleType \; \{ \; String \; \} \; \Rightarrow \; SimpleValue}{\text{simply validate as } SimpleType? \; \{ \; String \; \} \; \Rightarrow \; SimpleValue}$$

$$\frac{\text{simply validate as } SimpleType \; \{ \; String \; \} \; \Rightarrow \; SimpleValue}{\text{simply validate as } SimpleType+ \; \{ \; String \; \} \; \Rightarrow \; SimpleValue}$$

$$\frac{\text{simply validate as } SimpleType \; \{ \; String_1 \; \} \; \Rightarrow \; SimpleValue_1 \quad \text{simply validate as } SimpleType+ \; \{ \; String2 \; \} \; \Rightarrow \; SimpleValue_2}{\text{simply validate as } SimpleType+ \; \{ \; \texttt{concat}(String_1, "\; ", String_2) \; \} \; \Rightarrow \; SimpleValue_1 \; , \; SimpleValue_2}$$

$$\frac{\text{simply validate as } SimpleType+? \; \{ \; String \; \} \; \Rightarrow \; SimpleValue}{\text{simply validate as } SimpleType* \; \{ \; String \; \} \; \Rightarrow \; SimpleValue}$$

Simply validating a string against an atomic type derived from `xs:string` yields the string itself.

$$\frac{AtomicTypeName \text{ derives from } \texttt{xs:string}}{\texttt{simply validate as } AtomicTypeName \texttt{ \{ } String \texttt{ \} => } String}$$

Simply validating a string against an atomic type derived from `xs:float` yields the result of converting the string to a float.

$$\frac{AtomicTypeName \text{ derives from } \texttt{xs:float}}{\texttt{simply validate as } AtomicTypeName \texttt{ \{ } String \texttt{ \}}}$$
$$\texttt{=> float-of-string}(String)$$

8.2 Validate

The judgment

$$\texttt{validate as } Type \texttt{ \{ } UntypedValue \texttt{ \} => } Value$$

holds if validating the untyped value against the type succeeds and returns the value. For example,

```
validate as element of type xs:string {
  element author { "John Reynolds" }
}
=>
  element author of type xs:string { "John Reynolds" }
```

and

```
validate as element colorPoint {
  element colorPoint {
    element x { 1.0 }
    element y { 2.0 }
    element c { "blue" }
  }
}
=>
 element colorPoint of type colorPointType {
   element x of type xs:float { 1.0 }
   element y of type xs:float { 2.0 }
   element c of type color { "blue" }
 }
```

Validating the empty sequence as the empty type yields the empty sequence.

$$\frac{}{\texttt{validate as () \{ () \} => ()}}$$

Validating a concatenation of untyped values against a concatenation of types yields the concatenation of the validated values.

$$\frac{\text{validate as } Type_1 \text{ \{ } UntypedValue_1 \text{ \} } => Value_1 \qquad \text{validate as } Type_2 \text{ \{ } UntypedValue_2 \text{ \} } => Value_2}{\text{validate as } Type_1 \text{ , } Type_2 \text{ \{ } UntypedValue_1 \text{ , } UntypedValue_2 \text{ \} } => Value_1 \text{ , } Value_2}$$

Validating a value against a choice type yields the result of validating the value as either the first or second type in the choice.

$$\frac{\text{validate as } Type_1 \text{ \{ } UntypedValue \text{ \} } => Value}{\text{validate as } Type_1 \text{ | } Type_2 \text{ \{ } UntypedValue \text{ \} } => Value}$$

$$\frac{\text{validate as } Type_2 \text{ \{ } UntypedValue \text{ \} } => Value}{\text{validate as } Type_1 \text{ | } Type_2 \text{ \{ } UntypedValue \text{ \} } => Value}$$

The validation rules for occurrences are similar to the rules for occurrences in matching.

$$\frac{\text{validate as } (\text{() | } Type) \text{ \{ } UntypedValue \text{ \} } => Value}{\text{validate as } Type? \text{ \{ } UntypedValue \text{ \} } => Value}$$

$$\frac{\text{validate as } (Type \text{ , } Type*) \text{ \{ } UntypedValue \text{ \} } => Value}{\text{validate as } Type+ \text{ \{ } UntypedValue \text{ \} } => Value}$$

$$\frac{\text{validate as } Type+? \text{ \{ } UntypedValue \text{ \} } => Value}{\text{validate as } Type* \text{ \{ } UntypedValue \text{ \} } => Value}$$

Validating a string against a simple type is defined in the previous section.

$$\frac{\text{simply validate as } SimpleType \text{ \{ } String \text{ \} } => SimpleValue}{\text{validate as } SimpleType \text{ \{ } String \text{ \} } => SimpleValue}$$

Validating an element against an element type is described by the following rule.

$$\frac{\begin{array}{c} ElementType \text{ yields } ElementNameSet \text{ } TypeSpecifier \\ TypeSpecifier \text{ resolves to } BaseTypeName \text{ \{ } Type \text{ \} } \\ ElementName \text{ within } ElementNameSet \\ \text{validate as } Type \text{ \{ } UntypedValue \text{ \} } => Value \end{array}}{\begin{array}{c} \text{validate as } ElementType \text{ \{ element } ElementName \text{ \{ } UntypedValue \text{ \} \} } \\ => \text{ element } ElementName \text{ of type } BaseTypeName \text{ \{ } Value \text{ \} } \end{array}}$$

The element type yields an element name set and a type specifier, and the type specifier resolves to a base type name and a type. Then the given element matches the element type if two things hold: the element name must be within the element name set, and validating the untyped value against the type must yield a value. The resulting element has the element name, the base type name, and the validated value.

9   Ambiguity and the Validation Theorem

For a given type, validation takes an external representation (an untyped value) into an internal representation (a value annotated with types). For a given type, we would like each external representation to correspond to just one internal representation, and conversely. We show that this is the case if the type is unambiguous, using a characterization of validation in terms of erasure and matching.

Ambiguity. Validation is a judgment that relates a type and an untyped value to a value.

$$\text{validate as } \textit{Type} \ \{ \ \textit{UntypedValue} \ \} \ \texttt{=>} \ \textit{Value}$$

In most of the examples we have seen, validation behaves as a function. That is, for a given type, for every untyped value, there is at most one value such that the above judgment holds. In this case, we say the type is *unambiguous*. But just as there is more than one way to skin a cat, sometimes there is more than one way to validate a value.

Here is an example of an ambiguous complex type:

```
define element amb {
  element elt of type xs:float |
  element elt of type xs:string
}
```

```
  validate as amb { <amb><elt>1</elt></amb> }
=>
  element amb { element elt of type xs:float { 1 } }
```

```
  validate as amb { <elt>1</elt> }
=>
  element amb { element elt of type xs:string { "1" } }
```

Here is an example of an ambiguous simple type:

```
validate as xs:string* { "a b c" } => ("a b c")
validate as xs:string* { "a b c" } => ("a b", "c")
validate as xs:string* { "a b c" } => ("a", "b c")
validate as xs:string* { "a b c" } => ("a", "b", "c")
```

There are well known algorithms for determining when regular expressions are ambiguous, and there are similar algorithms for regular tree grammars [12, 7]. These are easily adapted to give an algorithm for determining when a given type is ambiguous.

In Schema, the issue of ambiguity is resolved differently than here. Complex types are required to be unambiguous. Simple types have rules that resolve the ambiguity: every space is taken as a list separator, and in a union the first alternative that matches is chosen. Thus, for the first example above Schema deems the type illegal, while for the second example above Schema validation yields the last of the four possibilities.

Our formal model differs from Schema for two reasons. First, while Schema is concerned solely with validation against types written by a user, XQuery must also support type inference. And while it may be reasonable to require that a user write types that are unambiguous, it is not reasonable to place this restriction on a type inference system. For example, if expression e_0 has type `xs:boolean` and e_1 has type t_1 and e_2 has type t_2, the expression `if` (e_0) `then` e_1 `else` e_2 has type $t_1 | t_2$, and it is not reasonable to require that t_1 and t_2 be disjoint.

Second, defining validation as a relation rather than a function permits a simple characterization of validation in terms of matching and erasure, as given in the next section.

The validation theorem. We can characterize validation in terms of erasure and matching.

Theorem 1. *We have that*
   validate as *Type* { *UntypedValue* } => *Value*
if and only if
   Value matches *Type*
and
   Value erases to *UntypedValue*

The proof is by induction over derivations.

We would like to know that if we convert an external value to an internal value (using validation) and then convert the internal value back to an external value (using erasure) that we end up back where we started. This follows immediately from the validation theorem.

Corollary 1. *If*
   validate as *Type* { *UntypedValue* } => *Value*
and
   Value erases to *UntypedValue'*
then
   UntypedValue = *UntypedValue'*

Proof. From the first hypothesis and the validation theorem we have that
   Value erases to *UntypedValue*
Taking this together with the second hypothesis and the fact that erasure is a function, the conclusion follows immediately. □

Similarly, we would like to know that if we convert an internal value of a given type to an external value (using erasure) and then convert the internal value back to an external value (using validation against that type) that we again end up back where we started, so long as the type is unambiguous. Again, this follows immediately from the validation theorem.

Corollary 2. *If*

   Value `matches` *Type*

and

   Value `erases to` *UntypedValue*

and

   `validate as` *Type* { *UntypedValue* } `=>` *Value'*

and

   Type is unambiguous

then

   Value = *Value'*

Proof. By the validation theorem, we have that the first two hypotheses are equivalent to

   `validate as` *Type* { *UntypedValue* } `=>` *Value*

Taking this together with the third hypothesis and the fact that validate is a function when the type is unambiguous, the conclusion follows immediately. □

References

[1] Tim Bray, Jean Paoli, and C. M. Sperberg-McQueen. Extensible Markup Language (XML) 1.0. W3C Recommendation, February 1998. 21

[2] Allen Brown, Matthew Fuchs, Jonathan Robie, and Philip Wadler. MSL - a model for W3C XML Schema. In *Proceedings of International World Wide Web Conference*, pages 191–200, Hong Kong, China, 2001. 22

[3] James Clarke. XSL Transformations (XSLT) version 1.0. W3C Proposed Recommendation, October 1999. 21

[4] James Clarke. TREX — Tree Regular Expressions for XML. Thai Open Source Software Center, February 2001. 21

[5] James Clarke and Murata Makoto. RELAX NG specification. Oasis, December 2001. 21, 22

[6] Sophie Cluet, Claude Delobel, Jérôme Siméon, and Katarzyna Smaga. Your mediators need data conversion! In *Proceedings of ACM Conference on Management of Data (SIGMOD)*, pages 177–188, Seattle, Washington, June 1998. 21

[7] H. Comon, M. Dauchet, R. Gilleron, F. Jacquemard, D. Lugiez, S. Tison, and M. Tommasi. Tree automata techniques and applications, 1997. 26, 30, 43

[8] Haruo Hosoya and Benjamin C. Pierce. XDuce: an XML processing language. In *International Workshop on the Web and Databases (WebDB'2000)*, Dallas, Texas, May 2000. 21, 22

[9] Michael Kay. XSL Transformations (XSLT) version 2.0. W3C Working Draft, April 2002. 21

[10] Murata Makoto. Document description and processing languages – regular language description for XML (relax), October 2000. 21

[11] Yannis Papakonstantinou and Victor Vianu. DTD inference for views of XML data. In *Proceedings of ACM Symposium on Principles of Database Systems (PODS)*, Dallas, Texas, May 2000. 26

[12] Grzegorz Rozenberg and Arto Salomaa, editors. *Handbook of Formal Languages.* Springer-Verlag, 1997. 30, 43

[13] Henri S. Thompson, David Beech, Murray Maloney, and N. Mendelsohn. XML Schema part 1: Structures. W3C Recommendation, May 2001. 21

[14] XPath 2.0. W3C Working Draft, April 2002. 21

[15] XQuery 1.0: An XML query language. W3C Working Draft, April 2002. 21

[16] XQuery 1.0 formal semantics. W3C Working Draft, March 2002. 22, 24

To the Gates of HAL: A HAL Tutorial

María García de la Banda[1], Bart Demoen[2],
Kim Marriott[1], and Peter J. Stuckey[3]

[1] School of Computer Science & Software Engineering
Monash University, Australia
[2] Dept. of Computer Science
K.U.Leuven, Belgium
[3] Dept. of Computer Science & Software Engineering
University of Melbourne, Australia

Abstract. Experience using constraint programming to solve real-life problems has shown that finding an efficient solution to the problem often requires experimentation with different constraint solvers or even building a problem-specific constraint solver. HAL is a new constraint logic programming language expressly designed to facilitate this process. It provides semi-optional type, mode and determinism declarations. These allow natural constraint specification by means of type overloading, better compile-time error checking and generation of more efficient run-time code. Importantly, it provides type classes which can be used to specify solver interfaces, allowing the constraint programmer to support modelling of a constraint problem independent of a particular solver, leading to easy "plug and play" experimentation with different solvers. Other interesting features include mutable global variables for implementing a constraint store, and dynamic scheduling and Constraint Handling Rules (CHRs) for combining, extending and writing new constraint solvers.

1 Introduction

Constraint logic programming (CLP) languages are evolving to support more flexible experimentation with constraint solvers. First generation CLP languages, such as CLP($\mathcal{R}$) [15], provided almost no support. They had a fixed underlying solver for each constraint domain which was viewed as a closed "black box." Second generation CLP languages, such as clpfd [6], provided more support by viewing the solver as a "glass box" which could be extended to support problem-specific complex constraints. However, CLP programmers want more than this: they want to be able to develop new problem-specific constraint solvers, for example by using "hybrid" methods that combine different constraint solving techniques. For this reason, recent versions of the CLP languages ECLiPSe and SICStus support the addition and specification of new constraint solvers by providing features such as dynamic scheduling, constraint handling rules [8] and attributed variables [12].

We describe the CLP language, HAL, which has been expressly designed to support experimentation with different constraint solvers and development of new solvers. Our specific design objectives were five-fold:

Z. Hu and M. Rodríguez-Artalejo (Eds.): FLOPS 2002, LNCS 2441, pp. 47–66, 2002.

- *Efficiency*: Current CLP languages are considerably slower than traditional imperative languages such as C. This efficiency overhead has limited the use of CLP languages, and becomes even more of an issue when constraint solvers are to be (partially) implemented in the language itself.
- *Integrability*: It should be easy to call solvers written in other languages, e.g. C, with little overhead. Conversely, it should be possible for HAL code to be readily called from other languages, facilitating integration into larger applications. Although most CLP languages provide a foreign language interface, it is often complex and may require rewriting the foreign language code to use "safe" memory management routines.
- *Robustness*: Current CLP languages provide little compile-time checking. However, when developing complex multi-layered software such as constraint solvers compile-time checking becomes crucial for improving program robustness.
- *Flexible choice of constraint solvers:* It should be easy to "plug and play" with different constraint solvers over the same domain.
- *Easy definition of new solvers:* it should be straightforward to extend an existing solver, create a hybrid solver by combining solvers and to write a new constraint solver.

HAL has four interesting features which allow it to meet these objectives. The first is semi-optional type, mode and determinism declarations for predicates and functions. Information from the declarations allows the generation of efficient target code, improves robustness by using compile-time tests to check that solvers and other procedures are being used in the correct way, and facilitates efficient integration with foreign language procedures. Type information also means that predicate and function overloading can be resolved at compile-time, allowing a natural syntax for constraints. For example, "=" is overloaded to be equality on all constraint domains, and type inference determines if this is equality over terms, reals etc.

The second feature is type classes. These allow specification of an abstract interface for solvers and so facilitate "plug and play" experimentation with different solvers over the same domain.

The third feature is support for "propagators" by means of a specialized delay construct. HAL allows the programmer to annotate goals with a delay condition which tells the system that execution of that goal should be delayed until the condition is satisfied. By default, the delayed goal remains active and is reexecuted whenever the delay condition becomes true again. Such dynamic scheduling of goals is useful for writing simple constraint solvers, extending a solver and combining different solvers. Importantly, delay conditions and the method for handling delayed goals is solver dependent, but with a common interface provided as a standard type class.

The fourth feature is "global variables." These behave a little like C's static variables and are only visible within a module. They are not intended for general use; rather they allow communication between search branches, and allow solver writers to efficiently implement a persistent constraint store.

Broadly speaking, HAL unifies two recent directions in constraint programming language research. The first direction is that of earlier CLP languages, including CLP($\mathcal{R}$), clpfd, ECLiPSe and SICStus. The second direction is that of logic programming languages with declarations as exemplified by Mercury [20]. Earlier CLP languages provided constraints and constraint solvers for pre-defined constraint domains and many provided dynamic scheduling. However, they did not allow type, mode, determinism or type class declarations. Providing such declarations has influenced the entire design of HAL, from the module system to delay constructs. Another important difference is explicit language support for extending or writing constraint solvers.

Like HAL, the Mercury language also provides type, mode, determinism and type class declarations. It is probably the most similar language to HAL, and we have leveraged greatly from its sophisticated compilation support by using it as an intermediate target language. The key difference is that Mercury is logic programming based and does not support constraints and constraint solvers. Indeed, it does not even fully support Herbrand constraints since it provides only a limited form of unification.

This paper provides a high-level introduction to HAL. For more detailed explanation of various aspects of HAL the interested reader is referred to our earlier publications [4, 3, 9, 2, 13]. In the next section we introduce the HAL language. In Section 3 we discuss the declarations supported by HAL, then in Section 4 we elaborate on how constraint solvers fit within in the language. In Section 5 we illustrate the user-extensible delay mechanism provided by HAL. Next in Section 6 we describe built-in Herbrand constraint solving facilities in HAL, then in Section 7 we examine the built-in solver hierarchy. Section 8 discusses how to build constraint solvers in HAL. In Section 9 we discuss the current implementation and Section 10 concludes with a discussion of future work.

2   A First Example

The basic HAL syntax follows the standard CLP syntax, with variables, literals, rules and predicates defined as usual (see, e.g., [18] for an introduction to CLP). Our philosophy has been to design a language which is as pure as possible, without unduly compromising efficiency. The module system in HAL is similar to that of Mercury. A module is defined in a file, it **imports** the modules it uses and has **export** annotations on the declarations for the objects that it wishes to be visible to those importing the module. Selective importation is also possible.

The core language supports the basic integer, float, string, and character data types plus polymorphic constructor types (such as lists) based on these basic types. This support is, however, limited to assignment, testing for equality, and construction and deconstruction of ground terms. More sophisticated constraint solving is provided by importing a constraint solver for each type involved.

As a simple example, the following program is a HAL version of the now classic CLP program **mortgage** for modelling the relationship between P the principal or amount owed, T the number of periods in the mortgage, I the interest rate of the mortgage, R the repayment due each period of the mortgage and B the balance owing at the end.

```
:- module mortgage.                                         (L1)
:- export pred mortgage(CF,CF,CF,CF,CF) <= float_solver(CF). (L2)
:-         mode mortgage(in,in,in,in,out) is nondet.        (L3)
:-         mode mortgage(oo,oo,oo,oo,oo) is nondet.         (L4)
mortgage(P,0.0,I,R,P).                                      (R1)
mortgage(P,T,I,R,B) :- T >= 1.0, NP = P + P * I - R,        (R2)
                       mortgage(NP,T-1.0,I,R,B).
```

The first line ($L1$) states that this is the definition of the module `mortgage`. Line ($L2$) declares that this module exports the predicate `mortgage` which is polymorphic in the type of its as argument but the type must be an instance of the `float_solver` type class. This is the *type* declaration for `mortgage`. Lines ($L3$) and ($L4$) are examples of *mode of usage* declarations. Since there are two declarations, `mortgage` has two possible modes of usage. In the first, the first four arguments have an `in` mode meaning their values are fixed when the predicate is called, and the last has a mode `out` which means it is uninitialized when called, and fixed on the return from the call to `mortgage`. Line ($L4$) gives another mode for the `mortgage` where each argument has mode `oo` meaning that each argument takes a "constrained" variable and returns a "constrained" variable. This is a more flexible mode of usage but will be less efficient to execute. The two declarations also state that for either mode `mortgage` is `nondet` meaning that the query may return 0 or more answers. Actually, in the case of ($L3$) it would be more precise to declare it as `semidet`, meaning that it either fails (for example `mortgage(0.0,-1.0,0.0,0.0,B)` fails) or succeeds with exactly one answer. However, HAL is currently unable to confirm it since this would require reasoning over numbers.

The rest of the file contains the standard two rules defining `mortgage`. The first states that when the number of repayments is 0, then the balance is simply the principal. The second states that if the number of repayments is greater than one, then we make one repayment, compute the new principle `NP` and take out a mortgage with this new principle for one less time period.

Since the definition of `mortgage` is polymorphic we can use it with any constraint solver for `floats`. In the following code we use the standard `clpr` solver, which provides a simplex-based arithmetic constraint solver for constrained floats, called `cfloats`. It is based on the CLP($\mathcal{R}$) solver.

```
:- module main.
:- import mortgage,clpr,io.
:- export io impure pred main.
:-                  mode main is cc_multi.
main :- ( mortgage(10000,10,0.10,1500,B), V = val(B) ->
          io write("The balance remaining is:"),
          io write(V)
        ; io write("No solution")).
```

The predicate `main` is declared to be `io` to indicate that it makes use of the I/O routines and hence an I/O state is implicitly threaded through the code.

It is also declared to be **impure** since it uses the impure **val** function. The **val** function returns the value of a solver variable if it is has a fixed value and fails otherwise. The determinism **cc_multi** means that **main** succeeds at least once, but we are interested in only the first solution.

3   Declarations

As we can see from the above example, one of the key features of HAL is that programmers may annotate predicate definitions with declarations. Information from the declarations allows the generation of efficient target code, compile-time tests to check that solvers and other predicates are being used in the correct way and facilitates integration with foreign language procedures. Currently the compiler supports type, mode, determinism, I/O and purity declarations, but the aim is to eventually support general user-defined declarations similar to those supported by the CIAO language [11].

By default, declarations are checked at compile-time, generating an error if they cannot be confirmed by the compiler. However, the programmer can also provide "trust me" declarations. These generate an error if the compiler can definitely prove they are wrong, but otherwise the compiler trusts the programmer and generates code according to the trusted declarations. A compile-time warning is issued if the declaration cannot be confirmed by the compiler.

Type declarations: These specify the representation format of a variable or argument. Thus, for example, the type system distinguishes between constrained floats provided by the **clpr** solver and the standard numerical float since these have a different representation. Types are specified using type definition statements. They are (polymorphic) regular tree type statements. For instance, lists are defined as:

```
:- typedef list(T) -> ([] ; [T|list(T)]).
```

Equivalence types are also supported. For example,

```
:- typedef vector = list(float).
```

Ad-hoc overloading of predicates is also allowed, although the predicates for different type signatures must be in different modules.

As an example, imagine that we wish to write a module for handling complex numbers. We can do this by leveraging from the **clpr** solver defining **cfloats**.

```
:- module complex.
:- import clpr.
:- export_abstract typedef complex -> c(cfloat,cfloat).
:- export pred cx(cfloat,cfloat,complex).       % access/creation
:-         mode cx(in,in,out) is det.
:-         mode cx(out,out,in) is det.
:-         mode cx(oo,oo,oo) is semidet.
cx(X,Y,c(X,Y)).
:- export func complex + complex --> complex.   % addition
:-         mode in + in --> out is det.
:-         mode oo + oo --> oo is semidet.
c(X1,Y1) + c(X2,Y2) --> c(X1+X2,Y1+Y2).
```

Note that the type definition for `complex` is exported abstractly, which means that the internal representation of a complex number is hidden within the module. This ensures that code cannot create or modify complex numbers outside of the `complex` module. Thus, this module also needs to export a predicate, `cx`, for accessing and creating a complex number. As this example demonstrates, HAL also allows the programmer to declare functions. The symbol "`-->`" should be read as "returns."

Using this module the programmer can now use complex arithmetic as if it were built into the language itself. If both `clpr` and `complex` are imported, type inference will determine the type of the arguments of each call to `+` and appropriately qualify the call with the correct module.

Mode declarations: These specify how execution of a predicate modifies the "instantiation state" of its arguments. A mode is associated with a predicate argument and has the form $Inst_1 \rightarrow Inst_2$, where $Inst_1$ and $Inst_2$ describe the input and output instantiation states of the argument, respectively.

The *base* instantiation states are **new**, **old** and **ground**. Variable X is **new** if it has not been seen by the constraint solver, **old** if it has, and **ground** if X has a known fixed value. Note that **old** is interpreted as **ground** for variables of non-solver types (i.e., types for which there is no solver).

The *base* modes are mappings from one base instantiation to another: we use two letter codes (**oo, no, og, gg, ng**) based on the first letter of the instantiation, e.g. **ng** is new→ground. The standard modes **in** and **out** are renamings of **gg** and **ng**, respectively. Therefore, line ($L3$) in our example program declares that each argument of `mortgage` has mode **oo**, i.e., takes an **old** variable and returns an **old** variable.

More sophisticated instantiation states (lying between **old** and **ground**) may be used to describe the state of complex terms. Instantiation state definitions look something like type definitions. For example, the instantiation definition

```
:- instdef fixed_length_list -> ([] ; [old | fixed_length_list]).
```

indicates that the variable is bound to either an empty list or a list with an **old** head and a tail with the same instantiation state.

Mode definitions have the following syntax:

```
:- modedef to_groundlist -> (fixed_length_list -> ground).
:- modedef same(I) -> (I -> I).
```

We have already seen examples of predicate mode declarations in the previous two programs. As another example, a mode declaration for an integer variable labelling predicate `labeling` would be

```
:- mode labeling(to_groundlist) is nondet.
```

Mode checking is a relatively complex operation involving reordering body literals in order to satisfy mode constraints, and inserting initialization predicates for solver variables. The compiler performs multi-variant specialization by generating different code for each declared mode for a predicate. The code corresponding to a mode is referred to as a "procedure" and calls to the original predicate are replaced by calls to the appropriate procedure.

Determinism declarations: These detail how many answers a predicate may have. We use the Mercury hierarchy: `nondet` means any number of solutions; `multi` at least one solution; `semidet` at most one solution; `det` exactly one solution; `failure` no solutions; and `erroneous` a runtime error. In addition the determinisms `cc_multi` and `cc_nondet` correspond to `multi` and `nondet` in a context where we are only interested in the first solution.

I/O declarations: Predicates and literals that use I/O safely must be annotated with `io`. The compiler will then automatically thread two extra arguments holding the I/O state before and after execution. Predicates can also use I/O unsafely by annotating calls to I/O literals with `unsafe_io`. The compiler will then build a dummy input I/O state for the literal and discard the resulting I/O state. This is useful, for example, for debug printing. I/O predicates are required to be `det` or `cc_multi`.

Purity declarations: These capture whether a predicate is `impure` (affects or is affected by the computation state), or `pure` (otherwise). By default predicates are pure. Any predicate that uses an impure predicate must have its predicate declaration annotated as either `impure` (so it is also impure) or `trust pure` (so even though it uses impure predicates it is considered pure). Note that all constraints are in some sense impure since they change the constraint store. However, for a correct solver, they act and should be treated as logically pure.

4 Constraint Solvers and Type Classes

As we have seen HAL provides type classes [17, 21]. These support *constrained* polymorphism by allowing the programmer to write code which relies on a parametric type having certain associated predicates and functions. More precisely, a *type class* is a name for a set of types for which certain predicates and/or functions, called the *methods*, are defined. Type classes were first introduced in functional programming languages Haskell and Clean, while Mercury [16] and CProlog [7] were the first logic programming languages to include them. One major motivation for providing type classes in HAL is that they provide a natural way of specifying a constraint solver's interface and separating this from its implementation and, therefore, support for "plug and play" with solvers.

A `class` declaration defines a new type class. It gives the names of the type variables which are parameters to the type class, and the methods which form its interface. As an example, one of the most important built-in type classes in HAL is that defining types which support equality testing:

```
:- class eq(T) where [
        pred T = T,
        mode oo = oo is semidet ].
```

Instances of this class can be specified, for example, by the declaration

```
:- instance eq(int).
```

which declares the `int` type to be an instance of the `eq/1` type class. For this to be correct, the current module must either define the method `=/2` with type `int=int` and mode `oo=oo is semidet` or indicate in the instance definition that the method is a renaming of another predicate.

Like Mercury, all types in HAL have an associated "equality" for modes `in=out` and `out=in`, which correspond to assignment, construction or deconstruction. These are implemented using specialised procedures rather than the `=/2` method. In addition, most types support testing for equality, the main exception being for types with higher-order subtypes. Thus, HAL automatically generates instances of `eq` for all constructor types which do not contain higher-order subtypes and for which the programmer has not already declared an instance.

Type classes allow us to naturally capture the notion of a type having an associated constraint solver: It is a type for which there is a method for initialising variables and a method for defining true equality. Thus, we define the `solver/1` type class to be:

```
:- class solver(T) <= eq(T) where [
        pred init(T::no) is det ].
```

Note the use of the abbreviated syntax for a single combined type, mode and determinism declaration. The above declaration indicates that the `solver/1` type class provides an initialisation method `init/1` and that `solver/1` is a subclass of `eq/1` and, thus, any instance of `solver/1` must also be an instance of `eq/1`. Therefore, for type `T` to be in the `solver/1` type class, there must exist methods `init/1` and `=/2` for this type with mode and determinism as shown.

A *solver type* is a type which is an instance of `solver/1`. The compiler distinguishes between variables of a solver type (*solver variables*) and other during mode analysis. The distinction first determines the interpretation of the instantiation `old`. Only solver variables can be truly `old`, for other variables `old` is interpreted as bound. Second, when necessary the compiler automatically inserts calls to `init` in order to change the instantiation of solver variables from `new` to `old`. See [9] for more details.

Class constraints can appear as part of a predicate or function's type signature. They constrain the variables in the type signature to belong to particular type classes. Class constraints are checked and inferred during the type checking phase except for those of type classes `solver/1` and `eq/1` which must be treated specially because they might vary for different modes of the same predicate. In the case of `solver/1`, this will be true if the HAL compiler inserts appropriate calls to `init/1` for some modes of usage but not in others. In the case of `eq/1`, this will be true if equalities are found to be simple assignments or deconstructions in some modes of usage but true equalities in others. As a result, it is not until after mode checking that we can determine which variables in the type signature should be instances of `eq/1` and/or `solver/1`. Unfortunately, mode checking requires type checking to have taken place. Hence, the HAL compiler includes an additional phase after mode checking, where newly inferred `solver/1` and `eq/1` class constraints are added to the inferred types of procedures for modes that require them. Note that, unlike for other classes, if the declared type for a predicate does not contain the inferred class constraints, this is not considered an error, unless the predicate is exported.[1]

To illustrate the problem, consider the predicate

```
:- pred append(list(T),list(T),list(T)).
:- mode append(in,in,out) is det.
:- mode append(in,out,in) is semidet.
append([],Y,Y).
append([A|X1], Y, [A|Z1]) :- append(X1,Y,Z1).
```

During mode checking, the predicate append is compiled into two different procedures, one for each mode of usage (indicated below by the keyword implemented_by). Conceptually, the code after mode checking is

```
:- pred append(list(T),list(T),list(T)) implemented_by [append_1, append_2].
:- pred append_1(list(T)::in,list(T)::in,list(T)::out) is det.
append_1(X,Y,Z) :- X =:= [], Z := Y.
append_1(X,Y,Z) :- X =: [A|X1], append_1(X1,Y,Z1), Z := [A|Z1].
:- pred append_2(list(T)::in,list(T)::out,list(T)::in) is semidet.
append_2(X,Y,Z) :- X =:= [], Y := Z.
append_2(X,Y,Z) :- X =: [A|X1], Z =: [B|Z1], A =:= B, append_2(X1,Y,Z1).
```

where =:=, :=, =: indicate calls to =/2 with mode (in,in), (out,in) and (in,out), respectively. It is only now that we see that for the second mode the parametric type T must allow equality testing (be an instance of the eq/1 class), because we need to compare A and B. Thus, in an additional phase of type inference the HAL compiler infers

```
:- pred append_2(list(T),list(T),list(T)) <= eq(T).
```

Any procedure calling append_2 will also inherit the eq(T) class constraint.

5   Dynamic Scheduling

An important feature of the HAL language is a form of "persistent" dynamic scheduling designed specifically to support constraint solving. A delay construct is of the form

$$cond_1 \texttt{ ==> } goal_1 \mid \cdots \mid cond_n \texttt{ ==> } goal_n$$

where the goal $goal_i$ will be executed when delay condition $cond_i$ is satisfied. By default, delayed goals remain active and are reexecuted every time the delay condition becomes true. This is useful, for example, if the delay condition is "the lower bound has changed." Delayed goals may also contain calls to the special predicate kill/0. When this is executed, all delayed goals in the immediate surrounding delay construct are killed; that is, will never be executed again.

For example, assume the delay conditions lbc(V), ubc(V) and fixed(V) are respectively satisfied when the lower bound changes for variable V, the upper bound changes for V, and V is given a fixed value. Assume also the given functions lb, ub and val respectively return the current lower bound, upper bound

---

[1] Exported predicates need to have all their information available to ensure correct modular compilation. We plan to remove this restriction when the compiler fully supports cross module optimizing compilation [1].

and value of their argument, while the predicates upd_lb, upd_ub and upd_val update these bounds. Then, the following delay construct implements bounds propagation for the constraint $X \leq Y$:

```
lbc(X) ==> upd_lb(Y,lb(X)) | fixed(X) ==> upd_lb(Y,val(X)), kill |
ubc(Y) ==> upd_ub(X,ub(Y)) | fixed(Y) ==> upd_ub(X,val(Y)), kill
```

The delay construct of HAL is designed to be extensible, so that programmers can build constraint solvers that support delay. In order to do so, one must create an instance of the delay type class defined as follows:

```
:- class delay(D,I) <= delay_id(I) where [
        pred delay(D, I, pred),
        mode delay(oo, in, in(pred is semidet)) is semidet ].
:- class delay_id(I) where [
        pred get_id(I::out) is det,
        pred kill(I::in) is det ].
```

where type I represents the unique identifier (id) of each delay construct, type D represents the supported delay conditions, delay/3 takes a delay condition, an id and a goal,[2] and stores the information in order to execute the goal whenever the delay condition holds, get_id/1 returns an unused id, and kill/1 causes all goals delayed for the input id to no longer wake up.

The HAL compiler translates the delay construct into the base delay methods provided by the classes. Thus, the delay construct shown above is translated into:

```
get_id(Id), delay(cond₁,Id,goal₁), ..., delay(condₙ,Id,goalₙ)
```

where each call to kill/0 in a $goal_i$ is replaced by a call to kill(Id). The separation of the delay type class into two parts allows different solver types to share delay ids. Thus, we can build delay constructs which involve conditions belonging to more than one solver as long as they use a common delay id.

Method delay/3 is an example of a higher-order predicate. Like Mercury, HAL supports higher-order programming through construction of higher-order objects and higher-order calls. For example, map/3 can be written as

```
:- export pred map(list(X), pred(X, Y), list(Y)).
:-       mode map(in, pred(in, out) is det, out) is det.
:-       mode map(in, pred(in, out) is semidet, out) is semidet.
map([],_,[]).
map([X | Xs], Pred, [Y | Ys]) :- call(Pred, X, Y), map(Xs, Pred, Ys).
```

Note the higher-order type pred(X,Y) and corresponding higher-order instantiations pred(in, out) is det and pred(in, out) is semidet which combine the mode and instantiation information of the higher-order argument.

HAL is designed to make it easy to combine constraint solvers into new hybrid constraint solvers. The delay construct is an important tool for doing this. Imagine combining an existing propagation solver (variable type cint in module bounds) and an integer linear programming solver (type ilpint in module

---

[2] To simplify analysis, each $goal_i$ must be semidet and may not change the instantiation state of variables. As a result, delayed code cannot invalidate the mode and determinism checking when woken up.

cplex) to create a combined solver (type `combint`). Each variable in the combined solver is a pair of variables, one from each of the underlying solvers. Constraints in the combined solver create corresponding constraints for both underlying solvers. Communication between the solvers is managed by goals delayed when a variable is initialized. A sketch of such a module (with communication only from the propagation solver to the ILP solver) is given below.

```
:- module combined.
:- import bounds, cplex.
:- export_abstract typedef combint -> p(cint,ilpint).
:- export pred combint >= combint.
:-          mode oo >= oo is semidet.
p(XB,XC) >= p(YB,YC) :- XB >= YB, XC >= YC.
:- export pred init(combint::no) is det.
init(p(XB,XC)) :- init(XB), init(XC), (communicate(XB,XC) -> true ; error).
:- trust pure pred communicate(cint::oo,ilpint::oo) is semidet.
communicate(XB,XC):-
            ( lbc(XB) ==> XC >= lb(XB)
            | ubc(XB) ==> ub(XB) >= XC
            | fixed(XB) ==> XC = val(XB), kill).
```

Note how the initialization sets up the delaying communiciation goal. Since its determinism is `semidet` it needs to be wrapped in an if-then-else to pass determinism checking. Similarly the use of impure functions `lb`, `ub` and `val` require the `trust pure` declaration.

6   Herbrand Constraint Solving

Most HAL types are structured data types defined using constructors. For example, earlier we defined the (polymorphic) `list/1` type using the constructors `[]` (nil) and "`.`" (cons). Elements of these type are the usual list terms. As indicated previously, the HAL base language only provides limited operations for dealing with such data structures unless their type is an instance of the `solver/1` class.

The `herbrand/1` type class captures those constructor types that are solver types. An instance of the `herbrand/1` type class is created by annotating the type definition with `deriving solver`. The compiler will then automatically generate appropriate instances for the `herbrand/1`, `solver/1` and `eq/1` classes (including the `=/2` and `init/1` predicates). Thus, the type declaration given earlier for lists

```
:- typedef list(T) -> ([] ; [T|list(T)]).
```

defines Mercury lists which have a fixed length while

```
:- typedef hlist(T) -> ([] ; [T|hlist(T)]) deriving solver.
```

defines true "Herbrand" lists.

The `herbrand/1` type class supports a number of other logical and non-logical operations commonly used in Prolog style programming. For instance, it provides impure methods `var/1` and `nonvar/1` to test if a variable is uninstantiated or not. It also provides the impure method `===/2` which succeeds only if its arguments are both variables and are identical.

Most modern logic programming languages allow predicates or goals to delay until a particular Herbrand variable is bound or is unified with another variable. In HAL a programmer can allow this by using the notation `deriving delay` when defining a type. The compiler will then automatically generate an instance of the `delay/2` class in addition to those of `herbrand/1`, `solver/1`, and `eq/1` classes for that type. All Herbrand types use the common delay conditions `bound(X)` and `touched(X)`, the common delay id type `system_delay_id`, and its system defined instance of `delay_id`. Note that `system_delay_id` can also be used by programmer defined solvers.

```
:- export_abstract typedef boolv -> ( f ; t ) deriving delay.
:- export pred and(boolv::oo,boolv::oo,boolv::oo) is semidet.
and(X,Y,Z) :-
  ( bound(X) ==> kill, (X = f -> Z = f ; Y = Z)
  | bound(Y) ==> kill, (Y = f -> Z = f ; X = Z)
  | bound(Z) ==> kill, (Z = t -> X = t, Y = t ; notboth(X,Y))).
:- export trust pure pred notboth(boolv::oo,boolv::oo) is semidet.
notboth(X,Y) :-
  ( bound(X) ==> kill, (X = t -> Y = f ; true)
  | bound(Y) ==> kill, (Y = t -> X = f ; true)
  | touched(X) ==> (X === Y -> kill, X = f ; true)
  | touched(Y) ==> (X === Y -> kill, X = f ; true)).
```

Fig. 1. Partial Boolean solver implemented by dynamic scheduling

As an example of the use of delay in constructing solvers, Figure 1 contains the code for (part of) a simple Boolean constraint solver. The constructor type `boolv` is used to represent Booleans. Notice how the `and/3` predicate delays until one argument has a fixed value, and then constrains the other arguments appropriately. In the case of predicate `notboth/2` we also test if two variables are identical, thus using an **impure** predicate. However, since the actions of `notboth` from outside are pure, we need to use a **trust pure** declaration.

7   The Solver Hierarchy

HAL is intended to provide a wide variety of different constraint solvers. It provides a rich collection of pre-defined type classes to allow the programmer to precisely describe the interface of a particular solver. One of the most important built-in type classes is `solver_for`. which connects a base type B with the corresponding solver type S:

```
solver_for(S,B) <= solver(S) where [
    func coerce(B::in) --> S::no is det,
    impure func val(S:oo) --> B::out is semidet,
]
```

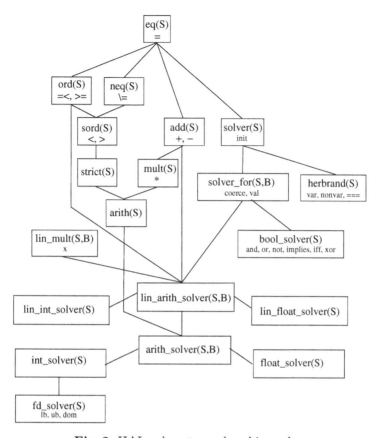

Fig. 2. HAL solver type class hierarchy

It provides methods to "coerce" an element of the base type to that of the solver type and to find the value of a variable.

Thus, we might use the following code to declare a restricted Boolean solver

```
:- export class my_bool_solv(BV) <= solver_for(BV,bool) where [
        and(BV::oo,BV::oo,BV::oo) is semidet,
        notboth(BV::oo,BV::oo,BV::oo) is semidet ].
```

We can then declare our previous Boolean solver to be an instance of this class and provide the coercion function and `val` functions

```
:- export func coerce(bool::in) --> boolv::no is det.
coerce(true) --> t.
coerce(false) --> f.
:- export impure func val(boolv:oo) --> bool:out is semidet.
val(X) --> B :- nonvar(X), (X = t, B = true ; X = f, B = false).
```

HAL provides a hierarchy of pre-defined type classes for common constraint domains which derive from the `solver` type class: `bool_solver`, `lin_float_solver`, `float_solver`, `lin_int_solver`, `int_solver`, and `fd_solver`. The solver type classes provide a standard interface to solvers which facilitates "plug and play" experimentation. The current[3] solver type class hierarchy is illustrated in Figure 2. The new predicates and functions are listed for each class, the modes for predicates have oo arguments and are `semidet`, while functions have their default mode: oo for inputs, no for outputs and are `det`. The exceptions are `init`, `coerce`, `val`, `lb`, `ub` defined previously, the linear multiplication function x which have type B x S --> S, and the impure function `dom` which returns the list of integers in a finite domain variables current domain.

8   Writing Constraint Solvers in HAL

As we have indicated, HAL is designed to allow the programmer to write their own constraint solver. This section discusses a number of additional features provided by HAL to support this.

One complication of writing a constraint solver in a CLP language itself is that solver variables will usually be viewed quite differently inside the solver module than outside. For example, externally a solver variable might be seen as an object of type `cint` while internally the solver variable might be a fixed integer index into a global variable tableau, and hence have type `int`. Abstract exportation of the type ensures that the different views of the type are handled correctly, but there is also the issue of the different views of instantiations.

Solver variables with abstract types can only be seen externally as having instantiation states `new`, `old`, or `ground`. However, the internal view associated to instantiations `old` and `ground` might be different to the external view. For example, if the solver variable is represented as an integer into a global variable tableau, what is externally viewed as `old` is internally viewed as `ground`. The same can happen for instantiation `ground`. Consider the following solver type:

```
:- export_abstract typedef cvar -> ( variable(int) ; fixed(float)).
```

which implements a float constraint variable using two functors: `fixed` which contains the value of the variable if it is known to be fixed, and `variable` which contains a pointer into a global variable tableau, otherwise. In this case, what is externally view as `ground` can be more accurately described by

```
:- instdef fixed -> fixed(ground).
```

HAL handles this by means of the `base_insts`(*Type*, *InstOld*, *InstGround*) declaration which provides the internal view of the `old` (*InstOld*) and `ground` (*InstGround*) instantiations for *Type*. For example,

```
:- base_insts(cvar,ground,fixed).
```

declares that the base instantiations `old` and `ground` for the type `cvar` are internally treated as `ground` and `fixed`.

Another complication of writing a constraint solver in a CLP language itself, is that we typically wish to be able to automatically coerce elements of the base-type into the solver type. Consider the following part of a simple integer bounds propagation solver:

---

[3] It seems clear to us that this will need to change in the future.

```
:- module bounds.
:- export_abstract typedef cint = ... %% internal cint representation
:- export instance fd_solver(cint).
:- export pred init(cint::no) is det.
:- export pred cint::oo = cint::oo is semidet.
:- export func coerce(int::in) --> cint::no is det.
```

We would then like to be able to write integer constants as `cint` arguments of predicates and functions, for example as in X + 3*Y >= Z + 2. Thus, we need to instruct the compiler to perform automatic coercion between an `int` and a `cint`. This is achieved by the existence of a declaration in the class `int_solver` which tells the compiler to support automatic coercion for instances of the method `coerce(int) --> S <= int_solver(S)`. The compiler then wraps integer constants in calls to coerce, and type inference determines if these are coercions or simply the identity. Thus the constraint above (assuming X, Y and Z are old) is translated to

```
T1=coerce(3), *(T1,Y,T2), +(X,T2,T3), T4=coerce(2), +(Z,T4,T5), >=(T3,T4).
```

The above translation may appear very inefficient, since many new solver variables are introduced, and many constraints each of which will involve propagation to solve. This is not necessarily the case. The solver could be defined so that `cints` are structured terms, which are built by coerce, + and *, and only the constraint relations build propagators. Thus, the + function would be defined as

```
:- export_abstract typedef cint -> (var(bvar) ; int(int)
                                     ; plus(cint,cint) ; times(cint,cint) ).
:- export func coerce(int::in) --> cint::no.
coerce(I) --> int(I).
:- export func cint::oo + cint::oo --> cint::no.
X + Y --> plus(X,Y).
```

Using this scheme, the goal above builds up a structure representing the terms of the constraint and then the equality predicate simplifies the structure and implements the appropriate propagation behaviour.[4]

When implementing constraint solvers or search strategies it is vital for efficiency to be able to destructively update a global data structure which might, for example, contain the current constraints in solved form.

To cater for this, HAL provides global variables. These are local to a module and cannot be accessed by name from outside the module, much like C's `static` variables. Global variables behave as references. They can never be directly passed as an argument to a predicate; they are always de-referenced at this point. They come in two flavours: backtracking and non-backtracking. Non-backtracking global variables must be ground. For example:

```
:- VarNo glob_var int = 0.
init(V) :- V = $VarNo, $VarNo := $VarNo + 1.
```

---

[4] It seems possible to build code to automatically extend a simple solver (e.g. `bvar`) to support this more efficient interface.

defines a backtracking global variable `VarNo` of type `int` initialised to value 0. This variable can be used, for example, to keep track of the number of variables encountered so far.

A major reason for designing HAL to be as pure as possible it that it simplifies the use of powerful compile-time optimizations such as unfolding, reordering and many low level optimizations. Typically a solver, though implemented using impure features, presents a "pure" interface to other modules that use it. For example, although the solver data structures are stored in a global variable, the solver will "behave" the same regardless of the order of external calls to primitive constraints. The purity declarations allow the user to control the inheritance of purity.

HAL also provides Constraint Handling Rules (CHRs) for defining new solvers. These have proven to be a very flexible formalism for writing incremental constraint solvers and other reactive systems. In effect, the rules define transitions from one constraint set to an equivalent constraint set. Rules are repeatedly applied until no new rule can be applied. Once applied, a rule cannot be undone. For more details the interested reader is referred to [8].

The simplest kind of rule is a *propagation* rule of the form

$$lhs \text{ ==> } guard \mid rhs$$

where *lhs* is a conjunction of CHR constraints, *guard* is a conjunction of constraints of the underlying language (in practice this is any goal not involving CHR constraints) and *rhs* is a conjunction of CHR constraints and constraints of the underlying language. The rule states that if there is a set S appearing in the global CHR constraint store G that matches *lhs* such that goal *guard* is entailed by the current constraints, then we should add the *rhs* to the store. *Simplification rules* have a similar form (replacing the `==>` with a `<=>`) and behavior except that the matching set S is deleted from G. A syntactic extension allows only part of the *lhs* to be eliminated by a simplification rule:

$$lhs_1 \setminus lhs_2 \text{ <=> } guard \mid rhs$$

indicates that only the set matching lhs_2 is eliminated.

As in most implementations, HAL CHRs [13] sit on top of the "host" language. More exactly, they may contain HAL code and are essentially compiled into HAL in a pre-processing stage of the HAL compiler. As a consequence, CHR constraints defined in HAL require the programmer to provide type, mode and determinism declarations.

In HAL, CHR constraints must have a mode which does not change the instantiation states of their arguments (like `oo` or `in`) to preserve mode safety, since the compiler is unlikely to statically determine when rules fire. Predicates appearing in the guard must also be `det` or `semidet` and not alter the instantiation of variables appearing in the left hand side of the CHR (this means they are implied by the store). This is a weak restriction since, typically, guards are simple tests.

The following code puts all of these elements together. It gives part of a Boolean solver implemented in HAL using CHRs.[5]

---

[5] Somewhat simplified for ease of exposition.

```
:- module bool_chr.
:- instance bool_solver(boolchr).
:- export_abstract typedef boolchr -> wrap(int).
:- base_insts(boolchr,ground,ground).
:- VNum glob_var int = 0.
:- export trust pure pred init(boolchr::no) is det.
init(V) :- V = wrap($VNum), $VNum := $VNum + 1.
:- export func coerce(bool::in) --> boolv::no is det
coerce(true) --> X :- init(X), (t(X) -> true ; error).
coerce(false) --> X :- init(X), (f(X) -> true ; error).
:- chr_constraints t/1, f/1, and/3, notboth/2.
:- export pred t(boolchr::oo) is semidet.
:- export pred f(boolchr::oo) is semidet.
t(X), f(X) <=> fail.
:- export pred and(boolchr::oo,boolchr::oo,boolchr::oo) is semidet.
t(X) \ and(X,Y,Z) <=> Y = Z.
t(Y) \ and(X,Y,Z) <=> X = Z.
f(X) \ and(X,Y,Z) <=> f(Z).
f(Y) \ and(X,Y,Z) <=> f(Z).
f(Z) \ and(X,Y,Z) <=> notboth(X,Y).
t(Z) \ and(X,Y,Z) <=> t(X), t(Y).
:- pred notboth(boolchr::oo,boolchr::oo) is semidet.
t(X) \ notboth(X,Y) <=> f(Y).
t(Y) \ notboth(X,Y) <=> f(X).
f(X) \ notboth(X,Y) <=> true.
f(Y) \ notboth(X,Y) <=> true.
```

In this case boolchrs are simply variable indices[6] and Boolean constraints and values are implemented using CHR constraints. Initialization simply builds a new term and increments the Boolean variable counter VNum which is a global variable. It must be declared trust pure to hide the use of impure global variables. Coercion returns a new boolchr which is appropriately constrained. The chr_constraint declaration lists which predicates are implemented by CHRs. The remaining parts are CHRs. The t and f constraints constrain a Boolean variable to have a fixed value. The first rule states that if a variable is given both truth values, true and false, we should fail. The next rule (for and/3) states that if the first argument is true we can replace the constraint by an equality of the remaining arguments. Note that equality is also implemented using CHRs.

9   Current System

The HAL compiler, system and libraries consists of some 60,000 lines of HAL code (which is also legitimate SICStus Prolog code). HAL programs may be compiled to either Prolog or Mercury. Mercury compiles to C and makes use of the information in declarations to produce efficient code. However, better debugging facilities in Prolog and the ability to handle code without type and

---

[6] HAL does not yet support CHRs on Herbrand types

mode declarations have made compilation to Prolog extremely useful in the initial development of the compiler.

Currently, we require full type, mode, determinism, I/O and purity declarations for exported predicates and functions. The HAL compiler performs type checking and inference. Partial type information may be expressed by using a '?' in place of an argument type or class constraint. The type checking algorithm is based on a constraint view of types and is described in [5]. The HAL compiler currently does not perform mode inference, but does perform mode checking [9]. The compiler performs determinism and purity inference and checking, using its generic analysis engine [19].

Compilation into Mercury required extending and modifying the Mercury language and its runtime system in several ways. Some of these extensions have now been incorporated into the Mercury release. The first extension was to provide an "any" instantiation, corresponding loosely to HAL's old instantiation. The second extension was to add purity declarations, as well as "trust me" declarations indicating to the Mercury compiler that it should just trust the declarations provided by the user (in our case the HAL compiler). The third extension was to provide support for global variables. The backtracking version needs to be trailed, while for the non-backtracking version the data needs to be stored in memory which will not be reclaimed on backtracking. Another extension was to provide run-time support for different equality operations. In order to support polymorphic operations properly, Mercury needs to know how to equate two objects of a (compile-time unknown) type. Mercury provides support for comparing two ground terms, but we needed to add similar support for equating two non-ground terms, as well as overriding the default ground comparison code to do the right thing for solver types.

Currently the HAL system provides four standard solvers: one for integers, two for floats and a Herbrand solver for term equations. The Herbrand solver is more closely built into the HAL implementation than the other two solvers, with support at the compiler level to leverage from the built-in term equation solving provided by Prolog and Mercury. One complicating issue has been that, as discussed earlier, Mercury only provides restricted forms of equality constraints. Since we wished to support full equality constraints, this required implementing a true unification based solver which interacted gracefully with the Mercury run-time system. This integration is described more fully in [3].

The integer solver is the same as that described in [10]. It is a bounds propagation solver which keeps linear constraints in a tableau form, and simplifies them during execution to improve further propagation. It was originally embedded in CLP($\mathcal{R}$)'s compiler and runtime system, yielding the language CLP($\mathcal{Z}$). It has since been interfaced to Mercury, and then to HAL via the Mercury interface. The first float solver is the solver from CLP($\mathcal{R}$), interfaced in the same way, while the second uses CPLEX [14] via the C foreign function interface.

10   Conclusion

We have introduced HAL, a language which extends existing CLP languages by providing semi-optional declarations, a well-defined solver interface, dynamic scheduling and global variables. These combine synergistically to give a language which is potentially more efficient than existing CLP languages, allows ready integration of foreign language procedures, is more robust because of compile-time checking, and, most importantly, allows flexible choice of constraint solvers which may either be fully or partially written in HAL. An initial empirical evaluation of HAL is very encouraging.

Despite several programmer years of effort, much still remains to be done on the HAL implementation. An important extension is to provide mutable data structures. Currently, only global variables are mutable but we would also like non-global mutable variables. One way is to provide references; another is to provide `unique` and `dead` declarations as is done in Mercury. We will explore both. We wish to support solver dependent compile-time analysis and specialization of solver calls. This is important since it will remove most of the runtime overhead of constructing arguments for constraints.

Apart for these specific aims, there are number of broader areas we are involved with. We are investigating how to extend the modelling capabilities of HAL, beyond the type class mechanism, to give simpler modelling of typical problems. We are exploring many further opportunities for global analyses and optimizations based on these analyses. We are in the process of building and integrating more solvers in the HAL system. Other important future research directions are debugging of constraint programs, and extended capabilities for programming search.

Acknowledgements

Many people have helped in the development of HAL. In particular they include Warwick Harvey, Christian Holzbaur, David Jeffery, Nick Nethercote, David Overton and Peter Schachte. We would also like to thank Zoltan Somogyi, Fergus Henderson and other members of the Mercury development team who have supported our (mis)use of Mercury.

References

[1] F. Bueno, M. Garcia de la Banda, M. Hermenegildo, K. Marriott, G. Puebla, and P. J. Stuckey. A model for inter-module analysis and optimizing compilation. In *Procs of LOPSTR2000*, volume 2042 of *LNCS*, pages 86–102, 2001. 55

[2] M. García de la Banda, D. Jeffery, K. Marriott, P. J. Stuckey, N. Nethercote, and C. Holzbaur. Building constraint solvers with HAL. In P. Codognet, editor, *Logic Programming: Proceedings of the 17th International Conference*, LNCS, pages 90–104. Springer-Verlag, 2001. 49

[3] B. Demoen, M. García de la Banda, W. Harvey, K. Marriott, and P. J. Stuckey. Herbrand constraint solving in HAL. In D. De Schreye, editor, *Logic Programming: Proceedings of the 16th International Conference*, pages 260–274. MIT Press, 1999. 49, 64

[4] B. Demoen, M. García de la Banda, W. Harvey, K. Marriott, and P. J. Stuckey. An overview of HAL. In J. Jaffar, editor, *Proceedings of the Fourth International Conference on Principles and Practices of Constraint Programming*, LNCS, pages 174–188. Springer-Verlag, October 1999. 49

[5] B. Demoen, M. García de la Banda, and P. J. Stuckey. Type constraint solving for parametric and ad-hoc polymorphism. In *Procs. of the 22nd Australian Comp. Sci. Conf.*, pages 217–228, 1999. 64

[6] D. Diaz and P. Codognet. A minimal extension of the WAM for clp(fd). In *Procs. of ICLP93*, pages 774–790, 1993. 47

[7] A. J. Fernández and B. C. Ruiz Jiménez. Una semántica operacional para CProlog. In *Proceedings of II Jornadas de Informática*, pages 21–30, 1996. 53

[8] T. Früwirth. Theory and practice of constraint handling rules. *Journal of Logic Programming*, 37:95–138, 1998. 47, 62

[9] M. García de la Banda, P. J. Stuckey, W. Harvey, and K. Marriott. Mode checking in HAL. In J. LLoyd et al., editor, *Proceedings of the First International Conference on Computational Logic*, LNCS 1861, pages 1270–1284. Springer-Verlag, July 2000. 49, 54, 64

[10] W. Harvey and P. J. Stuckey. Constraint representation for propagation. In *Procs. of PPCP98*, pages 235–249, 1998. 64

[11] M. Hermenegildo, F. Bueno, D. Cabeza, M. García de la Banda, P. López, and G. Puebla. The CIAO multi-dialect compiler and system. In *Parallelism and Implementation of Logic and Constraint Logic Programming*. Nova Science, 1999. 51

[12] C. Holzbaur. Metastructures vs. attributed variables in the context of extensible unification. In *Procs. of the PLILP92*, pages 260–268, 1992. 47

[13] C. Holzbaur, P. J. Stuckey, M. García de la Banda, and D. Jeffery. Optimizing compilation of constraint handling rules. In P. Codognet, editor, *Logic Programming: Proceedings of the 17th International Conference*, LNCS, pages 74–89. Springer-Verlag, 2001. 49, 62

[14] ILOG. CPLEX product page. http://www.ilog.com/products/cplex/. 64

[15] J. Jaffar, S. Michaylov, P. Stuckey, and R. Yap. The CLP($\mathcal{R}$) language and system. *ACM Transactions on Programming Languages and Systems*, 4(3):339–395, 1992. 47

[16] D. Jeffery, F. Henderson, and Z. Somogyi. Type classes in Mercury. Technical Report 98/13, University of Melbourne, Australia, 1998. 53

[17] S. Kaes. Parametric overloading in polymorphic programming languages. In *ESOP'88 Programming Languages and Systems*, volume 300 of *LNCS*, pages 131–141, 1988. 53

[18] K. Marriott and P. J. Stuckey. *Programming with Constraints: an Introduction*. MIT Press, 1998. 49

[19] N. Nethercote. The analysis framework for HAL. Master's thesis, Dept. of Comp. Sci and Soft. Eng, University of Melbourne, 2002. 64

[20] Z. Somogyi, F. Henderson, and T. Conway. The execution algorithm of Mercury: an efficient purely declarative logic programming language. *Journal of Logic Programming*, 29:17–64, 1996. 49

[21] P. Wadler and S. Blott. How to make *ad-hoc* polymorphism less *ad-hoc*. In *Proc. 16th ACM POPL*, pages 60–76, 1989. 53

Functional Logic Design Patterns[*]

Sergio Antoy[1] and Michael Hanus[2]

[1] Computer Science Department, Portland State University
P.O. Box 751, Portland, OR 97207, U.S.A.
antoy@cs.pdx.edu
[2] Institut für Informatik, Christian-Albrechts-Universität Kiel
Olshausenstr. 40, D-24098 Kiel, Germany
mh@informatik.uni-kiel.de

Abstract. We introduce a handful of software design patterns for functional logic languages. Following usual approaches, for each pattern we propose a name and we describe its intent, applicability, structure, consequences, etc. Our patterns deal with data type construction, identifier declarations, mappings, search, non-determinism and other fundamental aspects of the design and implementation of programs. We present some problems and we show fragments of programs that solve these problems using our patterns. The programming language of our examples is Curry. The complete programs are available on-line.

1 Introduction

A *design pattern* is a proven solution to a recurring problem in software design and development. A pattern itself is not primarily code. Rather it is an expression of design decisions affecting the architecture of a software system. A pattern consists of both ideas and recipes for the implementations of these ideas often in a particular language or paradigm. The ideas are reusable, whereas their implementations may have to be customized for each problem. For example, a pattern introduced in this paper expresses the idea of calling a data constructor exclusively indirectly through an intermediate function. The idea is applicable to a variety of problems, but the code of the intermediate function is highly dependent on each application.

Patterns originated from the development of object-oriented software [7] and became both a popular practice and an engineering discipline after [14]. As the landscape of programming languages evolves, patterns are "translated" from one language into another [12, 16]. Some patterns are primarily language specific, whereas others are fundamental enough to be largely independent of the language or programming paradigm in which they are coded. For example, the *Adapter* pattern, which solves the problem of adapting a service to a client coded for different interface, is language independent. The *Facade* pattern, which presents a

[*] This research has been partially supported by the DAAD/NSF grant INT-9981317, the German Research Council (DFG) grant Ha 2457/1-2 and the NSF grant CCR-0110496.

Z. Hu and M. Rodríguez-Artalejo (Eds.): FLOPS 2002, LNCS 2441, pp. 67–87, 2002.

set of separately coded services as a single unit, depends more on the modulariza-
tion features of a language than the language's paradigm itself. The *Composite*
and *Visitor* patterns are critically dependent on features of object orientation,
such as derivation and overriding, in the sense that other paradigms tend to triv-
ialize them. For example, Section 4 references programs that show the simplicity
of these patterns in a declarative paradigm.

In this paper, we present a handful of patterns intended for a declarative
paradigm—in most cases specifically for a functional logic one. High level languages are better suited for the implementation of reusable code than imperative
languages, see, e.g., parser combinators [10]. Although in some cases, e.g., search-
related patterns, we attempt to provide reusable code, the focus of our presentation is on the reusability of design and architecture which are more general than
the code itself. Our presentation of a pattern follows the usual (metapattern) approaches that provides, e.g., name, intent, applicability, structure, consequences,
etc. Some typical elements, such as "known uses," are sparse or missing because
of the novelty of our work. To our knowledge this is the first paper on patterns
for functional logic programming.

Section 2 briefly recalls some principles of functional logic programming and
the programming language Curry which we use to present the examples. Section 3 presents a small catalog of functional logic patterns together with motivating problems and implementation fragments. Section 4 contains references to
on-line versions of the entire programs whose fragments are interspersed in the
text. Section 5 concludes the paper. Appendix A further elaborates a framework
for search problems analyzed in relation to the Incremental Solution pattern.

2   Functional Logic Programming and Curry

This section provides both an introduction to the basic ideas of functional logic
programming and the elements of the programming language Curry that are
necessary to understand the subsequent examples.

Functional logic programming integrates in a single programming model the
most important features of functional and logic programming (see [18] for a
detailed survey). Thus, functional logic languages provide pattern matching in
the definition of functions and predicates as well as the use of logical variables
in expressions. The latter feature requires some built-in search principle in order
to guess the appropriate instantiations of logical variables. There are a number
of languages supporting functional logic programming in this broad sense, e.g.,
Curry [28], Escher [31], Le Fun [2], Life [1], Mercury [39], NUE-Prolog [34],
Oz [38], Toy [32], among others. Some of these proposals, as well as some Prolog
implementations (e.g., Ciao Prolog [9]), consider the functional notation only
as syntactic sugar for particular predicates. Functions with n arguments are
translated into predicates of arity $n + 1$ by including the result value as an
additional argument. This technique, known as naive *flattening*, does not exploit
the fact that in some situations the value of an argument of a function does not
affect the result. Computing these arguments would be a waste. For instance,

the *demand-driven* or *needed* evaluation strategy evaluates an argument of a function only if its value is needed to compute the result. An appropriate notion of "need" is a subtle point in the presence of a non-deterministic choice, e.g., a typical computation step, since the need of an argument might depend on the choice itself. [4] proposes a *needed narrowing* strategy to solve this problem. This strategy is optimal w.r.t. both the length of successful derivations and the disjointness of computed solutions. Narrowing is a combination of term reduction as in functional programming and (non-deterministic) variable instantiation as in logic programming. It exploits the presence of functions without transforming them into predicates which yields a more efficient operational behavior (e.g., see [17, 20]).

Functions can be also interpreted as a declarative notion to improve control in logic computations, i.e., functional logic languages do not include non-declarative control primitives like the Prolog's "cut" operator. The main reason is the dependency between input and output arguments which leads to needed evaluations. It is interesting to note that the *determinism* property of functions (i.e., there is at most one result value for fixed input arguments) is not strictly required. Actually, one can also deal with *non-deterministic functions* that deliver more than one result on a given input [3, 15]. This comes at no cost to the implementor since non-determinism is always available in functional logic languages. On the other hand, the combination of demand-driven evaluation and non-deterministic functions can result in a large reduction of the search space [3, 15].

It is well known that narrowing is an evaluation strategy that enjoys soundness and completeness in the sense of functional and logic programming, i.e., computed solutions/values are correct and correct solutions/values are computed. Nevertheless, narrowing is not able to deal with external functions. Therefore, [1, 2, 8, 31, 34] proposed alternative evaluation strategies based on *residuation*. The residuation principle delays a function call until the arguments are sufficiently instantiated so that the call can be deterministically reduced. Thus, residuation-based languages also support concurrent evaluations in order to deal with suspended computations. However, they do not ensure completeness in contrast to narrowing [19].

[21] proposes a seamless combination of needed narrowing with residuation-based concurrency. This is the basis of the programming language Curry [28], an attempt to provide a standard in the area of functional logic programming languages. The patterns presented in this paper are independent of Curry since they require only general features that can be found in many functional logic languages. Nevertheless, we use Curry for its dominant role in this field and due to its support for all typical features of functional logic languages. Thus, we provide in the following a short overview on Curry.

Curry has a Haskell-like syntax [35], i.e., (type) variables and function names usually start with lowercase letters and the names of type and data constructors start with an uppercase letter. The application of f to e is denoted by juxtaposition ("$f\ e$"). In addition to Haskell, Curry supports logic programming by means of free (logical) variables in both conditions and right-hand sides of defining rules. Thus, a Curry *program* consists of the definition of functions and the data types on which the functions operate. Functions are evaluated lazily and can be called with partially instantiated arguments. In general, functions are defined by conditional equations, or *rules*, of the form:

$$f\ t_1 \ldots t_n\ |\ c\ =\ e\ \text{ where } vs \text{ free}$$

where $t_1, \ldots, t_n$ are *data terms* (i.e., terms without defined function symbols), the *condition* c is a Boolean function or constraint, e is an expression and the `where` clause introduces a set of free variables. The condition and the `where` clause can be omitted. Curry defines *equational constraints* of the form $e_1 = := e_2$ which are satisfiable if both sides e_1 and e_2 are reducible to unifiable data terms. Furthermore, "c_1 & c_2" denotes the *concurrent conjunction* of the constraints c_1 and c_2 which is evaluated by solving both c_1 and c_2 concurrently.

The `where` clause introduces the free variables vs occurring in c and/or e but not in the left-hand side. Similarly to Haskell, the `where` clause can also contain other local function or pattern definitions. In contrast to Haskell, where the first matching function rule is applied, in Curry all matching (to be more precise, unifiable) rules are non-deterministically applied to support logic programming. This enables the definition of non-deterministic functions which may have more than one result on a given input.

Consider the following definition of lists and a function that non-deterministically inserts an element into a list:

```
data List a = [] | a : List a

insert :: a -> [a] -> [a]
insert e []     = [e]
insert e (x:xs) = e : x : xs
insert e (x:xs) = x : insert e xs
```

The data type declaration defines [] (empty list) and : (non-empty list) as the constructors of polymorphic lists. The symbol a is a type variable ranging over all types and the type "List a" is usually written as [a] for conformity with Haskell. The second line of the code declares the type of the function `insert`. This declaration is optional, since the compiler can infer it, and its is written for checkable redundancy. The type expression α->β denotes the type of all functions from type α to type β. Since the application of a function is curried, `insert` takes an element of type a, a list of elements of type a and returns a list of elements of type a, where a is any type.

A consequence of the rules defining `insert`, where the second and third rule overlap, is that the expression (`insert 1 [3,5]`) has three possible values: [1,3,5], [3,1,5], and [3,5,1]. Using `insert`, we define the possible permutations of a list by:

```
perm []     = []
perm (x:xs) = insert x (perm xs)
```

As an example of solving constraints, we want to define a function that checks whether some list starts with a permutation of another list and delivers the list of the remaining elements. For this purpose we use the concatenation of two lists which is defined by:

```
conc []     ys = ys
conc (x:xs) ys = x : conc xs ys
```

Now we can define the required function by a single conditional rule:

```
pprefix xs ys | conc (perm ys) zs =:= xs
              = zs                              where zs free
```

The operational semantics of Curry, precisely described in [21, 28], is a conservative extension of both lazy functional programming (if no free variables occur in the program or the initial goal) and (concurrent) logic programming. Since it is based on an optimal evaluation strategy [4], Curry can be considered a generalization of concurrent constraint programming [36] with a lazy (optimal) evaluation strategy. Furthermore, Curry also offers features for application programming like modules, monadic I/O, encapsulated search [27], ports for distributed programming [22], libraries for GUI [23] and HTML programming [24] etc. We do not discuss them here since they are not relevant for the subsequent examples.

There exist several implementations of Curry. The examples presented in this paper were all compiled and executed by PAKCS [25], a compiler/interpreter for a large subset of Curry.

3 Patterns

In this section we present a small catalog of patterns. Practitioners makes a distinction between the words *pattern* and *idiom*, although there are no formal definitions. An idiom is more language specific and addresses a smaller and less general problem than a pattern. An emblematic idiom of the C programming language is the code for copying a string:

```
while(*s++ = *t++) ;
```

The problem solved by this code is simple and the code relies on several peculiarities of the C language, e.g., the combination of the conventions of ending strings with a null character and representing the Boolean value *false* with the integer value zero. By contrast, patterns are more general both in applicability and scope. Many patterns of [14] were originally coded in C++ and/or Smalltalk. Later, they were easily ported to other object-oriented languages such as Java [16, 30]. Also, these patterns address design and/or architectural problems that often span across several classes with several methods each. The code of these classes and methods often depends on a specific application and, consequently, it is not easily reusable.

The same distinction between patterns and idioms holds for functional logic languages. To clarify the difference, we discuss an idiom in Curry. This idiom ensures that a function returns a value only if the value satisfies a certain property. The idiom is based on the following `suchthat` operator:

```
infix 0 'suchthat'
suchthat :: a -> (a->Bool) -> a
x 'suchthat' p | p x = x
```

For example, typical functional logic implementations of the n-queens puzzle generate a permutation of the input and test whether such permutation is "safe." Using the `suchthat` operator, the top-level function, `queens`, of an implementation of this puzzle looks like:

```
queens x = permute x 'suchthat' safe
```

where `permute` and `safe` have the expected meanings.

When appropriately used, this idiom yields terser and more elegant code, but hardly more than this. The patterns that we describe below address non-trivial solutions of some general and challenging problems.

3.1   Constrained Constructor

Name	*Constrained Constructor*
Intent	prevent invoking a constructor that might create invalid data
Applicability	a type is too general for a problem
Structure	define a function that either invokes a constructor or fails
Consequences	invalid instances of a type are never created by the function
Known uses	
See also	[30]; sometimes used with the Incremental Solution

The signature of a functional logic program is partitioned into *defined operations* and *data constructors*. They differ in that operations manipulate data by means of rewrite rules, whereas constructors create data and have no associated rewrite rules. Therefore, a constructor symbol cannot perform any checks on the arguments to which it is applied. If a constructor is invoked with arguments of the correct types, but inappropriate values, conceptually invalid data is created. We use an example to clarify this point.

The *Missionaries and Cannibals* puzzle is stated as follows. Three missionaries and three cannibals want to cross a river with a boat that holds up to two people. Furthermore, the missionaries, if any, on either bank of the river cannot be outnumbered by the cannibals (otherwise, as the intuition hints, they would be eaten by the cannibals).

A state of this puzzle is represented by the number of missionaries and cannibals and the presence of the boat on an arbitrarily chosen bank of the river, by convention the *initial* one:

```
data State = State Int Int Bool
```

For example, with suitable conventions, (State 3 3 True) represents the initial state. The simplicity of this representation has the drawback that invalid states, e.g., those with more than 6 people, can be created as well. Unless complex and possibly inefficient types for the state are defined, it is not possible to avoid the creation of invalid states using constructors alone.

Before completing the presentation of the *Constrained Constructor* pattern, consider one of the rewrite rules defining the operation that moves the boat and some people across the river:

```
move (State m c True)
   | m>=2 && (m-2==0 || m-2>=c) && (c==3 || m-2=<c)
   = State (m-2) c False          -- move 2 missionaries
 . . .
```

This rewrite rule abstracts moving two missionaries across the river. The complex guard ensures that before the move there are at least two missionaries on the originating bank of the river, m>=2, and that after the move, on each bank, the missionaries are not outnumbered by the cannibals. The second conjunct of the condition ensures that after the move either there are no missionaries left on the originating bank of the river, m-2==0, or the number of missionaries left is not smaller than the number of cannibals, m-2>=c. The third conjunct expresses a similar condition for the destination bank. Nine other rewrite rules with different, but similarly complex, guards are required to complete the definition of this operation.

Both the complexity of operation move and the creation of invalid states are avoided by the *Constrained Constructor* pattern. This pattern ensures that only states that are consistent with the conditions of the puzzle and are safe for the missionaries are created. For example, (State 2 1 _) is not safe since on one bank of the river the cannibals outnumber the missionaries and therefore should not be created. The function that constructs only desirable states is defined below:

```
makeState m c b | valid && safe = State m c b
    where valid = 0<=m && m<=3 && 0<=c && c<=3
          safe  = m==3 || m==0 || m==c
```

Using operation makeState, the definition of operation move is greatly simplified with a minimal loss of efficiency:[1]

```
move (State m c True)
    = makeState (m-2) c False      -- move 2 missionaries
    ! makeState (m-1) c False      -- move 1 missionary
    ! makeState m (c-2) False      -- move 2 cannibals
    ! ...
```

---

[1] The infix operator ! denotes the most fundamental non-deterministic function. It returns one of its arguments and is defined by the two rules:

```
x ! y = x
x ! y = y
```

Program *mission.curry*, referenced in Section 4, contains a second occurrence of the *Constrained Constructor* pattern. The program finds the solutions of the puzzle by constructing paths from the initial state (all the people and the boat on the initial bank) to the final state (no people and no boat on the initial bank). A path is defined by sequence of states as follows:

```
data Path = Initial State | Extend Path State
```

However, not all sequences of states are valid or desirable. In any path, any state except the initial one must be obtained from the preceding state by means of a move. Moreover, cycles in a path are undesirable since they unnecessarily consume memory and increase the size of the search space. Therefore, we have a second opportunity to use the *Constrained Constructor* pattern.

A crucial advantage of creating only valid paths with no cycles is that the search space of the puzzle changes from infinite to finite. This condition ensures that even naive strategies, e.g., depth-first search which may result from an incomplete implementation of a functional logic language such as a Prolog-based implementation [5], suffice to solve the puzzle. An implementation of the *n*-queens puzzle using the *Constrained Constructor* pattern, *queens.curry*, is referenced in Section 4. This implementation is structurally identical to that of the missionaries and cannibals and is much faster than implementations, e.g., *queens-permute.curry*, of the *n*-queens puzzle based directly on permutations.

This pattern, in the form here presented, is not available in functional languages. In a functional program, if a function call fails the entire execution of the program fails. The same problem does not occur in a logic language, though a new problem arises. In a functional language, constructor and function symbols are syntactically interchangeable in an expression. In a logic language they are not. Thus, replacing a constructor with a constrained constructor changes the structure of a logic program.

3.2 Concurrent Distinct Choices

Name	*Concurrent Distinct Choices*
Intent	ensure that a mapping from indexes to values is injective
Applicability	index-value pairs are computed concurrently
Structure	bind a unique token to a variable indexed by a value
Consequences	the index-value relation is an injective mapping
Known uses	
See also	

A *injective mapping* is a function from a set of *indexes* to a set of *values* such that distinct indexes are mapped to distinct values. Defining one such mapping is a component of the solution of many problems. For example, programs for both the *n*-queens and cryptarithmetic puzzles that are based on injective mappings are referenced in Section 4. A plausible representation of an injective mapping consists of a structure containing index-value pairs. Index-value pairs are computed during the execution of a program. To ensure injectivity, when an index-value pair is computed the program must check that no previously computed pair with the same index has the same value.

The *Concurrent Distinct Choices* pattern serves this purpose. One noteworthy feature of this pattern is that it allows the concurrent computation of the mapping. In other words, different portions of a program can compute index-value pairs in a non-sequential flow of control (e.g., due to residuation). With this condition, an implementation cannot pass around the structure containing the current index-value pairs in order to test the injectivity constraint.

In the simplest form of this pattern, the values are integer numbers in the range 0 to $n-1$. The representation of the mapping is a list referred to as the *store*. Initially, the elements of the store are n free variables. The *values* are used as indexes in the store. The elements in the store are referred to as *tokens*. A token represents the action of choosing a value that must be different from the value of any other choice. The type of the tokens is arbitrary. Often, the tokens are the *indexes* of the problem's mapping. Thus, the indexes and values of a problem are used as values and indexes respectively, i.e., the roles they have in the problem is reversed in the store.

To clarify this architecture, let us consider an example. A *cryptarithmetic puzzle* presents an arithmetic computation in which digits are replaced by letters. The problem is to find a correspondence from letters to digits that satisfies the computation. Different letters stand for different digits and leading zeros are disallowed in the encrypted representation of numbers. A well-know cryptarithmetic puzzle and its solution are shown in the following display:

```
SEND + MORE = MONEY
9567 + 1085 = 10652
```

In this case, the letters $S, E, N, \ldots$ are mapped to the digits $9, 5, 6, \ldots$

A program for this cryptarithmetic puzzle, *send-more.curry*, declares one variable for each letter:

```
vs,ve,vn,vd,vm,vo,vr,vy free
```

and defines, as a constraint, the set of equations that the variables must satisfy:

```
vd+ve     =:= c0*10+vy  &
vn+vr+c0 =:= c1*10+ve  &
ve+vo+c1 =:= c2*10+vn  &
vs+vm+c2 =:= c3*10+vo  &
       c3 =:= vm
```

where c0 is the carry of the units, c1 of the tens, etc. Each carry must be either 0 or 1 and consequently it is initialized as follows:

$$c_i = 0 ! 1 \qquad\qquad i = 0, \ldots, 3$$

It follows from the conventions of the problem that vm is not zero and consequently c3 is equal to one. In general, such precise inferences are not available and thus the program will ignore them.

The relation among the letters could be formulated as the single equation:

```
vd+ve + 10*(vn+vr) + 100*(ve+vo) + 1000*(vs+vm)
    =:= vy + 10*ve + 100*vn + 1000*vo + 10000*vm
```

Instead, we choose to split it into the conjunction of five simpler equations. This splitting enables the program to detect an incorrect mapping of letters to digits when fewer letters are mapped and consequently it improves considerably the efficiency of the execution. We will see shortly that these equations are not executed sequentially.

Since the variables, vs, ve, ..., that stand for the letters of the puzzle are initially unbound and the addition and multiplication operators are rigid, the execution of the equations that the variables must satisfy residuates, i.e., it is suspended until both the operands of an operator become bound. Each operand is a variable that is non-deterministically bound to a digit, similarly to the carries. However, in this case, different variables must be bound to different digits and the order in which variables are bound is not easily determined in advance. Here is where the *Concurrent Distinct Choices* pattern comes handy.

The initial store is a list of 10 free variables:

```
store = [s0,s1,s2,s3,s4,s5,s6,s7,s8,s9]
    where s0,s1,s2,s3,s4,s5,s6,s7,s8,s9 free
```

A letter of the cryptarithmetic puzzle is bound to a digit by the function `digit` defined as follows:

```
digit token | store !! x =:= token = x
    where x = 0!1!2!3!4!5!6!7!8!9
```

The argument `token` must be unique for each letter, hence, it is natural and convenient to represent it with the letter itself. The store, identified by the variable `store`, is defined in the scope of the function. The operator `!!` applied to arguments l and i returns the i-th element of the list l.

The letters of the cryptarithmetic puzzle are computed as follows:

```
vs = nzdigit 'S'
ve = digit   'E'
vn = digit   'N'
  ...
```

where `nzdigit` is a variant of `digit` that returns only non-zero digits. For example, (`digit 'Y'`) returns 2 if and only iff the second (starting from zero) element of the store is bound to `'Y'`. The entire program for this problem, *send-more.curry*, is referenced in Section 4.

The *n*-queens puzzle can be framed using the *Concurrent Distinct Choices* pattern, too, although concurrency is not a condition of this program. This program, *queenschoices.curry*, similar to many others for this problem, computes a permutation of the integers $0, 1, \ldots, n - 1$, where the i-th element of the permutation is the row in which the queen in the i-th column is placed. A permutation can be seen as an injective mapping of the values $0, 1, \ldots, n-1$ into themselves. In this case, both the indexes and the values of this problem's mapping are most naturally represented by the integer numbers in the range 0 through $n-1$.

This pattern is not available in functional languages since they lack free variables. On the other hand, pure logic languages do not support concurrency by residuation (although some implementations offer coroutining) and the functional notation.

3.3   Incremental Solution

Name	*Incremental Solution*
Intent	compute solutions in an incremental manner
Applicability	a solution consists of a sequence of steps
Structure	non-deterministically extend a partial solution stepwise
Consequences	avoid explicit representation of the search space
Known uses	[27, 37]
See also	often used with Constrained Constructor

A *solution* of a search problem is an element of a set, the search space, satisfying particular properties. To avoid both the enumeration of all the elements in the search space and the test of whether each element satisfies these properties, one defines a solution in an incremental manner, i.e., as a sequence of steps that extend a partial solution to a complete one. For instance, consider the problem, known as *stagecoach*, of constructing a path between two cities (see [29, p. 187]). The topology of a problem is represented by the connections between a set of cities using a `distance` function, e.g.:

```
distance Boston Chicago = 1500
distance Boston NewYork = 250
...
distance Denver LosAngeles = 1000
distance Denver SanFrancisco = 800
distance SanFrancisco LosAngeles = 300
```

An instance of this problem asks for a path from Boston to Los Angeles. A solution is a sequence of cities where Boston and Los Angeles are the first and last elements, respectively, and two consecutive elements are connected according to the `distance` function. Instead of this "monolithic" definition, it is preferable to define a solution in an incremental manner. A *partial solution* is any path from Boston to another city connected by `distance`. A complete solution is a partial solution with Los Angeles as the final element. A partial solution is extended, hopefully to a "more complete" one, by adding a new city reachable from the last one according to `distance`. It is convenient to represent a path as a list, in reverse order, of the cities of a partial solution. Extending a partial solution is implemented by the following function:

```
addCity (c:cs) | distance c c1 =:= d1
              = c1:c:cs                where c1,d1 free
```

Thus, a general search problem of this kind is specified by a triple: a function
extend that extends a partial solution, the initial partial solution, and a predicate complete that defines the completeness of a partial solution. Based on
such specification, the following non-deterministic search function computes a
solution:

```
searchNonDet :: (ps->ps) -> ps -> (ps->Bool) -> ps
searchNonDet extend initial complete = solve initial
  where
    solve psol = if complete psol then psol
                                  else solve (extend psol)
```

The function searchNonDet is equivalent, except for the order of the arguments,
to the function until found in the preludes of both Curry and Haskell. The
Incremental Solution pattern greatly simplies the structure of the code in that no
global search space is explicitly constructed. The function searchNonDet "sees"
only a partial solution, i.e., a single path originating from the initial state. This
works because the function extend is non-deterministic and the semantics of
functional logic languages ensure the completeness of the computation.

The following expression computes a solution of our reachability problem:

```
searchNonDet addCity [Boston] (\(c:_)->c==LosAngeles)
```

The entire program, *stagecoach.curry*, implementing this problem is referenced
in Section 4. This program has several advantages over a plausible formulation in a pure functional language. It is natural and convenient to define the
stepwise extension of partial solutions as a non-deterministic function, see the
definition of addCity and the examples of the Constrained Constructor pattern
in Section 3.1. Non-deterministic specifications are simpler and more adaptable
to new situations than equivalent deterministic specifications. For instance, the
distance between two cities is defined as a (partial) function on cities which can
be used in a narrowing-based functional logic language in a flexible way. To ex-
pand the topology of our sample problem with eastbound connections, it suffices
to add the following symmetric rule to the definition of addCity:

```
addCity (c:cs) | distance c1 c =:= d1
              = c1:c:cs                where c1,d1 free
```

Although this expansion generates paths of unbounded length, successful connections are nevertheless found with the proposed search function if the implementation either evaluates all the alternatives in a fair manner, as in [6, 26], or
appropriately uses the *Constrained Constructor* pattern discussed earlier.

Among the advantages of this pattern is a modular architecture that separates the definition or specification of a problem from the computation of its
solution. This separation makes different computations interchangeable. For instance, suppose that searchDepthFirst is a search strategy (its definition is

shown in Appendix A) computing the possibly infinite list of the solutions of the stagecoach problem in a depth-first order. The list of solutions is obtained by evaluating:

```
searchDepthFirst addCity [Boston] (\(c:_)->c==LosAngeles)
```

We can refine the problem by including in a path its length which is defined as the sum of the distances of consecutive cities:

```
data DPath = DPath Int [City]
extendPath (DPath d (c:cs)) | distance c c1 =:= d1
                        = DPath (d+d1) (c1:c:cs)
                        where c1,d1 free
startAtBoston = DPath 0 [Boston]
reachedLA (DPath _ (c:_)) = c == LosAngeles
```

Now, we compute solutions containing distance information by evaluating the expression:

```
searchNonDet extendPath startAtBoston reachedLA
```

In order to compute the solutions with the shortest distance first, we define an appropriate comparison predicate between partial solutions:

```
shorter (DPath d1 _) (DPath d2 _) = d1<d2
```

Now, we compute the shortest path by applying a "best-first" strategy (its implementation is shown in Appendix A) to the problem:

```
searchBestFirst extendPath startAtBoston reachedLA shorter
```

Many other search problems are conveniently implemented by programs, e.g., *mission.curry*, *queensincr.curry* and *waterjug.curry*, that use the *Incremental Solution* pattern.

3.4 Locally Defined Global Identifier

Name	*Locally Defined Global Identifier*
Intent	ensure that a local name is globally unique
Applicability	a global identifier is declared in a local scope
Structure	introduce local names as logical variables to be bound later
Consequences	local names are globally unique
Known uses	Curry's GUI library [23] and HTML/CGI library [24]
See also	often used with Opaque Type

Lists and trees are ubiquitous datatypes in functional and logic programming because of their simplicity. In many application areas, the use of these simple datatypes leads to unnatural models of a problem resulting in error-prone programs that are difficult to maintain. For instance, graphical user interfaces can be considered tree-like structures since widgets can be grouped in containers that are used as widgets themselves. However, these structures may include dependencies among each other, e.g., a button widget may manipulate another widget in a different hierarchy. Thus, a graph structure is a more appropriate model in this situation. The usual representation of a graph as an algebraic type is based on the definition of a pair consisting of nodes and edges:

```
data Graph = Graph [Node] [Edge]
```

Edges consist (at a minimum) of a source and a target node, i.e., we need a unique identification of nodes in order to specify the edges between them. If we identify nodes by unique integers, we obtain:

```
data Node = Node Int

data Edge = Edge Int Int
```

Depending on the application, additional information items are included into both nodes and edges, e.g., lengths of edges, names of nodes, etc., that we omit for the sake of clarity. With these assumptions, a simple graph instance is:

```
g1 = Graph [Node 1, Node 2, Node 3]
           [Edge 1 2, Edge 3 2, Edge 1 3, Edge 3 3]
```

Unfortunately, graph instances of this kind cannot be composed and lack desirable properties like functional abstraction. For instance, if `addGraphs` is a function that composes two graphs by joining their nodes and edges, respectively, the expression (`addGraphs g1 g1`) produces a non-intended graph containing supposedly different nodes with identical numbers.

This problem is avoided by passing a counter through all the nodes when all the graphs are defined. However, this solution leads to code that is non-reusable and difficult to both understand and maintain because two separate tasks are interleaved.

The *Locally Defined Global Identifier* pattern elegantly solves this problem. This pattern separates the local definition of names from the task of assigning globally unique identifiers. The idea is to use unbound local variables as names when defining or creating graphs. Following this idea, we define the graph of the previous example as follows:

```
g1 = Graph [Node n1, Node n2, Node n3]
           [Edge n1 n2, Edge n3 n2, Edge n1 n3, Edge n3 n3]
     where n1,n2,n3 free
```

Since n1, n2 and n3 are local variables, g1 becomes compositional as a list or a tree would be. For example, (`addGraphs g1 g1`) is a graph with six different nodes.

To connect two graphs of this kind with an additional edge, one "exposes" the nodes intended for the connection:

```
g2 = (Graph [Node n1, Node n2, Node n3]
             [Edge n1 n2, Edge n3 n2, Edge n1 n3, Edge n3 n3],
        n1)
      where n1,n2,n3 free
```

The following function connects graph/node pairs with an edge provided that addEdge is a function that adds a new edge between two nodes of a graph:

```
connectGraphs (g,m) (h,n) = addEdge m n (addGraphs g h)
```

Now, (connectGraphs g2 g2) defines a graph consisting of six nodes and nine edges. The locally defined identifiers n1, n2 and n3 act as global identifiers in the composition.

Since unbound variables are not expressive, one may wish to instantiate them in some applications, e.g., visualization. To visualize graphs, one instantiates the node identifiers to pairwise distinct numbers or strings as usually required by visualization tools. The following function implements this process:

```
finalizeGraph (Graph ns es) = Graph (numberNodes 1 ns) es
  where numberNodes _ [] = []
        numberNodes n (Node ni : nodes)
            | ni =:= n  -- assign unique identifier
          = Node ni : numberNodes (n+1) nodes
```

A skeletal program, *graph.curry*, showing the use of this pattern is referenced in Section 4.

This pattern is not only useful in graph-based applications, but also in applications where hierarchical (tree-like) data structures are appropriate, but additional references inside such structures are needed. As mentioned earlier, graphical user interfaces are one class of such applications. This pattern has been applied in this context in [23]. Another application area is dynamic web page generation with form-based input. HTML documents are structured as trees, but the input forms and their "submit" buttons contain dependencies between subtrees that can be appropriately described with this pattern [24].

The Graph datatype is only a simple example demonstrating the basic use of this pattern. In real world applications, this pattern is refined in various ways. For instance, the use of logical variables instead of concrete numbers in the definition of graphs is only a guideline for the programmer. By contrast, the *Opaque Type* pattern presented in the next section enforces the use of logical variables exclusively. A remaining problem not addressed by these patterns is ensuring that the variables used in different nodes are distinct. This situation occurs in other environments as well, e.g., Tcl/Tk or Perl/CGI programs, which use additional analysis to solve the problem. In functional logic programming, a convenient option is using the *Constrained Constructor* pattern discussed earlier.

This pattern is not available in functional languages since they lack free variables. As a consequence, functional approaches to GUI or HTML programming use a more imperative style and/or lack compositionality [11, 33]. Erwig [13] proposes an inductive definition of graphs that supports coding graph algorithms in a functional style. His approach is specific to graphs and does not lead to appropriate descriptions of the GUI and HTML applications that we mentioned.

3.5   Opaque Type

Name	*Opaque Type*
Intent	ensure that values of a datatype are hidden
Applicability	define instances of a type whose values are unknown
Structure	wrap values with a private constructor
Consequences	values can only be denoted by free variables
Known uses	Curry's GUI library [23] and HTML/CGI library [24]
See also	

In applications containing elements which are interesting only in relation to each other, it is often desirable to hide the values of these elements since they are either irrelevant or are computed by some function of the application. The construction of graphical user interfaces and interactive HTML documents mentioned in the previous section and abstracted by graphs are examples of this situation. A problem of this situation is that the programmer may have to construct instances of a type, but no value of that type is available.

In the graph example of the previous section, the values of the datatype that abstracts node identifiers should be hidden, but the datatype itself should be visible to construct the nodes. A convenient option to satisfy this condition is the use of unbound variables rather than literal values for node identifiers when a graph is defined. As an added bonus, this condition gives the implementor of a graph library the freedom to change this datatype, e.g., from Int to String whenever it is convenient, without affecting a client of the library.

The values of a datatype can be hidden by "wrapping" them with a private constructor of the datatype. This means that literal values are replaced by values of an abstract datatype that has no public constructors. The values of this datatype can be denoted by unbound variables.

For instance, consider the graph of Section 3.4. To hide the use of integers to identify nodes, we define in the graph library a datatype for *node identifiers*:

```
data NodeId = NodeId Int
```

where the constructor NodeId is not exported—a standard feature of module systems. Furthermore, we change the definition of nodes and edges so that we use the type NodeId wherever nodes are required:

```
data Node = Node NodeId

data Edge = Edge NodeId NodeId
```

These definitions are in the same module that declares NodeId and consequently may access it even though it is private. Finally, we adapt all the functions in the graph library where node identifiers are involved. These functions may access NodeId as well. In our example we slightly change the definition of finalizeGraph by replacing "ni =:= n" with "ni =:= NodeId n." This change is completely invisible to the user of the library. The coding of graphs remain identical, but the pattern ensures that the arguments of Node are exclusively unbound variables.

Program *graph.curry*, mentioned in the previous section and referenced in Section 4, shows an application of this pattern as well.

This pattern is not directly available in functional languages since they lack free variables. Although most functional languages have a module system that allows the programmer to hide values, using hidden values require accessor functions that may be more difficult to define when the values are distributed across tree-structured datatypes.

4 Exemplary Programs

The programs discussed in this paper are available at URL:

http://www.cs.pdx.edu/~antoy/flp/patterns/

5 Conclusion

We have presented five software design patterns specifically intended for a functional logic language. Our patterns are quite general. In the short programs referenced in Section 4, we find repeated opportunities of applications of our patterns. In several cases, more than one pattern is appropriately used in the same program.

This is the first paper on patterns for a functional logic language. Therefore, the patterns that we have selected for our small catalog address essential activities of program design and implementation. The *Constrained Constructor* offers a technique for using types that are more specialized than those directly available in functional and functional logic languages. The *Concurrent Distinct Choices* supports a simple and efficient implementation of an injective mapping where the mapping of indexes to values may occur concurrently or in no pre-established order. The *Incremental Solution* suggests a flexible general architecture for non-deterministic search problems which avoids the explicit manipulation of a global search space. The *Locally Defined Global Identifier* and the *Opaque Type* are intended for the definition of respectively global identifiers in local scopes and instances of a type whose values are hidden. These patterns simplify data construction in a way that promotes code modularity and reuse.

Object-oriented patterns are classified according to tasks, e.g., creational patterns for the construction of objects, behavioral patterns for the execution of code, etc., and develop some general themes, e.g., replacement of inheritance, a static property, with delegation, a dynamic property. Our catalog is yet too small for meaningful classifications, but it already outlines two general themes. The theme of the first three patterns that we presented is the use of non-determinism in computations. The theme of the last two patterns is the use of logical variables in expressions.

The elegance of some of our patterns and the ease with which they solve some difficult problems highlight the features that distinguish a functional logic language from other paradigms. Of course, the functional evaluation is an essential aspect since it provides sophisticated efficient control of execution, through lazy evaluation, in a purely declarative manner, e.g., without the Prolog "cut." A related important aspect is non-determism, specifically the integration of non-determinism with functional evaluation. This combination supports implicit search in the logic programming style without sacrificing the efficient control of execution discussed earlier. Another essential aspect are logic variables, specifically the integration of logic variables with functional evaluation. This combination, made possible by narrowing, supports both equational reasoning and functional inversion in the logic programming style. The final aspect is concurrency, specifically the interleaving of different computations. The interleaving of deterministic and non-deterministic computations may reduce the size of the search space and consequently improve the overall efficiency of a program.

Our patterns rely on these essential aspects of functional logic languages. Consequently, they can be used in any functional logic language that supports these characterizing aspects. Curry supports all these aspects. For this reason, and for the availability of an efficient, robust and fairly complete implementation, PAKCS, we have chosen Curry as the presentation language.

Industry is showing a growing interest in programming with patterns. The proved or perceived benefits of using patterns for software development include clarity of design, faster development, lower costs, robustness, efficiency and ease of maintenance. Although most often the programming language used in industry is object oriented, patterns are more concerned with ideas than with code and many benefits of using patterns are largely independent of the language.

We plan to continue maintaining our on-line catalog and to add new functional logic patterns as they become recognized and documented.

References

[1] H. Aït-Kaci. An overview of LIFE. In J. Schmidt and A. Stogny, editors, *Proc. Workshop on Next Generation Information System Technology*, pages 42–58. Springer LNCS 504, 1990. 68, 69

[2] H. Aït-Kaci, P. Lincoln, and R. Nasr. Le Fun: Logic, equations, and functions. In *Proc. 4th IEEE Internat. Symposium on Logic Programming*, pages 17–23, San Francisco, 1987. 68, 69

[3] S. Antoy. Optimal non-deterministic functional logic computations. In *Proc. International Conference on Algebraic and Logic Programming (ALP'97)*, pages 16–30. Springer LNCS 1298, 1997. 69

[4] S. Antoy, R. Echahed, and M. Hanus. A needed narrowing strategy. *Journal of the ACM*, 47(4):776–822, 2000. 69, 71

[5] S. Antoy and M. Hanus. Compiling multi-paradigm declarative programs into Prolog. In *Proc. International Workshop on Frontiers of Combining Systems (FroCoS'2000)*, pages 171–185. Springer LNCS 1794, 2000. 74

[6] S. Antoy, M. Hanus, B. Massey, and F. Steiner. An implementation of narrowing strategies. In *Proc. of the 3rd International ACM SIGPLAN Conference on Principles and Practice of Declarative Programming (PPDP 2001)*, pages 207–217. ACM Press, 2001. 78

[7] K. Beck and W. Cunningham. Using pattern languages for object-oriented programs. In *Specification and Design for Object-Oriented Programming (OOPSLA-87)*, 1987. 67

[8] J. Boye. S-SLD-resolution – an operational semantics for logic programs with external procedures. In *Proc. of the 3rd Int. Symposium on Programming Language Implementation and Logic Programming*, pages 383–393. Springer LNCS 528, 1991. 69

[9] F. Bueno, D. Cabeza, M. Carro, M. Hermenegildo, P. López-García, and G. Puebla. The Ciao Prolog system. Reference manual. Technical report CLIP3/97.1, School of Computer Science, Technical University of Madrid (UPM), 1997. 68

[10] R. Caballero and F. López-Fraguas. A functional-logic perspective of parsing. In *Proc. of the 4th Fuji Int'l Symposium on Functional and Logic Programming*, pages 85–99, Tsukuba, Japan, 1999. Springer LNCS 1722. 68

[11] K. Claessen, T. Vullinghs, and E. Meijer. Structuring graphical paradigms in TkGofer. In *Proc. of the International Conference on Functional Programming (ICFP'97)*, pages 251–262. ACM SIGPLAN Notices Vol. 32, No. 8, 1997. 81

[12] J.W. Cooper. *Java Design Patterns*. Addison Wesley, 2000. 67

[13] M. Erwig. Functional programming with graphs. In *2nd ACM SIGPLAN Int. Conf. on Functional Programming (ICFP'97)*, pages 52–65, 1997. 81

[14] E. Gamma, R. Helm, R. Johnson, and J. Vlissides. *Design Patterns: Elements of Reusable Object-Oriented Software*. Addison Wesley, 1994. 67, 71

[15] J. González-Moreno, M. Hortalá-González, F. López-Fraguas, and M. Rodríguez-Artalejo. An approach to declarative programming based on a rewriting logic. *Journal of Logic Programming*, 40:47–87, 1999. 69

[16] M. Grand. *Patterns in Java*. J. Wiley, 1998. 67, 71

[17] M. Hanus. Improving control of logic programs by using functional logic languages. In *Proc. of the 4th International Symposium on Programming Language Implementation and Logic Programming*, pages 1–23. Springer LNCS 631, 1992. 69

[18] M. Hanus. The integration of functions into logic programming: From theory to practice. *Journal of Logic Programming*, 19&20:583–628, 1994. 68

[19] M. Hanus. Analysis of residuating logic programs. *Journal of Logic Programming*, 24(3):161–199, 1995. 69

[20] M. Hanus. Efficient translation of lazy functional logic programs into Prolog. In *Proc. Fifth International Workshop on Logic Program Synthesis and Transformation*, pages 252–266. Springer LNCS 1048, 1995. 69

[21] M. Hanus. A unified computation model for functional and logic programming. In *Proc. of the 24th ACM Symposium on Principles of Programming Languages (Paris)*, pages 80–93, 1997. 69, 71

[22] M. Hanus. Distributed programming in a multi-paradigm declarative language. In *Proc. of the International Conference on Principles and Practice of Declarative Programming (PPDP'99)*, pages 376–395. Springer LNCS 1702, 1999. 71

[23] M. Hanus. A functional logic programming approach to graphical user interfaces. In *International Workshop on Practical Aspects of Declarative Languages (PADL'00)*, pages 47–62. Springer LNCS 1753, 2000. 71, 79, 81, 82

[24] M. Hanus. High-level server side web scripting in Curry. In *Proc. of the Third International Symposium on Practical Aspects of Declarative Languages (PADL'01)*, pages 76–92. Springer LNCS 1990, 2001. 71, 79, 81, 82

[25] M. Hanus, S. Antoy, K. Höppner, J. Koj, P. Niederau, R. Sadre, and F. Steiner. PAKCS: The Portland Aachen Kiel Curry System. Available at http://www.informatik.uni-kiel.de/~{}pakcs/, 2002. 71

[26] M. Hanus and R. Sadre. An abstract machine for Curry and its concurrent implementation in Java. *Journal of Functional and Logic Programming*, 1999(6), 1999. 78

[27] M. Hanus and F. Steiner. Controlling search in declarative programs. In *Principles of Declarative Programming (Proc. Joint International Symposium PLILP/ALP'98)*, pages 374–390. Springer LNCS 1490, 1998. 71, 77, 87

[28] M. Hanus (ed.). Curry: An integrated functional logic language (vers. 0.7). Available at http://www.informatik.uni-kiel.de/~curry, 2000. 68, 69, 71

[29] E. Horowitz and S. Sahni. *Fundamentals of Computer Algorithms*. Computer Science Press, 1978. 77

[30] J. Langr. *Essential Java Style: Patterns for Implementation*. Prentice Hall, 2000. 71, 72

[31] J. Lloyd. Programming in an integrated functional and logic language. *Journal of Functional and Logic Programming*, (3):1–49, 1999. 68, 69

[32] F. López-Fraguas and J. Sánchez-Hernández. TOY: A Multiparadigm Declarative System. In *Proc. of RTA'99*, pages 244–247. Springer LNCS 1631, 1999. 68

[33] E. Meijer. Server side web scripting in Haskell. *Journal of Functional Programming*, 10(1):1–18, 2000. 81

[34] L. Naish. Adding equations to NU-Prolog. In *Proc. of the 3rd Int. Symposium on Programming Language Implementation and Logic Programming*, pages 15–26. Springer LNCS 528, 1991. 68, 69

[35] S. Peyton Jones and J. Hughes. Haskell 98: A non-strict, purely functional language. http://www.haskell.org, 1999. 69

[36] V. Saraswat. *Concurrent Constraint Programming*. MIT Press, 1993. 71

[37] C. Schulte and G. Smolka. Encapsulated search for higher-order concurrent constraint programming. In *Proc. of the 1994 International Logic Programming Symposium*, pages 505–520. MIT Press, 1994. 77

[38] G. Smolka. The Oz programming model. In J. van Leeuwen, editor, *Computer Science Today: Recent Trends and Developments*, pages 324–343. Springer LNCS 1000, 1995. 68

[39] Z. Somogyi, F. Henderson, and T. Conway. The execution algorithm of Mercury, an efficient purely declarative logic programming language. *Journal of Logic Programming*, 29(1-3):17–64, 1996. 68

A Further Search Strategies for the Incremental Solution Pattern

In this appendix we show the implementation of additional search strategies to compute solutions to problems suitable for the *Incremental Solution* pattern. These strategies are variations or refinements of the *Incremental Solution* in the sense that they compute solutions by incremental steps.

First, we show the implementation of a *depth-first* strategy which enumerates the possibly infinite list of all the solutions in a depth-first order. We make use of

the predefined operation `findall` for encapsulating search [27]. The expression
`findall \`x`->c` computes the list of all the solutions for x w.r.t. a constraint c.
The depth-first strategy is implemented by:

```
searchDepthFirst :: (ps->ps) -> ps -> (ps->Bool) -> [ps]
searchDepthFirst extend initial complete = solve [initial]
    where
        solve []      = []
        solve (st:sts) = if complete st
                          then st : solve sts
                          else solve (expand (st:sts))

        nextstates st = findall \x -> extend st =:= x

        expand (st:sts) = nextstates st ++ sts
```

A *breadth-first* search strategy is similarly defined by swapping the order of
the concatenation of the partial solutions in the local function `expand`. This
has the advantage that solutions are computed even in the presence of infinite
expansions of partial solutions. On the other hand, it requires more memory to
store all intermediate partial solutions.

A *best-first* search strategy that expands the "best" partial solutions first
requires an additional parameter. This parameter is a predicate, `better`, that
determines which of two partial solutions is better according to an arbitrary
general criterion. Namely, "`better s1 s2`" where `s1` and `s2` are partial solutions
is intended to be true if `s1` is better than `s2`. The definition of this search
strategy is similar to `searchDepthFirst`, the difference being that the list of
partial solutions that are candidate for expansion is sorted according to `better`.
The best first strategy is implemented by:

```
searchBestFirst :: (ps->ps) -> ps ->
                   (ps->Bool) -> (ps->ps->Bool) -> [ps]
searchBestFirst extend initial complete better
    = solve [initial]
    where
        solve []      = []
        solve (st:sts) = if complete st
                          then st : solve sts
                          else solve (expand (st:sts))

        nextstates st = findall \x -> extend st =:= x

        expand (st:sts) =
            merge (sort better(nextstates st)) sts

        merge []          sts       = sts
        merge (st:sts)    []        = st:sts
        merge (st1:sts1) (st2:sts2) =
          if better st1 st2 then st1 : merge sts1 (st2:sts2)
                            else st2 : merge (st1:sts1) sts2
```

On Consistency and Width Notions for Constraint Programs with Algebraic Constraints

Klaus Meer[*]

Department of Mathematics and Computer Science
Syddansk Universitet, Campusvej 55, 5230 Odense M, Denmark
meer@imada.sdu.dk

Abstract. Width notions have been studied in the framework of constraint satisfaction problems in order to exhibit subclasses of problems which allow backtrack-free solution algorithms. Among the most prominent such notions is the tree-width of the constraint graph studied, for example, by Freuder [6, 7]. However, Freuder's results heavily rely on constraint programs over finite domains, where each constraint is given as a list of admissible tuples and therefore fails, for example, if continuous domains are considered. Faltings [5] introduced an arc consistency notion for constraints over continuous domains that are given in a more complicated form using formulas $c(x, y) \geq 0$ for continuously differentiable functions c. He then showed for such binary constraints how arc consistency can be established and guarantees solvability of tree-structured problems.
In this paper we want to study a generalization of Freuder's and Faltings' notions to problems with algebraic constraints. We show that an analog notion of k-consistency guarantees backtrack-free solution algorithms for tree-structured problems, but argue that already for binary constraints and a tree as structure of the constraint graph there arise unavoidable complexity problems in achieving k-consistency. We then propose a new width notion based on [10] which in certain situations even allows to include global constraints without yielding a complexity explosion - something not true within the above mentioned setting.

Keywords: algebraic constraint satisfaction problems, width, consistency, backtrack-free algorithms

1 Introduction

An important branch of the analysis of constraint programs is the study of consistency notions. Certain local and global consistency notions were introduced. Here, one goal is to find subclasses of constraint programs for which validity of

[*] partially supported by EU ESPRIT project NeuroCOLT2, by the Future and Emerging Technologies programme of the EU under contract number IST-1999-14186 (ALCOM-FT) and by the Danish Natural Science Research Council SNF.

(some of) the former imply validity of (some of) the latter. Such results, for example, can be used in order to either perform a backtrack-free solution algorithm for the constraint program or to at least simplify the problem.

Among local consistency notions we can find node consistency, arc consistency, path consistency and, most general, k-consistency, see [11, 6]. Freuder [6, 7] has studied k-consistency and related it to the structure of a so called (primal) constraint graph. The latter has the problem variables as vertices; two variables are joined by an edge iff they occur together in a single constraint. Introducing a width notion for the constraint graph Freuder was able to establish certain subclasses of constraint programs which can be solved without backtracking, see section 2. Freuder's approach heavily relies on the variable domains and the way constraints are given: for each variable x_i there is a *finite* set D_i as its domain; a constraint c over variables $x_{i_1}, \dots, x_{i_k}, i_j \in \{1, \dots, n\}$ is then given by explicitly listing the elements of a corresponding subset of $D_{i_1} \times \dots \times D_{i_k}$. This approach is problematic, for example, if one deals with continuous constraints or if it is not ad hoc possible to list a constraint because it is given in an algebraic form (say as solution of an equation). In [5], Faltings defines arc consistency for certain classes of continuous constraint satisfaction programs. The (binary) constraints there are given as formulas $c(x, y) \geq 0$, where $c(x, y) = 0$ determines a differentiable curve. For binary problems whose constraint graph is a tree Faltings presents a finite algorithm yielding arc consistency (which in this situation implies global consistency). However, non-binary programs are not treated.

Part of the present paper is devoted to generalize and homogenize both Freuder's and Faltings' approaches to constraint programs (both discrete and continuous) for which the constraints are given in an algebraic manner. By the latter, we mean formulas of the form $c(x_{i_1}, \dots, x_{i_k}) \Delta 0$, where c is a polynomial with real coefficients and $\Delta \in \{=, \neq, \geq \leq, >, <\}$. After recalling the main concepts of [7, 5] in section 2, we shall extend the notions of width of the constraint graph and k-consistency to such constraint programs and study their relation. We shall see that both above approaches can be captured. Even though in [5] there was given a refinement procedure to achieve arc consistency, it turns out that the related algorithm is problematic already in the binary case and for algebraic constraints (i.e. instead of the more general constraints Faltings is considering); in general, an exploding complexity cannot be avoided. This is due to problems resulting from quantifier elimination.

Another problem with the width notion used so far is the fact that it is only useful (w.r.t. efficient solution algorithms) if no global constraints are present in the program. We therefore consider in section 3 a new width notion for such constraint programs. The latter was introduced in [10] in an algebraic-complexity framework. We propose its study also in the area of constraint programming problems. In some situations, it allows backtrack-free algorithms even though global (algebraic) constraints occur.

2   Algebraic Constraint Satisfaction Problems; Width-Notion and Consistency

We start by recalling some basic definitions, including Freuder's width notion for finite domain programs and Faltings' arc consistency notion for certain continuous variable programs. We then extend it to general algebraic constraint programs.

2.1   Freuder's and Faltings' Settings

We start with

Definition 1. *a) A* constraint satisfaction problem *(CSP) $\mathcal{P}$ is given as a finite set $X := \{x_1, \ldots, x_n\}$ of variables which can take values from finite domains $D_1, \ldots, D_n$ together with a set $\mathcal{C} := \{c_1, \ldots, c_m\}$ of constraints. Each c_i is given as a pair $(var(c_i), r_i)$, where $var(c_i) \subseteq X$ denotes the variables of constraint c_i and $r_i \subseteq \bigotimes_{x_j \in var(c_i)} D_j$ is a relation representing the admissible tuples for constraint c_i. The points satisfying relation r_i are listed one by one.*
b) A solution of a CSP is an assignment $x_i := a_i \in D_i$ such that for each constraint c_j the projection of $(a_1, \ldots, a_n)$ to the corresponding components belongs to r_j. Solving a CSP means to decide existence of a solution. (One could as well ask for finding at least one or all solutions.)
c) The constraint graph *(also called* primal constraint graph*) of a CSP $\mathcal{P}$ is the graph $G = (V, E)$ with $V := X$ and two vertices x_i, x_j are joined in E iff there exists a constraint c such that $\{x_i, x_j\} \subseteq var(c)$.*

In order to identify subclasses of CSPs being solvable without backtracking Freuder [6] studied the tree-width of the primal graph.

Definition 2. *a) A* tree decomposition *of a graph $G = (V, E)$ is a tree $T = (V_T, E_T)$ satisfying the following conditions:*

i) to each node $t \in V_T$ there corresponds a subset $V_t \subseteq V$;
ii) $\bigcup_{t \in V_T} V_t = V$;
iii) $\forall (i, j) \in E$ there exists a node $t \in V_t$ such that $\{i, j\} \subseteq V_t$;
iv) for each $i \in V$ the subgraph of T induced by those $t \in V_T$ such that $i \in V_t$ is connected.

b) The width *of a tree decomposition T is given as $\max\{|V_t|, t \in V_T\} - 1$. The* tree-width *$twd(G)$ of a graph G is the minimal width of one of its tree decompositions.*

In recent years the notion of tree-width has played an important role in the design of efficient algorithms for certain subclasses of hard problems; for a good introduction into tree-width issues (which mainly focusses on parametrized complexity) see [4] and the literature cited in there. In relation with CSPs, Freuder has shown the following (see also [2] for the issue of constructing decompositions):

Theorem 1. *(Freuder [7]) Let $k \in \mathbb{N}$ be a fixed constant. Given a CSP whose constraint graph has tree-width at most k, there exists linear (in the number of variables) time algorithms finding all solutions of the problem.*

The solution algorithm is based on climbing up an optimal decomposition tree, each step taking care of the tuples satisfying those constraints which only relate variables covered by V_t for the current node t. This update heavily relies on the fact that the admissible tuples are listed explicitly (and thus, the domains have to be finite). Note as well that a single global constraint (i.e. a constraint including $O(n)$ many variables) results in a tree-width of order n and thus forbids the application of the above theorem.

In order to obtain similar results as well for continuous CSPs Faltings [5] has introduced an arc consistency notion for the following type of problems:

Definition 3. *A continuous binary CSP is given by a set $X := \{x_1, \ldots, x_n\}$ of variables with associated domains $D_1, \ldots, D_n, D_i \subseteq \mathbb{R}$ and a finite set $\mathcal{C}$ of constraints $c_i(x, y) \geq 0, 1 \leq i \leq m$, where each c_i determines a differentiable curve $c_i(x, y) = 0$.*
The constraint graph of such a problem is defined as above.

Due to the fact that the functions c_i are rather general, numerical issues enter into the analysis of such CSPs. The domains D_i are represented by so called interval labels L_{x_i} which describe a finite set of bounded intervals from which assignments for x_i can be chosen. Arc consistency is then defined in the following way: the label L_x of a variable x is arc consistent with the label L_y of variable y iff $(\forall x_0 \in L_x)$ $(\exists\ y_0 \in L_y)$ such that for all constraints c which relate x and y it is $c(x_0, y_0) \geq 0$. Faltings then shows that for constraint graphs of tree-width 1 (i.e. trees) arc consistency for all pairs of variables guarantees global consistency; moreover, arc consistency can be obtained by making use of a linear (in the number of variables) number of applications of a procedure REFINE(x,y). The latter procedure propagates admissible values for one of the variables taking the labels for the other one and considering all constraints in both.

2.2   Extension to Algebraic CSPs; Consistency and Complexity

We shall now define and analyze algebraic CSPs relying on Faltings' approach. The special problems we consider are at the same time more restricted and more general ones. More restrictive because we only allow constraints involving polynomials instead of general differentiable functions; more general because we consider arbitrary arities in the constraints as well as a k-consistency notion. Note also that algebraic constraints can express all properties being definable via semi-algebraic sets.

The above mentioned refinement procedure from [5], when applied to a polynomial c, is strongly related to a restricted kind of quantifier elimination. As we shall see, this actually is the reason why in certain situations the task to make a

binary CSP arc consistent cannot be afforded efficiently even if the constraints
are polynomials. Thus, reaching arc consistency with a linear number of refinement procedures in general does not result in suitable solution algorithms: the
application of these operations might be as expensive as solving the entire CSP
without taking into account any local consistency consideration, see Theorem 3
below.

Let us first define the corresponding notions.

Definition 4. *a) An algebraic constraint satisfaction problem $\mathcal{P}$ is given as a
tuple $\mathcal{P} = (X, \psi_1, \ldots, \psi_{|X|}, c_1, \ldots, c_m)$, where $X := \{x_1, \ldots, x_n\}$ is a finite set
of variables each of which ranging over a domain $D_i \subseteq \mathbb{R}$. Every D_i is (finitely)
represented via a first-order formula $\psi_i(x)$ over the real numbers, i.e. a Boolean
combination of (in-)equalities $q(x) \Delta 0$ for polynomials q and $\Delta \in \{=, \neq, \geq, \leq,
>, <\}$. Then $D_i = \{x \in \mathbb{R} \mid \psi_i(x)\}$. The finitely many constraints c_i are of the
form $c_i(x_{i_1}, \ldots, x_{i_{j_i}}) \Delta_{c_i} 0$, where c_i is a real polynomial and Δ_{c_i} is as above.
Again, $var(c_i) = \{x_{i_1}, \ldots, x_{i_{j_i}}\}$ denotes the variables constraint c_i depends on.
b) The size of an algebraic CSP $\mathcal{P}$ is given as*

$$size(\mathcal{P}) := \sum_{i=1}^{m} size(c_i) + \sum_{i=1}^{n} size(\psi_i).$$

*Here, the size of a constraint c_i in j_i variables is defined to be $j_i \cdot degree(c_i)$, and
the size of a first-order formula ψ is the number of involved basic (in-)equalities
multiplied with the maximal degree occurring.*

Remark 1. The size of a first-order formula could be defined in a different manner; for example, if all coefficients are rationals one could include the bit-sizes of
these coefficients as well. We restrict ourselves to the above algebraic measure
which is appropriate to explain the ideas.

Example 1. a) We want to express a finite CSP in our setting. If the finite
domains are given by $D_1, \ldots, D_n$ each D_i can be represented by a first-order
formula

$$\psi_i(x_i) \equiv \prod_{a \in D_i} (x_i - a) = 0$$

of degree $|D_i|$. A relation r in variables $x_1, \ldots, x_s$ can be described by a polyno-
mial equation

$$0 = p_r(x_1, \ldots, x_s) := \prod_{(a_1, \ldots, a_s) \in r} \sum_{i=1}^{s} (x_i - a_i)^2$$

of degree $2 \cdot |r|$. Supposing d to be an upper bound on the domains' cardinalities
the size of the entire algebraic CSP with m constraints is of order $O(m \cdot d^n)$. If
all constraints relate at most k different variables each, then the size reduces to
$O(m \cdot d^k)$.
b) A system of linear inequalities can be represented in a straightforward manner

by defining every inequality as a constraint. The domains can either be described via a tautology (if we are looking for real solutions) or as in part a) if we look for 0-1 or other integral solutions.

Definition 5. *Let $k \in \mathbb{N}$ and an algebraic CSP $\mathcal{P} = (X, \psi_1, \ldots, \psi_n, c_1, \ldots, c_m)$ over n variables be given. Problem $\mathcal{P}$ is strongly k-consistent iff for all constraints in at most k many variables the following holds: w.l.o.g. let $x_1, \ldots, x_\ell$ denote an arbitrary set of ℓ variables, $\ell \leq k - 1$. Then for all choices $x_i = a_i, 1 \leq i \leq \ell$ which are admissible (i.e. $\psi_i(a_i)$ is true) and which satisfy all constraints c with $var(c) \subseteq \{x_1, \ldots, x_\ell\}$ and for any additional variable $y \notin \{x_1, \ldots, x_\ell\}$ there is an admissible assignment $y := a$ such that $(a_1, \ldots, a_\ell, a)$ satisfies all the constraints among those $\ell + 1$ variables.*

Though the above definition is straightforward, the necessity to represent domains in algebraic CSPs in a different manner than by elementwise listing results in severe differences and difficulties being not present in the finite case. We analyze some of the latter in the rest of this section.

The (primal) constraint graph of an algebraic CSP is defined as before.

Theorem 2. *Let $k \in \mathbb{N}$ be fixed.*

a) Given an algebraic CSP $\mathcal{P}$ it is decidable in polynomial time in size$(\mathcal{P})$ whether $\mathcal{P}$ is strongly k-consistent.

b) If $\mathcal{P}$ is strongly k-consistent and if its constraint graph has tree-width at most $k - 1$, then it is decidable in polynomial time whether $\mathcal{P}$ is solvable.

Proof. Ad a) Let $\underline{x} := (x_{i_1}, \ldots, x_{i_\ell}), i_1 < \ldots < i_\ell$ denote a tuple of $\ell \leq k - 1$ variables and let $C_{\underline{x}} := \{c_1, \ldots, c_s\}$ denote those constraints of $\mathcal{P}$ only depending on variables of $\underline{x}$. For sake of notational simplicity we write $c(\underline{x}) \Delta_c 0$ for such a constraint $c \in C_{\underline{x}}$, even though c might not depend on all components of $\underline{x}$. Let y be an arbitrary additional variable and denote by $C_{\underline{x} \cup \{y\}}$ the constraints among variables $\underline{x}$ and y. Consistency for $\underline{x}, y$ asks for truth of the following formula:

$$(*) \; \forall \, a_{i_1}, \ldots, a_{i_\ell} \; \{\rho_{\underline{x}}(a_{i_1}, \ldots, a_{i_\ell}) \Rightarrow \exists \, a \; \rho_{\underline{x} \cup \{y\}}(a_{i_1}, \ldots, a_{i_\ell}, a)\}.$$

Here, for a subset $\tilde{X}$ of variables the formula $\rho_{\tilde{X}}$ denotes the conjunction of the domain formulas ψ_i for $x_i \in \tilde{X}$ and the formulas given by any constraint c that satisfies $var(c) \subseteq \tilde{X}$. Thus,

$$\rho_{\underline{x}}(a_{i_1}, \ldots, a_{i_\ell}) \equiv \bigwedge_{j=1}^{\ell} \psi_{i_j}(a_{i_j}) \wedge \bigwedge_{var(c) \subseteq \underline{x}} c(a_{i_1}, \ldots, a_{i_\ell}) \Delta_c 0$$

and

$$\rho_{\underline{x} \cup \{y\}}(a_{i_1}, \ldots, a_{i_\ell}, a) \equiv \rho_{\underline{x}}(a_{i_1}, \ldots, a_{i_\ell}) \wedge \psi_y(a) \wedge$$

$$\bigwedge_{var(c) \subseteq \underline{x} \cup \{y\}} c(a_{i_1}, \ldots, a_{i_\ell}, a) \Delta_c 0.$$

Checking $(*)$ to hold can be done by eliminating the ℓ universal and the single existential quantifier. Note that k is a constant and $\ell \leq k - 1$, so we have to eliminate a constant number of quantifiers only. Applying well known results concerning quantifier elimination over the reals (see, for example, [12]) this can be accomplished in polynomial time w.r.t. $size(\mathcal{P})$ (and exponential time in k). Now a formula like $(*)$ has to be checked for all possible choices of k many variables. Again, taking into account k's role as a fixed constant, we have to perform the above elimination algorithm a polynomial number of times: there are $O(n^k)$ possible choices (actually, the latter only has to be done for those subsets of variables commonly occurring in a single constraint).

Ad b) Given $\mathcal{P}$ we consider, for each single variable x_i, the proposition

$$\theta_i \equiv \exists\, a\; \psi_i(a) \;\wedge\; \bigwedge_{var(c)=\{x_i\}} c\Delta_c 0$$

and eliminate in polynomial time the existential quantifier. Then $\mathcal{P}$ is solvable (under the assumption of strong k-consistency) iff

$$\bigwedge_{i=1}^{n} \theta_i$$

is a true proposition. The latter equivalence can be seen in exactly the same way as for discrete programs using a top-down evaluation in the decomposition tree.   □

Whereas the above results seem to be similar to those for finite programs, the question how to obtain strong k-consistency for a given program results in difficulties.

Theorem 3. *Given as input an algebraic CSP $\mathcal{P}$ whose primal constraint graph has tree-width ≤ 2, there is no general polynomial time (in $size(\mathcal{P})$) algorithm computing an equivalent arc consistent program. Here, we call a two algebraic CSPs equivalent if they have the same solution set.*

Proof. Consider the following algebraic CSP: there are $n + 1$ many variables $x_0, \ldots, x_n$ with binary constraints $c_1, \ldots, c_n$, where

$$c_i(x_i, x_{i-1}) \;\equiv\; (x_i - x_{i-1}) \cdot (x_i - x_{i-1} - \frac{1}{10^i}) = 0 \;,\; 1 \leq i \leq n.$$

The domains are defined via

$$\psi_0(x_0) \;\equiv\; (x_0 - 1) \cdot (x_0 - 2) = 0$$

for x_0 and as $\mathbb{R}$ for the other variables (but could be a finite interval such as $[0, 10]$ as well). The size of $\mathcal{P}$ is of order $O(n)$.

An easy calculation now shows that there are $O(2^n)$ admissible values for variable x_n which can be extended to solution vectors of $\mathcal{P}$. Thus, any quantifier-free first order-formula which describes the domain of x_n in an equivalent, arc consistent program must have exponential size as well. This is due to well-known results about semi-algebraic sets (a set A in some $\mathbb{R}^n$ is called semi-algebraic if it can be defined as the set of all points in $\mathbb{R}^n$ which satisfy a first-order formula over $\mathbb{R}$ with n free variables). Since the domain of x_n consists of 2^n isolated points and since a sign condition on any univariate polynomial of degree d can at most define a semi-algebraic set with d many connected components, the statement follows (see, for example, [1]).

$\square$

The last result shows that even if the constraint graph of an algebraic CSP is well-structured efficiency problems can arise due to the computation of a description of the corresponding projection sets.

Remark 2. i) The above result does, of course, not mean that there is no efficient algorithm deciding solvability. It just addresses the question of designing such an algorithm along the line of establishing strong k-consistency.
ii) The importance of projection sets in the finite framework was studied in [9]. Once again, the above problems do not occur in that setting, compare Example 1.

An additional condition sufficient to guarantee a better complexity performance for such problems can be derived as follows.

Suppose T to be a tree decomposition of width k for the constraint graph. W.l.o.g. assume T to be binary, and if t is a branch node in T with children t_1, t_2, then the sets V_{t_1}, V_{t_2} are equal. If $\tilde{t}$ is the only child of t the sets V_T and $V_{\tilde{t}}$ differ only in one element. All these conditions can be fulfilled without problems, see [4]. As, for example, described in [5] consistency can be obtained by first performing a bottom-up and thereafter a top-down computation in T. At each step we have to perform a restricted quantifier elimination. Suppose that we want to pass from a leaf $\tilde{t}$ in T to its father t, and assume $V_t = \{x_1, \ldots, x_s, y\}, V_{\tilde{t}} = \{x_1, \ldots, x_s, z\}$. Let the first-order formulas $\tilde{c}(x_1, \ldots, x_s, z)$ and $c(x_1, \ldots, x_s, y)$ denote the conjunction of all constraints in $\mathcal{P}$ only involving variables $(x_1, \ldots, x_s, z)$ and $(x_1, \ldots, x_s, y)$, respectively. Given the defining formulas ψ_v for the domain of each variable v, passing from $\tilde{c}$ to c can be done by propagating a quantifier free description of the projection to $x_1, \ldots, x_s$ of the feasible set for

$$\tilde{c}(x_1, \ldots, x_s, z) \wedge \bigwedge_{i=1}^{s} \psi_{x_i} \wedge \psi_z$$

to the upper level, i.e. apply quantifier elimination to

$$\exists z \; \tilde{c}(x_1, \ldots, x_s, z) \wedge \bigwedge_{i=1}^{s} \psi_{x_i} \wedge \psi_z$$

and add the resulting formula, say $\rho_{\tilde{c}}(x_1, \ldots, x_s)$, by conjunction to c.

If we climb the tree, then other variables might be replaced. This results in an elimination in the last obtained formula of the variable to be replaced next. If a branch node is reached, by our initial assumption on T we just have to join the corresponding sub-formulas by conjunction and potentially simplify the resulting one. After reaching the root a top-down computation is performed in the same manner, this time applying appropriate quantifier eliminations in the reverse variable order (and to possibly different formulas). This process will finally give a k-consistent algebraic CSP.

The above algorithm runs in polynomial (linear in n) time if all first-order formulas computed in between have a size bounded by an (arbitrary) function in k. We have thus proven:

Theorem 4. *Let $k \in \mathbb{N}$ be fixed. Under the above boundedness condition, an algebraic CSP can be transformed to an equivalent strongly k-consistent one in polynomial time. If, in addition, the constraint graph has tree-width $\leq k - 1$ the algebraic CSP can be solved in polynomial time.*

Note that a direct application of the existing complexity estimates for quantifier elimination does not guarantee that during the above procedure formula sizes will remain polynomially bounded in the initial problem size (see Theorem 3).

We close this section by giving two examples where the above Theorem can be applied and thus, efficient algorithms exist on instances of bounded-width constraint graphs.

Example 2. a) The finite CSP setting (see Example 1) is captured by the above approach. Updating the describing formulas when moving bottom up or top down here results in removing certain tuples which turned out to be infeasible. With respect to the describing quantifier free formulas this leads to the deletion of certain factors in the polynomials. Therefore, the sizes of the formulas produced will never be longer than the initial formulas defining the variable domains, and are thus bounded by $O(m \cdot d^k)$. There is no blow up and the above arguments re-establish Freuder's result.

b) Consider a generalization of "simple temporal problems" studied in [3]. A constraint c is given as a linear inequality of the form

$$a^T \cdot x + d \leq \tilde{a}^T \cdot x$$

for vectors $a, \tilde{a} \in \{0, 1\}^n, d \in \mathbb{R}$. Quantifier elimination for a single variable can be done by Fourier-Motzkin elimination (see [13]). This method eliminates a variable y in a set of formulas

$$a_i^T \cdot x + d_i \leq y \leq \tilde{a}_j^T \cdot x + \tilde{d}_j,$$

where $i \in I, j \in J, I, J$ are finite index sets, each $a_i, \tilde{a}_j \in \{0, 1\}^n, d_i, \tilde{d}_j \in \mathbb{R}$, by replacing them with

$$a_i^T \cdot x + d_i \leq \tilde{a}_j^T \cdot x + d_j \quad \forall \, i \in I, j \in J \, .$$

But the special form of the coefficients implies that for a set of k many variables we shall never get more than $O(2^k)$ many inequalities. So for constraint graphs of bounded tree-width the algebraic CSP can be solved in linear time (even with computing an interval representation of all solutions).

Note that the above argument works in a complexity theoretic setting where only the number of arithmetic operations is counted. In such a framework it is an open problem whether (general) Linear Programming is polynomial time solvable.

A challenging problem is certainly provided by finding classes of algebraic CSPs for which the above condition on formula sizes is fulfilled.

3   A New Width Notion for Algebraic CSPs

In the previous section we have seen that a straightforward generalization of the width notion for the constraint graph of algebraically given constraints leads to difficulties. In addition, this approach cannot be used as soon as global constraints (i.e. constraints combining $O(n)$ many variables) are present.

In this section we want to consider another width notion which was first introduced in [10] in an algebraic complexity framework. It takes into account the special algebraic form of the constraints. In addition, up to a certain extend also global constraints can be treated in a backtrack-free manner.

We present the main ideas behind this new notion. Instead of considering a constraint as an entity its special structure will be analyzed more precisely. As we are dealing with algebraic constraints, the latter refers to the structure of the monomials in a constraint such as $p(x_1, \ldots, x_n)\Delta 0$, p a polynomial. In particular, we are not so much interested in how variables are mixed in single constraints (as it is the case with Freuder's width notion) but how they are mixed within each monomial of a constraint. To a certain extend this point of view allows more general constraints to be treated efficiently, and even certain global ones can be admitted.

Let us now define the *algebraic width* of an algebraic CSP $\mathcal{P}$. Suppose the latter to be of the form $\mathcal{P} = (X, \psi_1, \ldots, \psi_{|X|}, c_1, \ldots, c_m)$, see Definition 4. We assume all constraints to have a degree at most $d \in \mathbb{N}$. We consider each constraint c in $\mathcal{P}$ as a weighted hypergraph (V, E), $V := \{x_0, x_1, \ldots, x_n\}$, $E_c \subseteq V^{d+1}$. The weights on each hyperedge e of E_c are given by a function $w_c : E \to \mathbb{R}$. This weight function represents the coefficients of monomials in c in the following way: for a hyperedge $e := x_0^{\alpha_0} \cdot x_1^{\alpha_1} \cdot \ldots \cdot x_n^{\alpha_n}$, $\sum_{i=0}^{n} \alpha_i = d$, the value $w_c(e)$ represents the coefficient of monomial $x_1^{\alpha_1} \cdot \ldots \cdot x_n^{\alpha_n}$ in c. Note that the vertex x_0 in V is only used for dehomogenization of the given constraint.

Definition 6. *Let $d \in \mathbb{N}$ be fixed and let $\mathcal{P} := (X, \psi_1, \ldots, \psi_{|X|}, c_1, \ldots, c_m)$ be given as above, all c_i of degree at most d. Let $V := \{x_0, \ldots, x_n\}$, E_{c_i} be the set of hyperedges for constraint c_i and w_{c_i} its weight function, $1 \le i \le m$.*
a) An algebraic tree decomposition *of $\mathcal{P}$ is a tree $T = (V_T, E_T)$ satisfying the following conditions:*

i) to each node $t \in V_T$ there corresponds a subset $V_t \subseteq \{c_1, \ldots, c_m\} \cup V$;
ii) $\bigcup_{t \in V_T} V_t = \{c_1, \ldots, c_m\} \cup V$;

iii) for every constraint c and for all $(x_{i_1}, \ldots, x_{i_d}) \in E_c$ there exists a node $t \in V_t$ such that $\{c, x_{i_1}, \ldots, x_{i_d}\} \subseteq V_t$;

iv) for every $i \in \{c_1, \ldots, c_m\} \cup V$ the subgraph of T induced by those $t \in V_T$ such that $i \in V_t$ is connected.

b) The algebraic width of a tree decomposition T is given as $\max\{|V_t|, t \in V_T\} - 1$. The algebraic tree-width $twd(\mathcal{P})$ of $\mathcal{P}$ is the minimal width of one of its tree decompositions.

Remark 3. A few remarks are necessary here.

i) The above way to define an algebraic width notion logically corresponds to the consideration of two-sorted structures: one sort being represented by the variables and the constraints, the other by the monomials involved in the constraints, see [10]. This is different from studying the primal graph of a constraint satisfaction program, which takes the variables as the only sort.

ii) Formalizing a CSP in different ways, especially with respect to the constraint graph, is not a new idea. A survey on such approaches in the framework of finite constraint programs and database theory can be found, for example, in [8]. There, a hypergraph width is studied. However, when applied to an algebraic setting, these notions create similar problems like those mentioned in section 2. For example, a single global constraint has a bounded hypertree width. This is, of course, in an algebraic setting not sufficient to guarantee efficient solution algorithms because already one global algebraic constraint can express an **NP**-hard problem. In addition, the hypertree-width still treats a whole constraint as an entity (which is, of course, appropriate if the constraint is listed elementwise). Therefore, for algebraic constraints we believe our notion to be more suitable taking into account also the structure of each single constraint.

The above width notion was introduced in [10] in order to deal with algebraic problems such as solving polynomial systems of equations over finite fields or the reals. In such a framework, it seems to be necessary to incorporate a significant part of logical methods (basically, an adaption of the theorem by Feferman and Vaught for the particular logical structures coming into play when describing such algebraic problems). In order to concentrate on the main ideas for using this approach to solve algebraic CSPs, here we will deal with the **NP**-complete 0-1 integer programming problem only.

Theorem 5. *Let $k \in \mathbb{N}$ be fixed. Let an algebraic CSP $\mathcal{P} = (X, \psi_1, \ldots, \psi_{|X|}, c_1, \ldots, c_m)$ be given such that*

i) all the constraints c_i are linear inequalities and all ψ_j define the domain $\{0, 1\}$;

ii) $\mathcal{P}$ has algebraic width at most k;

iii) the coefficients of the c_i are integers in $\{-q(|X|), \ldots, q(|X|)\}$ for a polynomial q.

Then $\mathcal{P}$ can be solved without backtracking in linear time in the number $n := |X|$ of variables.

Proof. The algorithm starts by producing a tree-decomposition T of algebraic width k, this time w.r.t. the hypergraph representing the set of constraints. This can be done as usual, see [4]. The propagation will work bottom up along the nodes of T. However notice that, because of the fact that the width notion is based on monomials in a constraint, we have to take care about how a single constraint is decomposed as well by T. Consider a node in T with the corresponding set $V_t, |V_t| \leq k + 1$. Therefore, V_t represents parts of constraints in a bounded number of variables together with monomials combining precisely these variables. Given a fixed bound d on the degrees for the constraints, here $d = 1$, the number of different monomials in those variables occurring in V_t is constant w.r.t. the total number n of variables. We now start the evaluation of these monomials and their sum on the substructure induced by V_t. It is important to note that on the substructures obtained by the decomposition the algebraic task to perform is that of partially evaluating the entire constraint (this might not be the same in general for arbitrary algebraic constraints, see the remarks following the proof).

Since we finally have to check an algebraic condition we have to store the different results intermediately obtained on the substructures for the different choices of assignments. The coefficient condition iii) on the c_i's guarantees that at most polynomially many different subresults occur: if the possible assignments for the x_i are taken from $\{0, 1\}$, then there are only polynomially many subresults occurring when adding arbitrary monomials of a constraint. Therefore, if we climb up the decomposition tree and replace a variable already treated by a new one, then dealing with the new variable will not result in more than polynomially many different subresults. Backtracking as usual is avoided since a variable which was removed once will never reoccur. Finally, at the root we check whether there was an assignment meeting the required inequalities for all constraints.   □

The above result is formulated in such a way that major problems with applying similar techniques to more general algebraic problems remain hidden. The approach can be extended to other algebraic CSPs, but then including a broader study of the logical framework in which such problems have to be expressible. The latter involves the introduction of a monadic second order logic on so-called meta-finite structures. This logic is used in order to specify which kind of algebraic problems can be treated with our approach. For the above 0-1 programming problem these difficulties lie quiet. For linear or quadratic programs where real solutions are looked for, the same becomes much more difficult due to the fact that the corresponding logical descriptions now include quantifiers over the reals ('there exists a real solution') instead of 'discrete' quantifiers (there exists a 0-1 solution). We postpone the treatment of such problems to an extended version. For the principle ideas behind such logical aspects related to our algebraic width notion see [10].

Let us mention that the above coefficient condition iii) is somehow related to the kind of problems we encountered in the proof of Theorem 3. Such a condition seems to be needed in order to avoid an explosion of the complexity even when variable backtracking does not occur.

We close with an example which shows that the above result captures certain constraint programs involving global constraints and thus extends the range of applicability of related techniques.

Example 3. Consider once more the generalization of simple temporal problems introduced in Example 2. The single constraints are of the form

$$(*) \quad c(x_1, \ldots, x_n) := \sum_{i \in \tilde{S}} x_i - \sum_{j \in S} x_j + d \ \geq \ 0 \text{ for } S, \tilde{S} \subseteq \{1, \ldots, n\}, S \cap \tilde{S} = \emptyset$$

and satisfy condition iii) in Theorem 5.

We construct a class of such algebraic CSPs where the algorithm of Example 2 b) cannot be applied but Theorem 5 can. Let $m, k \in \mathbb{N}$ be constants independent of $n, k \cdot s = n$ for some $s \in \mathbb{N}, s > 1$. First, consider a set of m arbitrary (global) constraints $\tilde{c}_1, \ldots, \tilde{c}_m$ of form $(*)$. Next, consider quadratic blocks of $2k$ inequalities each, where block i represents $2k$ constraints $c_{(i-1)k+1}, \ldots, c_{(i+1)k}$ of form $(*)$ only involving variables $x_{(i-1)k+1}, \ldots, x_{(i+1)k}$. The structure of this algebraic CSP is indicated in the next figure, where the boxes represent non-zero coefficients.

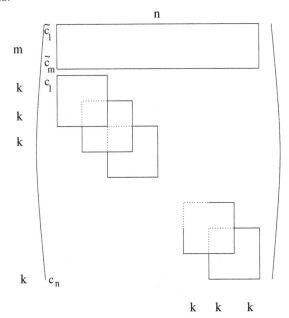

The usual tree-width of the primal constraint graph of such problems is n because of the global constraints $\tilde{c}_1, \ldots, \tilde{c}_m$; however, it is easy to sea that the algebraic width is bounded by the constant $m + 4k - 1$: a corresponding decomposition places $\tilde{c}_1, \ldots, \tilde{c}_m$; into each box V_t of a decomposition for the algebraic program represented by the constraints $c_1, \ldots, c_n$.

If we look for a 0-1 solution or, more general, a solution with integer components in a set $\{-q(n), \ldots, q(n)\}$ for a polynomial q we obtain an efficient solution algorithm.

In the present paper we studied generalization of the commonly used width notion for the (primal) constraint graph of a CSP to algebraic CSPs. Though, in principle, the definitions can easily be generalized, we showed that significant problems w.r.t. the complexity of propagation algorithms might occur even if the constraint graph is a tree. We then proposed the study of a new algebraic width notion in the framework of algebraic CSPs and showed how some problems can be solved efficiently by that approach, even though they might contain global constraints.

It is not completely clear how far the present approach can be pushed further. This is related to the above mentioned way of defining a monadic second order logic for meta-finite structures; there are different ways to define specific logics in such a way that similar decomposition ideas as those used in Theorem 5 work. It might be interesting to study several such different notions as well as to include algorithms based on the latter into an algebraic constraint solver.

Acknowledgement

Thanks are due to the anonymous referees for some helpful remarks.

References

[1] J. Bochnak, M. Coste, M. F. Roy, Real Algebraic Geometry. Springer, 1998. 95
[2] H. Bodlaender, Treewidth: Algorithmic techniques and results. In I. Privara, P. Ruzicka, editors, Proc. 22nd Symposium *Mathematical Foundation of Computer Science*, volume 1295 of *Lecture Notes in Computer Science*, Springer, 19–36, 1997. 90
[3] R. Dechter, I. Meiri, J. Pearl, Temporal constraint networks. Artificial intelligence 49 (1-3), 61–95 (1991). 96
[4] R. G. Downey, M.F Fellows, Parametrized Complexity. Springer, 1999. 90, 95, 99
[5] B. Faltings, Arc-consistency for continuous variables. Artificial Intelligence 65, 363–376, 1994. 88, 89, 91, 95
[6] E. C. Freuder, A sufficient condition for backtrack-free search. Journal of the ACM 29 (1), 61–95, 1982. 88, 89, 90
[7] E. C. Freuder, Complexity of k-tree structured constraint satisfaction problems. Proc. of the 8th National Conference on AI, 4–9, 1990. 88, 89, 91
[8] G. Gottlob, N. Leone, F. Scarcello, Hypertree Decompositions: A Survey. In J. Sgall, A. Pultr, P. Kolman, editors, Proc. 26nd Symposium *Mathematical Foundation of Computer Science*, volume 2136 of *Lecture Notes in Computer Science*, Springer, 37–57, 2001. 98
[9] P. Jeavons, D. Cohen, M. Cooper, Constraints, Consistency, and Closure. Artificial Intelligence 101, 251–265, 1998. 95
[10] J. A. Makowsky, K. Meer, Polynomials of bounded tree-width. Foundations of Computational Mathematic: Proceedings of the Smalefest 2000, World Scientific, 211–250, 2002. 88, 89, 97, 98, 99
[11] K. Marriott, P. J. Stuckey, Programming with Constraints. The MIT Press, Cambridge, Massachusetts and London, England 1998 89

[12] J. Renegar, On the computational Complexity and Geometry of the first-order Theory of the Reals, I - III, *Journal of Symbolic Computation*, Vol. 13, 255–352, 1992. 94

[13] A. Schrijver, Theory of Linear and Integer Programming. Wiley, Chichester, 1986. 96

Solving Mixed Quantified Constraints over a Domain Based on $\mathcal{R}$eal Numbers and $\mathcal{H}$erbrand Terms

Miguel García-Díaz and Susana Nieva

Dpto. Sistemas Informáticos y Programación
Universidad Complutense de Madrid
{miguel,nieva}@sip.ucm.es

Abstract. Combining the logic of hereditary Harrop formulas *HH* with a constraint system, a logic programming language is obtained that extends Horn clauses in two different directions, thus enhancing substantially the expressivity of Prolog. The implementation of this new language requires the ability to test the satisfiability of constraints built up by means of terms and predicates belonging to the domain of the chosen constraint system, and by the connectives and quantifiers usual in first-order logic. In this paper we present a constraint system called $\mathcal{R}\mathcal{H}$ for a hybrid domain that mixes Herbrand terms and real numbers. It arises when joining the axiomatization of the arithmetic of real numbers and the axiomatization of the algebra of finite trees. We have defined an algorithm to solve certain constraints of this kind. The novelty relies on the combination of two different mechanisms, based on elimination of quantifiers, one used for solving unification and disunification problems, the other used to solve polynomials. This combination provides a procedure to solve $\mathcal{R}\mathcal{H}$-constraints in the context of *HH* with constraints.
Keywords: constraint systems, hereditary Harrop formulas, real numbers, finite symbolic trees, first-order logic.

1 Introduction

Constraint logic programming *CLP* [10] arises as an extension of the traditional logic programming (based on Horn clauses) with the purpose of overcoming its inherent limitations in dealing efficiently with elements of domains different from Herbrand terms. In order to build an implementation, it is necessary to find a combination of the goal solving procedure, concerning the logic part of the language (e.g. *SLD*-resolution [14] for Horn clauses), with a decision mechanism for constraint satisfiability, capable of generating the set of valid answer constraints for any goal, which will depend on the specific domain of the constraint system.

This kind of extension is also dealt with in the papers [13] and [12] but, in both cases, the base language is the logic of Hereditary Harrop formulas *HH* (first-order and higher-order, respectively). This logic is in addition an extension of the logic of Horn clauses in which implications and universal quantification

Z. Hu and M. Rodríguez-Artalejo (Eds.): FLOPS 2002, LNCS 2441, pp. 103–118, 2002.
© Springer-Verlag Berlin Heidelberg 2002

are allowed in goals [16]. *SLD*-resolution, which deals with equality between Herbrand terms by using unification, is no longer valid in this extension, mainly due to the existence of prefixes with mixed quantifications, i. e. prefixes containing both ∃ and ∀ arbitrarily ordered. In [17], a method based on labeled unification is used for *HH*. But, in *HH(C)*, the extension of *HH* including constraints, the technique to obtain answer substitutions using unification is replaced by the checking of the satisfiability of constraints under a mixed prefix. As a consequence, the specific mechanism to decide the satisfiability should be able to deal with complex formulas, which may contain occurrences of all the connectives in first-order logic, equations between Herbrand terms and, moreover, other relations belonging to the constraint signature between terms of the instance domain.

Following one of the open research lines mentioned in [13], we intended to find decidable theories which could be the basis of a first-order constraint system for the abstract logic programming language *HH(C)*, but which are also useful programming domains. The domain traditionally used in declarative programming is the Herbrand universe, which consists of symbolic terms built up with constants and the application of function symbols to other terms. We must be able to solve equality constraints between such terms, but we also intend to deal with disequalities, and, of course, these relations may occur embedded in expressions together with several connectives and quantifiers, as reasoned before. This domain has been axiomatized and decision mechanisms have been defined for the corresponding theory [15, 6]. However, our approach demands an enlargement of it that provides more expressiveness, but simultaneously keeping the good properties and efficiency inherent to *CLP*, in which the tests for constraint satisfiability and the general goal solving procedure respect to a program are separated. The fields of application of *CLP* with constraint domains related to real numbers are abundant and very well known [10, 11]. In addition, thanks to the results due to Tarski about the decidability of the theory of the field of real numbers [19], this domain becomes a good choice as a constraint system instance. In this article we aimed to join the theory of the arithmetic of real numbers and the one of Herbrand terms, to produce a mixed constraint system called $\mathcal{RH}$ and so the instance *HH($\mathcal{RH}$)* of the language of *HH* with constraints. An algorithm to solve constraints for this language has been described. There are other works in the literature that introduce mixed numeric and symbolic domains (see e.g. [2, 5, 9]), but all of them deal with the logic of Horn clauses, which implies that quantifiers in the goals are limited to be existential. Other approaches of decision procedures for combined theories, as [18], apply only to universal quantified formulas.

The structure of the rest of this article is as follows: In Section 2, the constraint system $\mathcal{RH}$ is introduced in the context of the logic of hereditary Harrop formulas with constraints. The main results of the paper appear in Section 3. First we present two rules that constitute the core of a procedure to solve $\mathcal{RH}$-constraints. In order to give the foundations of these rules, several definitions and technical results are needed, their proofs appear in [7]. Then the algorithm that constitutes this procedure is detailed. In Section 4, its behavior is shown through examples. We end summarizing the contributions of our work, and stating future research, in Section 5.

2   The Constraint System $\mathcal{RH}$

The logic of Hereditary Harrop formulas HH [16] arises when extending the logic of Horn clauses, on which the traditional logic programming language is based, relaxing the conditions over the structure of clauses and goals. Specifically, the connectives $\Rightarrow$ and $\forall$ are allowed in goals. In [13] a logic programming language called $HH(\mathcal{C})$ is defined by adding constraints of a generic constraint system $\mathcal{C}$ to HH. In it, the language and the conditions of a system $\mathcal{C}$ to be a constraint system are specified, but no constraint solver for any particular system is studied. Here we will concentrate on an specific constraint system denoted by $\mathcal{RH} = \langle \mathcal{L}_{\mathcal{RH}}, \vdash_{\mathcal{RH}} \rangle$, which mixes $\mathcal{R}$eal numbers and finite symbolic trees (or $\mathcal{H}$erbrand terms). $\mathcal{L}_{\mathcal{RH}}$ denotes the set of formulas allowed as constraints, and $\vdash_{\mathcal{RH}}$ is the entailment relation that represents deducibility of a constraint formula C from a set of constraints Γ. $\mathcal{L}_{\mathcal{RH}}$ is a set of first-order formulas whose terms and atoms are built up using typed symbols belonging to a signature $\Sigma_{\mathcal{RH}}$. We agree on the existence of two sorts: r for real numbers, and h for Herbrand terms. Combining these basic types, types $\tau_1 \times \ldots \times \tau_n$ for predicate symbols and $\tau_1 \times \ldots \times \tau_n \to \tau$ for function symbols are built, where $\tau, \tau_i \in \{r, h\}$, $1 \leq i \leq n$. τ will stand for any type, and $o : \tau$ specifies that object o is of type τ. $\Sigma_{\mathcal{RH}}$ will contain:

- Constants, denoted by c. Some of them represent real numbers (-4.32, $1/2$, ...), and there is also a denumerable set of symbolic constants.
- Arithmetic operators $+, -, * : r \times r \to r$, and a finite or denumerable set of symbolic function $f : \tau_1 \times \ldots \times \tau_n \to h$, where $\tau_i \in \{r, h\}, 1 \leq i \leq n$.
- The predicate symbol $\approx: \tau \times \tau$, where $\tau \in \{r, h\}$, for equality between terms of the same type.
- The symbols $<, >, \leq, \geq : r \times r$, for the relations of order between real numbers.

Let $\mathcal{V} = \mathcal{V}_h \cup \mathcal{V}_r$ be the set of variables ν, where $\mathcal{V}_h$ is a denumerable set of variables of sort h, called symbolic variables, denoted with uppercase letters, and $\mathcal{V}_r$ is a denumerable set of variables of sort r, denoted with lowercase letters. The set of terms $\mathcal{T}_{\mathcal{RH}}$, with elements denoted t, is defined by:

$$t ::= \nu \mid c \mid f(t_1, \ldots, t_n) \mid t_1 + t_2 \mid t_1 - t_2 \mid t_1 * t_2$$

where $f : \tau_1 \times \ldots \times \tau_n \to h$ and $t_i : \tau_i, 1 \leq i \leq n$. Notice that infix notation is used for arithmetic operators, and that the included terms, t_1 and t_2, must be of type r.

The atoms of $\mathcal{L}_{\mathcal{RH}}$ are built up using the predicate symbols in $\Sigma_{\mathcal{RH}}$ (with infix notation) and the terms in $\mathcal{T}_{\mathcal{RH}}$. It also contains the constraints $\top$ and $\bot$, which stand for *true* and *false*, respectively. The existence of different connectives and quantifiers in the goals forces the constraint system to be able to express and deduce complex constraints during the process of goal solving, that specifically contain a mixed prefix of quantifiers. So, we should impose to $\mathcal{L}_{\mathcal{RH}}$ to be closed under $\wedge, \vee, \exists, \forall$ and $\neg$. For instance, if the signature contains the symbols $cons$: $r \times h \to h$ and $nil : h$ for the list constructor and the empty list, respectively, the formula

$$\forall x \exists X (X \approx cons(x * (2 - z), cons(-10.3, cons(z, nil)z)) \wedge \exists y(z \geq x + y))$$

is an $\mathcal{RH}$-constraint. The constraints with the form $t_1 \approx t_2$, where $t_1, t_2 : h$, will be referred to as *equalities*, and the ones with the form $\neg(t_1 \approx t_2)$ as *disequalities*. A *polynomial*, denoted by p, is any quantifier free constraint, such that its atomic subformulas are built up exclusively with real predicate symbols and real terms. For instance, the constraint

$$(x \approx z * z - (x * (2.5 + (1/5) * y)) \vee z \geq x) \Rightarrow y * y > 4.24$$

is a polynomial. The notation $t(\overline{v})$ or $p(\overline{v})$ will specify that $\overline{v}$ is a set of variables comprising the ones in t, or p, respectively. The substitution of a set of variables $\overline{v}$ by a set of terms $\overline{t}$ of the same cardinality and corresponding types will be denoted by $[\overline{t}/\overline{v}]$, and its application to a term or formula, denoted $F[\overline{t}/\overline{v}]$, is defined in the usual way, avoiding the capture of free variables. $[\overline{t}/\overline{v}]$ is said to be a *symbolic ground substitution* if $\overline{t}$ does not contain symbolic variables. It must be understood in the sequel that $\overline{X} \approx \overline{t}$ stands for a (possibly empty) conjunction of equalities of the form $X \approx t$.

The deducibility relation between constraints, $\vdash_{\mathcal{RH}}$, is defined as the result of combining the classic deducibility relation with equality, $\vdash_{\approx}$, with the axiomatization for the field of real numbers due to Tarski [19], plus the axiomatization for the Herbrand universe due to Clark [4]. I. e., if $Ax_{\mathcal{R}}$ and $Ax_{\mathcal{H}}$ denote respectively the sets of axioms for these two theories, then, for any set of constraints Γ and any constraint C, $\Gamma \vdash_{\mathcal{RH}} C$ if and only if $\Gamma \cup Ax_{\mathcal{R}} \cup Ax_{\mathcal{H}} \vdash_{\approx} C$. The relation $\vdash_{\mathcal{RH}}$ verifies that $C_1 \vdash_{\mathcal{RH}} C_2$, if and only if, for any symbolic ground substitution σ, $C_1\sigma \vdash_{\mathcal{RH}} C_2\sigma$ holds.

C is said to be $\mathcal{RH}$-satisfiable when $\emptyset \vdash_{\mathcal{RH}} \overline{\exists} C$, where $\overline{\exists} C$ represents the existential closure of C. We say that C and C' are $\mathcal{RH}$-equivalent, denoted by $C \equiv_{\mathcal{RH}} C'$, when $C \vdash_{\mathcal{RH}} C'$ and $C' \vdash_{\mathcal{RH}} C$. $\vdash_{\mathcal{RH}}$ verifies that if $C_1 \equiv_{\mathcal{RH}} C_2$ and $C \vdash_{\mathcal{RH}} C'[C_1]$ (C_1 is a subformula of C'), then $C \vdash_{\mathcal{RH}} C'[C_2]$ (C_1 is replaced by C_2 in C').

Using this mixed constraint system as parameter, we obtain the instance $HH(\mathcal{RH})$ of the logic programming language of hereditary Harrop formulas with constraints. As in CLP, the result of solving a goal using a program will be an *answer constraint*. Any goal solving procedure for $HH(\mathcal{RH})$ (such as the general one defined in [13] for $HH(\mathcal{C})$) should incorporate a constraint solver capable of dealing with the satisfiability of partially or totally calculated answer constraints. Therefore, our aim in this paper has been to find a procedure to determine whether a constraint of the system $\mathcal{RH}$ is $\mathcal{RH}$-satisfiable. It is important to notice that due to the mixed quantifier prefix binding real and symbolic variables, no separate solvers dealing with Herbrand terms and reals, respectively, can be used. Specifically, it is not possible to take advantage directly of the mechanism defined in [18] for combining decision procedures for several theories into a single solver for their combination.

3   A Solving Procedure for $\mathcal{RH}$-Constraints

The procedure that will be described is based on a transformation of constraints into simpler $\mathcal{RH}$-equivalent ones called *elemental constraints*, in which the real and symbolic parts are arranged in such a way that its $\mathcal{RH}$-satisfiability can be deduced. Some steps in this transformation make use exclusively of properties of the connectives in first-order logic; others are based on the axiomatization of the algebra of finite trees and of the field of real numbers; the essential part attempts to eliminate quantifiers. It combines the techniques of Maher [15] for symbolic quantified variables, with the elimination of real quantified variables using *Cylindrical Algebraic Decomposition (CAD)* [3].

We have found a condition, with respect to the order on the occurrence of the real and symbolic quantifications, which guarantees that the solving procedure finishes obtaining an elemental constraint. Nevertheless, the procedure can also happen to end in some other cases for which that condition is not fulfilled. This is the case when the included polynomials can be simplified, by eliminating a variable that can be represented in function of the others by means of a finite number of equations. This problem can be decided using techniques based on Gröebner bases, see for instance the works included in [1].

Some definitions are needed prior to the presentation of the procedure.

3.1   Solved Forms, Basic Formulas and Elemental Constraints

In order to define elemental constraints, for which $\mathcal{RH}$-satisfiability may be decided, we previously introduce some concepts concerning constraints that are conjunctions of equalities and polynomials.

Definition 1 *A system of equalities E is a conjunction of a finite number of equalities. A system of equalities and polynomial E is a conjunction of a system of equalities and a polynomial.*

Definition 2 *E is said to be a* solved form *if $E \equiv \overline{X} \approx \overline{t}(\overline{U}, \overline{x}) \wedge p(\overline{x})$, where each variable in $\overline{X}$ appears exactly once. The variables in $\overline{U}$ will be referred to as* parameters *of the system, and the ones in $\overline{X}$ as its* eliminable variables. *If $X \approx t$ appears in E and V occurs in t, we say that X depends on V. Given two systems of equalities and polynomial, E_1 and E_2, E_2 is said to be a* solved form *of E_1 if $E_1 \equiv_{\mathcal{RH}} E_2$ and E_2 is a solved form.*

In the following, we describe an algorithm whose purpose is to find a solved form of a system of equalities and polynomial. It is based on the common rules for equality solving in the algebra of finite trees [8]. The algorithm, designated by *Solve-Tree*, simply consists in the sequential, nondeterministic application of the rules immediately presented, until none of them can be applied. These rules are written in the form $\frac{E_1}{E_2}$, which means that the system of equalities and polynomial E_1 may be transformed by the rule into the $\mathcal{RH}$-equivalent system E_2.

The Algorithm Solve-Tree

1) $\dfrac{f(t_1,\dots,t_n)\approx f(t'_1,\dots,t'_n)\wedge E}{t_1\approx t'_1\wedge\dots\wedge t_n\approx t'_n\wedge E}$, for any symbolic function symbol f.

2) $\dfrac{f(t_1,\dots,t_n)\approx g(t'_1,\dots,t'_m)\wedge E}{\perp}$, if f and g are different symbolic function symbols.

3) $\dfrac{c\approx c'\wedge E}{\perp}$, if c and c' are different symbolic constants.

4) $\dfrac{X\approx X\wedge E}{E}$

5) $\dfrac{t\approx X\wedge E}{X\approx t\wedge E}$, if t is not a variable.

6) $\dfrac{X\approx t\wedge E}{X\approx t\wedge E[t/X]}$, if X does not occur in t, and X occurs in some equality in E.

7) $\dfrac{X\approx t\wedge E}{\perp}$, if t is not a variable and X occurs in t.

In the rule 1), the expressions $t_i \approx t'_i$, $t_i, t'_i : r$, obtained by decomposition, are conjunctively added to the polynomial of E.

For any E used as input, the algorithm terminates, producing a solved form for E if there is any, and $\perp$ otherwise. In the latter case, we say that the algorithm *fails*. It must also be noticed that a system of equalities and polynomial $\overline{X} \approx \overline{t}\wedge p$ is a solved form, if and only if, no rule can be applied to it, and that a system of equalities and polynomial is $\mathcal{RH}$-satisfiable if and only if it has a solved form $\overline{X} \approx \overline{t}\wedge p$ and p is $\mathcal{RH}$-satisfiable.

Definition 3 *A basic formula is* $\top$, *or a constraint of the form* $\exists \overline{U} E$, *where* E *is a system of equalities in solved form and* $\overline{U}$ *its set of parameters.*

The set of boolean combinations of basic formulas *is defined as the minimum set closed under* $\vee$, $\wedge$ *and* $\neg$ *that contains every basic formula.*

In the sequel, basic formulas will be denoted by b, possibly ornate with sub or superindexes.

Definition 4 *An* $\mathcal{RH}$-*normal form is a constraint of the form* $C_1 \vee \dots \vee C_n$, $n \geq 1$, *where* $C_i \equiv b^i \wedge \neg b^i_1 \wedge \dots \wedge \neg b^i_k \wedge p^i$, $k \geq 0$, $1 \leq i \leq n$. *A quantified* $\mathcal{RH}$-*normal form is a constraint of the form* ΠC, *where* C *is an* $\mathcal{RH}$-*normal form and* Π *is a sequence of quantifications. An elemental constraint is a quantified* $\mathcal{RH}$-*normal form* $\Pi\Pi' C$, *in which* Π *is a sequence of existential quantifications and* Π' *binds only real variables.*

We are able to decide the $\mathcal{RH}$-satisfiability of elemental constraints[1]. Therefore, the first aim of the $\mathcal{RH}$-constraint solver will be to reach elemental constraints eliminating quantifiers of quantified $\mathcal{RH}$-normal forms. During the process, it will often be necessary to transform boolean combinations of basic formulas and polynomials into $\mathcal{RH}$-equivalent normal forms. This normalization will be easily accomplished following the steps of the next algorithm.

$\mathcal{RH}$-Normalization

1. All negations are distributed, until the scope of each negation is a unique basic formula. The result is transformed into a disjunction of constraints of the form $b_1 \wedge \dots \wedge b_n \wedge \neg b'_1 \wedge \dots \wedge \neg b'_m \wedge p$.

---

[1] Due to lack of space we have not included the corresponding decision procedure.

2. Each constraint $C \equiv b_1 \wedge \ldots \wedge b_n \wedge \neg b'_1 \wedge \ldots \wedge \neg b'_m \wedge p$ in such disjunction with $n > 1$ is replaced by $b \wedge \neg b'_1 \wedge \ldots \wedge \neg b'_m \wedge (p \wedge p')$, where b and p' are obtained as follows.

   (a) Let $b_i \equiv \exists \overline{U}^i (\overline{X}_i \approx \overline{t}_i)$, $1 \leq i \leq n$, and let $E \wedge p'$ be the solved form of $\overline{X}_1 \approx \overline{t}_1 \wedge \ldots \wedge \overline{X}_n \approx \overline{t}_n$, produced by *Solve-Tree*, if it does not fail. Otherwise, C is simply removed from the original disjunction.

   (b) Let $\overline{U} = \overline{U}^1 \cup \ldots \cup \overline{U}^n$. Let E' be the result of eliminating in E all the equalities concerning the eliminable variables of E belonging to $\overline{U}$, and let $\overline{W}$ be the set of variables of $\overline{U}$ not appearing in E'. Then, $b \equiv \exists \overline{U} \backslash \overline{W} E'$.

In the special case in which all the constraints C in the disjunction were removed, the output is defined as $\neg \top$.

In the search process for $\mathcal{RH}$-equivalent elemental constraints, there are two ways of eliminating real quantifiers, one of them will simplify constraints containing polynomials following the definition below.

Definition 5 *A solved polynomial on x is a polynomial of the form $(x \approx t_1 \wedge p_1) \vee \ldots \vee (x \approx t_l \wedge p_l)$, where x does not appear in $t_1, \ldots, t_l, p_1, \ldots, p_l$.*

3.2 Eliminating Quantifiers

The solving procedure for $\mathcal{RH}$-constraints transforms, under certain conditions on the order of the quantified variables, a constraint into an $\mathcal{RH}$-equivalent elemental constraint. It proceeds by eliminating quantifiers of quantified $\mathcal{RH}$-normal forms. Quantifiers over real variables are eliminated using algebraic methods as *CAD*, [3]. The elimination of symbolic quantifiers is based on two rules, *(Pair)* and *(Elim)*. They transform constraints into $\mathcal{RH}$-equivalent simpler ones that are boolean combinations of basic formulas. The rules *(Pair)* and *(Elim)* will be presented together with the theorems that constitute their theoretical foundations. The theorem that is the foundation of the first rule is similar to that presented in [15] for symbolic terms, because in some sense, the polynomial has been isolated. Nevertheless, we have elaborated an original proof, based on the entailment relation $\vdash_{\mathcal{RH}}$, instead of on the semantics, as it was done in [15], since that specific semantics is not valid for $\mathcal{RH}$-constraints, due to the presence of real terms inside symbolic functions. The following lemma is required in such proof.

Lemma 1 *Let t be a term of type h, with free symbolic variables $\overline{X}$, and let Γ be a set of $\mathcal{RH}$-constraints, with no free symbolic variables in $\overline{X}$. Let t_1, t_2 be terms with no free symbolic variables, and such that t_2 results from t_1, replacing one or more symbolic subterms by new terms whose principal function symbol, or constant, does not appear in t, t_1, Γ. Then, if there is no substitution σ with domain $\overline{X}$, such that $\Gamma \vdash_{\mathcal{RH}} t\sigma \approx t_1$, there is also no substitution θ with domain $\overline{X}$, such that $\Gamma \vdash_{\mathcal{RH}} t\theta \approx t_2$.*

Theorem 2 (Pair) *Let $b, b_1, \ldots, b_n$ be basic formulas, $n \geq 1$. Then,*

$$F_1 \equiv \exists Y(b \wedge \neg b_1 \wedge \ldots \wedge \neg b_n) \equiv_{\mathcal{RH}} \exists Y(b \wedge \neg b_1) \wedge \ldots \wedge \exists Y(b \wedge \neg b_n) \equiv F_2.$$

Proof: Without loss of generality, we can suppose that the sets of parameters in the basic formulas $b \wedge b_1 \wedge \ldots \wedge b_n$ are disjoint, not containing occurrences of the variable Y. It can also be supposed that Y appears as eliminable in all of them, since, for any basic formula b^* not containing occurrences of Y, $b^* \equiv \exists Y'(b^* \wedge Y \approx Y')$, where Y' is a variable not occurring in b^*. Thereafter, b^* may be replaced by $\exists Y'(b^* \wedge Y \approx Y')$, and conversely. Let us write $b \equiv \exists \overline{U}, \overline{W}\ E$, where $E \equiv \overline{X} \approx \overline{t}(\overline{U}, \overline{x}) \wedge Y \approx s(\overline{V}, \overline{W}, \overline{x})$. $\overline{U}$ is the set of symbolic variables in $\overline{t}$. $\overline{x}$ is the set of variables of sort r in E. The set of symbolic variables in the term s is divided in two, $\overline{V}$ and $\overline{W}$, depending on whether variables belong to $\overline{U}$ or not, respectively. Thus, $\overline{V} \subseteq \overline{U}$, and $\overline{W} \cap \overline{U} = \emptyset$. For each $1 \le i \le n$, we write b_i in an analogous way, adding the superindex i to every set of symbolic variables. Let $\overline{X}^* = (\overline{X} \cup \overline{X}^1 \cup \ldots \cup \overline{X}^n)/Y$.

$F_1 \vdash_{\mathcal{RH}} F_2$ is trivial. We will prove $F_2 \vdash_{\mathcal{RH}} F_1$. Let σ be a symbolic ground substitution with domain $\overline{X}^*$ and let σ^* be a symbolic ground substitution, extending σ to $\overline{U}, \overline{W}, Y$, and such that for $\overline{U}$ it is defined in such a way that $F_2\sigma \vdash_{\mathcal{RH}} (\overline{X} \approx \overline{t})\sigma^*$ holds; for each $W \in \overline{W}$, let $W\sigma^*$ be a term whose principal function symbol, or constant, does not appear in $F_1\sigma$, $F_2\sigma$. Finally, let $Y\sigma^* = s\sigma^*$. Our goal is to prove that $F_2\sigma \vdash_{\mathcal{RH}} (E \wedge \neg b_1 \wedge \ldots \wedge \neg b_n)\sigma^*$. Once this is proved, $F_2\sigma \vdash_{\mathcal{RH}} F_1\sigma$ will be straightforward, and $F_2 \vdash_{\mathcal{RH}} F_1$ is followed by the properties of $\mathcal{RH}$.

Due to the definition of σ^*, $F_2\sigma \vdash_{\mathcal{RH}} E\sigma^*$ holds trivially. Therefore, it only remains to provide a proof for

$$F_2\sigma \vdash_{\mathcal{RH}} \neg b_i\sigma^*, \ 1 \le i \le n \qquad (\dagger).$$

Let i, $1 \le i \le n$, then $F_2\sigma \vdash_{\mathcal{RH}} (\exists Y(b \wedge \neg b_i))\sigma$ holds. Hence, the entailment relation $\vdash_{\mathcal{RH}}$ verifies that there is a ground symbolic substitution σ_i, extending σ to $\overline{U}, \overline{W}, Y$ such that:

$$F_2\sigma \vdash_{\mathcal{RH}} (E \wedge \neg b_i)\sigma_i \qquad (\ddagger).$$

Let σ_i' be a substitution that extends σ_i to $\overline{U}^i$ for which $F_2\sigma \vdash_{\mathcal{RH}} (\overline{X}^i \approx \overline{t}^i)\sigma_i'$, if there is any. Otherwise, $F_2\sigma \vdash_{\mathcal{RH}} (\neg \overline{X}^i \approx \overline{t}^i)\sigma'$ for every substitution σ' extending σ, and $(\dagger)$ is straightforward. But if such σ_i' exists, since $(\ddagger)$ implies $F_2\sigma \vdash_{\mathcal{RH}} \neg b_i\sigma_i$, there can be no further extension σ_i'' of it to $\overline{W}^i$ such that

$$F_2\sigma \vdash_{\mathcal{RH}} Y\sigma_i \approx s^i(\overline{V}^i\sigma_i', \overline{W}^i\sigma_i'', \overline{x}) \qquad (\sharp).$$

Now, in order to prove $(\dagger)$, we will show that there is no extension θ of σ^* to $\overline{U}^i, \overline{W}^i$ such that $F_2\sigma \vdash_{\mathcal{RH}} E_i\theta$. Let us suppose that there is an extension θ' of σ^* to $\overline{U}^i$ such that $F_2\sigma \vdash_{\mathcal{RH}} (\overline{X}^i \approx \overline{t}^i)\theta'$. We conclude if we show that there is no such θ extending θ' to $\overline{W}^i$, for which $F_2\sigma \vdash_{\mathcal{RH}} Y\sigma^* \approx s^i(\overline{V}^i\theta', \overline{W}^i\theta, \overline{x})$ holds.

From $(\ddagger)$ we deduce that $F_2\sigma \vdash_{\mathcal{RH}} (\overline{X} \approx \overline{t})\sigma_i$, but σ^* is a substitution for $\overline{U}$ verifying $F_2\sigma \vdash_{\mathcal{RH}} (\overline{X} \approx \overline{t})\sigma^*$, thus $F_2\sigma \vdash_{\mathcal{RH}} \overline{U}\sigma_i \approx \overline{U}\sigma^*$ holds. On the other hand σ_i' is a substitution for $\overline{U}^i$ satisfying $F_2\sigma \vdash_{\mathcal{RH}} (\overline{X}^i \approx \overline{t}^i)\sigma_i'$, and we are supposing $F_2\sigma \vdash_{\mathcal{RH}} (\overline{X}^i \approx \overline{t}^i)\theta'$, hence $F_2\sigma \vdash_{\mathcal{RH}} \overline{U}^i\sigma_i' \approx \overline{U}^i\theta'$. Therefore, it will be enough to prove that there is no such extension θ for which $F_2\sigma \vdash_{\mathcal{RH}} Y\sigma^\star \approx s^i(\overline{V}^i\sigma_i', \overline{W}^i\theta, \overline{x})$ holds. From ($\ddagger$) we obtain $F_2\sigma \vdash_{\mathcal{RH}} Y\sigma_i \approx s(\overline{V}\sigma_i, \overline{W}\sigma_i, \overline{x})$, and using ($\sharp$) we deduce that there is no substitution σ_i'' extending σ_i' to $\overline{W}^i$ such that $F_2\sigma \vdash_{\mathcal{RH}} s(\overline{V}\sigma_i, \overline{W}\sigma_i, \overline{x}) \approx s^i(\overline{V}^i\sigma_i', \overline{W}^i\sigma_i'', \overline{x})$. Hence, since $s(\overline{V}\sigma^\star, \overline{W}\sigma^\star, \overline{x})$ can be obtained from $s(\overline{V}\sigma_i, \overline{W}\sigma_i, \overline{x})$ by replacing some subterms by terms whose principal symbol function, or constant, does not appear in the previous formulas, Lemma 1 can be applied, and states that there is no extension θ of θ' to $\overline{W}^i$ satisfying $F_2\sigma \vdash_{\mathcal{RH}} s(\overline{V}\sigma^\star, \overline{W}\sigma^\star, \overline{x}) \approx s^i(\overline{V}^i\sigma_i', \overline{W}^i\theta, \overline{x})$, concluding the proof since $F_2\sigma \vdash_{\mathcal{RH}} \overline{V}^i\sigma_i' \approx \overline{V}^i\theta'$, and $F_2\sigma \vdash_{\mathcal{RH}} s(\overline{V}\sigma^\star, \overline{W}\sigma^\star, \overline{x}) \approx Y\sigma^\star$, by definition of $\sigma^\star$. $\square$

We are finally ready to define the rule $(Pair)$, whose purpose is to eliminate conjunctions of negated basic formulas under the same existential quantifier.

Definition 6 *The rule $(Pair)$ replaces a formula of the form $\exists Y (b \wedge \neg b_1 \wedge \ldots \wedge \neg b_n)$ by the $\mathcal{RH}$-equivalent formula provided by Theorem 2.*

The second rule in which the main procedure is based requires the following definition.

Definition 7 *Given two sets of symbolic variables $\overline{V}$ and $\overline{W}$, and a system of equalities and polynomial E, we say that E constrains $\overline{V}$ w.r.t. $\overline{W}$ if, for every solved form of E, either some $V \in \overline{V}$ is eliminable, or some $W \in \overline{W}$ is eliminable and depends on some $V \in \overline{V}$. Otherwise, we say that E does not constrain $\overline{V}$ w.r.t. $\overline{W}$.*

This definition depends on the verification of some properties for every solved form of E, which is difficult to check directly. However, it is possible to provide for a characterization of this concept very easy to check. Moreover, if E_1 and E_2 are two solved forms such that $E_1 \equiv_{\mathcal{RH}} E_2$, then E_1 constrains $\overline{V}$ w.r.t. $\overline{W}$ if and only if E_2 constrains $\overline{V}$ w.r.t. $\overline{W}$.

Proposition 3 (Characterization) *Let $E(\overline{V}, \overline{W}, \overline{Z}, \overline{x})$ be a solved form. E constrains $\overline{V}$ w.r.t. $\overline{W}$ if and only if one of the conditions below holds for E.*

1) *E contains $W \approx t$, where $W \in \overline{W}$ and some variable in $\overline{V}$ occurs in t.*
2) *E contains $V \approx t$, where $V \in \overline{V}$ and t is not a variable.*
3) *E contains $V \approx X$, where $V \in \overline{V}, X \in \overline{V} \cup \overline{W}$.*
4) *E contains $V \approx Z$ and $X \approx t$, where $V \in \overline{V}, Z \in \overline{Z}, X \in \overline{V} \cup \overline{W}$ and X depends on Z.*

The next theorem will be the core of the transformation rule $(Elim)$, which is the responsible for the elimination of symbolic quantifiers. Its proof requires several technicalities, which are detailed on [7].

Theorem 4 (Elim) *Let b and b' be basic formulas. Let Y be a variable that may appear in them only as eliminable variable. Then, the formula $F \equiv \exists Y(b \wedge \neg b')$ is $\mathcal{RH}$-equivalent to one of the next constraints, depending on the case:*

1. *Y does not appear in b nor in b'. Then, trivially $F \equiv_{\mathcal{RH}} b \wedge \neg b'$.*
2. *Y appears in b, but not in b'. Let b have the form $\exists \overline{U}(\overline{X} \approx \overline{t}(\overline{U}, \overline{x}) \wedge Y \approx s(\overline{U}, \overline{x}))$. Then, $F \equiv_{\mathcal{RH}} \exists \overline{U}(\overline{X} \approx \overline{t}(\overline{U}, \overline{x})) \wedge \neg b'$.*
3. *Y appears in b', but not in b. Let b' have the form $\exists \overline{U}(\overline{X} \approx \overline{t}(\overline{U}, \overline{x}) \wedge Y \approx s(\overline{U}, \overline{x}))$. If $\overline{X} \approx \overline{t}(\overline{U}, \overline{x}) \wedge Y \approx s(\overline{U}, \overline{x})$ constrains Y w.r.t. $\overline{X}$, then $F \equiv_{\mathcal{RH}} b$. Otherwise, $F \equiv_{\mathcal{RH}} b \wedge \neg \exists \overline{U}(\overline{X} \approx \overline{t}(\overline{U}, \overline{x}))$.*
4. *Y appears in both b and b', with forms $b \equiv \exists \overline{U}, \overline{V}(\overline{X} \approx \overline{t}(\overline{U}, \overline{x}) \wedge Y \approx s(\overline{U}, \overline{V}, \overline{x}))$ and $b' \equiv \exists \overline{U}^1(\overline{X}^1 \approx \overline{t}^1(\overline{U}^1, \overline{x}) \wedge Y \approx s^1(\overline{U}^1, \overline{x}))$.*

    a) *If $\overline{X} \approx \overline{t}(\overline{U}, \overline{x}) \wedge \overline{X}^1 \approx \overline{t}^1(\overline{U}^1, \overline{x}) \wedge s(\overline{U}, \overline{V}, \overline{x}) \approx s^1(\overline{U}^1, \overline{x})$ constrains $\overline{V}$ w.r.t. $\overline{X}$. Then $F \equiv_{\mathcal{RH}} \exists \overline{U}(\overline{X} \approx \overline{t}(\overline{U}, \overline{x}))$.*

    b) *If $\overline{X} \approx \overline{t}(\overline{U}, \overline{x}) \wedge \overline{X}^1 \approx \overline{t}^1(\overline{U}^1, \overline{x}) \wedge s(\overline{U}, \overline{V}, \overline{x}) \approx s^1(\overline{U}^1, \overline{x})$ does not constrain $\overline{V}$ w.r.t. $\overline{X}$. Then, if the algorithm Solve-Tree fails when processing $\overline{X} \approx \overline{t}(\overline{U}, \overline{x}) \wedge \overline{X}^1 \approx \overline{t}^1(\overline{U}^1, \overline{x}) \wedge s(\overline{U}, \overline{V}, \overline{x}) \approx s^1(\overline{U}^1, \overline{x})$, $F \equiv_{\mathcal{RH}} \exists \overline{U}(\overline{X} \approx \overline{t}(\overline{U}, \overline{x}))$. Otherwise, $F \equiv_{\mathcal{RH}} \exists \overline{U}(\overline{X} \approx \overline{t}(\overline{U}, \overline{x})) \wedge \neg \exists \overline{V}, \overline{U}, \overline{U}^1 \backslash \overline{W} E$, where E is obtained by removing in the result produced by Solve-Tree all the equalities corresponding to the eliminable variables belonging to $\overline{V} \cup \overline{U} \cup \overline{U}^1$, and $\overline{W}$ is the subset of $\overline{V} \cup \overline{U} \cup \overline{U}^1$ of the variables not occurring in E.*

Definition 8 *The rule* (Elim) *replaces a formula in the form $\exists Y(b \wedge \neg b')$ by the $\mathcal{RH}$-equivalent boolean combination of basic formulas with a polynomial provided by Theorem 4.*

Notice that the resulting polynomial is a conjunction of real equalities that is obtained only in the case 4.b) of Theorem 4. The rule *(Elim)* will be also applied when b' does not exist, since that can be considered as a particular case of the item 2.

3.3   The Transformation Algorithm

As we have mentioned before, the algorithm to check $\mathcal{RH}$-satisfiability should be classified as a quantifier elimination technique. That referred elimination can be performed only in some cases, depending on the order of the symbolic and real quantifications, and under some conditions of solvability over the included polynomials, which will be shown during the description of the algorithm. The process requires a prior manipulation that converts the initial constraint into a quantified $\mathcal{RH}$-normal form, for which the elimination quantifier techniques can be applied. In the following, we detail the whole algorithm. Its input is an arbitrary constraint C, its output is an $\mathcal{RH}$-equivalent elemental constraint.

Phase I: Preprocessing.

1) Producing a constraint in prenex form $\mathcal{RH}$-equivalent to C. In this way, a formula $\Pi C'$ is obtained so that $C \equiv_{\mathcal{RH}} \Pi C'$, where Π is a sequence of quantifiers and C' is quantifier-free.

2) Transforming $\Pi C'$ into $\Pi(C_1 \vee \ldots \vee C_n)$, where, for each $1 \le i \le n$, C_i is a conjunction of equalities, disequalities and polynomials.

3) Transforming $\Pi(C_1 \vee \ldots \vee C_n)$ into an $\mathcal{RH}$-equivalent quantified $\mathcal{RH}$-normal form, modifying each C_i, $1 \le i \le n$ as follows.

   3.1) Let E be a solved form for the system of equalities and polynomial in C. C_i is removed from the disjunction if such solved form E does not exist. Otherwise, let $\overline{W}$ be the set of parameters in E, free in C_i, and let $\overline{W'}$ be a set of variables not occurring in E, in bijection with $\overline{W}$. Now, replace, in the system E, each variable $W \in \overline{W}$ with the corresponding $W' \in \overline{W'}$. Later, augment the result with the equalities $\overline{W} \approx \overline{W'}$. Finally, quantify existentially the conjunction of the equalities over all its parameters, leaving the polynomial unaffected, therefore rendering a constraint of the form $p \wedge b$ ($b \equiv \top$ if there are no equalities in C_i).

   3.2) For each disequality in C_i remove the outermost negation and proceed as in step 3.1). Add conjunctively the result, preceded by the negation, to $p \wedge b$.

   3.3) At this stage, C_i has been removed or transformed to some $p \wedge b \wedge \neg(p_1 \wedge b_1) \wedge \ldots \wedge \neg(p_s \wedge b_s)$, $s \ge 0$, which is finally $\mathcal{RH}$-normalized.

The result of this transformation is a constraint $\Pi C''$ in quantified $\mathcal{RH}$-normal form, where $C'' \equiv D_1 \vee \ldots \vee D_m$ and each D_i is of the form $p' \wedge b \wedge \neg b'_1 \wedge \ldots \wedge \neg b'_k$.

Phase II: Quantifier elimination algorithm.

4) Eliminating the innermost quantifier.

   Let $\Pi = \Pi' Q \nu$, where $Q \in \{\exists, \forall\}$ and $\nu \in \mathcal{V}$. We intend to eliminate the quantification $Q \nu$, obtaining an $\mathcal{RH}$-normal form $\mathcal{RH}$-equivalent to $Q \nu C''$. If $\nu : h$, the algorithm can perform this task for any constraint. However, if $\nu : r$, it may or may not be able to do it, depending on C''. If $Q \nu$ cannot be eliminated by the following criteria, but $\Pi' = \Pi'' Q \nu_1 \ldots Q \nu_l$, $l \ge 1$, and for some i, $1 \le i \le l$, $Q \nu_i$ does verify some of those criteria, then move $Q \nu_i$ to the right of $Q \nu$, and proceed. If no such quantifier is found, stop.

   4.1) $\nu = x : r$, $Q \equiv \exists$. In this case, $Q \nu C'' \equiv \exists x (D_1 \vee \ldots \vee D_m) \equiv_{\mathcal{RH}} \exists x D_1 \vee \ldots \vee \exists x D_m$. Now, it is required that for each D_i, one of the next two conditions holds, otherwise, the algorithm stops without success.

   (a) x occurs, at most, in p'. Therefore, $\exists x D_i \equiv \exists x p' \wedge b \wedge \neg b'_1 \wedge \ldots \wedge \neg b'_k$. $\exists x p'$ can be replaced by an $\mathcal{RH}$-equivalent, quantifier-free Tarski formula, obtained by applying a CAD, then producing the elimination of the quantification $\exists x$.

   (b) x occurs also in $b \wedge \neg b'_1 \wedge \ldots \wedge \neg b'_k$, and a polynomial of the form $(x \approx t_1 \wedge q_1) \vee \ldots \vee (x \approx t_l \wedge q_l)$ solved for x, $\mathcal{RH}$-equivalent to p', can be found. Then, $\exists x D_i$ is replaced by the $\mathcal{RH}$-equivalent constraint $(q_1 \wedge (b \wedge \neg b'_1 \wedge \ldots \wedge \neg b'_k)[t_1/x]) \vee \ldots \vee (q_l \wedge (b \wedge \neg b'_1 \wedge \ldots \wedge \neg b'_k)[t_l/x])$.

4.2) $\nu = X : h$, $Q \equiv \exists$. Introducing the existential quantifier over X in the disjunction, $\exists X\, D_1 \vee \ldots \vee \exists X D_m$ is obtained. The aim of this step is to replace every $\exists X\, D_i$, $1 \leq i \leq m$, by a boolean combination of basic formulas and polynomials. Let $D_i'' \equiv b \wedge \neg b_1' \wedge \ldots \wedge \neg b_k'$, $1 \leq i \leq m$, and thus $\exists X\, D_i \equiv_{\mathcal{RH}} p' \wedge \exists X\, D_i''$. Now, if $k = 0$, $\exists X\, D_i''$ can be easily transformed into a basic formula, otherwise the rule $(Pair)$ must be applied, replacing $\exists X\, D_i''$ by $\exists X\, (b \wedge \neg b_1') \wedge \ldots \wedge \exists X\, (b \wedge \neg b_k')$. Each member of this conjunction is further transformed by means of the rule $(Elim)$, rendering a boolean combination of polynomials and basic formulas, therefore eliminating the quantifier over X.

4.3) $Q \equiv \forall$. $Q\,\nu C''$ is $\mathcal{RH}$-equivalent to $\neg \exists \nu \neg C''$. Now, $\neg C''$ is $\mathcal{RH}$-normalized, producing $D' \equiv D_1' \vee \ldots \vee D_u'$. Next, the quantifier $\exists \nu$ is eliminated, following 4.1) or 4.2), depending on the type of ν.

5) The constraint produced is a boolean combination of polynomials and basic formulas, which must be $\mathcal{RH}$-normalized. We denote the resulting constraint by C'''. Since $Q\,\nu C'' \equiv_{\mathcal{RH}} C'''$, $\Pi C''$ has been replaced by the constraint $\Pi' C'''$, therefore removing the innermost quantifier.

6) If Π' is empty, stop. Otherwise, go on processing $\Pi' C'''$ starting at step 4).

It must be noticed that termination of the transformation algorithm is guaranteed, because the length of the quantifier prefix decreases on every loop. It will successfully finish when the obtained constraint is elemental.

The algorithm just described constitutes the basis of the constraint solver. The next phase of the solving procedure should be to check the $\mathcal{RH}$-satisfiability of the output of the transformation. When such tansformation is successful, the checking will be carried out by the corresponding decision algorithm dealing with elemental constraints.

4   Examples

The aim of this section is just to show, using examples, the mechanism of the transformation algorithm. In order to find examples of programs of $HH(\mathcal{RH})$, see [13]. There it is also described the goal solving procedure, which will call the constraint solver to check $\mathcal{RH}$-satisfiability of answer constraints. More examples illustrating the expressivity of $HH(\mathcal{RH})$ can be found in [7].

Example 1 Let C_1 be the constraint below, where $f : r \to h$, $g : h \times h \to h$.

$$C_1 \equiv \exists X (\exists x, y (g(X, Y) \approx g(f(x), f(y)) \wedge x + y \approx 1) \wedge \forall Z \neg (g(X, Y) \approx g(Z, Z))).$$

The algorithm would transform C_1 as follows. The preprocessing phase yields:

$$\exists X \exists x, y \forall Z \Big((X \approx f(y) \wedge Y \approx f(x)) \wedge \neg \exists Z_1 (X \approx Z_1 \wedge Y \approx Z_1 \wedge Z \approx Z_1) \wedge x + y \approx 1 \Big).$$

According to 4.3), the quantification $\forall Z$ is transformed into $\exists Z$, and then $\mathcal{RH}$-normalization is carried out, rendering:

$$\exists X \exists x, y \neg \exists Z \Big(\neg (X \approx f(y) \wedge Y \approx f(x)) \vee \exists Z_1 (X \approx Z_1 \wedge Y \approx Z_1 \wedge Z \approx Z_1) \vee \neg (x + y \approx 1) \Big)$$

$\exists Z$ must be distributed, the subconstraint $\exists Z, Z_1(X \approx Z_1 \wedge Y \approx Z_1 \wedge Z \approx Z_1)$ is simplified to $\exists Z_1(X \approx Z_1 \wedge Y \approx Z_1)$ according to 4.2) $(k = 0)$.

Applying 5), the $\mathcal{RH}$-normalization yields:

$$\exists X \exists x \exists y \Big((X \approx f(y) \wedge Y \approx f(x)) \wedge \neg \exists Z_1(X \approx Z_1 \wedge Y \approx Z_1) \wedge x + y \approx 1 \Big).$$

Step 4.2) is applied after moving $\exists X$ to the right, and the rule $(Elim)$ produces:

$$\exists x \exists y ((Y \approx f(x)) \wedge \neg(Y \approx f(x) \wedge x \approx y) \wedge x + y \approx 1).$$

This transformation comprises several steps, immediately detailed. First, the constraint

$$\exists x \exists y \Big((Y \approx f(x)) \wedge \neg \exists Z_1(Y \approx f(x) \wedge Y \approx Z_1 \wedge f(y) \approx Z_1) \wedge x + y \approx 1 \Big)$$

is obtained, which does not already contain quantifiers over X. Then, $Solve$-$Tree$ must be applied to $Y \approx f(x) \wedge Y \approx Z_1 \wedge f(y) \approx Z_1$. The result is simplified eliminating the equality for Z_1 and its quantifier.

Now, carrying out step 5), the quantified $\mathcal{RH}$-normal form below is obtained:

$$\exists x \exists y \Big((x + y \approx 1 \wedge Y \approx f(x) \wedge \neg Y \approx f(x)) \vee (x + y \approx 1 \wedge Y \approx f(x) \wedge \neg x \approx y) \Big).$$

Following 4.1), it is transformed into:

$$\exists x \Big(\exists y(x + y \approx 1 \wedge Y \approx f(x) \wedge \neg Y \approx f(x)) \vee \exists y(x + y \approx 1 \wedge Y \approx f(x) \wedge \neg x \approx y) \Big).$$

For the first constraint in the disjunction, step 4.1.(a) can be now applied, transforming $\exists y(x + y \approx 1)$ into $\top$. With regard to the second one, following 4.1.(a) again, $\exists y(x + y \approx 1 \wedge \neg(x \approx y))$ is transformed into $\neg(x \approx 1/2)$. Therefore,

$$C_1 \equiv_{\mathcal{RH}} \exists x \Big((Y \approx f(x) \wedge \neg Y \approx f(x)) \vee (Y \approx f(x) \wedge \neg(x \approx 1/2)) \Big).$$

The $\mathcal{RH}$-satisfiability of this elemental constraint can be proved.

Example 2 In this example, we will deal with symbolic terms built up using the list constructor to handle lists of reals. For the sake of readability, we will use the usual notation of PROLOG for them. Let us begin with the constraint C_2:

$$\exists L(\exists x_2, L_2(L \approx [x_1, x_2|L_2] \wedge x_1 + x_2 \approx 4) \wedge \neg \exists x_3, L_3(L \approx [x_3|L_3] \wedge x_3 \times x_3 \approx 1)).$$

The preprocessing phase yields:

$$\exists x_2, L \forall x_3 (x_1 + x_2 \approx 4 \wedge \exists L_2(L \approx [x_1, x_2|L_2]) \wedge \neg(x_3 \times x_3 \approx 1 \wedge \exists L_3(L \approx [x_3|L_3]))).$$

The negation was not distributed because the next step will be to transform the quantifier $\forall$ into the corresponding $\exists$, and this would imply to undo this distribution.

Now, according to 4.3), after the implicit $\mathcal{RH}$-normalization and the distribution of the existential quantification $\exists x_3$ the current constraint is:

$$\exists x_2, L\neg(\exists x_3(x_1 + x_2 \not\approx 4) \vee \exists x_3(\neg\exists L_2(L \approx [x_1, x_2|L_2]))\vee$$
$$\exists x_3(x_3 \times x_3 \approx 1 \wedge \exists L_3(L \approx [x_3|L_3]))).$$

The quantification $\exists x_3$ is trivially removed in the first two cases. For the last one, the polynomial $x_3 \times x_3 \approx 1$ can be transformed into $x_3 \approx 1 \vee x_3 \approx -1$, which is solved for x. Therefore, steps 4.1.(b), followed by 5). are carried out, rendering:

$$\exists x_2 \exists L(x_1 + x_2 \approx 4 \wedge \exists L_2(L \approx [x_1, x_2|L_2])\wedge$$
$$\neg\exists L_3(L \approx [1|L_3]) \wedge \neg\exists L_3(L \approx [-1|L_3])).$$

At this stage, in order to eliminate the quantifier $\exists L$, step 4.2) is considered, and the application of the rule $(Pair)$ yields:

$$\exists x_2(x_1 + x_2 \approx 4 \wedge \exists L(\exists L_2(L \approx [x_1, x_2|L_2]) \wedge \neg\exists L_3(L \approx [1|L_3]))\wedge$$
$$\exists L(\exists L_2(L \approx [x_1, x_2|L_2]) \wedge \neg\exists L_3(L \approx [-1|L_3])))).$$

The rule $(Elim)$ must be applied to

$$\exists L(\exists L_2(L \approx [x_1, x_2|L_2]) \wedge \neg\exists L_3(L \approx [1|L_3])),$$

producing $\neg x_1 \approx 1$. This constraint is obtained applying *Solve Tree* to $[x_1, x_2|L_2] \approx [1|L_3]$, and simplifying trivial equalities and quantifiers. Analogously, applying $(Elim)$ to

$$\exists L(\exists L_2(L \approx [x_1, x_2|L_2]) \wedge \neg\exists L_3(L \approx [-1|L_3])),$$

it is reduced to $\neg x_1 \approx -1$. Thus the constraint produced in this step is

$$\exists x_2(x_1 + x_2 \approx 4 \wedge \neg x_1 \approx 1 \wedge \neg x_1 \approx -1).$$

Finally, using 4.1(a), the current constraint is converted to:

$$C_2 \equiv_{\mathcal{RH}} \neg x_1 \approx 1 \wedge \neg x_1 \approx -1.$$

5   Conclusion

The constraint system $\mathcal{RH}$ has been defined joining the axiomatization of the algebra of finite trees together with the axiomatization of the field of real numbers. Both theories are decidable, and our interest is to find a decision procedure for the combination of both theories. The framework of the constraint system $\mathcal{RH}$ is the *CLP* scheme, and it can be considered as a domain that produces a particular instance. In this field, there is a variety of works dealing with different constraint domains [11, 2, 5, 9]. Our contribution relies on the fact that we have dealt with a harder, more general satisfiability problem, because, having the domain in the context of a logic programming language based on hereditary Harrop formulas, any occurrence of existential and universal quantifiers is allowed in the constraints, instead of only existential ones as in Horn clauses. On the other hand, comparing our method with the decision procedure for combined theories proposed in [18], it is remarkable that the latter applies only to quantifier-free formulas, and the technique of propagation of equalities on which it leans is not useful here when quanifier elimination is carried ot, since this propagation incorporates equalities implied from the polynomial, but does not replace it, which does not help to the elimination of a quantifier. However, it could be used to check $\mathcal{RH}$-satisfiability of constraints with no mixed quantifier prefix.

Starting from the decision procedure due to Maher [15] for the theories of the algebras of finite, rational and infinite trees, based on elimination of quantifiers, we have extended it to dealing with quantifiers over real variables, using CAD based techniques [19, 3]. The incorporation of real variables and polynomials to the formulas to be treated is not trivial at all, and its effect on the original algorithm due to Maher has been studied. A procedure to solve a subclass of the set of $\mathcal{RH}$-constraints has been defined based on the reduction of the original constraints to simpler ones, for which a satisfiability decision method has been found. This procedure can be considered as the basis of a solver for the constraint logic programming language $HH(\mathcal{RH})$. In this paper we have focused on its foundations, which are proved in an original way. So, it has been defined as simple as possible to facilitate this study. However, regarding implementation, many refinements and improvements, as the incorporation of heuristics, would be necessary. With respect to the efficiency, the algorithm is very naïve, since it incorporates parts like the *Solve-Tree* algorithm, which is exponential. The tasks concerning elimination of real quantifiers computing a CAD have polynomial complexity [3], but they can be reused when the following real quantifier is eliminated. Another desirable feature concerning to the implementation of the solver in the context of $HH(\mathcal{RH})$ is the incrementality. The goal-solving procedure presented in [13] handles prenex constraints as partial calculated answers, which evidently benefits the phase of preprocessing, although it must be studied how that may be useful for the quantifier elimination phase, in order to profit the calculus performed for the constraints of previous steps.

Our interest as future related research consists in the dealing, if possible, with a greater class of $\mathcal{RH}$-constraints, as well as to improve the efficiency of our procedure, in order to implement it as a proper $\mathcal{RH}$-constraint solver.

Acknowledgements

We are grateful to Jacobo Torán, Javier Leach and Jesús Escribano for their collaboration during the first stages of the development of this work.

References

[1] Buchberger, B. and , Winkler, F. (eds.) *Gröebner Bases and Applications*, Cambridge Univ. Press, 1998. 107
[2] Caprotti, O. *Extending RISC-CLP(Real) to Handle Symbolic Functions*, A. Miola (ed.) DISCO 1993. LNCS 722, Springer, 1993, 241–255. 104, 116
[3] Caviness, B. F. and Johnson, J. R. *Quantifier Elimination and Cylindrical Algebraic Decomposition*, Springer, 1998. 107, 109, 117

[4] Clark, K. L., *Negation as Failure*, in: H. Gallaire and J. Minker (eds.) *Logic and Databases* 293-322, Plenum Press, 1978. 106

[5] Colmerauer, A. *An introduction to PROLOG III*, Commun. ACM 33(7), 1990, 69–90. 104, 116

[6] Comon, H. and Lescanne, P. *Equational problems and disunification*, J. of Symbolic Computation 7, 1989, 371–425. 104

[7] García-Díaz, M. and Nieva, S. *Solving mixed quantified constraints over a domain based on real numbers and Herbrand terms*, Technical Report 01-121, Dep. of Computer Science, Univ. Complutense of Madrid, 2001. 104, 111, 114

[8] Herbrand, J. *Researches sur la theorie de la demonstration*. In: Ecrits logiques de Jacques Herbrand, Paris, PUF, 1968. 107

[9] Hong, M., *RISC-CLP(CF) Constraint Logic Programming over Complex Functions*, Frank Pfenning (ed.) Logic Programming and Automated Reasoning, LPAR'94. LNCS 822, Springer, 1994, 99-113. 104, 116

[10] Jaffar, J. and Maher, M. *Constraint Logic Programming: A Survey*, J. of Logic Programming 19(20), 1994, 503–581. 103, 104

[11] Jaffar, J., Michaylov, S., Stuckey, P. and Yap, R. *The CLP(R) Language and System* , ACM Transactions on Programming Languages 14(3), 1992, 339–395. 104, 116

[12] Leach, J. and Nieva, S. *A Higher-Order Logic Programming Language with Constraints*, Kuchen, H. and Ueda, K. (eds.) FLOPS'01. LNCS 2024, Springer, 2001, 102–122. 103

[13] Leach, J., Nieva, S. and Rodríguez-Artalejo, M. *Constraint Logic Programming with Hereditary Harrop Formulas*, Theory and Practice of Logic Programming 1(4), Cambridge University Press, 2001, 409–445. 103, 104, 105, 106, 114, 117

[14] Lloyd, J. W. *Foundations of Logic Programming*, Springer-Verlag, 1987. 103

[15] Maher, M. *Complete axiomatizations of the algebras of finite, rational and infinite trees*, in Procs. of the Third Annual Symposium on Logic in Computer Science, Edinburgh, 1988. IEEE Computer Society, 348–357. 104, 107, 109, 117

[16] Miller, D., Nadathur, G., Pfenning, F. and Scedrov, A. *Uniform Proofs as a Foundation for Logic Programming*, Annals of Pure and Applied Logic 51, 1991, 125–157. 104, 105

[17] Nadathur, G. *A Proof Procedure for the Logic of Hereditary Harrop Formulas*, J. of Automated Reasoning 11, 1993, 111–145. 104

[18] Nelson, G. and Oppen, D. *Simplification by Cooperating Decision Procedures*, ACM Transactions on Programming Languages and Systems 1(2), 1979, 245–257. 104, 106, 116

[19] Tarski, A. *A Decision Method for Elementary Algebra and Geometry*, University of California Press, 1951. 104, 106, 117

On the Correctness
of the Factoring Transformation

Pascual Julián Iranzo[*]

Departamento de Informática, Universidad de Castilla–La Mancha
Ciudad Real, Spain
pjulian@inf-cr.uclm.es

Abstract. Non-deterministic computations greatly enhance the expressive power of functional logic programs, but are often computationally expensive. Recently we analyzed a program transformation, called *factoring* transformation [4], that may save both execution time and memory occupation in a non-deterministic computation. In this paper we study the formal properties of our transformation, proving its correctness for constructor-based left linear rewriting systems, under some well established conditions. We also introduce some proof techniques that help us to reason with this kind of rewriting systems.

1 Introduction

The aim of functional logic programming is to integrate the best features of both functional and logic programming. Logic programming provides the use of predicates and logical formulas. Logic programs have a great expressive power thanks to the ability of logic languages of computing using logical variables, partial data structures and an operational mechanism that permits a non-deterministic search for answers. Functional programming is based on the concept of function. In a functional program functions are defined by means of equations. The deterministic evaluation of ground expressions increases the efficiency of functional programs. The concept of evaluation strategies, that also increase the efficiency of functional computations, relays on the existence and manipulation of nested terms. The combination of these features makes functional logic languages both more expressive than functional languages and more efficient than traditional logic languages.

Non-determinism is an essential feature of these integrated languages, since it allows problem solving using programs that are textually shorter, easier to understand and maintain, and more declarative than their deterministic counterparts (see [2], [9] or [14] for several motivating examples).

---

[*] Supported by the Spanish Research Funding Agency (CICYT) TIC 2001-2705-C03-01, by Acción Integrada Hispano-Italiana HI2000-0161, by Acción Integrada Hispano-Alemana HA2001-0059, and the Valencian Research Council under grant GV01-424.

Z. Hu and M. Rodríguez-Artalejo (Eds.): FLOPS 2002, LNCS 2441, pp. 119–133, 2002.
© Springer-Verlag Berlin Heidelberg 2002

In a functional logic programming language, non-deterministic computations are modeled by the defined operations of a constructor-based left linear rewrite system [2, 8]. The following emblematic example [8, Ex. 2] defines an operation, *coin*, that non-deterministically returns either zero or one.

$$coin \rightarrow 0$$
$$coin \rightarrow s(0)$$

Rewrite systems with operations such as `coin` are non-confluent. A computation in these rewrite systems may have distinct normal forms and/or does not terminate. Non-determinism abstracts the choice of one of several outcomes of a computation. The outcome of a non-deterministic computation is selected somewhat randomly. For example, for the operation *coin* defined above, each solution, 0 or $s(0)$, is equally likely to be produced. There is no feasible means of deciding which replacement should be chosen at the time `coin` is evaluated. Therefore, evaluation under both replacements must be considered. In general, to ensure operational completeness, all the possible replacements of a non-deterministic computation must be executed fairly. In fact, if one replacement is executed only after the computation of another replacement is completed, the second replacement will never be executed if the computation originated by a first replacement does not terminate.

This approach, which we refer to as *fair independent computations*, captures the intended semantics, but clearly it is computationally costly. For example, consider the following operations, where "bigger" is a variant of `coin`:

$$add(0, Y) \rightarrow Y$$
$$add(s(X), Y) \rightarrow s(add(X, Y))$$
$$positive(0) \rightarrow false$$
$$positive(s(X)) \rightarrow true$$
$$bigger \rightarrow s(0)$$
$$bigger \rightarrow s(s(0))$$

The evaluation of the term $positive(add(bigger, 0))$ requires the evaluation of the subterm *bigger*. Therefore, one must compute fairly and independently both $positive(add(s(0), 0))$ and $positive(add(s(s(0)), 0))$.

However, in a situation like the one just described, the cost of fair independent computations might be avoided by means of a programming technique that facilitates the use of deterministic choices. Our programming technique is based on the introduction of a new symbol, denoted by the infix operator " ! " and read as *alternative*, into the signature of the TRS modeling a functional logic program. We treat the new symbol as a polymorphic operation[1], defined by the rules [8, 14]:

$$ALT1 : X!Y \rightarrow X$$
$$ALT2 : X!Y \rightarrow Y$$

---

[1] The reader can see another different approach in [4], where we also consider the alternative symbol as an overloaded constructor.

The *alternative* operation allows us to give an equivalent definition of the operation `bigger`:

$$bigger \rightarrow s(0!s0)$$

where a common context of the right-hand sides of the rules defining the operation *bigger*, in the original term rewriting system, has been "factored". The advantage of this new definition of *bigger* with respect to the original one is that, using a *needed* strategy [2] or the constructor-based lazy narrowing of [9], only the factored portion of the two alternative right-hand sides of the rewrite rules of *bigger* is needed by a context and no fair independent computations are created. As it is shown by the following (needed) derivation:

$$positive(add(bigger, 0)) \rightarrow positive(add(s(0!s(0)), 0))$$
$$\rightarrow positive(s(add(0!s(0)), 0))$$
$$\rightarrow true.$$

where two non-deterministic fair independent computations have been merged. Roughly speaking, if we "factor out" the common part of a set of non-deterministic choices, when it is possible, we can avoid the replication of the choice's context obtaining a gain. For this example, the cost criteria developed in [4] reveal that our programming technique cuts the number of steps in half and reduces the memory consumption by 25% w.r.t. a computation performed using the original program. On the other hand, in cases where factoring the right-hand sides of two rewrite rules does not eliminate the need of fair independent computations, the run-time cost of factoring is a single additional rewrite step. For realistic programs, this cost is negligible. Hence, the factorization of right-hand sides is a source of potential improvement. In the best case, it saves computing time and/or storage for representing terms. In the worst case, it costs one extra step and very little additional memory (see [4] for some examples on larger benchmark programs, coded using the functional logic language Curry [11], that illustrate in more detail the impact on the efficiency produced by our factoring technique).

We can see all this process as a program transformation that starting from an original program produce a new and, in many cases, more efficient program. In this paper, we define our program transformation in a formal setting and we prove its correctness under precise conditions. That is, we prove that the original and the transformed program are semantically equivalent. In order to obtain this result it is convenient to introduce some proof techniques that help us to reason with non-confluent constructor-based rewrite systems, where the concept of *descendants* of a redex [12] is not well established.

The plan of the paper is as follows: Section 2 introduces some preparatory concepts that are used in the rest of the paper. Section 3 gives a formal definition of our transformation. Section 4 discusses the conditions under our transformation is sound and complete and we introduce some concepts to facilitate our proofs: namely, an embedding relation, that abstracts the intuitive notion of "containment" between terms with alternative symbols and the concept of non-factorized program, that defines a standard form of program. Finally, Section 5 contains our conclusions.

A full version with missing proofs can be found as a wed document at the URL address http://www.inf-cr.uclm.es/www/pjulian.

2   Preliminaries

In this section we briefly summarize some well-known notations and concepts about term rewriting systems [5] and functional logic programming [10].

2.1   Terms, Substitutions and Positions

Throughout this paper, $\mathcal{X}$ denotes a countably infinite set of *variables* and $\mathcal{F}$ denotes a set of *function symbols* (also called the *signature*), each of which has a fixed associated arity. We assume that the signature $\mathcal{F}$ is partitioned into two disjoint sets $\mathcal{F} = \mathcal{C} \uplus \mathcal{D}$. Symbols in $\mathcal{C}$ are called *constructors* and symbols in $\mathcal{D}$ are called *defined functions*. $\mathcal{T}(\mathcal{F}, \mathcal{X})$ denotes the set of *terms* or *expressions* built from $\mathcal{F}$ and $\mathcal{X}$. $\mathcal{T}(\mathcal{F})$ denotes the set of *ground terms*, while $\mathcal{T}(\mathcal{C}, \mathcal{X})$ denotes the set of *constructor* terms. If $t \notin \mathcal{X}$, then $\mathcal{R}oot(t)$ is the function symbol heading the term t, also called the *root symbol* of t. A term t is *linear* if t does not contain multiple occurrences of the same variable. $\mathcal{V}ar(o)$ is the set of variables occurring in the syntactic object o.

A *substitution* is a mapping from the set of variables $\mathcal{X}$ to the set of terms $\mathcal{T}(\mathcal{F}, \mathcal{X})$ such that its *domain* $\mathcal{D}om(\sigma) = \{x \in \mathcal{X} \mid \sigma(x) \neq x\}$ is finite. We frequently identify a substitution σ with the set $\{x/\sigma(x) \mid x \in \mathcal{D}om(\sigma)\}$. We denote the identity substitution by id. We say that σ is a *constructor substitution* if $\sigma(x)$ is constructor term for each $x \in \mathcal{D}om(\sigma)$. We define the composition of two substitutions σ and θ, denoted $\sigma \circ \theta$ as usual: $\sigma \circ \theta(x) = \hat{\sigma}(\theta(x))$, where $\hat{\sigma}$ is the extension of σ to the domain of the terms $\mathcal{T}(\mathcal{F}, \mathcal{X})$. We say that θ is *more general* than σ (in symbols $\theta \leq \sigma$) iff $(\exists \gamma)\ \sigma = \gamma \circ \theta$. The *restriction* $\sigma_{\restriction V}$ of a substitution σ to a set V of variables is defined by $\sigma_{\restriction V}(x) = \sigma(x)$ if $x \in V$ and $\sigma_{\restriction V}(x) = x$ if $x \notin V$. We write $\sigma = \theta[V]$ iff $\sigma_{\restriction V} = \theta_{\restriction V}$. A *renaming* is a substitution ρ such that there exists the inverse substitution ρ^{-1} and $\rho \circ \rho^{-1} = \rho^{-1} \circ \rho = id$. Given a set S of terms and a substitution σ, $\sigma(S) = \{\sigma(t) \mid t \in S\}$.

A term t is *more general* than s (or s is an *instance* of t), in symbols $t \leq s$, if $(\exists \sigma)\ s = \sigma(t)$. Two terms t and t' are *variants* if there exists a renaming ρ such that $t' = \rho(t)$. A *unifier* of a pair of terms $\langle t_1, t_2 \rangle$ is a substitution σ such that $\sigma(t_1) = \sigma(t_2)$. A unifier σ is called *most general unifier* (*mgu*) if $\sigma \leq \sigma'$ for every other unifier σ'.

Positions of a term t (also called *occurrences*) are represented by sequences of natural numbers used to address subterms of t. The concatenation of the sequences p and w is denoted by $p.w$. We let Λ denote the empty sequence. $\mathcal{P}os(t)$ and $\mathcal{F}\mathcal{P}os(t)$ denote, respectively, the set of positions and the set of nonvariable positions of the term t. If $p \in \mathcal{P}os(t)$, $t|_p$ denotes the subterm of t at position p and $t[s]_p$ denotes the result of replacing the subterm $t|_p$ by the term s.

2.2 Term Rewriting, Classes of Term Rewrite Systems and Programs

We limit the discussion to unconditional term rewriting systems. A *rewrite rule* is a pair $l \rightarrow r$ with $l, r \in \mathcal{T}(\mathcal{F}, \mathcal{X})$, $l \notin \mathcal{X}$, and $Var(r) \subseteq Var(l)$. l and r are called the *left-hand side* (lhs) and *right-hand side* (rhs) of the rewrite rule, respectively. A *term rewriting system* (TRS) $\mathcal{R}$ is a finite set of rewrite rules.

Rewrite rules in a TRS define a *rewriting relation* $\rightarrow$ between terms which can be defined as follows: $t \rightarrow_{p, l \rightarrow r} s$ if there exists a position $p \in \mathcal{P}os(t)$, a rewrite rule $l \rightarrow r$, and a substitution σ with $t|_p = \sigma(l)$ and $s = t[\sigma(r)]_p$. We say that s is reduced to t in a *rewrite step*, $t \rightarrow_{p, l \rightarrow r} s$ and the subterm $t|_p = \sigma(l)$ is a *redex* (reducible expression) of t. A sequence of (zero or more) rewriting steps is denoted by $(t \rightarrow^* s)$ $t \rightarrow^+ s$. A term t is in *normal form* if t is a term without redexes. A term s has a normal form if there exists a reduction sequence $s \rightarrow^* t$, where t is a normal form.

A TRS is *terminating* or *noetherian* if there are no infinite reduction sequences. Since in this work we do not impose the requirement of terminating rules, normal forms may not exist.

A TRS is called *confluent* if, whenever a term s reduces to two terms t_1 and t_2, both t_1 and t_2 reduce to the same term. Confluence is a decidable property for terminating TRSs. Confluent TRSs have unique normal forms, when they exist. The confluence property is lost when non convergent critical pairs appear. Given two rules $l_1 \rightarrow r_1$ and $l_2 \rightarrow r_2$ if there exists a position $p \in \mathcal{F}\mathcal{P}os(l_1)$ such that $l_1|_p$ and l_2 unify with *mgu* σ, then the pair of terms $\langle \sigma(r_1), l_1[\sigma(r_2)]_p \rangle$ is a *critical pair*. If two rules have a critical pair, we say that they *overlap*. A special case of overlapping rules are, those what we call *variant overlapping* rules, that is, overlapping rules whose lhss are variants one of each other [2]. We call a TRS with overlapping rules *overlapping* TRS.

A TRS is said to be *constructor-based* (CB) if the "arguments" of the lhs of its rules are constructor terms or variables.

A TRS is said to be *left-linear* (resp. *rigth-linear*) if for each rule $l \rightarrow r$ in the TRS, the lhs l (resp. rhs r) is a linear term.

Since, in this paper, we are interested in non-determinism we are going to work with overlapping CB and left linear TRSs that we assimilate to *programs*. This is a suitable class of programs for integrating functional and logic languages and modeling a non-deterministic behavior [2, 8].

2.3 Functional Logic Programming

Functional logic languages can be considered as an extension of functional languages with principles derived from logic programming. Most of this languages use TRSs as programs and (some variant) of narrowing as operational semantics. Narrowing generalizes the *rewriting* operational mechanism of functional

---

[2] Rules of this kind are not unusual in practical programs. This is the only kind of overlapping allowed in *overlapping inductively sequential* rewrite systems, a class that supports both non-deterministic computations and optimal lazy evaluation [2].

languages. The narrowing relation induced by a TRS is defined as follows: a term t is reduced to the term s in a *narrowing step*, denoted $t \leadsto_{[p,R,\sigma]} s$, if there exists a position $p \in \mathcal{FP}os(t)$, a variant program rule $R = (l \rightarrow r)$ and a unifier σ of the terms $t|_p$ and l, such that $s = \sigma(t[r]_p)$. We say that there exists a *narrowing derivation* from a term t to a term s, if there exists a sequence of narrowing steps $t = t_0 \leadsto_{[p_1,R_1,\sigma_1]} t_1 \leadsto_{[p_2,R_2,\sigma_2]} \cdots \leadsto_{[p_n,R_n,\sigma_n]} t_n = s$ and we write $t \leadsto_\sigma^* s$, where $\sigma = \sigma_n \circ \ldots \circ \sigma_2 \circ \sigma_1$. We say that the pair $\langle s, \sigma \rangle$ is the *outcome* of the derivation. Usually we say that the term s is the *result* of the derivation and the substitution σ is the *computed answer*. Mostly, we are interested in derivations to constructor terms, that we call *values*.

Intuitively, narrowing computes a suitable substitution, σ, which when it is applied to a term t, the term $\sigma(t)$ can be reduced on a rewriting step $\sigma(t) \rightarrow_{p,R} s$. Note that, usually, the substitution σ computed by a narrowing step is a most general unifier, i.e., $\sigma = mgu(\{l = t|_p\})$. However we have relaxed this restriction to support narrowing strategies, such as needed narrowing [3] or INS [2], that may compute substitutions which are not most general unifiers.

Narrowing provides completeness in the sense of logic programming (computation of answers) and also in the sense of functional programming (computation of values or normal forms).

3   The Factoring Transformation

The aim of *program transformation* [6, 18] is to derive a program semantically equivalent to the original program. More accurately, given an initial program $\mathcal{R}$, we want to derive a new program $\mathcal{R}'$ which computes the same results and answers as $\mathcal{R}$ for any input term, but with a better behavior w.r.t. some determined properties (usually, we want the transformed program may be executed more efficiently than the initial one).

We are interested in the transformation of overlapping, CB and left linear TRSs modeling functional logic programs with a non-deterministic behavior [2, 9]. Beginning from this point, by abuse of language, and in order to lighten our discourse, we use the word "program" as a synonym of "overlapping, CB and left linear TRS". In a program, variant overlapping rules can be "merged" and expressed in a more concise way by means of the introduction of the alternative operation " ! ". We consider the alternative operation " ! " as defined by the pair of variant overlapping rules introduced in Section 1. Also, we consider that this pair of rules is present in all our programs. This assumption is harmless, since the operation can be added to any program that does not already define it without changing the meaning of existing operations.

We formalize our transformation, intuitively introduced in Section 1, by means of the foollowing definitions.

Definition 1. *[Term factoring] Let t, u and v be terms. We say that t is a product of u and v if and only if one of the following conditions hold:*

1. $t = u \, ! \, v$ or $t = v \, ! \, u$.

2. $t = f(t_1, \ldots, t_n)$, where f is a symbol of arity n and $t_1, \ldots, t_n$ are terms, $u = f(u_1, \ldots, u_n)$, $v = f(v_1, \ldots, v_n)$, where $u_1, \ldots, u_n, v_1, \ldots, v_n$ are terms, and for all $i \in \{1, \ldots, n\} \backslash \{j\}$, with $j \in \{1, \ldots, n\}$, $t_i = u_i = v_i$ and t_j is a product of u_j and v_j.

Conversely we say that u and v are factors *of t.*

Observe that the last case of Definition 1 may apply when f is " ! ".

Example 1. Both $s(0) \, ! \, s(s(0))$ and $s(0 \, ! \, s(0))$ are products of the terms $s(0)$ and $s(s(0))$. The term $f(X, s(0 \, ! \, s(0)))$ is a product of the terms $f(X, s(0))$ and $f(X, s(s(0)))$. Note also that, for the terms $f(0,0)$ and $f(s(0), s(0))$ it is impossible to construct a product other that the trivial $f(0,0) \, ! \, f(s(0), s(0))$.

Intuitively, a factor t is built by sharing a common context of u and v over a `single` common position of both u and v. In the simplest case the context is a vacuum context and the single common position is the top position of the factors.

Definition 2. *[Program factoring] Let $\mathcal{R}$ be a program defining the alternative operation " ! ", and $l_1 \to r_1$ and $l_2 \to r_2$ are variant overlapping rules of $\mathcal{R}$. Without loss of generality we assume that $l_1 = l_2$ (since renaming the variables of a rule does not change the rewrite relation). A program $\mathcal{R}'$ factors $\mathcal{R}$ if and only if either $\mathcal{R}' = \mathcal{R} \backslash \{l_1 \to r_1, l_2 \to r_2\} \cup \{l_1 \to r\}$, where r is a product of r_1 and r_2, or $\mathcal{R}'$ factors some program $\mathcal{R}''$ and $\mathcal{R}''$ factors $\mathcal{R}$.*

Informally, the factoring transformation can be seen as a process that starting with an overlapping, left linear and CB TRS (the original program) produce a new TRS (the transformed program) by application of a sequence of the following transformation steps:

1. `merging step`: we arbitrarily select two variant overlapping rules (different from *ALT*) $l \to u$ and $l \to v$ that are merged into a new single rule $l \to u \, ! \, v$ and the old rules are erased;
2. `factoring step`: if possible, we push the root alternative operator down the term by factoring some common part of the rhs.

This transformation process always terminates, provided that we work with finite programs and terms. Although we let unspecified both the starting program and the final program, it should be intuitively clear that the deeper the alternative operator can be pushed down the right-hand side, the more likely it will be to replace two fair independent computations by a single computation.

Example 2. Considering once more again the program $\mathcal{R} = \{bigger \to s(0),$ $bigger \to s(s(0))\}$ (augmented with the *ALT* rules), the free application of the aforementioned transformation steps leads to the following residual programs:

$$\mathcal{R}'_1 = \{bigger \to s(0) \, ! \, s(s(0))\} \quad \text{and} \quad \mathcal{R}'_2 = \{bigger \to s(0 \, ! \, s(0))\}.$$

Both $\mathcal{R}'_1$ and $\mathcal{R}'_2$ factors $\mathcal{R}$ (according to Definition 2), but only $\mathcal{R}'_2$ can effectively produce a gain by merging two fair independent computations into a single computation. Finally, it is worthy to say that $\mathcal{R}'_2$ factors $\mathcal{R}'_1$ and $\mathcal{R}'_2$ cannot be further transformed.

Note that, since we introduce the *ALT* rules in the transformed program as well as in the original one, both programs derive the same signature and can be used to reduce the same kind of terms. Therefore, it is not necessary any kind of renaming transformation as it is the case of other more complex transformation techniques, e.g., the partial evaluation transformation of [1].

4   Correctness of the Factoring Transformation

From an operational semantics point of view, we say that a transformation is *sound* when, given a term, the results and answers computed by the transformed program are exactly the same as the ones computed by the original program for that term. The definition of *completeness* is the reverse of the last concept.

Definition 3. *Let $\Im$ be a mapping from programs to programs. Let $\mathcal{R}$ and $\mathcal{R}'$ be programs (with the same signature) such that $\mathcal{R}' = \Im(\mathcal{R})$. $\Im$ is* complete *if and only if for every term t and value v, $t \leadsto^*_\sigma v$ in $\mathcal{R}$ implies $t \leadsto^*_{\sigma'} v$ in $\mathcal{R}'$ where $\sigma = \sigma'[\mathcal{V}ar(t)]$. $\Im$ is* sound *if and only if for every term t and value v, $t \leadsto^*_{\sigma'} v$ in $\mathcal{R}'$ implies $t \leadsto^*_\sigma v$ in $\mathcal{R}$ where $\sigma = \sigma'[\mathcal{V}ar(t)]$.*

In this section we are interested in the study of the correctness properties of the factoring transformation given by Definition 2.

4.1   Embedding Relation

For the class of programs we are working on there is not a notion of descendants [12] of a redex. Therefore, it is difficult to reason about the correctness properties of our transformation. To facilitate our proofs of correctness we introduce an intuitive notion of ordering, for terms with alternative symbols, in which a term that is "contained" inside another, it is smaller than the other.

Definition 4 (embedding relation).
The embedding relation $\trianglelefteq$ on terms in $\mathcal{T}(\mathcal{F}, \mathcal{X})$ is defined as the smallest relation satisfying: $x \trianglelefteq x$ for all $x \in \mathcal{X}$, and $s \trianglelefteq t$, if and only if:

1. *if $\mathcal{R}oot(s) \neq !$ and $t = u \,!\, v$ then $s \trianglelefteq u$ or $s \trianglelefteq v$;*
2. *if $s = f(s_1, \ldots, s_n)$ and $t = f(t_1, \ldots, t_n)$ then $s_i \trianglelefteq t_i$ for all $i = 1, \ldots, n$.*

The strict embedding *relation $\lhd$ is defined, in terms of the embedding relation $\trianglelefteq$, as follows: $s \lhd t$, if and only if $s \trianglelefteq t$ and $s \neq t$.*

The above definition differs from the homeomorphic embedding relation of [7] or [16]. Note also that, for the second case, the operation symbol f may be an alternative symbol.

Example 3. These terms are in the embedding relation: $0 \trianglelefteq 0 \,!\, s(X)$; $f(a) \trianglelefteq a \,!\, f(a \,!\, b)$ and $0 \,!\, f(X) \trianglelefteq (0 \,!\, s(0)) \,!\, f(X)$.

The embedding relation $\trianglelefteq$ is a partial order over the set $\mathcal{T}(\mathcal{F}, \mathcal{X})$. Clearly, the relation is reflexive, transitive, and antisymmetric.

Definition 5 (minimal element).
Let t be a term, we call minimal element of t, a term u such that $u \trianglelefteq t$ and there no exists a term $v \trianglelefteq t$ such that $v \vartriangleleft u$

The notion of minimal element can be extended to substitutions in a natural way: a substitution σ is *minimal* w.r.t. the substitution θ iff $Dom(\sigma) = Dom(\theta)$ and, for all $x \in Dom(\sigma)$, $\sigma(x)$ is a minimal element of $\theta(x)$.

Lemma 1. *If s and t are terms such that $s \trianglelefteq t$, then there exists a reduction sequence from t to s using only ALT rules.*

Corollary 1. *If u is a minimal element of t, then u is a normal form of t w.r.t. reduction sequences using only ALT rules.*

4.2 Completeness

The following lemma establishes the precise relation between a step in the original program and a reduction sequence in the transformed one.

Lemma 2. *Let $\mathcal{R}$ be a program, $\mathcal{R}'$ be a program that factors $\mathcal{R}$. If there exists a reduction step $A = t \rightarrow s$ in $\mathcal{R}$ then there exists a reduction sequence $D' = t \rightarrow^+ s$ in $\mathcal{R}'$.*

Now it is immediate to establish the equivalence between reduction sequences leading to a value in both the original and the transformed program.

Proposition 1. *Let $\mathcal{R}$ be a program and $\mathcal{R}'$ be a program that factors $\mathcal{R}$. If there exists a reduction sequence $D = t \rightarrow^* s$ in $\mathcal{R}$, where s is a value then there exists a reduction sequence $D' = t \rightarrow^* s$ in $\mathcal{R}'$.*

Finally, the completeness of the transformation is an easy consequence of the correctness of narrowing.

Theorem 1. *The factoring transformation is complete.*

Note that it was not necessary to impose additional requirements to the programs (such as right linearity) or to use a special semantics (see Section 4.4) in order to obtain the completeness result.

4.3 Soundness

As we are going to see, our transformation does not preserve the soundness property in all cases. The following example points out this drawback and permit us to understand the kind of restrictions that are necessary to introduce to preserve this property.

Example 4. Given the initial program $\mathcal{R}$

$$R_1 : double(X) \rightarrow X + X$$
$$R_2 : f \rightarrow double(0) \qquad R_3 : f \rightarrow double(s(0))$$

extended with the usual rules for the addition, and the input term f, only the following results are possible: $\{0, s(s(0))\}$. On the other hand, the factored version of $\mathcal{R}$, namely $\mathcal{R}'$, is

$$R_1 : \ double(X) \rightarrow X + X$$
$$R_{23} : f \rightarrow double(0 \ ! \ s(0))$$

and it can compute the additional result s(0) (twice) for the input term f.

This example reveals that, in general, our transformation is unsound, because there exists derivations in $\mathcal{R}'$ that cannot be reproduced in $\mathcal{R}$. At the first sight, a possible solution for this drawback might be to restrict the kind of operations that can be used in the transformation. Note that, the operation *double*, defined by rule R_1, is not right linear and this is the main source of our problem: the subterm at position 1 of $double(0 \ ! \ s(0))$ is duplicate, introducing new alternatives that are not produced when the reduction of f is done using the original program $\mathcal{R}$. Therefore, the solution might be to impose as a restriction that only operations defined by right linear rules should be part of a context containing a product. Unfortunately, a stronger restriction, namely the right linearity of the program, must be imposed. Suppose that we change the rule R_1, in $\mathcal{R}$, by this right linear rule

$$R_1 : double(X) \rightarrow s(s(0)) \times X,$$

we also introduce in our program the suitable rules for the operation $\times$ and we transform the resulting program to obtain a new factored version of it. Then when we proceed with the computation of f, due to the lack of right linearity of one of the rules defining the operation $\times$, the same problem is reproduced again (the original program computes the results $\{0, s(s(0))\}$ whereas the transformed program computes the results $\{0, s(0), s(s(0))\}$).

For the class of programs we use, the concept of right linearity must be revised, considering that the variables occurring in different alternatives of a rhs of a variant overlapping rule are completely independent. Certainly, since this kind of rules are the result of merging several rules whose lhss are variants [2], this distintion corresponds with the intended semantics of the original program.

Example 5. Given the program

$$R_1 : f(X) \rightarrow g(X)$$

it can be transformed in this other program

$$R_{12} : f(X) \rightarrow g(X) \ ! \ h(X)$$

The variables of the rules R_1 and R_2 of the original program are independent and, indeed, we have to select a variant of these rules when they are applied to perform a computation step. Therefore, it is meaningless to consider the variable X of the rule R_{12} as the same variable for both alternatives.

On the other hand, the situation illustrated by Example 5 does not lead to the unsoundness problem as we have been discussing above. Although the rule R_{12} of Example 5 is not right linear, at most one of both alternatives of the function f is needed in a computation to a value. Therefore, we assume that the apparition of this kind of rules in the transformed program doesn't break the good properties provided by the right linearity of the original program. Certainly, this kind of rules preserve an important compositional property that we are going to establish in Lemma 5.

In order to prove the soundness of our transformation we need the following auxiliary lemmas. The first lemma points out the existence of a compositional property between the minimal elements of a linear term t, the minimal substitutions w.r.t. a substitution σ and the minimal elements of the term $\sigma(t)$.

Lemma 3. *Let t be a linear term and σ a substitution. Let M be the set of all minimal elements of t and $\bigcup_{i=1}^n \{\sigma_i\}$ be the set of all minimal substitutions w.r.t. σ. Then, $\bigcup_{i=1}^n \sigma_i(M)$ is the set of all minimal elements of the term $\sigma(t)$.*

The intuitive idea behind Lemma 3 is to avoid problems like the one illustrated in the following example:

Example 6. Suppose the non-linear term $t = X + X$ (possibly a rhs of a rule) and a substitution $\sigma = \{X/(0 \,!\, s(0))\}$. Then, t is minimal, $\{\{X/0\}, \{X/s(0)\}\}$ is the set of minimal substitutions w.r.t. σ, but $\{\{X/0\}(t), \{X/s(0)\}(t)\} = \{0 + 0, s(0) + s(0)\}$ is not the set of all minimal elements of $\sigma(t)$.

Lemma 3 can be extended to a product where each factor is linear, although some of these factors may share some variables in common.

Lemma 4. *Let $t = u \,!\, v$ be a product where u and v are linear terms such that $\mathcal{V}ar(u) \cap \mathcal{V}ar(v) \neq \emptyset$. Let U and V be the set of all minimal elements of u and v respectively. Let σ be a substitution and $\bigcup_{i=1}^n \{\sigma_i\}$ be the set of all minimal substitutions w.r.t. σ. Then, $(\bigcup_{i=1}^n \sigma_i(U)) \cup (\bigcup_{i=1}^{n_i} \sigma_i(V))$ is the set of all minimal elements of the term $\sigma(t)$.*

Note that, in Lemma 4, the only requirement for the subterms u and v is linearity and, therefore, they can contain occurrences of the alternative symbol. The following lemma is a generalization of Lemma 4.

Lemma 5. *Let $t = t_1 \,!\,, \ldots, \,!\, t_m$ be a product where each factor t_j, $j \in \{1, \ldots, m\}$, is a linear term such that $\bigcap_{j=1}^m \mathcal{V}ar(t_j) \neq \emptyset$. Let M_j be the set of all minimal elements of t_j, $j \in \{1, \ldots, m\}$. Let σ be a substitution and $\bigcup_{i=1}^n \{\sigma_i\}$ be the set of all minimal substitutions w.r.t. σ. Then, $\bigcup_{i=1}^n \bigcup_{j=1}^m \sigma_i(M_j)$ is the set of all minimal elements of the term $\sigma(t)$.*

Note that our transformation produce, mostly, transformed rules whose rhss fulfills the conditions of Lemma 5. Therefore, the last result can be use to obtain all minimal elements of a rhs $\sigma'(r')$ applying the minimal substitutions σ w.r.t. σ' to the minimal elements r of r'. This is one of the keys to prove Lemma 6. But, we first need the introduction of a new concept.

As we said, Definition 2 lets unspecified the shape of the original program as well as the way the transformation steps are applied. Managing this great freedom in the use of our transformation when we try to prove its soundness can increase unnecessarily the difficulty of the proof without produce, as we are going to reason, a real gain. Therefore, in order to maintain the proof as simple as possible, we first assume that the original program is in a "non-factorized" form and we prove some auxiliary results that are extended to arbitrary programs later.

Definition 6 (non-factorized program). *A non-factorized program is a program where the rhs of its rules don't contain occurrences of the alternative symbol.*

That is, a non-factorized program is a program where the variant overlapping rules are in the simplest possible form and none factoring transformation was previously applied.

Example 7. The program $\{bigger \to s(0), bigger \to s(s(0))\}$ is a non-factorized version of bigger whereas $\{bigger \to s(0) \, ! \, s(s(0))\}$ or $\{bigger \to s(0 \, ! \, s(0))\}$ are not.

It is clear that the non-factorized form of a program is unique, since the factoring transformation does not erase factors and it can be undone following this sequence of steps: i) given a rule $R = l \to r$, where r contains the alternative operator, find the set $\{r_1, \ldots, r_n\}$ of minimal elements of r (w.r.t. embedding relation); ii) replace the rule R by the set of rules $\{l \to r_1, \ldots, l \to r_n\}$.

Now, we are ready to prove the following auxiliary lemmas.

Lemma 6. *Let $\mathcal{R}$ be a non-factorized and right linear program and $\mathcal{R}'$ be a program that factors $\mathcal{R}$. If there exists a reduction step $t' \to u'$ in $\mathcal{R}'$ then, for any minimal element u of u' there exists a minimal element t of t' and a reduction step $t \to u$ in $\mathcal{R}$ or $t = u$.*

Lemma 7. *Let $\mathcal{R}$ be a non-factorized and right linear program and $\mathcal{R}'$ be a program that factors $\mathcal{R}$. If there exists a reduction sequence $t' \to^* u'$ in $\mathcal{R}'$ then, for any minimal element u of u' there exists a minimal element t of t' and a reduction sequence $t \to^* u$ in $\mathcal{R}$*

The following lemma establishes the relation between the reduction sequences leading to a value in both the transformed and the original program.

Lemma 8. *Let $\mathcal{R}$ be a non-factorized and right linear program and $\mathcal{R}'$ be a program that factors $\mathcal{R}$. If there exists a reduction sequence $t \to^* s$ in $\mathcal{R}'$, where s is a value then there exists a reduction sequence $t \to^* s$ in $\mathcal{R}$*

Now, we lift the last result to arbitrary right linear programs.

Proposition 2. *Let $\mathcal{R}$ be a right linear program and $\mathcal{R}'$ be a program that factors $\mathcal{R}$. If there exists a reduction sequence $t \to^* s$ in $\mathcal{R}'$, where s is a value then there exists a reduction sequence $t \to^* s$ in $\mathcal{R}$*

The soundness of the transformation is an easy consequence of the correctness of narrowing and Proposition 2

Theorem 2. *The factoring transformation is sound for right linear programs.*

4.4   Discussion

As we have seen, factoring is generally unsound, but soundness can be recovered in some cases of practical interest. In the following discussion, the notions of *descendant* of a redex is informal, as this notion has been rigorously defined only for orthogonal rewrite systems [12]. The unsoundness of factoring originates from computations in which some redex r generates several descendants, and distinct descendants are reduced to different terms. Thus, two simple independent solutions to the unsoundness problem are to avoid distinct descendants of a redex or to ensure that all the descendants of a redex are contracted using the same rewrite rule.

The first condition holds, as we have just proved, for right-linear rewrite systems. But the restriction to right linear systems is unacceptable from a programming point of view.

The second condition is ensured by the use of a call-time choice semantics or sharing. These solutions were proposed to manage similar but distinct issues in the context of overlapping TRSs by Hussmann [14]. Informally, the *call-time choice* semantics consists of "committing" to the value of an argument of a symbol (either operation or constructor) at the time of the symbol's application. The value of the argument does not need to be computed at application time: thus, the laziness of computations is not jeopardized. This semantics is the most appropriate for some computations, but it fails to capture the intuitive meaning of others. Nevertheless, there are formalisms, such as [9], and languages, like Toy [17] (based on the aforementioned formalism) and Curry [11], that adopt the call-time choice as the only semantics of non-deterministic computations. On the other hand, *sharing* is a technique where all occurrences of the same variable in a rhs of a rule are shared, i.e. all these occurrences are replaced by a pointer to the same subterm after a rewriting step. Sharing is effectively implemented using term graphs.

Hence, both approaches, call-time choice semantics or sharing, are useful to resolve the problems discussed w.r.t. Example 4: they avoid the strong syntactic restriction of right linearity while keep the factoring transformation sound.

5   Conclusions

Non-deterministic computations are an essential feature of functional logic programming languages but its implementation may be very costly, since, usually it is necessary to compute a set of fair independent computations whose results are used, and possibly discarded, by a context.

In this paper, we have defined a program transformation, called factoring transformation, that can be fully automated or used as a programming technique. The factoring transformation is based on the introduction of a new symbol, called *alternative*, into the signature of a program. The alternative symbol is a polymorphic defined operation. This symbol allows a program to factor a common portion of the non-deterministic replacements of a redex. This transformation may improve the efficiency of a computation by reducing the number of computation steps or the memory used in representing terms. Savings are obtained when fair independent computations are avoided because only the factored portion of non-deterministic replacements is needed.

We have studied the formal properties of the factoring transformation, proving its correctness for right linear programs. Afterwards, we have discussed how this impractical syntactic restriction can be overcome if sharing or call-time choice semantics is used as an implementation device of the functional logic language. Therefore, our transformation can be applied safely to the Constructor-based (conditional) ReWriting Logic (CRWL) programs of [9] as well as to Curry programs [11], since they adopt the call-time choice semantics for non-deterministic functions.

Also, in order to prove our results we have introduced an embedding relation that have shown its usefulness to reason with non-confluent constructor-based TRSs, where the notion of descendants of a redex [12] is not well established.

Finally note that, although the process of factoring a program can remind, in some aspects, the full laziness transformation of Functional Programming [13, 15], at the best of our knowledge, it is a novel transformation that can be applied to a high programming language as well as to a core language, producing an effective improvement of the efficiency of the programs.

Acknowledgments

I wish to thank Sergio Antoy the discussion of technical aspects of this paper that greatly improve it. Part of this research was done while the author was visiting the Department of Computer Science at Portland State University. The author gratefully acknowledges the hospitality of that department.

References

[1] M. Alpuente, M. Falaschi, P. Julián, and G. Vidal. Specialization of Lazy Functional Logic Programs. In *Proc. of PEPM'97*, volume 32, 12 of *Sigplan Notices*, pages 151–162, New York, 1997. ACM Press. 126

[2] S. Antoy. Optimal non-deterministic functional logic computations. In *Proc. of ALP'97*, pages 16–30. Springer LNCS 1298, 1997. 119, 120, 121, 123, 124, 128

[3] S. Antoy, R. Echahed, and M. Hanus. A Needed Narrowing Strategy. *Journal of the ACM*, 47(4):776–822, July 2000. 124

[4] S. Antoy, P. Julián Iranzo, and B. Massey. Improving the efficiency of non-deterministic computations. *Electronic Notes in Theoretical Computer Science*,

64:22, 2002. URL: `http://www.elsevier.nl/locate/entcs/volume64.html`. 119, 120, 121

[5] F. Baader and T. Nipkow. *Term Rewriting and All That*. Cambridge University Press, 1998. 122

[6] R. M. Burstall and J. Darlington. A Transformation System for Developing Recursive Programs. *Journal of the ACM*, 24(1):44–67, 1977. 124

[7] N. Dershowitz and J.-P. Jouannaud. Rewrite Systems. In J. van Leeuwen, editor, *Handbook of Theoretical Computer Science*, volume B: Formal Models and Semantics, pages 243–320. Elsevier, Amsterdam, 1990. 126

[8] J. C. González-Moreno, M. T. Hortalá-González, F. J. López-Fraguas, and M. Rodríguez-Artalejo. A rewriting logic for declarative programming. In *Proc. ESOP'96*, pages 156–172. Springer LNCS 1058, 1996. 120, 123

[9] J. C. González-Moreno, F. J. López-Fraguas, M. T. Hortalá-González, and M. Rodríguez-Artalejo. An approach to declarative programming based on a rewriting logic. *The Journal of Logic Programming*, 40:47–87, 1999. 119, 121, 124, 131, 132

[10] M. Hanus. The Integration of Functions into Logic Programming: From Theory to Practice. *Journal of Logic Programming*, 19&20:583–628, 1994. 122

[11] M. Hanus (ed.). Curry: An Integrated Functional Logic Language (Ver. 0.71). Web document http://www.informatik.uni-kiel.de/ mh/curry/report.html, 2000. 121, 131, 132

[12] G. Huet and J.-J. Lévy. Computations in orthogonal term rewriting systems. In J.-L. Lassez and G. Plotkin, editors, *Computational logic: essays in honour of Alan Robinson*. MIT Press, Cambridge, MA, 1991. 121, 126, 131, 132

[13] R. Hughes. *The Design and Implementation of Programming Languages*. PhD thesis, University of Oxford, 1984., 1984. 132

[14] H. Hussmann. Nondeterministic Algebraic Specifications and nonconfluent term rewriting. *Journal of Logic Programming*, 12:237–255, 1992. 119, 120, 131

[15] S. L. Peyton Jones and D. Lester. A modular fully-lazy lambda lifter in HASKELL. *Software, Practice and Experience*, 21(5):479–506, 1991. 132

[16] M. Leuschel and B. Martens. Global Control for Partial Deduction through Characteristic Atoms and Global Trees. In *Proc. of the 1996 Dagstuhl Seminar on Partial Evaluation*, pages 263–283. Springer LNCS 1110, 1996. 126

[17] F. López-Fraguas and J. Sánchez-Hernández. TOY: A Multiparadigm Declarative System. In *Proceedings of RTA '99*, pages 244–247. Springer LNCS 1631, 1999. 131

[18] A. Pettorossi and M. Proietti. A Comparative Revisitation of Some Program Transformation Techniques. In O. Danvy, R. Glück, and P. Thiemann, editors, *Partial Evaluation, Int'l Seminar, Dagstuhl Castle, Germany*, pages 355–385. Springer LNCS 1110, 1996. 124

Lambda-Lifting in Quadratic Time[*]

Olivier Danvy[1] and Ulrik P. Schultz[2]

[1] BRICS[**]
Department of Computer Science, University of Aarhus
Ny Munkegade, Building 540, DK-8000 Aarhus C, Denmark
danvy@daimi.au.dk
[2] Center for Pervasive Computing
Department of Computer Science, University of Aarhus
IT-Byen, Aabogade 34, DK-8200 Aarhus C, Denmark
ups@daimi.au.dk

Abstract. Lambda-lifting is a program transformation used in compilers and in partial evaluators and that operates in cubic time. In this article, we show how to reduce this complexity to quadratic time.
Lambda-lifting transforms a block-structured program into a set of recursive equations, one for each local function in the source program. Each equation carries extra parameters to account for the free variables of the corresponding local function *and of all its callees*. It is the search for these extra parameters that yields the cubic factor in the traditional formulation of lambda-lifting, which is due to Johnsson. This search is carried out by a transitive closure.
Instead, we partition the call graph of the source program into strongly connected components, based on the simple observation that *all functions in each component need the same extra parameters and thus a transitive closure is not needed*. We therefore simplify the search for extra parameters by treating each strongly connected component instead of each function as a unit, thereby reducing the time complexity of lambda-lifting from $\mathcal{O}(n^3 \log n)$ to $\mathcal{O}(n^2 \log n)$, where n is the size of the program.
Since a lambda-lifter can output programs of size $\mathcal{O}(n^2)$, we believe that our algorithm is close to optimal.

1 Lambda-Lifting

1.1 Setting and Background

Lambda-lifting: what. In the mid 1980's, Augustsson, Hughes, Johnsson, and Peyton Jones devised 'lambda-lifting', a meaning-preserving transformation from block-structured programs to recursive equations [6, 17, 18, 25]. Recursive equations provide a propitious format because they are scope free. Today, a number of

---

[*] An extended version of this article is available in the BRICS Research Series [14].
[**] Basic Research in Computer Science (www.brics.dk), funded by the Danish National Research Foundation.

Z. Hu and M. Rodríguez-Artalejo (Eds.): FLOPS 2002, LNCS 2441, pp. 134–151, 2002.
© Springer-Verlag Berlin Heidelberg 2002

systems use lambda-lifting as an intermediate phase. For example, partial evaluators such as Schism, Similix, and Pell-Mell lambda-lift source programs and
generate scope-free recursive equations [8, 10, 22]. Compilers such as Larceny
and Moby use local, incremental versions of lambda-lifting in their optimizations [9, 26], and so did an experimental version of the Glasgow Haskell Compiler [27]. Program generators such as Bakewell and Runciman's least general
common generalization operate on lambda-lifted programs [7].

Lambda-lifting: how. Lambda-lifting operates in two stages: *parameter lifting*
and *block floating*.

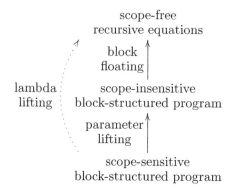

A block-structured program is scope-sensitive because of free variables in local
functions. Parameter lifting makes a program scope-insensitive by passing extra
variables to each function. These variables account both for the free variables of
each function but also for variables occurring free further in the call path. Block
floating erases block structure by making each local function a global recursive
equation.

Parameter lifting. Parameter-lifting a program amounts to making all the free
variables of a function formal parameters of this function. All callers of the
function must thus be passed these variables as arguments as well. A set of
solutions is built by traversing the program. A solution pairs each function with
a least set of additional parameters. Each block of locally defined functions gives
rise to a collection of set equations describing which variables should be passed
as arguments to its local functions. The names of functions, however, are not
included in the sets, since all functions become globally visible when the lambda-
lifting transformation is complete. The solution of each set equation extends the
current set of solutions, which is then used to analyze the header and the body
of the block.

Block floating. After parameter lifting, a program is scope insensitive. Block
floating is thus straightforward: the program is merely traversed, all local functions are collected and all blocks are replaced by their bodies. The collected
function definitions are then appended to the program as global mutually recursive functions, making all functions globally visible.

Lambda-lifting: when. In a compiler, the effectiveness of lambda-lifting hinges on the tension between passing many actuals vs. passing few actuals, and between referring to an actual parameter vs. referring to a free variable.

In practice, though, programmers often stay away both from recursive equations and from maximally nested programs. Instead, they write in a mixed style that both abides by Perlis's epigram "If you have a procedure with ten parameters, you probably missed some." and by Turner's recommendation that good Miranda style means little nesting. In this mixed style, and to paraphrase another of Perlis's epigrams, one man's parameter is another man's free variable.

1.2   Three Examples

We first illustrate lambda-lifting with the classical `foldr` functional, and then with two examples involving multiple local functions and mutual recursion. Throughout, we use Standard ML.

Example 1: We consider the classical fold function for lists, defined with a local function.

```
fun foldr f b xs
    = let fun walk nil
              = b
          | walk (x :: xs)
              = f (x, walk xs)
      in walk xs
      end
```

Lambda-lifting this block-structured program yields two recursive equations: the original entry point, which now serves as a wrapper to invoke the other function, and the other function, which has been extended with two extra parameters.

```
fun foldr f b xs
    = foldr_walk f b xs
and foldr_walk f b []
    = b
  | foldr_walk f b (x :: xs)
    = f (x, foldr_walk f b xs)
```

Example 2: The following token program adds its two parameters.

```
fun main x y
    = let fun add p
              = add_to_x p
          and add_to_x q
              = q + x
      in add y
      end
```

Lambda-lifting this block-structured program yields three recursive equations:

```
fun main x y
    = main_add x y
and main_add x p
    = main_add_to_x x p
and main_add_to_x x q
    = q + x
```

As a local function, add_to_x has a free variable, x, and thus it needs to be passed the value of x. Since add calls add_to_x, it needs to pass the value of x to add_to_x and thus to be passed this value, even though x is not free in the definition of add. During parameter lifting, each function thus needs to be passed not only the value of its free variables, but also the values of the free variables of all its callees.

Example 3: The following token program multiplies its two parameters with successive additions, using mutual recursion.

```
fun mul x y
    = let fun loop z
             = if z=0 then 0 else add_to_x z
          and add_to_x z
             = x + loop (z-1)
      in loop y
      end
```

Again, lambda-lifting this block-structured program yields three recursive equations:

```
fun mul x y
    = mul_loop x y
and mul_loop x z
    = if k=0 then 0 else mul_add_to_x x z
and mul_add_to_x x z
    = x + mul_loop x (z-1)
```

As before, the free variable x of add_to_x has to be passed as a formal parameter, through its caller loop. When add_to_x calls loop recursively, it must pass the value of x to loop, so that loop can pass it back in the recursive call.

This third example illustrates our key insight: during parameter lifting, mutually recursive functions must be passed the same set of variables as parameters.

1.3 Overview

Lambda-lifting, as specified by Johnsson, takes cubic time (Section 2). In this article, we show how to reduce this complexity to quadratic time (Section 3).

Throughout the main part of the article, we consider Johnsson's algorithm [18, 19]. Other styles of lambda-lifting, however, exist: we describe them as well, together with addressing related work (Section 4).

2   Lambda-Lifting in Cubic Time

2.1   Johnsson's Parameter-Lifting Algorithm

Johnsson's algorithm descends recursively through the program structure, calculating the set of variables that are needed by each function. This is done by solving set equations describing the dependencies between functions. These dependencies may be arbitrarily complex, since a function can depend on any variable or function that is lexically visible to it. In particular, mutually recursive functions depend upon each other, and so they give rise to mutually recursive set equations.

The mutually recursive set equations are solved using fixed-point iteration. A program containing m function declarations gives rise to m set equations. In a block-structured program the functions are distributed across the program, so we solve the set equations in groups, as we process each block of local functions. Each set equation unifies $\mathcal{O}(m)$ sets of size $\mathcal{O}(n)$, where n is the size of the program. However, the total size of all equations is bounded by the size of the program n, so globally each iteration takes time $\mathcal{O}(n \log n)$. The number of set union operations needed is $\mathcal{O}(n^2)$, so the time needed to solve all the set equations is $\mathcal{O}(n^3 \log n)$, which is the overall running time of lambda-lifting.

2.2   An Alternative Specification Based on Graphs

Rather than using set equations, one can describe an equivalent algorithm using graphs. We use a graph to describe the dependencies between functions. Peyton Jones names this representation a *dependency graph* [25], but he uses it for a different purpose (see Section 4.1). Each node in the graph corresponds to a function in the program, and is associated with the free variables of this function. An edge in the graph from a node f to a node g indicates that the function f depends on g, because it refers to g. Mutually recursive dependencies give rise to cycles in this graph. Rather than solving the mutually recursive equations using fixed-point iteration, we propagate the variables associated with each node backwards through the graph, from callee to caller, merging the variable sets, until a fixed point is reached.

2.3   Example

Figure 1 shows a small program, defined using three mutually recursive functions, each of which has a different free variable.

We can describe the dependencies between the local block of functions using set equations, as shown in Figure 2. To solve these set equations, we need to perform three fixed-point iterations, since there is a cyclic dependency of size three. Similarly, we can describe these dependencies using a graph, also shown in Figure 2. The calculation of the needed variables can be done using this representation, by propagating variable sets backwards through the graph. A single propagation step is done by performing a set union over the variables

```
fun main x y z n
    = let fun f1 i
               = if i=0 then 0 else x + f2 (i-1)
           and f2 j
               = let fun g2 b = b * j
                 in if j=0 then 0 else g2 y + f3 (j-1)
                 end
           and f3 k
               = let fun g3 c = c * k
                 in if k=0 then 0 else g3 z + f1 (k-1)
                 end
      in f1 n
      end
```

Fig. 1. Three mutually recursive functions

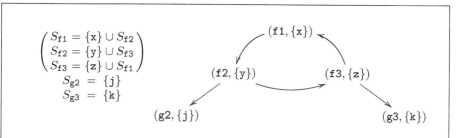

$$\left(\begin{array}{l} S_{f1} = \{x\} \cup S_{f2} \\ S_{f2} = \{y\} \cup S_{f3} \\ S_{f3} = \{z\} \cup S_{f1} \end{array} \right)$$

$S_{g2} = \{j\}$

$S_{g3} = \{k\}$

$(f1, \{x\})$

$(f2, \{y\})$ $(f3, \{z\})$

$(g2, \{j\})$ $(g3, \{k\})$

Fig. 2. Dependencies between the local functions of the program of Figure 1

```
fun main x y z n
    = f1 x y z n
and f1 x y z i
    = if i=0 then 0 else x + f2 x y z (i-1)
and f2 x y z j
    = if j=0 then 0 else g2 y j + f3 x y z (j-1)
and g2 b j
    = b * j
and f3 x y z k
    = if k=0 then 0 else g3 z k + f1 x y z (k-1)
and g3 c k
    = c * k
```

Fig. 3. Lambda-lifted counterpart of Figure 1

associated with a node and the variables associated with its successors. Similarly to the case of the set equations, each node must be visited three times before a fixed point is reached.

When the set of needed variables has been determined for each function, solutions describing how each function must be expanded with these variables are added to the set of solutions. The result is shown in Figure 3.

3   Lambda-Lifting in Quadratic Time

We consider the variant of the parameter-lifting algorithm that operates on a dependency graph. It propagates needed variables backwards through the graph since the caller needs the variables of each callee.

It is our observation that functions that belong to the same strongly connected component of the call graph must be parameter-lifted with the same set of variables (as was illustrated in Section 1.2). We can thus treat these functions in a uniform fashion, by coalescing the strongly connected components of the dependency graph. Each function must define at least its free variables together with the free variables of the other functions of the strongly connected component. Coalescing the strongly connected components of the dependency graph produces a DAG with sets of function names for nodes. A breadth-first backwards propagation of variables can then be done in linear time, which eliminates the need for a fixed-point computation.

3.1   Complexity Analysis

The parameter-lifting algorithm must first construct the dependency graph, which takes time $\mathcal{O}(n \log n)$, where n is the size of the program. The strongly connected components of the graph can then be computed in time $\mathcal{O}(n)$. The ensuing propagation requires a linear number of steps since we are now operating on a DAG. Each propagation step consists of a number of set-union operations, each of which takes $\mathcal{O}(n \log n)$ time, i.e., the time to unify two sets of variables of size $\mathcal{O}(n)$. Globally, a number of set-union operations linear in the size of the program needs to be performed, yielding a time complexity of $\mathcal{O}(n^2 \log n)$. The overall running time is thus $\mathcal{O}(n^2 \log n)$, where n is the size of the program.

3.2   Lower Bound

Consider a function with m formal parameters $\{v_1, \ldots, v_m\}$ that declares m mutually recursive local functions, each of which has a different variable from $\{v_1, \ldots, v_m\}$ as a free variable. The size of the program n is $\mathcal{O}(m)$. The output program contains the m functions, each of which needs to be expanded with the m formal parameters of the enclosing function. The output program is therefore of size $\mathcal{O}(m^2)$, which is also $\mathcal{O}(n^2)$. One thus cannot perform lambda-lifting faster than $\mathcal{O}(n^2)$. Since one needs $\mathcal{O}(n \log n)$ time to compute the sets of free variables of the program, our complexity of $\mathcal{O}(n^2 \log n)$ must be close to optimal.

3.3   Contribution

Our contribution is

- to characterize the fixed-point operations on the set equations as propagation through the dependency graph, and
- to recognize that functions in the same strongly connected component require the same set of variables.

We can therefore first determine which variables need to be known by each function in a strongly connected component, and then add them as formal parameters to these functions. In each function, those variables not already passed as parameters to the function should be added as formal parameters.

This approach can be applied locally to work like Johnsson's algorithm, processing each block independently. It can also be applied globally to the overall dependency graph. The global algorithm, however, must explicitly limit the propagation of free variables, so that they are not propagated beyond their point of definition.

3.4   The New Algorithm

We operate on programs conforming to the simple syntax of Figure 4.

$$
\begin{aligned}
p \in \mathsf{Program} &::= \{d_1, \ldots, d_m\} \\
d \in \mathsf{Def} &::= f \equiv \lambda v_1. \ldots \lambda v_n.e \\
e \in \mathsf{Exp} &::= e_0 \ldots e_n \\
&\quad | \ \mathsf{LetRec}\,\{d_1, \ldots, d_k\}\, e_0 \\
&\quad | \ \mathsf{If}\, e_0\, e_1\, e_2 \\
&\quad | \ f \\
&\quad | \ v \\
&\quad | \ \underline{\text{literal}} \\
v &\in \mathsf{Variable} \\
f &\in \mathsf{FunctionName} \cup \mathsf{PredefinedFunction}
\end{aligned}
$$

Fig. 4. Simplified syntax of source programs

The set $\mathrm{FV}(f)$ denotes the set of free variables in the function f, and the set $\mathrm{FF}(f)$ denotes the set of free functions in f (note that $\mathrm{FV}(f) \cap \mathrm{FF}(f) = \emptyset$). In our algorithm, we assume variable hygiene, i.e., that no name clashes can occur. Figure 5 shows our (locally applied) $\mathcal{O}(n^2 \log n)$ parameter-lifting algorithm. It makes use of several standard graph and list operations that are described in the appendix. Figure 6 shows the standard linear-time (globally applied) block-floating algorithm. Johnsson's original lambda-lifting algorithm includes steps to explicitly name anonymous lambda expressions and replace non-recursive let blocks by applications. These steps are trivial and omitted from the figures.

parameterLiftProgram :: Program $\rightarrow$ Program
parameterLiftProgram p = map (parameterLiftDef $\emptyset$) p
parameterLiftDef :: Set(FunName,Set(Variable)) $\rightarrow$ Def $\rightarrow$ Def
parameterLiftDef S $(f \equiv \lambda v_1. \ldots \lambda v_n.e)$ =
$\qquad$ applySolutionToDef S $(f \equiv \lambda v_1. \ldots \lambda v_n.(\text{parameterLiftExp } S\ e))$
parameterLiftExp :: Set(FunName,Set(Variable)) $\rightarrow$ Exp $\rightarrow$ Exp
parameterLiftExp S $(e_0 \ldots e_n)$ =
$\qquad$ **let** $e_i' = \text{parameterLiftExp } S\ e_i$, **for each** $e_i \in \{e_0, \ldots, e_n\}$
$\qquad$ **in** $(e_0' \ldots e_n')$
parameterLiftExp S (LetRec $\{d_1, \ldots, d_k\}\, e_0$) =
$\quad$ **let** $G = \mathbf{ref}\ (\emptyset, \emptyset)$
$\qquad$ $V_{f_i} = \mathbf{ref}\ (\text{FV}(f_i))$, **for each** $(d_i = (f_i \equiv \lambda v_1. \ldots \lambda v_n.e)) \in \{d_1, \ldots, d_k\}$
$\qquad$ $P_{f_i} = \{v_1, \ldots, v_n\}$, **for each** $(d_i = (f_i \equiv \lambda v_1. \ldots \lambda v_n.e)) \in \{d_1, \ldots, d_k\}$
$\quad$ **in foreach** $f_i \in \{f_1, \ldots, f_k\}$ **do**
$\qquad\quad$ **foreach** $g \in \text{FF}(f_i) \cap \{f_1, \ldots, f_k\}$ **do**
$\qquad\qquad$ Graph.add-edge $G\ f_i\ g$
$\qquad$ **let** $(G'\ \mathbf{as}\ (V', E')) = \text{Graph.coalesceSCC } G$
$\qquad\quad$ $\text{succ}_p = \{q \in V' | (p, q) \in E'\}$, **for each** $p \in V'$
$\qquad\quad$ $F_p = \bigcup_{q \in \text{succ}_p} q$, **for each** $p \in V'$
$\qquad\quad$ propagate :: List(Set(FunName)) $\rightarrow$ ()
$\qquad\quad$ propagate $[\,] = ()$
$\qquad\quad$ propagate $(p :: r)$ =
$\qquad\qquad$ **let** $V = (\bigcup_{f \in p} V_f) \cup (\bigcup_{g \in F_p} V_g)$
$\qquad\qquad$ **in foreach** $f \in p$ **do**
$\qquad\qquad\qquad$ $V_f := V \backslash P_f$;
$\qquad\qquad$ (propagate r)
$\qquad$ **in** (propagate (List.reverse (Graph.breadthFirstOrdering G')));
$\qquad\quad$ **let** $S' = S \cup \{(f_1, V_{f_1}), \ldots, (f_k, V_{f_k})\}$
$\qquad\qquad$ $f_s = \text{map (parameterLiftDef } S')\ \{d_1, \ldots, d_k\}$
$\qquad\qquad$ $e_0' = \text{parameterLiftExp } S'\ e_0$
$\qquad\quad$ **in** (LetRec $f_s\ e_0'$)
parameterLiftExp S (If $e_0\ e_1\ e_2$) =
$\qquad$ **let** $e_i' = \text{parameterLiftExp } S\ e_i$, **for each** $e_i \in \{e_0, e_1, e_2\}$
$\qquad$ **in** (If $e_0'\ e_1'\ e_2'$)
parameterLiftExp S f = applySolutionToExp S f
parameterLiftExp S v = v
parameterLiftExp S (x **as** literal) = x
applySolutionToDef :: Set(FunName,Set(Variable)) $\rightarrow$ Def $\rightarrow$ Def
applySolutionToDef $(S\ \mathbf{as}\ \{\ldots, (f, \{v_1, \ldots, v_n\}), \ldots\})$ $(f \equiv \lambda v_1'. \ldots \lambda v_n'.e)$ =
$\qquad$ $(f \equiv \lambda v_1. \ldots \lambda v_n.\lambda v_1'. \ldots \lambda v_n'.e)$
applySolutionToDef S $d = d$
applySolutionToExp :: Set(FunName,Set(Variable)) $\rightarrow$ Exp $\rightarrow$ Exp
applySolutionToExp $(S\ \mathbf{as}\ \{\ldots, (f, \{v_1, \ldots, v_n\}), \ldots\})$ $f = (f\ v_1\ \ldots\ v_n)$
applySolutionToExp S $e = e$

Fig. 5. Parameter lifting: free variables are made parameters

blockFloatProgram :: Program → Program
blockFloatProgram p = foldr makeUnion (map blockFloatDef p) $\emptyset$
blockFloatDef :: Def → (Set(Def),Def)
blockFloatDef $(f \equiv \lambda v_1 \ldots \lambda v_n.e)$ = **let** (F_{new}, e') = blockFloatExp e
$\qquad\qquad\qquad\qquad\qquad\qquad$ **in** $(F_{\text{new}}, f \equiv \lambda v_1 \ldots \lambda v_n.e')$
blockFloatExp :: Exp → (Set(Def),Exp)
blockFloatExp $(e_0 \ldots e_n)$ =
$\qquad\qquad$ **let** (F_i, e_i') = blockFloatExp e_i, **for each** $e_i \in \{e_0, \ldots, e_n\}$
$\qquad\qquad\qquad$ F_{new}= foldr $(\cup)$ $\{F_1, \ldots, F_n\}$ $\emptyset$
$\qquad\qquad$ **in** $(F_{\text{new}}, e_0' \ldots e_n')$
blockFloatExp $(\text{LetRec} \{d, \ldots\} e_0)$ =
$\qquad\qquad$ **let** (F_{new}, e) = blockFloatExp $(\text{LetRec} \{\ldots\} e_0)$
$\qquad\qquad$ **in** $(\{d\} \cup F_{\text{new}}, e)$
blockFloatExp $(\text{LetRec} \emptyset e_0)$ = blockFloatExp e_0
blockFloatExp $(\text{If } e_0 e_1 e_2)$ =
$\qquad\qquad$ **let** (F_i, e_i') = blockFloatExp e_i, **for each** $e_i \in \{e_0, e_1, e_2\}$
$\qquad\qquad$ **in** $(F_0 \cup F_1 \cup F_2, (\text{If } e_0' e_1' e_2'))$
blockFloatExp f = $(\emptyset, f)$
blockFloatExp v = $(\emptyset, v)$
blockFloatExp $(x \text{ as } \underline{\text{literal}})$ = $(\emptyset, x)$
makeUnion :: ((Set(Def),Def),Set(Def)) → Set(Def)
makeUnion $((F_{\text{new}}, d), S)$ = $F_{\text{new}} \cup \{d\} \cup S$

Fig. 6. Block floating: block structure is flattened

When parameter-lifting a set of mutually recursive functions $\{f_1, \ldots, f_k\}$, and some function f_i defines a variable x that is free in one of its callees f_j, a naive algorithm expands the parameter list of the function with x. The sets P_{f_i} used in our parameter-lifting algorithm serve to avoid this problem.

3.5   Revisiting the Example of Section 2.3

Applying the algorithm of Figure 5 to the program of Figure 1 processes the main function by processing its body. The letrec block of the body is processed by first constructing a dependency graph similar to that shown in Figure 2 (except that we simplify the description of the algorithm to not include the sets of free variables in the nodes). Coalescing the strongly connected components of this graph yields a single node containing the three functions. Since there is only a single node, the propagation step only serves to associate each function in the node with the union of the free variables of each of the functions in the component. These variable sets directly give rise to a new set of solutions.

Each of the functions defined in the letrec block and the body of the letrec block are traversed and expanded with the variables indicated by the set of solutions. Block floating according to the algorithm of Figure 6 yields the program of Figure 3.

4   Related Work

We review alternative approaches to handling free variables in higher-order, block-structured programming languages, namely supercombinator conversion, closure conversion, lambda-dropping, and incremental versions of lambda-lifting and closure conversion. Finally, we address the issue of formal correctness.

4.1   Supercombinator Conversion

Peyton Jones's textbook describes the compilation of functional programs towards the G-machine [25]. Functional programs are compiled into supercombinators, which are then processed at run time by graph reduction. Supercombinators are closed lambda-expressions. Supercombinator conversion [17, 24] produces a series of closed terms, and thus differs from lambda-lifting that produces a series of mutually recursive equations where the names of the equations are globally visible.

Peyton Jones also uses strongly connected components for supercombinator conversion. First, dependencies are analyzed in a set of recursive equations. The resulting strongly connected components are then topologically sorted and the recursive equations are rewritten into nested letrec blocks. There are two reasons for this design:

1. it makes type-checking faster and more precise; and
2. it reduces the number of parameters in the ensuing supercombinators.

Supercombinator conversion is then used to process each letrec block, starting outermost and moving inwards. Each function is expanded with its own free variables, and made global under a fresh name. Afterwards, the definition of each function is replaced by an application of the new global function to its free variables, including the new names of any functions used in the body. This application is mutually recursive in the case of mutually recursive functions, relying on the laziness of the source language; it effectively creates a closure for the functions.

Peyton Jones's algorithm thus amounts to first applying dependency analysis to a set of mutually recursive functions and then to perform supercombinator conversion. As for dependency analysis, it is only used to optimize type checking and to minimize the size of closures.

In comparison, applying our algorithm locally to a letrec block would first partition the functions into strongly connected components, like dependency analysis. We use the graph structure, however, to propagate information, not to obtain an ordering of the nodes for creating nested blocks. We also follow Johnsson's algorithm, where the names of the global recursive equations are free in each recursive equations, independently of the evaluation order. Instead,

Johnsson's algorithm passes all the free variables that are needed by a function and its callees, rather than just the free variables of the function.

To sum up, Peyton Jones's algorithm and our revision of Johnsson's algorithm both coalesce strongly connected components in the dependency graph, but for different purposes, our purpose being to reduce the time complexity of lambda-lifting from cubic to quadratic.

4.2 Closure Conversion

The notion of closure originates in Landin's seminal work on functional programming [20]. A closure is a functional value and consists of a pair: a code pointer and an environment holding the denotation of the variables that occur free in this code. Efficient representations of closures are still a research topic today [31].

Closure conversion is a key step in Standard ML of New Jersey [4, 5], and yields scope-insensitive programs. It is akin to supercombinator conversion, though rather than creating a closure through a mutually recursive application, the closure is explicitly created as a vector holding the values of the free variables of the possibly mutually recursive functions.

In his textbook [25], Peyton Jones concluded his discussion between lambda-lifting and supercombinator/closure conversion by pointing out a tension between

- passing all the [denotations of the] free variables of all the callees but not the values of the mutually recursive functions (in lambda-lifting), and
- passing all the values of the mutually recursive functions but not the free variables of the callees (in closure conversion).

He left this tension unresolved, stating that future would tell which algorithm (lambda-lifting or closure conversion) would prevail.

Today we observe that in the compiler world (Haskell, ML, Scheme), closure conversion has prevailed, with only one exception in Scheme [9]. Conversely, in the program-transformation world [8, 10, 22], lambda-lifting has prevailed. We also observe that only for lambda-lifting has an inverse transformation been developed: lambda-dropping.

4.3 Lambda-Dropping

Lambda-dropping is the inverse of lambda-lifting [13]:

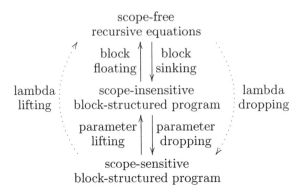

Block floating is reversed by block sinking, which creates block structure by making functions used in only one function local to this function. Parameter lifting is reversed by parameter dropping, which removes redundant formal parameters that are originally defined in an outer scope and that always take on the same value.

Lambda-lifting simplifies the structure of a program. However, a program transformation that employs lambda-lifting as a preprocessing phase tends to output a lambda-lifted program rather than a block-structured one. For one point, the resulting programs are less readable. For another point, compilers are often geared for source programs with few parameters.[1] Therefore, increased numbers of formal parameters often form a major overhead in procedure invocation at run time. Against these odds, lambda-dropping can be applied to re-create block structure and reduce the number of formal parameters.

A few years ago, Appel has pointed out a correspondence between imperative programs in SSA form and functional programs using block structure and lexical scope [2]. Specifically, he has shown how to transform an SSA program into its functional representation.[2] We were struck by the fact that this transformation corresponds to performing block sinking on the recursive equations defining the program. As for the transformation into optimal SSA form (which diminishes the number of Φ-nodes), it is equivalent to parameter dropping. This made us conclude that lambda-dropping can be used to transform programs in SSA form into optimal SSA form [13].

This conclusion prompted us to improve the complexity of the lambda-dropping algorithm to $\mathcal{O}(n \log n)$, where n is the size of the program, by using the dominance graph of the dependency graph. We then re-stated lambda-lifting in a similar framework using graph algorithms, which led us to the result presented in the present article.

Even with the improvement presented in this article, we are still left in an asymmetric situation where lambda-lifting and lambda-dropping do not have

---

[1] For example, the magic numbers of parameters, in OCaml, are 0 to 7.

[2] The point is made comprehensively in his SIGPLAN Notices note, which is also available in his home page [3].

the same time complexity. With some thought, though, this asymmetry is not so surprising, since lambda-dropping is applied to the output of lambda-lifting, and the complexity is measured in terms of the size of the output program. Measuring the complexity of lambda-dropping in terms of the size of the program before lambda-lifting yields a relative time complexity of lambda-dropping of $\mathcal{O}((n^2)\log(n^2))$, which is $\mathcal{O}(n^2 \log n)$, a fitting match for the $\mathcal{O}(n^2 \log n)$ time complexity of lambda-lifting.

4.4 Mixed Style

In order to preserve code locality, compilers such as Twobit [9] or Moby [26] often choose to lift parameters only partially. The result is in the mixed style described at the end of Section 1.1.

In more detail, rather than lifting all the free variables of the program to become formal parameters, parameter lifting is used incrementally to transform programs by lifting only a subset of the free variables of each function. If a function is to be moved to a different scope, however, it needs to be passed the free variables of its callees as parameters. As was the case for global lambda-lifting, propagating the additional parameters through the dependency graph requires cubic time. To improve the time complexity, our quadratic-time parameter-lifting algorithm can be applied to the subsets of the free variables instead. The improvement in time complexity for incremental lambda-lifting is the same as what we observed for the global algorithm.

We note that a partial version of closure conversion also exists, namely Steckler and Wand's [32], that leaves some variables free in a closure because this closure is always applied in the scope of these variables. We also note that combinator-based compilers [34] could be seen as using a partial supercombinator conversion.

4.5 Correctness Issues

Only idealized versions of lambda-lifting and lambda-dropping have been formally proven correct. Danvy has related lambda-lifted and lambda-dropped functionals and their fixed point [12]. Fischbach and Hannan have capitalized on the symmetry of lambda-lifting and lambda-dropping to formalize them in a logical framework, for a simply typed and recursion-free source language [15].

Overall, though, and while there is little doubt about Johnsson's original algorithm, its semantic correctness still remains to be established.

5 Conclusion and Future Work

We have shown that a transitive closure is not needed for lambda-lifting. In this article, we have reformulated lambda-lifting as a graph algorithm and improved its time complexity from $\mathcal{O}(n^3 \log n)$ to $\mathcal{O}(n^2 \log n)$, where n is the size of the program. Based on a simple example where lambda-lifting generates a program of size $\mathcal{O}(n^2)$, we have also demonstrated that our improved complexity is close to optimal.

The quadratic-time algorithm can replace the cubic-time instances of lambda-lifting in any partial evaluator or compiler, be it for global or for incremental lambda-lifting.

As for future work, we are investigating lambda-lifting in the context of object-oriented languages. Although block structure is instrumental in object-oriented languages such as Java, Beta and Simula [11, 16, 21], existing work on partial evaluation for object-oriented languages has not addressed the issue of block structure [28, 29, 30]. Problems similar to those found in partial evaluation for functional languages appear to be unavoidable: residual methods generated in a local context may need to be invoked outside of the scope of their class. Side effects, however, complicate matters.

Acknowledgements

We are grateful to Lars R. Clausen, Daniel Damian, and Laurent Réveillère for their comments on an earlier version of this article. Thanks are also due to the anonymous referees for very perceptive and useful reviews.

This work is supported by the ESPRIT Working Group APPSEM (http://www.md.chalmers.se/Cs/Research/Semantics/APPSEM/).

A   Graph Algorithms

The description of the algorithm for parameter lifting (Figure 5) makes use of a number of graph and list algorithms. We give a short description of each of these algorithms in Figure 7.

Graph.add-edge :: $\mathsf{Graph}(\alpha) \to (\alpha, \alpha) \to (\alpha, \alpha)$
Graph.add-edge G (n_1, n_2) : Updates G to contain the nodes n_1 and n_2 as well as an edge between the two.
Graph.coalesceSCC :: $\mathsf{Graph}(\alpha) \to \mathsf{Graph}(\mathsf{Set}(\alpha))$
Graph.coalesceSCC G : Returns G with its strongly connected components coalesced into sets [1].
Graph.breadthFirstOrdering :: $\mathsf{Graph}(\alpha) \to \mathsf{List}(\alpha)$
Graph.breadthFirstOrdering G : Returns a list containing the nodes of G, in a breadth-first ordering.
List.reverse :: $\mathsf{List}(\alpha) \to \mathsf{List}(\alpha)$
List.reverse L : Returns L with its elements reversed.

Fig. 7. Graph and list functions

References

[1] Alfred V. Aho, Ravi Sethi, and Jeffrey D. Ullman. *Compilers: Principles, Techniques and Tools*. Addison-Wesley, 1986. 148

[2] Andrew W. Appel. *Modern Compiler Implementation in {C, Java, ML}*. Cambridge University Press, New York, 1998. 146

[3] Andrew W. Appel. SSA is functional programming. *ACM SIGPLAN Notices*, 33(4):17–20, April 1998. 146

[4] Andrew W. Appel and Trevor Jim. Continuation-passing, closure-passing style. In Michael J. O'Donnell and Stuart Feldman, editors, *Proceedings of the Sixteenth Annual ACM Symposium on Principles of Programming Languages*, pages 293–302, Austin, Texas, January 1989. ACM Press. 145

[5] Andrew W. Appel and David B. MacQueen. Standard ML of New Jersey. In Jan Małuszyński and Martin Wirsing, editors, *Third International Symposium on Programming Language Implementation and Logic Programming*, number 528 in Lecture Notes in Computer Science, pages 1–13, Passau, Germany, August 1991. Springer-Verlag. 145

[6] Lennart Augustsson. A compiler for Lazy ML. In Guy L. Steele Jr., editor, *Conference Record of the 1984 ACM Symposium on Lisp and Functional Programming*, pages 218–227, Austin, Texas, August 1984. ACM Press. 134

[7] Adam Bakewell and Colin Runciman. Automatic generalisation of function definitions. In Middeldorp and Sato [23], pages 225–240. 135

[8] Anders Bondorf and Olivier Danvy. Automatic autoprojection of recursive equations with global variables and abstract data types. *Science of Computer Programming*, 16:151–195, 1991. 135, 145

[9] William Clinger and Lars Thomas Hansen. Lambda, the ultimate label, or a simple optimizing compiler for Scheme. In Talcott [33], pages 128–139. 135, 145, 147

[10] Charles Consel. A tour of Schism: A partial evaluation system for higher-order applicative languages. In David A. Schmidt, editor, *Proceedings of the Second ACM SIGPLAN Symposium on Partial Evaluation and Semantics-Based Program Manipulation*, pages 145–154, Copenhagen, Denmark, June 1993. ACM Press. 135, 145

[11] Ole-Johan Dahl, Bjørn Myhrhaug, and Kristen Nygaard. *Simula: Common Base Language*. Norwegian Computing Center, October 1970. 148

[12] Olivier Danvy. An extensional characterization of lambda-lifting and lambda-dropping. In Middeldorp and Sato [23], pages 241–250. Extended version available as the technical report BRICS RS-99-21. 147

[13] Olivier Danvy and Ulrik P. Schultz. Lambda-dropping: Transforming recursive equations into programs with block structure. *Theoretical Computer Science*, 248(1-2):243–287, 2000. 145, 146

[14] Olivier Danvy and Ulrik P. Schultz. Lambda-lifting in quadratic time. Technical Report BRICS RS-02-30, Department of Computer Science, University of Aarhus, Aarhus, Denmark, June 2002. 134

[15] Adam Fischbach and John Hannan. Specification and correctness of lambda lifting. In Walid Taha, editor, *Proceedings of the First Workshop on Semantics, Applications, and Implementation of Program Generation (SAIG 2000)*, number 1924 in Lecture Notes in Computer Science, pages 108–128, Montréal, Canada, September 2000. Springer-Verlag. 147

[16] James Gosling, Bill Joy, and Guy Steele. *The Java Language Specification*. Addison-Wesley, 1996. 148

[17] John Hughes. Super combinators: A new implementation method for applicative languages. In Daniel P. Friedman and David S. Wise, editors, *Conference Record of the 1982 ACM Symposium on Lisp and Functional Programming*, pages 1–10, Pittsburgh, Pennsylvania, August 1982. ACM Press. 134, 144

[18] Thomas Johnsson. Lambda lifting: Transforming programs to recursive equations. In Jean-Pierre Jouannaud, editor, *Functional Programming Languages and Computer Architecture*, number 201 in Lecture Notes in Computer Science, pages 190–203, Nancy, France, September 1985. Springer-Verlag. 134, 137

[19] Thomas Johnsson. *Compiling Lazy Functional Languages*. PhD thesis, Department of Computer Sciences, Chalmers University of Technology, Göteborg, Sweden, 1987. 137

[20] Peter J. Landin. The mechanical evaluation of expressions. *Computer Journal*, 6:308–320, 1964. 145

[21] Ole L. Madsen, Birger Møller-Pedersen, and Kristen Nygaard. *Object-oriented programming in the Beta programming language*. Addison-Wesley, Reading, MA, USA, 1993. 148

[22] Karoline Malmkjær, Nevin Heintze, and Olivier Danvy. ML partial evaluation using set-based analysis. In John Reppy, editor, *Record of the 1994 ACM SIGPLAN Workshop on ML and its Applications, Rapport de recherche N° 2265, INRIA*, pages 112–119, Orlando, Florida, June 1994. Also appears as Technical report CMU-CS-94-129. 135, 145

[23] Aart Middeldorp and Taisuke Sato, editors. *Fourth Fuji International Symposium on Functional and Logic Programming*, number 1722 in Lecture Notes in Computer Science, Tsukuba, Japan, November 1999. Springer-Verlag. 149

[24] Simon L. Peyton Jones. An introduction to fully-lazy supercombinators. In Guy Cousineau, Pierre-Louis Curien, and Bernard Robinet, editors, *Combinators and Functional Programming Languages*, number 242 in Lecture Notes in Computer Science, pages 176–208, Val d'Ajol, France, 1985. Springer-Verlag. 144

[25] Simon L. Peyton Jones. *The Implementation of Functional Programming Languages*. Prentice Hall International Series in Computer Science. Prentice-Hall International, 1987. 134, 138, 144, 145

[26] John Reppy. Local CPS conversion in a direct-style compiler. In Amr Sabry, editor, *Proceedings of the Third ACM SIGPLAN Workshop on Continuations*, Technical report 545, Computer Science Department, Indiana University, pages 1–6, London, England, January 2001. 135, 147

[27] André Santos. *Compilation by transformation in non-strict functional languages*. PhD thesis, Department of Computing, University of Glasgow, Glasgow, Scotland, 1996. 135

[28] Ulrik P. Schultz. *Object-Oriented Software Engineering Using Partial Evaluation*. PhD thesis, University of Rennes I, Rennes, France, 2000. 148

[29] Ulrik P. Schultz. Partial evaluation for class-based object-oriented languages. In Olivier Danvy and Andrzej Filinski, editors, *Programs as Data Objects, Second Symposium, PADO 2001*, number 2053 in Lecture Notes in Computer Science, pages 173–197, Aarhus, Denmark, May 2001. Springer-Verlag. 148

[30] Ulrik P. Schultz, Julia Lawall, Charles Consel, and Gilles Muller. Towards automatic specialization of Java programs. In Rachid Guerraoui, editor, *Proceedings of the European Conference on Object-oriented Programming (ECOOP'99)*, volume 1628 of *Lecture Notes in Computer Science*, pages 367–390, Lisbon, Portugal, June 1999. Springer-Verlag. 148

[31] Zhong Shao and Andrew W. Appel. Space-efficient closure representations. In Talcott [33], pages 150–161. 145

[32] Paul A. Steckler and Mitchell Wand. Lightweight closure conversion. *ACM Transactions on Programming Languages and Systems*, 19(1):48–86, 1997. 147

[33] Carolyn L. Talcott, editor. *Proceedings of the 1994 ACM Conference on Lisp and Functional Programming*, LISP Pointers, Vol. VII, No. 3, Orlando, Florida, June 1994. ACM Press. 149, 151

[34] Mitchell Wand. From interpreter to compiler: a representational derivation. In Harald Ganzinger and Neil D. Jones, editors, *Programs as Data Objects*, number 217 in Lecture Notes in Computer Science, pages 306–324, Copenhagen, Denmark, October 1985. Springer-Verlag. 147

The Well-Founded Semantics in Normal Logic Programs with Uncertainty

Yann Loyer and Umberto Straccia

Istituto di Elaborazione della Informazione -C.N.R.
Via G. Moruzzi,1 I-56124 Pisa (PI) ITALY

Abstract. Many frameworks of logic programming have been proposed to manage uncertain information in deductive databases and expert systems. Roughly, on the basis of how uncertainty is associated to facts and the rules in a program, they can be classified into *implication-based* (IB) and *annotation-based* (AB). However, one fundamental issue that remains unaddressed in the IB approach is the representation and the manipulation of the non-monotonic mode of negation, an important feature for real applications. Our focus in this paper is to introduce non-monotonic negation in the *parametric* IB framework, a unifying umbrella for IB frameworks. The semantical approach that we will adopt is based on the well-founded semantics, one of the most widely studied and used semantics of (classical) logic programs with negation.

1 Introduction

The management of uncertainty within deduction systems is an important issue in all those AI application domains in which the real world information to be represented is of imperfect nature (which is likely the rule rather than an exception). An impressive work has been carried out in the last decades, resulting in a number of concepts being investigated, a number of problems being identified and a number of solutions being developed (see, *e.g.* [1, 6, 17, 29]).

First-Order Logic (FOL) has been the basis for most knowledge representation formalisms. Its basic units –individuals, their properties, and the relationship between them– naturally capture the way in which people encode their knowledge. Unfortunately, it is severely limited in its ability to represent our uncertainty about the world: a fact can only be known to be true, known to be false or neither. By contrast, most of our knowledge about the real world is not absolutely true. Additionally, practical considerations dictate that the framework used for knowledge representation with uncertainty admit efficient implementation and efficient computations. Logic database programming, with its advantage of modularity and its powerful top-down and bottom-up query processing techniques, has attracted the attention of researchers and numerous frameworks for deductive databases with uncertainty have been proposed [2, 4, 5, 9, 10, 14, 15, 16, 18, 19, 20, 21, 22, 25, 26, 27, 35, 36, 37, 38, 39], where the underlying uncertainty formalism include probability theory [10, 19, 22, 25, 26, 27, 39], fuzzy set theory [2, 35, 37, 38], multi-valued logic [9, 15, 16, 20, 21] and possibilistic

Z. Hu and M. Rodríguez-Artalejo (Eds.): FLOPS 2002, LNCS 2441, pp. 152–166, 2002.

logic [5]. Roughly, based on the way in which uncertainty is associated with the facts and rules of a program, these frameworks can be classified into *annotation based* (AB) and *implication based* (IB).

In the AB approach (se *e.g.* [15, 16, 25, 26, 27, 36]), a rule is of the form

$$A : f(\beta_1, \ldots, \beta_n) \leftarrow B_1 : \beta_1, \ldots, B_n : \beta_n$$

which asserts "the certainty of the atom A is at least (or is in) $f(\beta_1, \ldots, \beta_n)$, whenever the certainty of the atom B_i is at least (or is in) β_i, $1 \leq i \leq n$", where f is an n-ary computable function and β_i is either a constant or a variable ranging over an appropriate certainty domain.

On the other hand, in the IB approach (see *e.g.* [7, 9, 18, 19, 20, 37]), a rule is of the form

$$A \stackrel{\alpha}{\leftarrow} B_1, \ldots, B_n$$

which says that the certainty associated with the implication $B_1 \wedge \ldots \wedge B_n \to A$ is α. Computationally, given an assignment I of certainties to the B_is, the certainty of A is computed by taking the "conjunction" of the certainties $I(B_i)$ and then somehow "propagating" it to the rule head. It is not our aim to compare the two approaches in this paper. Refer to [20] for an exhaustive comparison. We limit our contribution in this sense to recall the following facts [20]: (i) while the way implication is treated in the AB approach is closer to classical logic, the way rules are fired in the IB approach has a definite intuitive appeal and (ii) the AB approach is strictly more expressive than the IB. The down side is that query processing in the AB approach is more complicated, *e.g.* the fixpoint operator is not continuous in general, while it is in the IB approaches. From the above points, it is believed that the IB approach is easier to use and is more amenable for efficient implementation.

However, one fundamental issue that remains still unaddressed in the IB approach is the representation and the manipulation of the non-monotonic mode of *default negation, not A*, an without doubts important feature to be used in applications. The major distinctive feature is that *not A* is assumed in the absence of sufficient evidence to the contrary. The meaning of "sufficient evidence" depends on the specific semantics used. Due to its importance, the problem of negation in logic programs has attracted many researchers and a broad variety of semantical approaches have been invented. For example, in Reiter's *Closed World Assumption* [34], *not A* is assumed for atomic A if A is not provable, or, equivalently, if there is a minimal model in which A is false. On the other hand, in Minker's *Generalised Closed World Assumption* [24, 13], or in McCarthy's *Circumscription*, [23], *not A* is assumed only if A is false in *all* minimal models. In Clark's *Predicate Completion* semantics for logic programs [3] this form of negation is called *negation-as-failure* because *not A* is derived whenever attempts to prove A finitely fail. The more recent semantics proposed for logic programs and deductive databases, such as the *stable semantics* [12], *well-founded semantics* [28], *partial stable* or *stationary semantics* [33], and *static semantics* [30], propose even more sophisticated meanings for default negation.

Contributions: We will extend the *parametric* IB framework [20], a unifying umbrella for IB frameworks, with default negation. The semantical approach that we will adopt is based on the well-founded semantics, one of the most widely studied and used semantics of (classical) logic programs with negation. From a semantics point of view, we will combine an alternating fixpoint semantics similar to [11] with the fixpoint characterisation of [20]. We will show that in case of positive programs, the *parametric* IB framework is obtained, while restricting logic programs to Datalog programs, the classical well-founded semantics is obtained, *i.e.* our extension is a conservative extension.

The use of default negation has already been considered in some deductive databases with uncertainty frameworks. For instance, in [25], the stable semantics has been considered within the AB approach, but limited to the case where the underlying uncertainty formalism is probability theory. The stable semantics has been considered also in [38], where a semi-possibilistic logic has been proposed. In it, a particular negation operator has been introduced and a fixed min/max-evaluation of conjunction and disjunction is adopted. To the best of our knowledge, there is no work dealing with default negation within the parametric IB approach.

The remaining part of the paper is organized as follows. The syntax of programs, called normal parametric programs, is given in Section 2. In Section 3 the notions of interpretation and model of a program are defined, while Section 4, we define the intended model of a normal parametric program and show that our semantics extends the well-founded semantics [28] and the Shiri-Lakshmanan's semantics [20] to normal parametric programs. Section 5 contains concluding remarks.

2   Preliminaries

We recall the syntactical aspects of the parametric IB framework presented in [20] and extend it with negation.

Consider an arbitrary first order language that contains infinitely many variable symbols, finitely many constants, and predicate symbols, but no function symbols. The predicate symbol $\pi(A)$ of an atomic formula A given by $A = p(X_1, \ldots, X_n)$ is defined by $\pi(A) = p$. While the language does not contain function symbols, it contains symbols for families of propagation ($\mathcal{F}_p$), conjunction ($\mathcal{F}_c$) and disjunction functions ($\mathcal{F}_d$), called *combination functions*.

Let $\mathcal{L} = \langle \mathcal{T}, \preceq, \otimes, \oplus \rangle$ be a certainty lattice (a complete lattice), where $\mathcal{T}$ is a set of truth values, and let $\mathcal{B}(\mathcal{T})$ the set of finite multisets over $\mathcal{T}$ (multisets are indicated with $\{\cdot\}$). With $\perp$ and $\top$ we denote the least and greatest element in $\mathcal{T}$, respectively. A *propagation function* is a mapping from $\mathcal{T} \times \mathcal{T}$ to $\mathcal{T}$ and a *conjunction* or *disjunction* function is a mapping from $\mathcal{B}(\mathcal{T})$ to $\mathcal{T}$. Each kind of function must verify some of the following properties[1]:

---

[1] For simplicity, we formulate the properties treating any function as a binary function on $\mathcal{T}$.

1. monotonicity w.r.t. (with respect to) each one of its arguments;
2. continuity w.r.t. each one of its arguments;
3. bounded-above: $f(\alpha_1, \alpha_2) \preceq \alpha_i$, for $i = 1, 2, \forall \alpha_1, \alpha_2 \in \mathcal{T}$;
4. bounded-below: $f(\alpha_1, \alpha_2) \succeq \alpha_i$, for $i = 1, 2, \forall \alpha_1, \alpha_2 \in \mathcal{T}$;
5. commutativity: $f(\alpha_1, \alpha_2) = f(\alpha_2, \alpha_1), \forall \alpha_1, \alpha_2 \in \mathcal{T}$;
6. associativity: $f(\alpha_1, f(\alpha_2, \alpha_3)) = f(f(\alpha_1, \alpha_2), \alpha_3), \forall \alpha_1, \alpha_2, \alpha_3 \in \mathcal{T}$;
7. $f(\{\alpha\}) = \alpha, \forall \alpha \in \mathcal{T}$;
8. $f(\emptyset) = \bot$;
9. $f(\emptyset) = \top$;
10. $f(\alpha, \top) = \alpha, \forall \alpha \in \mathcal{T}$;

As postulated in [20]:

1. a conjunction function in $\mathcal{F}_c$ should satisfy properties 1, 2, 3, 5, 6, 7, 9 and 10;
2. a propagation function in $\mathcal{F}_p$ should satisfy properties 1, 2, 3 and 10;
3. a disjunction function in $\mathcal{F}_d$ should satisfy properties 1, 2, 4, 5, 6, 7 and 8.

We also assume that there is a function from $\mathcal{T}$ to $\mathcal{T}$, called *negation function* and denoted $\neg$, that is anti-monotone w.r.t. $\preceq$ and satisfies $\neg\neg\alpha = \alpha, \forall \alpha \in \mathcal{T}$ and $\neg\bot = \top$.

Definition 1 (Normal parametric program). *A normal parametric program P (np-program) is a 5-tuple $\langle \mathcal{L}, \mathcal{R}, \mathcal{C}, \mathcal{P}, \mathcal{D} \rangle$, whose components are defined as follows:*

1. *$\mathcal{L} = \langle \mathcal{T}, \preceq, \otimes, \oplus \rangle$ is a complete lattice, where $\mathcal{T}$ is a set of truth-values partially ordered by $\preceq$, $\otimes$ is the meet operator and $\oplus$ the join operator. We denote the least element of the lattice by $\bot$ and the greatest element by $\top$;*
2. *$\mathcal{R}$ is a finite set of* normal parametric rules *(np-rules), each of which is a statement of the form:*

$$r : A \xleftarrow{\alpha_r} B_1, ..., B_n, \neg C_1, ..., \neg C_m$$

   where A is an atomic formula and $B_1, ..., B_n, C_1, ..., C_m$ are atomic formulas or values in $\mathcal{T}$ and $\alpha_r \in \mathcal{T} \setminus \{\bot\}$ is the certainty of the rule;
3. *$\mathcal{C}$ is a mapping that associates with each np-rule a conjunction function in $\mathcal{F}_c$;*
4. *$\mathcal{P}$ is a mapping that associates with each np-rule a propagation function in $\mathcal{F}_p$;*
5. *$\mathcal{D}$ is a mapping that associates with each predicate symbol in P a disjunction function in $\mathcal{F}_d$.* □

For ease of presentation, we write

$$r : A \xleftarrow{\alpha_r} B_1, ..., B_n, \neg C_1, ..., \neg C_m; \langle f_d, f_p, f_c \rangle$$

to represent a np-rule in which $f_d \in \mathcal{F}_d$ is the disjunction function associated with the predicate symbol $\pi(A)$ of A and, $f_c \in \mathcal{F}_c$ and $f_p \in \mathcal{F}_p$ are respectively the conjunction and propagation functions associated with r. The intention is that the conjunction function ($e.g.$ $\otimes$) determines the truth value of the conjunction of $B_1, ..., B_n, \neg C_1, ..., \neg C_m$, the propagation function ($e.g.$ $\otimes$) determines how to "propagate" the truth value resulting from the evaluation of the body to the head, by taking into account the certainty α_r associated to the rule r, while the disjunction function ($e.g.$ $\oplus$) dictates how to combine the certainties in case an atom appears in the heads of several rules.

We further define the *Herbrand base* $\mathcal{HB}_P$ of an np-program P as the set of all instantiated atoms corresponding to atoms appearing in P and define P^* to be the *Herbrand instantiation of P*, $i.e.$ the set of all ground instantiations of the rules in P. We can note that any classical logic program P is equivalent to the np-program constructed by replacing each classical rule in P of the form

$$A \leftarrow B_1, ..., B_n, \neg C_1, ..., \neg C_m$$

by the rule

$$r : A \overset{t}{\leftarrow} B_1, ..., B_n, \neg C_1, ..., \neg C_m; \langle \oplus, \otimes, \otimes \rangle$$

where $\mathcal{T} = \{f, t\}$, $\preceq$ is defined by $f \preceq t$, $\oplus = max_\preceq$, $\otimes = min_\preceq$, $\neg f = t$ and $\neg t = f$.

Example 1. The following example describes a legal case where a judge has to decide whether to charge a person named John accused of murder. To do so, the judge collects facts that he combines using an np-program in order to reach a decision.

Consider the complete lattice $\langle \mathcal{T}, \preceq, \otimes, \oplus \rangle$, where $\mathcal{T}$ is $[0,1]$, $\forall, a, b \in [0,1]$, $a \preceq b$ iff $a \leq b$, $a \otimes b = \min(a, b)$, and $a \oplus b = \max(a, b)$. Consider the disjunction function $f_d(\alpha, \beta) = \alpha + \beta - \alpha \cdot \beta$, the conjunction function $f_c(\alpha, \beta) = \alpha \cdot \beta$ and the propagation function $f_p = f_c$. The negation function is the usual function $\neg(\alpha) = 1 - \alpha$. Then the following is an np-program P:[2]

$$
P = \left\{
\begin{array}{lll}
\texttt{suspect(X)} & \overset{0.6}{\leftarrow} \texttt{motive(X)} & \langle f_d, \otimes, - \rangle \\
\texttt{suspect(X)} & \overset{0.8}{\leftarrow} \texttt{witness(X)} & \langle f_d, \otimes, - \rangle \\
\texttt{innocent(X)} & \overset{1}{\leftarrow} \texttt{alibi(X,Y)} \wedge \neg\texttt{friends(X,Y)} & \langle f_d, f_p, \otimes \rangle \\
\texttt{friends(X,Y)} & \overset{1}{\leftarrow} \texttt{friends(Y,X)} & \langle \oplus, f_p, - \rangle \\
\texttt{friends(X,Y)} & \overset{0.7}{\leftarrow} \texttt{friends(X,Z)} \wedge \texttt{friends(Z,Y)} & \langle \oplus, f_p, f_c \rangle \\
\texttt{charge(X)} & \overset{1}{\leftarrow} \texttt{suspect(X)}, \neg\texttt{innocent(X)} & \langle \oplus, f_p, - \rangle \\
\texttt{motive(John)} & \overset{1}{\leftarrow} 0.8 & \langle \oplus, f_p, - \rangle \\
\texttt{alibi(John,Sam)} & \overset{1}{\leftarrow} 1 & \langle \oplus, f_p, - \rangle \\
\texttt{friends(John,Ted)} & \overset{1}{\leftarrow} 0.8 & \langle \oplus, f_p, - \rangle \\
\texttt{friends(Sam,Ted)} & \overset{1}{\leftarrow} 0.6 & \langle \oplus, f_p, - \rangle
\end{array}
\right\}
$$

---

[2] The symbol $-$ instead of a function denotes the facts that this function is not relevant. Note that any conjunction function is also a propagation function.

Some comments on the rules. The two first rules of R describe how a person X is shown to be a suspect, *i.e.* by providing a motive (first rule) or a witness against X (second rule). The third rule of R describes how a person X is shown to be innocent, *i.e.* by providing an alibi for X by a person who is not a friend of X. The fourth and fifth rules describe the relation `friend`. Finally, the sixth rule of P is the "decision making rule" and the last rules are the facts collected by the judge. Note that *e.g.* for predicate `suspect`, the disjunction function f_d is associated, as if there are different ways to infer that someone is suspect, then we would like to increase (summing up) our suspicion and not just to choose the maximal value. In the fifth rule, the function f_p allows us to infer some friendship relations taking into account the fact that friendship decreases with transitivity. Moreover, the rules are associated to different propagation coefficients and functions corresponding to the reliability we associate to the information inferred from those rules.   □

3   Interpretations of Programs

An interpretation of an np-program P is a function that assigns to all atoms of the Herbrand base of P a value in $\mathcal{T}$. We denote $\mathcal{V}_P(\mathcal{T})$ the set of all interpretations of P.

An important issue is to determine which is the intended meaning or semantics of an np-program. Following the usual approach, the semantics of a program P is determined by selecting a particular interpretation of P in the set of models of P. In logic programs without negation, as well as in the parametric IB framework, that chosen model is usually the least model of P w.r.t. $\preceq$.

Introducing negation in classical logic programs, some np-programs do not have a unique minimal model, as shown in the following examples.

Example 2. Let P be the classical program defined by the two rules

$$A \leftarrow \neg B$$
$$B \leftarrow \neg A$$

The program P has two minimal models: $I_1 = \{A\colon f, B\colon t\}$ and $I_2 = \{A\colon t, B\colon f\}$ that are not comparable w.r.t. the truth ordering.   □

Of course, we can observe the same problem in our parametric IB framework as shown in the following example.

Example 3. Let $\mathcal{T}$ be $[0,1]$. Consider, as usual, $f_c(\alpha, \beta) = \min(\alpha, \beta)$, $f_d(\alpha, \beta) = \max(\alpha, \beta)$, $f_p(\alpha, \beta) = \alpha \cdot \beta$ and the usual negation function. Consider the program P defined by the following rules :

$$A \xleftarrow{1} \neg B; \langle f_d, f_p, - \rangle$$
$$B \xleftarrow{1} \neg A; \langle f_d, f_p, - \rangle$$
$$A \xleftarrow{1} 0.2; \langle f_d, f_p, - \rangle$$
$$B \xleftarrow{1} 0.3; \langle f_d, f_p, - \rangle$$

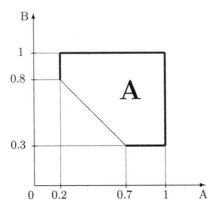

Fig. 1. Infinite minimal models

This program will have an infinite number of models I_x^y, where $0.2 \leq x \leq 1$, $0.3 \leq y \leq 1$, $y \geq 1 - x$, $I_x^y(A) = x$ and $I_x^y(B) = y$ (those in the A area in Figure 1). There are also an infinite number of minimal models (those on the thin diagonal line) according to the order $(a, b) \preceq (c, d)$ iff $a \preceq c$ and $b \preceq d$. These minimal models I_x^y are such that $y = 1 - x$. □

Concerning the previous example we may note that the truth value of A in the minimal models is in the interval $[0.2, 0.7]$, while for B the interval is $[0.3, 0.8]$. An obvious question is: what should the response to a query A to the program in Example 3 be? There are at least two answers:

1. the truth value of A is *undefined*, as there is no unique minimal model. This is clearly a conservative approach, which in case of ambiguity prefers to leave A unspecified;
2. the truth value of A is in $[0.2, 0.7]$, which means that even if there is no unique value for A, in all minimal models the truth of A is in $[0.2, 0.7]$. In this approach we still try to provide some information. Of course, some care should be used. Indeed from $I(A) \in [0.2, 0.7]$ and $I(B) \in [0.3, 0.8]$ we should not conclude that $I(A) = 0.2$ and $I(B) = 0.3$ is a model of the program.

In this paper we address solution 1. and leave solution 2. for future work. In order to allow some atom's truth value to be unspecified, we will introduce *partial interpretations*: partial interpretations correspond to interpretations that assign values only to some atoms of $\mathcal{HB}_P$ and are not defined for the other atoms.

Definition 2 (Partial interpretation). *Let P be an np-program. A partial interpretation I of P is a partial function from $\mathcal{HB}_P$ to $\mathcal{T}$.* □

A partial interpretation I can be seen as a set $\{A : \mu \mid A \in \mathcal{HB}_P \text{ and } \mu \in \mathcal{T}\}$, such that each atom in $\mathcal{HB}_P$ appears at most once in that set, defined by: for all ground atoms A, $A : \mu \in I$ if $I(A) = \mu$. Of course, an interpretation is a partial interpretation. Interpretations and partial interpretations will be used as functions or as sets following the context.

In the following, given an np-program P, given an interpretation I such that each premise in the body is defined under I, (i) with r_A we denote a rule $(r : A \xleftarrow{\alpha_r} B_1, ..., B_n, \neg C_1, ..., \neg C_m; \langle f_d, f_p, f_c \rangle) \in P^*$, whose head is A; and (ii) with $I(r_A)$ we denote the evaluation of the body of r_A w.r.t. I, $i.e.$

$$I(r_A) = f_p(\alpha_r, f_c(\{I(B_1), \ldots, I(B_n), \neg I(C_1), \ldots, \neg I(C_m)\}))$$

$I(r_A)$ is undefined in case some premise in the body is undefined in I, except for the case where there is an i such that $I(B_i) = \bot$ or $I(C_i) = \top$. In that case, we define $I(r_A) = \bot$.

Definition 3 (Satisfaction of an np-program). *Let P be an np-program and let I be a partial interpretation of P. Then we say that I satisfies (is a model of) P, denoted $\models_I P$, iff $\forall A \in \mathcal{HB}_P$:*

1. *if there is a rule $r_A \in P^*$ such that $I(r_A) = \top$, then $I(A) = \top$;*
2. *if $I(r_A)$ is defined for all rules $r_A \in P^*$, then $I(A) \succeq f_d(\{I(r_A)|r_A \in P^*\})$, where f_d is the disjunction function associated with $\pi(A)$, the predicate symbol of A.* □

Example 4. For the program P in Example 2, it is easily verified that the interpretations $I_1 = \{A\colon f, B\colon t\}$, $I_2 = \{A\colon t, B\colon f\}$ and $I_3 = \emptyset$ are models of P.

For the program P in Example 3, the interpretations I_x^y such that $0.2 \leq x \leq 1$, $0.3 \leq y \leq 1$, $y \geq 1 - x$, $I_x^y(A) = x$ and $I_x^y(A) = y$ are all models of P. Note that the interpretation $I_4 = \emptyset$ is also a model of P. □

It is worth noting that if we restrict our attention to positive programs only then the definition reduces to that presented in [20] if the interpretation I is not partial but defined for all atoms in $\mathcal{HB}_P$.

4   Alternating Fixpoint and Compromise Semantics

In this section we will define our well-founded semantics for np-programs.

4.1   Immediate Consequence Operators

First, we extend the ordering on $\mathcal{T}$ to the space of interpretations $\mathcal{V}_P(\mathcal{T})$. Let I_1 and I_2 be in $\mathcal{V}_P(\mathcal{T})$, then $I_1 \preceq I_2$ if and only if $I_1(A) \preceq I_2(A)$ for all ground atoms A. Under this ordering $\mathcal{V}_P(\mathcal{T})$ becomes a complete lattice, and we have $(I_1 \otimes I_2)(A) = I_1(A) \otimes I_2(A)$, and similarly for the other operators. The actions of functions can be extended from atoms to formulas as follows: $I(f_c(X, Y)) = f_c(I(X), I(Y))$, and similarly for the other functions. Finally, for all α in $\mathcal{T}$ and for all I in $\mathcal{V}_P(\mathcal{T})$, $I(\alpha) = \alpha$.

We now define a new operator T_P inspired by [8, 30, 31, 32]. It infers new information from two interpretations: the first one is used to evaluate the positive literals, while the second one is used to evaluate the negative literals of the bodies of rules in P.

Definition 4. *Let P be any np-program. The* immediate consequence operator *T_P is a mapping from $\mathcal{V}_P(\mathcal{T}) \times \mathcal{V}_P(\mathcal{T})$ to $\mathcal{V}_P(\mathcal{T})$, defined as follows: for every pair (I, J) of interpretations in $\mathcal{V}_P(\mathcal{T})$, for every atom A, $T_P(I, J)(A) = f_d(X)$, where f_d is the disjunction function associated with $\pi(A)$, the predicate symbol of A, and*

$$X = \{f_p(\alpha_r, f_c(\{I(B_1), \ldots, I(B_n), \neg J(C_1), \ldots, \neg J(C_m)\})) :$$
$$(r : A \stackrel{\alpha_r}{\leftarrow} B_1, \ldots, B_n, \neg C_1, \ldots, \neg C_m; \langle f_d, f_p, f_c \rangle) \in P^*\}$$

□

Note that the T_P operator applies to interpretations only and not to partial interpretations. Additionally, the interpretation $T_P(I, J)$ is in $\mathcal{V}_P(\mathcal{T})$.

It is easy to prove that

Proposition 1. *Let P be any np-program. T_P is monotonic in its first argument, and anti-monotone in its second argument w.r.t. $\preceq$.*   □

4.2   Compromise Semantics of an np-Program

Using Proposition 1 and the Knaster-Tarski theorem, we can define an operator S_P, inspired from [11] and derived from T_P, that takes an interpretation J as input, first evaluates the negative literals of the program w.r.t. J, and then returns the minimal model of the resulting "positive" np-program w.r.t. $\preceq$.

Let $I_\perp$ be the interpretation that assigns the value $\perp$ to all atoms of $\mathcal{HB}_P$, *i.e.* the minimal element of $\mathcal{V}_P(\mathcal{T})$ w.r.t. $\preceq$, while let $I_\top$ be the interpretation that assigns the value $\top$ to all atoms of $\mathcal{HB}_P$, *i.e.* the maximal element of $\mathcal{V}_P(\mathcal{T})$ w.r.t. $\preceq$.

Definition 5. *Let P be any np-program. We define $S_P(J) = T_P^\infty(I_\perp, J)$, i.e. the least fixpoint of T_P w.r.t. $\preceq$ for a given interpretation J.*   □

Intuitively, $S_P(J)$ is the interpretation that assigns to negative literals the evaluation of them in the fixed interpretation J and then applies the usual T_P operator. Note that the closure ordinal is at most the first ordinal limit ω.

Example 5. Let P be the np-program of Example 1, then we have[3]

$$S_P(I_\perp) = \{\ \texttt{friends(John, Ted)} : 0.8, \quad \texttt{motive(John)} : 0.8,$$
$$\texttt{friends(Ted, John)} : 0.8, \quad \texttt{alibi(John, Sam)} : 1,$$
$$\texttt{friends(Sam, Ted)} : 0.6, \quad \texttt{suspect(John)} : 0.6,$$
$$\texttt{friends(Ted, Sam)} : 0.6, \quad \texttt{innocent(John)} : 1,$$
$$\texttt{friends(John, Sam)} : 0.336, \quad \texttt{charge(John)} : 0.6,$$
$$\texttt{friends(Sam, John)} : 0.336 \quad\quad\quad\quad\quad \}$$

□

---

[3] $S_P(I_\perp)$ is a total interpretation, but we will indicate only the atoms whose values are different from 0.

From Proposition 1, we easily derive the following property of S_P.

Proposition 2. *Let P be any np-program, then S_P is anti-monotone w.r.t. $\preceq$ and, thus, $S_P \circ S_P$ is monotone.*   □

There is a well-know property, which derives from the Knaster-Tarski theorem and deals with anti-monotone functions on complete lattices:

Proposition 3 ([40]). *Suppose that a function f is anti-monotone on a complete lattice $\mathcal{L} = \langle \mathcal{T}, \preceq, \otimes, \oplus \rangle$. Then there are two unique elements μ and ν of $\mathcal{T}$, called extreme oscillation points of f, such that the following hold:*

- *μ and ν are the least and greatest fixpoint of $f \circ f$ (i.e. of f composed with f;*
- *f oscillates between μ and ν in the sense that $f(\mu) = \nu$ and $f(\nu) = \mu$;*
- *if x and y are also elements of $\mathcal{T}$ between which f oscillates then x and y lie between μ and ν.*   □

Under the ordering $\preceq$, S_P is anti-monotone and $\mathcal{V}_P(\mathcal{T})$ is a complete lattice, so S_P has two extreme oscillation points under this ordering.

Proposition 4. *Let P be any np-program, S_P has two extreme oscillation points under $\preceq$, $S_P^\perp = (S_P \circ S_P)^\infty(I_\perp)$ and $S_P^\top = (S_P \circ S_P)^\infty(I_\top)$, with $S_P^\perp \preceq S_P^\top$.*   □

As in Van Gelder's alternated fixpoint approach [11], $S_P^\perp$ and $S_P^\top$ are respectively an under-estimation and an over-estimation of P. As the meaning of P, we propose to consider the consensus or compromise between those two interpretations, *i.e.* to consider as defined only the atoms whose values coincide in both limit interpretations. We define the *compromise* between $S_P^\perp$ and $S_P^\top$ to be the intersection between $S_P^\perp$ and $S_P^\top$.

Definition 6. *Let P be any np-program, the* compromise *semantics of P, denoted $CS(P)$, is defined by $CS(P) = S_P^\perp \cap S_P^\top$.*   □

The following theorem asserts that, for any np-program P, $CS(P)$ satisfies P and will be seen as its the intended meaning or semantics.

Theorem 1. *Let P be any np-program, then $\models_{CS(P)} P$.*

Sketch of proof. Given an np-program P, it can be proved that for all rules $r_A \in P^*$, if $CS(P)(r_A)$ is defined, then it means that either there is one literal L in the body of r_A such that $CS(P)(L) = \perp$, or all the literals are defined in $CS(P)$. In the first case, we have $S_P^\perp(L) = S_P^\top(L) = \perp$, and it follows that $S_P^\perp(r_A) = S_P^\top(r_A) = \perp$. In the second case, for all literals $L \in r_A$, $S_P^\perp(L) = S_P^\top(L)$, so $S_P^\perp(r_A) = S_P^\top(r_A)$. It follows that for all atoms $A \in \mathcal{HB}_P$,

- if there is a rule $r_A \in P^*$ such that $CS(P)(r_A) = \top$, then it means that $S_P^\perp(A) = S_P^\top(A) = \top$, thus $CS(P)(A) = \top$;

– if $CS(P)(r_A)$ is defined for all rules $r_A \in P^*$, then $S_P^\perp(r_A) = S_P^\top(r_A)$ for all rules $r_A \in P^*$, and we have

$$f_d(\{CS(P)(r_A)|r_A \in P^*\}) = f_d(\{S_P^\perp(r_A)|r_A \in P^*\})$$
$$= f_d(\{S_P^\top(r_A)|r_A \in P^*\})$$
$$= CS(P)(A)$$

We can conclude that $CS(P)$ satisfies P.   □

Example 6. Let P be the np-program of Example 1, then we have[4]

$$CS(P) = \{\, \texttt{friends(John, Ted)} : 0.8, \quad \texttt{motive(John)} : 0.8,$$
$$\texttt{friends(Ted, John)} : 0.8, \quad \texttt{alibi(John, Sam)} : 1,$$
$$\texttt{friends(Sam, Ted)} : 0.6, \quad \texttt{suspect(John)} : 0.6,$$
$$\texttt{friends(Ted, Sam)} : 0.6, \quad \texttt{innocent(John)} : 0.664,$$
$$\texttt{friends(John, Sam)} : 0.336, \quad \texttt{charge(John)} : 0.336,$$
$$\texttt{friends(Sam, John)} : 0.336 \qquad \}$$

□

Example 7. For the program P in Example 2, $CS(P) = \emptyset$, and for the program P in Example 3, $CS(P) = \emptyset$.   □

Example 8. Consider the following np-program P on $\mathcal{T} = [0,1]$, with the disjunction function $f_d(\alpha, \beta) = \max(\alpha, \beta)$, the conjunction function $f_c(\alpha, \beta) = \min(\alpha, \beta)$ and the propagation function $f_p(\alpha, \beta) = \alpha \cdot \beta$. Negation is as usual. All rules have the same functions associated, so we omit them for readability.

$$A \stackrel{0.8}{\leftarrow} B, \neg C$$
$$B \stackrel{0.9}{\leftarrow} A, D$$
$$D \stackrel{0.6}{\leftarrow} 0.2$$

It can be shown that $CS(P) = I$, where $I(A) = I(B) = I(C) = 0$ and $I(D) = 0.12$.   □

4.3   Comparison with Existing Semantics

We conclude this section by showing that our extension is a conservative one.

Our semantics extends the Lakshmanan and Shiri's semantics of parametric programs presented in [20] to normal parametric programs. This is due to the fact that the machinery developed in order to deal with negation has no effect in positive programs.

---

[4] Note that it follows from $S_P^\perp = S_P^\top$ that $CS(P)$ is a totally defined interpretation. But, for ease of presentation, we will indicate only the atoms whose values are different from 0.

Proposition 5. *If P is an np-program without negation then the compromise semantics $CS(P)$ of P coincides with the Lakshmanan and Shiri's semantics of P.*   □

Example 9. Consider the following np-program P on $\mathcal{T} = [0, 1]$, with the disjunction function $f_d(\alpha, \beta) = \alpha + \beta - \alpha \cdot \beta$, the conjunction function $f_c(\alpha, \beta) = \alpha \cdot \beta$ and the propagation function $f_p = f_c$. Negation is as usual.

$$A \overset{0.6}{\leftarrow} B, C$$
$$A \overset{1}{\leftarrow} D$$
$$B \overset{0.5}{\leftarrow} 0.4$$
$$D \overset{0.3}{\leftarrow} 0.2$$
$$C \overset{1}{\leftarrow} 0.5$$

It is easily to be verified that $CS(P) = I$, where $I(A) = 0.1164$, $I(B) = 0.2$, $I(C) = 0.5$ and $I(D) = 0.06$ □

Finally, we compare our semantics with the well-founded semantics of classical logic programs defined in [28].

Proposition 6. *Let P be a Datalog program with negation. The compromise semantics $CS(P)$ of P coincides with the well-founded semantics of P.*   □

Example 10. Consider the Boolean lattice and the classical logic program P defined by :

$$A \leftarrow B, \neg C$$
$$B \leftarrow A, D$$
$$D \leftarrow$$

Then $CS(P) = I$, where $I(A) = I(B) = I(C) = f$ and $I(D) = t$. This corresponds exactly to the well-founded semantics of the program P.   □

5   Conclusions

We have extended the parametric IB approach [20], a general framework for the representation and the manipulation of uncertainty in logic databases and expert systems, with default negation. The semantical approach that we adopted for default negation in logic programs is based on the well-founded semantics, a widely studied and used semantics of classical logic programs with negation. Technically, we integrated the fixpoint semantics of the parametric IB approach with the alternating fixpoint techniques proposed in [11]. We have also shown that our extension is a conservative extension.

In the future we will address the issue in which intervals are specified for those atoms for which no consensus exists.

References

[1] Fahiem Bacchus. *Representing and Reasoning with Probabilistic Knowledge.* The MIT Press, 1990. 152

[2] True H. Cao. Annotated fuzzy logic programs. *Fuzzy Sets and Systems,* 113(2):277–298, 2000. 152

[3] K. L. Clark. On closed world data bases. In Hervé Gallaire and Jack Minker, editors, *Logic and data bases,* pages 293–322. Plenum Press, New York, NY, 1978. 153

[4] Alex Dekhtyar and V. S. Subrahmanian. Hybrid probabilistic programs. In *Proc. of the 13th Int. Conf. on Logic Programming (ICLP-97),* Leuven, Belgium, 1997. The MIT Press. 152

[5] Didier Dubois, Jérome Lang, and Henri Prade. Towards possibilistic logic programming. In *Proc. of the 8th Int. Conf. on Logic Programming (ICLP-91),* pages 581–595. The MIT Press, 1991. 152, 153

[6] Didier Dubois and Henri Prade. Approximate and commonsense reasoning: From theory to practice. In Zbigniew W. Ras and Michalewicz Maciek, editors, *Proc. of the 9th Int. Sym. on Methodologies for Intelligent Systems (ISMIS-96),* number 1079 in Lecture Notes in Artificial Intelligence, pages 19–33. Springer-Verlag, 1996. 152

[7] Gonzalo Escalada-Imaz and Felip Manyà. Efficient interpretation of propositional multiple-valued logic programs. In *Proc. of the 5th Int. Conf. on Information Processing and Managment of Uncertainty in Knowledge-Based Systems, (IPMU-94),* number 945 in Lecture Notes in Computer Science, pages 428–439. Springer-Verlag, 1994. 153

[8] M. C. Fitting. The family of stable models. *Journal of Logic Programming,* 17:197–225, 1993. 159

[9] Melvin Fitting. Bilattices and the semantics of logic programming. *Journal of Logic Programming,* 11:91–116, 1991. 152, 153

[10] Norbert Fuhr. Probabilistic datalog: Implementing logical information retrieval for advanced applications. *Journal of the American Society for Information Science,* 51(2):95–110, 2000. 152

[11] Allen Van Gelder. The alternating fixpoint of logic programs with negation. In *Proc. of the 8th ACM SIGACT SIGMOD Sym. on Principles of Database Systems (PODS-89),* pages 1–10, 1989. 154, 160, 161, 163

[12] M. Gelfond and V. Lifschitz. Logic programs with classical negation. In David H. D. Warren and Peter Szeredi, editors, *Proceedings of the Seventh International Conference on Logic Programming,* pages 579–597, Jerusalem, 1990. The MIT Press. 153

[13] Michael Gelfond, Halina Przymusinska, and Teodor C. Przymusinski. On the relationship between circumscription and negation as failure. *Artificial Intelligence,* 38:75–94, 1989. 153

[14] Mitsuru Ishizuka and Naoki Kanai. Prolog-ELF: incorporating fuzzy logic. In *Proc. of the 9th Int. Joint Conf. on Artificial Intelligence (IJCAI-85),* pages 701–703, Los Angeles, CA, 1985. 152

[15] M. Kifer and Ai Li. On the semantics of rule-based expert systems with uncertainty. In *Proc. of the Int. Conf. on Database Theory (ICDT-88),* number 326 in Lecture Notes in Computer Science, pages 102–117. Springer-Verlag, 1988. 152, 153

[16] Michael Kifer and V. S. Subrahmanian. Theory of generalized annotaded logic programming and its applications. *Journal of Logic Programming*, 12:335–367, 1992. 152, 153

[17] R. Kruse, E. Schwecke, and J. Heinsohn. *Uncertainty and Vagueness in Knowledge Based Systems*. Springer-Verlag, Berlin, Germany, 1991. 152

[18] Laks Lakshmanan. An epistemic foundation for logic programming with uncertainty. In *Foundations of Software Technology and Theoretical Computer Science*, number 880 in Lecture Notes in Computer Science, pages 89–100. Springer-Verlag, 1994. 152, 153

[19] Laks V. S. Lakshmanan and Nematollaah Shiri. Probabilistic deductive databases. In *Int'l Logic Programming Symposium*, pages 254–268, 1994. 152, 153

[20] Laks V. S. Lakshmanan and Nematollaah Shiri. A parametric approach to deductive databases with uncertainty. *IEEE Transactions on Knowledge and Data Engineering*, 13(4):554–570, 2001. 152, 153, 154, 155, 159, 162, 163

[21] James J. Lu. Logic programming with signs and annotations. *Journal of Logic and Computation*, 6(6):755–778, 1996. 152

[22] Thomas Lukasiewicz. Probabilistic logic programming. In *Proc. of the 13th European Conf. on Artificial Intelligence (ECAI-98)*, pages 388–392, Brighton (England), August 1998. 152

[23] John McCarthy. Circumscription - a form of nonmonotonic reasoning. *Artificial Intelligence*, 13:27–39, 1980. 153

[24] Jack Minker. On indefinite data bases and the closed world assumption. In Springer-Verlag, editor, *Proc. of the 6th Conf. on Automated Deduction (CADE-82)*, number 138 in Lecture Notes in Computer Science, 1982. 153

[25] Raymond Ng and V. S. Subrahmanian. Stable model semantics for probabilistic deductive databases. In Zbigniew W. Ras and Maria Zemenkova, editors, *Proc. of the 6th Int. Sym. on Methodologies for Intelligent Systems (ISMIS-91)*, number 542 in Lecture Notes in Artificial Intelligence, pages 163–171. Springer-Verlag, 1991. 152, 153, 154

[26] Raymond Ng and V. S. Subrahmanian. Probabilistic logic programming. *Information and Computation*, 101(2):150–201, 1993. 152, 153

[27] Raymond Ng and V. S. Subrahmanian. A semantical framework for supporting subjective and conditional probabilities in deductive databases. *Journal of Automated Reasoning*, 10(3):191–235, 1993. 152, 153

[28] Allen nva Gelder, Kenneth A. Ross, and John S. Schlimpf. The well-founded semantics for general logic programs. *Journal of the ACM*, 38(3):620–650, January 1991. 153, 154, 163

[29] J. Pearl. *Probabilistic Reasoning in Intelligent Systems: Networks of Plausible Inference*. Morgan Kaufmann, Los Altos, 1988. 152

[30] T. Przymusinski. Static semantics for normal and disjunctive logic programs. *Annals of Mathematics and Artificial Intelligence*, 14:323–357, 1995. 153, 159

[31] T. C. Przymusinski. Extended stable semantics for normal and disjunctive programs. In D. H. D. Warren and P. Szeredi, editors, *Proceedings of the Seventh International Conference on Logic Programming*, pages 459–477. MIT Press, 1990. 159

[32] T. C. Przymusinski. Stationary semantics for disjunctive logic programs and deductive databases. In S. Debray and H. Hermenegildo, editors, *Logic Programming, Proceedings of the 1990 North American Conference*, pages 40–59. MIT Press, 1990. 159

[33] Teodor C. Przymusinski. The well-founded semantics coincides with the three-valued stable semantics. *Fundamenta Informaticae*, 13(4):445–463, 1990. 153

[34] Raymond Reiter. On closed world data bases. In Hervé Gallaire and Jack Minker, editors, *Logic and data bases*, pages 55–76. Plenum Press, New York, NY, 1978. 153

[35] Ehud Y. Shapiro. Logic programs with uncertainties: A tool for implementing rule-based systems. In *Proc. of the 8th Int. Joint Conf. on Artificial Intelligence (IJCAI-83)*, pages 529–532, 1983. 152

[36] V. S. Subramanian. On the semantics of quantitative logic programs. In *Proc. 4th IEEE Symp. on Logic Programming*, pages 173–182. Computer Society Press, 1987. 152, 153

[37] M. H. van Emden. Quantitative deduction and its fixpoint theory. *Journal of Philosophical Logic*, (1):37–53, 1986. 152, 153

[38] Gerd Wagner. Negation in fuzzy and possibilistic logic programs. In T. Martin and F. Arcelli, editors, *Logic programming and Soft Computing*, pages –. Research Studies Press, 1998. 152, 154

[39] Beat Wüttrich. Probabilistic knowledge bases. *IEEE Transactions on Knowledge and Data Engineering*, 7(5):691–698, 1995. 152

[40] S. Yablo. Truth and reflection. *Journal of Philosophical Logic*, 14:297–349, 1985. 161

Linearly Used Effects:
Monadic and CPS Transformations into the Linear Lambda Calculus

Masahito Hasegawa

Research Institute for Mathematical Sciences, Kyoto University
hassei@kurims.kyoto-u.ac.jp

Abstract. We propose a semantic and syntactic framework for modelling *linearly used effects*, by giving the monadic transforms of the computational lambda calculus (considered as the core calculus of typed call-by-value programming languages) into the linear lambda calculus. As an instance Berdine et al.'s work on *linearly used continuations* can be put in this general picture. As a technical result we show the full completeness of the CPS transform into the linear lambda calculus.

1 Introduction

1.1 Background: Linearly Used Effects

Many higher-order applicative programming languages like ML and Scheme enjoy imperative features like states, exceptions and first-class continuations. They are powerful ingredients and considered as big advantages in programming practice. However, it is also true that unrestricted use of these features (in particular the combination of first-class continuations with other features) can be the source of very complicated ("higher-order spaghetti") programs. In fact, it has been observed that only the styled use of these imperative features is what we actually need in the "good" or "elegant" programming practice. There can be several points to be considered as "stylish", but in this work we shall concentrate on a single (and simple) concept: *linearity*. To be more precise, we consider the *linear usage of effects* (note that we do not say that the effects themselves should be implemented in a linear manner – but they should be *used* linearly).

The leading examples come from the recent work on *linearly used continuations* by Berdine, O'Hearn, Reddy and Thielecke [3]. They observe:

> ...in the many forms of control, continuations are used *linearly*. This is true for a wide range of effects, including procedure call and return, exceptions, goto statements, and coroutines.

They then propose linear type systems (based on a version of intuitionistic linear logic [9, 1]) for capturing the linear usage of continuations. Note that the linear types are used for typing the target codes of continuation passing style (CPS) transforms, rather than the source (ML or Scheme) programs. Several "good"

Z. Hu and M. Rodríguez-Artalejo (Eds.): FLOPS 2002, LNCS 2441, pp. 167–182, 2002.
© Springer-Verlag Berlin Heidelberg 2002

examples are shown to typecheck, while examples which duplicate continuations do not.

There are several potential benefits of picking up the linearly used effects using (linear) type systems. First, such type systems can be used to detect certain ill-behaving programs at the compile time. Furthermore, if we only consider the programs with linearly used effects, the linear type systems often capture the nature of compiled codes very closely, as the following full completeness result on the CPS transform suggests. Such tight typing on the compiled codes should be useful for better analysis and optimisation. Also the verification of the correctness of the compilation phase can be simplified.

1.2   A Framework for Linearly Used Effects

In the present paper, we propose a semantics-oriented framework for dealing with linearly used effects in a coherent way. Specifically, we adopt Moggi's monad-based approach to computational effects [Mog88].

In Moggi's work, a strong monad on a cartesian closed category (a model of the simply typed lambda calculus) determines the semantics of computational effects. If we concentrate on the syntactic case (monads syntactically defined on the term model), this amounts to give a monadic transform (monad-based compilation) of call-by-value programs into the simply typed lambda calculus.

Basically we follow this story, but in this work we consider cartesian closed categories induced from models of intuitionistic linear logic (ILL) and, most importantly, monads on these cartesian closed categories induced from the monads on models of ILL. In this way we can make use of monads determined by primitives of ILL like linear function type $\multimap$ to capture the linearity of the usage of computational effects. Syntactically, this precisely amounts to give a monadic transformation into the linear lambda calculus.

In summary, our proposal is to model linearly used effects by monads on models of ILL, which, if presented syntactically (as will be done in this paper), amounts to consider monadic transformations into the linear lambda calculus.

1.3   Fully Complete CPS Transformation

To show how this framework neatly captures the compiled codes of the linearly used effects, we give a technical result which tells us a sort of "no-junk" property of the CPS transform: *full completeness*.

Though the standard call-by-value CPS transformation from the computational lambda calculus [14] (considered as the core calculus of typed call-by-value programming languages) into the simply typed lambda calculus has been shown to be equationally sound and complete (Sabry and Felleisen [16]), it is not *full*: there are inhabitants of the interpreted types which are not in the image of the transformation. As the case of the full abstraction problem of PCF, there are at least two ways to obtain full completeness for the transformation: either

1. enrich the source calculus by adding first-class continuations, or
2. restrict the target calculus by some typing discipline.

The first approach is standard. In this paper we show how the second approach can be carried out along the line of work by Berdine et al. [4], as mentioned above. The basic idea is surprisingly simple (and old): since a continuation is used precisely once (provided there is no controls), we can replace the interpretation $(Y \to R) \to (X \to R)$ of a (call-by-value) function type $X \to Y$ by $(Y \to R) \multimap (X \to R)$ using the linear function type $\multimap$ – and it does work.

Our framework allows us to formulate this CPS transformation as an instance of the monadic transformations into the linear lambda calculus arising from a simple monad. The type soundness and equational soundness then follow immediately, as they are true for any of our monadic transformations. On top of this foundation, we show that this CPS transformation is fully complete.

Organization of This Paper. In Sec. 2 we recall the semantic background behind our development, and explain how the considerations on the category-theoretic models lead us to the monadic transformations into the linear lambda calculus. Sec. 3 recalls the source and target calculi of our transformations. We then present the monadic and CPS transformations and some basic results in Sec. 4. Sec. 5 is devoted to the full completeness result of our CPS transformation. Sec. 6 discusses a way to add recursion to our framework. Sec. 7 sketches a generalisation of our approach for some "non-linearly used" effects. We conclude the paper with some discussions in Sec. 8.

2   Semantics of Linearly Used Effects

2.1   Models of Linear Type Theory, and Monads

A *model of propositional intuitionistic linear type theory* (with multiplicatives I, $\otimes$, $\multimap$, additives 1, & and the modality !) can be given as a symmetric monoidal closed category $\mathcal{D}$ with finite products and a monoidal comonad ! (subject to certain coherence conditions, see e.g. [6] for relevant category theoretic notions and results). The symmetric monoidal closure is used for modelling multiplicatives, while products and the comonad for additive products and the modality respectively.

Benton and Wadler [2] observe that such a structure is closely related to a model of Moggi's *computational lambda calculus* [14] described as a cartesian closed category with a strong monad.[1] The result below is well-known (and is the semantic counterpart of Girard's translation from intuitionistic logic to linear logic):

---

[1] To be minimal, for modelling the computational lambda calculus, it suffices to have a category with finite products, Kleisli exponentials and a strong monad [14]; but in this paper we do not make use of this full generality.

Lemma 1. *Suppose that $\mathcal{D}$ is a model of intuitionistic linear type theory with a monoidal comonad* !. *Then the co-Kleisli category $\mathcal{D}_!$ of the comonad* ! *on $\mathcal{D}$ is cartesian closed.*   □

Also general category theory tells us that the monoidal comonad ! on $\mathcal{D}$ induces a *strong monad* on $\mathcal{D}_!$: the comonad ! gives rise to the co-Kleisli adjunction $F \dashv U : \mathcal{D}_! \to \mathcal{D}$

$$\mathcal{D}_! \; \xrightleftharpoons[\;U\;]{\;F\;} \; \mathcal{D}$$

such that the composition FU is the comonad !, and the composition UF is a strong monad on $\mathcal{D}_!$. We also note that this adjunction is symmetric monoidal, which means that the cartesian products in $\mathcal{D}_!$ and the tensor products in $\mathcal{D}$ are naturally related by coherent natural transformations.

  Therefore, from a model of intuitionistic linear type theory, we can derive a model of computational lambda calculus for free. Benton and Wadler have observed that this setting induces a call-by-value translation $(A \to B)^\circ =\,!A^\circ \multimap\,!B^\circ$ into the linear lambda calculus [2]. However, they also observe that, since the derived monad is commutative (which means that we cannot distinguish the order of computational effects), this setting excludes many of the interesting examples, including continuations as well as global states.

  Now we add one more twist. Let us additionally suppose that our model of intuitionistic linear type theory $\mathcal{D}$ has a strong monad T (on the symmetric monoidal closed category $\mathcal{D}$, rather than on the cartesian closed category $\mathcal{D}_!$). We observe that

Lemma 2. *Given a symmetric monoidal adjunction $F \dashv U : \mathcal{C} \to \mathcal{D}$ together with a strong monad T on $\mathcal{D}$, the induced monad UTF on $\mathcal{C}$ is also a strong monad.*   □

$$\mathcal{C} \; \xrightleftharpoons[\;U\;]{\;F\;} \; \mathcal{D} \;\supset\; T$$

As a special case, in our situation we have a strong monad $T!$ on the cartesian closed category $\mathcal{D}_!$ (by taking $\mathcal{D}_!$ as $\mathcal{C}$ and the co-Kleisli adjunction between $\mathcal{D}_!$ and $\mathcal{D}$ as the symmetric monoidal adjunction):

Proposition 1. *Given a model of intuitionistic linear type theory $\mathcal{D}$ with a monoidal comonad* ! *and a strong monad T on $\mathcal{D}$, the induced monad on $\mathcal{D}_!$ is also a strong monad.*   □

Then we can model the computational lambda calculus using the derived monad. The induced translation on arrow types takes the form $(A \to B)^\circ =\,!A^\circ \multimap T(!B^\circ)$. (Note that the Benton-Wadler translation can be understood as the case of T being the identity monad.) The details of the translation will be described in Section 4.1.

The merit of considering monads on the symmetric monoidal closed category $\mathcal{D}$ instead of the cartesian closed category $\mathcal{D}_!$ is that we can use linear type constructors for describing the monads. We should warn that no extra generality is obtained by this approach; we only claim that this can be a convenient way to concentrate on the special form of effects (the linearly used ones), especially on the situations like CPS transform, to be spelled out below.

2.2   A Monad for Linearly Used Continuations

The motivating example in this paper is the *(linear) continuation monad* $TX = (X \multimap R) \multimap R$. As will be explained in detail in Section 4.2, the induced translation is the call-by-value CPS transformation (of Plotkin [15]), regarded as a translation from the computational lambda calculus to the linear lambda calculus. The translation of arrow types is: $(A \to B)^\circ = !A^\circ \multimap (!B^\circ \multimap R) \multimap R$. This can be rewritten as $A^\circ \to (B^\circ \to R) \multimap R$ if we write $X \to Y$ for $!X \multimap Y$, which is of course isomorphic to $(B^\circ \to R) \multimap A^\circ \to R$, the CPS transformation (of Fischer) used by Berdine et al. for explaining the linear usage of continuations [3]. (Another good example might be the state monad $TX = S \multimap (X \otimes S)$ which induces the translation $(A \to B)^\circ = !A^\circ \multimap S \multimap (!B^\circ \otimes S) \simeq (!A^\circ \otimes S) \multimap (!B^\circ \otimes S)$, though in this paper we spell out only the case of continuation monads – but see also the concluding remarks.)

It follows that Plotkin's CPS transformation from the computational lambda calculus to the linear lambda calculus is type sound (straightforward), and equationally complete (by modifying Sabry and Felleisen's equational completeness [16]). As mentioned in the introduction, following the work by Berdine et al. [4], we show that this CPS transformation is *fully complete*, meaning that each term of an interpreted type is provably equal to an interpreted term (Section 5). Although the present proof is a mixture of syntactic and semantic techniques, we expect that a fully semantic (and transparent) proof will be available by axiomatic considerations on the semantic structures described in this section.

3   The Calculi

We shall consider the minimal setting for discussing the monadic and CPS transformations, thus that involving only the (call-by-value) function type, linear function type and the modality !. (For ease of presentation we omit the product types which, however, can be routinely added.) We use the (simply typed) computational lambda calculus [14] as the source language. The target language is the fragment of intuitionistic linear logic with $\multimap$ and !, formulated as a linear lambda calculus below. Our presentation is based on a dual-context type system for intuitionistic linear logic (called DILL) due to Barber and Plotkin [1].

A set of *base types* (b ranges over them) is fixed throughout this paper.

3.1   The Computational Lambda Calculus

We employ a fairly standard syntax:

Types, Terms and Values

$$\sigma ::= b \mid \sigma \to \sigma$$
$$M ::= x \mid \lambda x^\sigma.M \mid MM$$
$$V ::= x \mid \lambda x^\sigma.M$$

We may omit the type superscripts of the lambda abstraction for ease of presentation. As an abbreviation, we write let x^σ be M in N for $(\lambda x^\sigma.N)M$. $\mathrm{FV}(M)$ denotes the set of free variables in M.

Typing

$$\frac{}{\Gamma_1, x : \sigma, \Gamma_2 \vdash x : \sigma} \qquad \frac{\Gamma, x : \sigma_1 \vdash M : \sigma_2}{\Gamma \vdash \lambda x^{\sigma_1}.M : \sigma_1 \to \sigma_2} \qquad \frac{\Gamma \vdash M : \sigma_1 \to \sigma_2 \quad \Gamma \vdash N : \sigma_1}{\Gamma \vdash MN : \sigma_2}$$

where Γ is a context, i.e. a finite list of variables annotated with types, in which a variable occurs at most once. We note that any typing judgement has a unique derivation.

Axioms

let x^σ be V in $M = M[V/x]$
$\lambda x^\sigma.V\, x \qquad\quad = V$ $\qquad\qquad\qquad\qquad\qquad (x \notin \mathrm{FV}(V))$
let x^σ be M in $x = M$
let y^{σ_2} be (let x^{σ_1} be L in M) in N = let x^{σ_1} be L in let y^{σ_2} be M in N
$\qquad\qquad\qquad\qquad\qquad\qquad\qquad\qquad\qquad\qquad\qquad (x \notin \mathrm{FV}(N))$
$M\, N = $ let $f^{\sigma_1 \to \sigma_2}$ be M in let x^{σ_1} be N in $f\, x \qquad (M : \sigma_1 \to \sigma_2, N : \sigma_1)$

We assume usual conditions on variables for avoiding undesirable captures. The equality judgement $\Gamma \vdash M = N : \sigma$, where $\Gamma \vdash M : \sigma$ and $\Gamma \vdash N : \sigma$, is defined as the congruence relation on well-typed terms of the same type under the same context, generated from these axioms.

3.2   The Linear Lambda Calculus

In this formulation of the linear lambda calculus, a typing judgement takes the form Γ ; $\Delta \vdash M : \tau$ in which Γ represents an intuitionistic (or additive) context whereas Δ is a linear (multiplicative) context.

Types and Terms

$$\tau ::= b \mid \tau \multimap \tau \mid !\tau$$
$$M ::= x \mid \lambda x^\tau.M \mid MM \mid !M \mid \text{let } !x^\tau \text{ be } M \text{ in } M$$

Typing

$$\overline{\Gamma \; ; \; x : \tau \vdash x : \tau} \qquad\qquad \overline{\Gamma_1, x : \tau, \Gamma_2 \; ; \; \emptyset \vdash x : \tau}$$

$$\frac{\Gamma \; ; \; \Delta, x : \tau_1 \vdash M : \tau_2}{\Gamma \; ; \; \Delta \vdash \lambda x^{\tau_1}.M : \tau_1 \multimap \tau_2} \qquad \frac{\Gamma \; ; \; \Delta_1 \vdash M : \tau_1 \multimap \tau_2 \quad \Gamma \; ; \; \Delta_2 \vdash N : \tau_1}{\Gamma \; ; \; \Delta_1 \sharp \Delta_2 \vdash MN : \tau_2}$$

$$\frac{\Gamma \; ; \; \emptyset \vdash M : \tau}{\Gamma \; ; \; \emptyset \vdash !M : !\tau} \qquad \frac{\Gamma \; ; \; \Delta_1 \vdash M : !\tau_1 \quad \Gamma, x : \tau_1 \; ; \; \Delta_2 \vdash N : \tau_2}{\Gamma \; ; \; \Delta_1 \sharp \Delta_2 \vdash \text{let } !x^{\tau_1} \text{ be } M \text{ in } N : \tau_2}$$

where $\Delta_1 \sharp \Delta_2$ is a merge of Δ_1 and Δ_2 [1]. Thus, $\Delta_1 \sharp \Delta_2$ represents one of possible merges of Δ_1 and Δ_2 as finite lists. We assume that, when we introduce $\Delta_1 \sharp \Delta_2$, there is no variable occurring both in Δ_1 and in Δ_2. We write $\emptyset$ for the empty context. Again we note that any typing judgement has a unique derivation.

Axioms

$$
\begin{array}{ll}
(\lambda x.M)N & = M[N/x] \\
\lambda x.Mx & = M \\
\text{let } !x \text{ be } !M \text{ in } N & = N[M/x] \\
\text{let } !x \text{ be } M \text{ in } !x & = M \\
C[\text{let } !x \text{ be } M \text{ in } N] & = \text{let } !x \text{ be } M \text{ in } C[N]
\end{array}
$$

where $C[-]$ is a linear context (no $!$ binds $[-]$); formally it is generated from the following grammar.

$$C ::= [-] \mid \lambda x.C \mid CM \mid MC \mid \text{let } !x \text{ be } C \text{ in } M \mid \text{let } !x \text{ be } M \text{ in } C$$

The equality judgement $\Gamma \; ; \; \Delta \vdash M = N : \tau$ is defined in the same way as the case of the computational lambda calculus.

It is convenient to introduce syntax sugars for "intuitionistic" or "non-linear" function type

$$
\begin{array}{c}
\tau_1 \to \tau_2 \equiv !\tau_1 \multimap \tau_2 \\
\boldsymbol{\lambda} x^\tau.M \equiv \lambda y^{!\tau}.\text{let } !x^\tau \text{ be } y \text{ in } M \\
M^{\tau_1 \to \tau_2} \text{@} N^{\tau_1} \equiv M\,(!N)
\end{array}
$$

which enjoy the following typing derivations.

$$\frac{\Gamma, x : \tau_1 \; ; \; \Delta \vdash M : \tau_2}{\Gamma \; ; \; \Delta \vdash \boldsymbol{\lambda} x^{\tau_1}.M : \tau_1 \to \tau_2} \qquad \frac{\Gamma \; ; \; \Delta \vdash M : \tau_1 \to \tau_2 \quad \Gamma \; ; \; \emptyset \vdash N : \tau_1}{\Gamma \; ; \; \Delta \vdash M \text{@} N : \tau_2}$$

As one expects, the usual $\beta\eta$-equalities $(\boldsymbol{\lambda} x.M) \text{@} N = M[N/x]$ and $\boldsymbol{\lambda} x.M \text{@} x = M$ (with x not free in M) are easily provable from the axioms above.

4   Monadic and CPS Transformations

4.1   Monadic Transformations

By a *(linearly strong) monad* on the linear lambda calculus, we mean a tuple of a type constructor T, type-indexed terms $\eta_\tau : \tau \multimap T\tau$ and $(-)^*_{\tau_1, \tau_2} : (\tau_1 \multimap$

$T\tau_2) \multimap T\tau_1 \multimap T\tau_2$ satisfying the *monad laws*:

$$\eta_\tau^* = \lambda x^{T\tau}.x : T\tau \multimap T\tau$$
$$f^* \circ \eta_{\tau_1} = f \qquad : \tau_1 \multimap T\tau_2$$
$$(g^* \circ f)^* = g^* \circ f^* : T\tau_1 \multimap T\tau_3 \quad (f : \tau_1 \multimap T\tau_2,\ g : \tau_2 \multimap T\tau_3)$$

For a monad $T = (T, \eta, (-)^*)$, the *monadic transformation* $(-)^\circ$ from the computational lambda calculus to the linear lambda calculus sends a typing judgement $\Gamma \vdash M : \sigma$ to $\Gamma^\circ\, ;\, \emptyset \vdash M^\circ : T(!\sigma^\circ)$, where Γ° is defined by $\emptyset^\circ = \emptyset$ and $(\Gamma, x : \sigma)^\circ = \Gamma^\circ, x : \sigma^\circ$.

$$b^\circ = b$$
$$(\sigma_1 \to \sigma_2)^\circ = !\sigma_1^\circ \multimap T(!\sigma_2^\circ)$$
$$= \sigma_1^\circ \to T(!\sigma_2^\circ)$$

$$x^\circ \equiv \eta\,(!x)$$
$$= \eta\,@\,x$$
$$(\lambda x^\sigma.M)^\circ \equiv \eta\,(!(\lambda a^{!\sigma^\circ}.\mathsf{let}\ !x^{\sigma^\circ}\ \mathsf{be}\ a\ \mathsf{in}\ M^\circ))$$
$$= \eta\,@\,(\boldsymbol{\lambda} x^{\sigma^\circ}.M^\circ)$$
$$(M^{\sigma_1 \to \sigma_2}\ N^{\sigma_1})^\circ \equiv (\lambda h^{!(\sigma_1 \to \sigma_2)^\circ}.\mathsf{let}\ !f^{(\sigma_1 \to \sigma_2)^\circ}\ \mathsf{be}\ h\ \mathsf{in}\ f^*\ N^\circ)^*\ M^\circ$$
$$= (\boldsymbol{\lambda} f^{(\sigma_1 \to \sigma_2)^\circ}.f^*\ N^\circ)^*\ M^\circ$$

We shall note that $(\mathsf{let}\ x\ \mathsf{be}\ M\ \mathsf{in}\ N)^\circ = (\boldsymbol{\lambda} x.N^\circ)^*\ M^\circ$ holds.

Proposition 2 (type soundness). *If $\Gamma \vdash M : \sigma$ is derivable in the computational lambda calculus, then $\Gamma^\circ\, ;\, \emptyset \vdash M^\circ : T(!\sigma^\circ)$ is derivable in the linear lambda calculus.* □

Proposition 3 (equational soundness). *If $\Gamma \vdash M = N : \sigma$ holds in the computational lambda calculus, so is $\Gamma^\circ\, ;\, \emptyset \vdash M^\circ = N^\circ : T(!\sigma^\circ)$ in the linear lambda calculus.* □

As an easiest example, one may consider the identity monad ($T\tau = \tau$, $\eta = \lambda x.x$ and $f^* = f$). In this case we have $(\sigma_1 \to \sigma_2)^\circ = !\sigma_1^\circ \multimap !\sigma_2^\circ = \sigma_1^\circ \to !\sigma_2^\circ$ and

$$x^\circ = !x$$
$$(\lambda x.M)^\circ = !(\boldsymbol{\lambda} x.M^\circ)$$
$$(M\ N)^\circ = (\boldsymbol{\lambda} f.f\ N^\circ)\ M^\circ$$
$$(\mathsf{let}\ x\ \mathsf{be}\ M\ \mathsf{in}\ N)^\circ = \mathsf{let}\ !x\ \mathsf{be}\ M^\circ\ \mathsf{in}\ N^\circ$$

This translation is *not* equationally complete – it validates the *commutativity axiom* $\mathsf{let}\ x\ \mathsf{be}\ M\ \mathsf{in}\ \mathsf{let}\ y\ \mathsf{be}\ N\ \mathsf{in}\ L = \mathsf{let}\ y\ \mathsf{be}\ N\ \mathsf{in}\ \mathsf{let}\ x\ \mathsf{be}\ M\ \mathsf{in}\ L$ (with x, y not free in M, N) which is not provable in the computational lambda calculus. Also it is *not* full, as there is a term $f : (\sigma_1 \to \sigma_2)^\circ\, ;\, \emptyset \vdash !(\boldsymbol{\lambda} x^{\sigma_1^\circ}.!(\mathsf{let}\ !y^{\sigma_2^\circ}\ \mathsf{be}\ f\,@\,x\ \mathsf{in}\ y)) : !(\sigma_1 \to \sigma_2)^\circ$ which does not stay in the image of the translation if σ_2 is a base type (note that $!(\mathsf{let}\ !y\ \mathsf{be}\ M\ \mathsf{in}\ y) = M$ does not hold in general, cf. Note 3.6 of [1]).

Remark 1. The reason of the failure of fullness of this translation can be explained as follows. In the source language, we can turn a computation at the function types to a value via the η-expansion – but not at the base types. On the other hand, in the target language, we can do essentially the same thing at every types of the form $!\tau$ (by turning $\Gamma \ ; \ \emptyset \vdash M :!\tau$ to $\Gamma \ ; \ \emptyset \vdash !(\text{let } !y^\tau \text{ be } M \text{ in } y) :!\tau$) which are strictly more general than the translations of function types. This mismatch does create junks which cannot stay in the image of the translation. (In terms of monads and their algebras: while the base types of the term model of the (commutative) computational lambda calculus do not have an algebra structure, all objects of the Kleisli category of the term model of DILL are equipped with an algebra structure given by the term $x :!\tau \ ; \ \emptyset \vdash \text{let } !y^\tau \text{ be } x \text{ in } y : \tau$ for the monad induced by the monoidal comonad.) We conjecture that, if we enrich the commutative computational lambda calculus with the construct $\text{val}_b(M) : b$ for base type b and $M : b$, with axioms $\text{let } x^b \text{ be } \text{val}_b(M) \text{ in } N = N[\text{val}_b(M)/x]$ (i.e. $\text{val}_b(M)$ is a value) and $\text{val}_b(\text{val}_b(M)) = \text{val}_b(M)$, then the translation extended with $(\text{val}_b(M))^\circ =!(\text{let } !x^b \text{ be } M^\circ \text{ in } x)$ is fully complete. For example, for $f : \sigma \to b$ we have $(\lambda x^\sigma.\text{val}_b(f\,x))^\circ =!(\boldsymbol{\lambda} x^{\sigma^\circ}.!(\text{let } !y^b \text{ be } f \circledcirc x \text{ in } y))$.   □

4.2 The CPS Transformation

By specialising the monadic transformation to that of the continuation monad, we obtain Plotkin's CPS transformation [15] from the computational lambda calculus to the linear lambda calculus. Let o be a type of the linear lambda calculus. Define a monad $(T, \eta, (-)^*)$ by

$$T\tau = (\tau \multimap o) \multimap o$$
$$\eta = \lambda x.\lambda k.k\,x$$
$$f^* = \lambda h.\lambda k.h\,(\lambda x.f\,x\,k)$$

Lemma 3. *The data given above specify a monad.*   □

Now we have the monadic transformation of this monad as follows:

$$b^\circ = b$$
$$(\sigma_1 \to \sigma_2)^\circ - !\sigma_1^\circ \multimap (!\sigma_2^\circ \ \circ o) \multimap o$$
$$= \sigma_1^\circ \to (\sigma_2^\circ \to o) \multimap o$$

$$x^\circ \equiv \lambda k.k\,(!x)$$
$$= \lambda k.k \circledcirc x$$
$$(\lambda x^\sigma.M)^\circ \equiv \lambda k.k\,(!(\lambda a^{!\sigma^\circ}.\text{let } !x^{\sigma^\circ} \text{ be } a \text{ in } M^\circ))$$
$$= \lambda k.k \circledcirc (\boldsymbol{\lambda} x^{\sigma^\circ}.M^\circ)$$
$$(M^{\sigma_1 \to \sigma_2}\,N^{\sigma_1})^\circ \equiv \lambda k.M^\circ\,(\lambda h^{!(\sigma_1 \to \sigma_2)^\circ}.\text{let } !f^{(\sigma_1 \to \sigma_2)^\circ} \text{ be } h \text{ in } N^\circ\,(\lambda a^{!\sigma_1^\circ}.f\,a\,k))$$
$$= \lambda k.M^\circ\,(\boldsymbol{\lambda} f^{(\sigma_1 \to \sigma_2)^\circ}.N^\circ\,(\boldsymbol{\lambda} a^{\sigma_1^\circ}.f \circledcirc a\,k))$$

This is no other than the call-by-value CPS transformation of Plotkin. Note that $(\text{let } x \text{ be } M \text{ in } N)^\circ = \lambda k.M^\circ\,(\boldsymbol{\lambda} x.N^\circ\,k)$ holds (as expected).

Proposition 4 (type soundness). *If $\Gamma \vdash M : \sigma$ is derivable in the computational lambda calculus, then $\Gamma^\circ ; \emptyset \vdash M^\circ : (\sigma^\circ \to o) \multimap o$ is derivable in the linear lambda calculus.* □

Proposition 5 (equational completeness of Sabry and Felleisen [16]).
$\Gamma \vdash M = N : \sigma$ *holds in the computational lambda calculus if and only if* $\Gamma^\circ ; \emptyset \vdash M^\circ = N^\circ : (\sigma^\circ \to o) \multimap o$ *holds in the linear lambda calculus.* □

5 Full Completeness

Following the work by Berdine et al. [4], we show that this CPS transformation is in fact *fully complete*: supposing that o is a base type of the linear lambda calculus but not of the computational lambda calculus, we claim

> If $\Gamma^\circ ; \emptyset \vdash N : (\sigma^\circ \to o) \multimap o$ is derivable in the linear lambda calculus, then there exists $\Gamma \vdash M : \sigma$ in the computational lambda calculus such that $\Gamma^\circ ; \emptyset \vdash M^\circ = N : (\sigma^\circ \to o) \multimap o$ holds in the linear lambda calculus.

The proof is done as follows. First, we note that the image of the CPS transform involves only the types of the form b, $\tau_1 \multimap \tau_2$ and $\tau_1 \to \tau_2$, but no $!\tau$ – in contrast to the case of the identity monad or the state monad. By modifying the full completeness proof for the Girard translation in [10] (via a Kripke logical relation), we are able to show that the inhabitants of these types are provably equal to terms constructed from x, $\lambda x.M$, $M\,N$, $\boldsymbol{\lambda} x.M$ and $M \otimes N$.

Proposition 6 (fullness of Girard translation, extended version).
Given $\Gamma ; \Delta \vdash M : \sigma$ in the linear lambda calculus such that types in Γ, Δ and σ are constructed from base types, linear function type $\multimap$ and intuitionistic function type $\to$, M is provably equal to a term constructed from variables x, linear lambda abstraction $\lambda x.N$, linear application $N_1\,N_2$, intuitionistic lambda abstraction $\boldsymbol{\lambda} x.N$ and intuitionistic application $N_1 \otimes N_2$. □

Then we have only to consider the long $\beta\eta$-normal forms of the types o (answers), σ° (values), $\sigma^\circ \to o$ (continuations) and $(\sigma^\circ \to o) \multimap o$ (programs) (with intuitionistic free variables of σ°'s, and one linear free variable of $\sigma^\circ \to o$ in the cases of answers and continuations), and define the inversion function on them, as done in [16, 4]. This inversion function $(-)^*$ for the long $\beta\eta$-normal forms of the answers, values, continuations and programs are given as follows (see Appendix for the typing).

	types	
answers	o	$A ::= k \otimes V \mid x \otimes V\,C$
values	σ°	$V ::= x \mid \boldsymbol{\lambda} x.P$
continuations	$\sigma^\circ \to o$	$C ::= k \mid \boldsymbol{\lambda} x.A$
programs	$(\sigma^\circ \to o) \multimap o$	$P ::= \lambda k.A \mid x \otimes V$

answers	$(k \mathbin{@} V)^* = V^*$	$(x \mathbin{@} V\, C)^* = C^*\,(x\, V^*)$
values	$x^* = x$	$(\boldsymbol{\lambda}x.P)^* = \lambda x.P^*$
continuations	$k^* = \lambda x.x$	$(\boldsymbol{\lambda}x.A)^* = \lambda x.A^*$
programs	$(\lambda k.A)^* = A^*$	$(x \mathbin{@} V)^* = x\, V^*$

Lemma 4.

- For Γ° ; $k : \theta^\circ \to o \vdash A : o$ we have $\Gamma \vdash A^* : \theta$.
- For Γ° ; $\emptyset \vdash V : \sigma^\circ$ we have $\Gamma \vdash V^* : \sigma$.
- For Γ° ; $k : \theta^\circ \to o \vdash C : \sigma^\circ \to o$ we have $\Gamma \vdash C^* : \sigma \to \theta$.
- For Γ° ; $\emptyset \vdash P : (\sigma^\circ \to o) \multimap o$ we have $\Gamma \vdash P^* : \sigma$. $\square$

Proposition 7. For $\Gamma \vdash M : \sigma$ in the computational lambda calculus, we have $\Gamma \vdash M^{\circ *} = M : \sigma$. $\square$

Lemma 5.

- For Γ° ; $k : \theta^\circ \to o \vdash A : o$ we have Γ° ; $\emptyset \vdash A^{*\circ} = \lambda k.A : (\theta^\circ \to o) \multimap o$.
- For Γ° ; $\emptyset \vdash V : \sigma^\circ$ we have Γ° ; $\emptyset \vdash V^{*\circ} = \lambda k.k \mathbin{@} V : (\sigma^\circ \to o) \multimap o$.
- For Γ° ; $k : \theta^\circ \to o \vdash C : \sigma^\circ \to o$ we have
  Γ° ; $\emptyset \vdash C^{*\circ} = \lambda m.m \mathbin{@} (\boldsymbol{\lambda}x.\lambda k.C \mathbin{@} x) : ((\sigma \to \theta)^\circ \to o) \multimap o$.
- For Γ° ; $\emptyset \vdash P : (\sigma^\circ \to o) \multimap o$ we have Γ° ; $\emptyset \vdash P^{*\circ} = P : (\sigma^\circ \to o) \multimap o$. $\square$

Theorem 1 (full completeness of the CPS transform). *Given* Γ° ; $\emptyset \vdash N : (\sigma^\circ \to o) \multimap o$ *in the linear lambda calculus, we have* $\Gamma \vdash M : \sigma$ *in the computational lambda calculus such that* Γ° ; $\emptyset \vdash N = M^\circ : (\sigma^\circ \to o) \multimap o$. $\square$

6   Adding Recursion

Following the results in [12], we can enrich our transformations with recursion while keeping the type-soundness and equational soundness valid. For interpreting a call-by-value fixpoint operator on function types

$$\mathsf{fix}^{\mathsf{v}}_{\sigma_1 \to \sigma_2} : ((\sigma_1 \to \sigma_2) \to \sigma_1 \to \sigma_2) \to \sigma_1 \to \sigma_2$$

it suffices to add a fixpoint operator on types of the form $T!\tau$

$$\mathsf{fix}^{\mathsf{L}}_\tau : (T!\tau \to T!\tau) \to T!\tau$$

to the linear lambda calculus.

$$(\mathsf{fix}^{\mathsf{v}}_{\sigma_1 \to \sigma_2})^\circ =$$
$$\eta \mathbin{@} (\boldsymbol{\lambda}F.\eta \mathbin{@} (\alpha \mathbin{@} (\mathsf{fix}^{\mathsf{L}}_{(\sigma_1 \to \sigma_2)^\circ} \mathbin{@} (\boldsymbol{\lambda}g^{T!(\sigma_1 \to \sigma_2)^\circ}.\eta \mathbin{@} (\alpha \mathbin{@} (F \mathbin{@} (\alpha \mathbin{@} g)))))))$$
$$: T!(((\sigma_1 \to \sigma_2)^\circ \to T!(\sigma_1 \to \sigma_2)^\circ) \to T!(\sigma_1 \to \sigma_2)^\circ)$$

$$\text{where } \alpha = \boldsymbol{\lambda}g^{T!(\sigma_1 \to \sigma_2)^\circ}.\boldsymbol{\lambda}x^{\sigma_1^\circ}.(\lambda f^{(\sigma_1 \to \sigma_2)^\circ}.f \mathbin{@} x)^* g$$
$$: T!(\sigma_1 \to \sigma_2)^\circ \to (\sigma_1 \to \sigma_2)^\circ$$

The fixpoint equation $\mathsf{fix}^\mathsf{L} \odot M = M \odot (\mathsf{fix}^\mathsf{L} \odot M)$ is necessary and sufficient for justifying the call-by-value fixpoint equation $\mathsf{fix}^\mathsf{V} F = \lambda x.F(\mathsf{fix}^\mathsf{V} F) x$ as well as the stability axiom $\mathsf{fix}^\mathsf{V} F = \mathsf{fix}^\mathsf{V}(\lambda f.\lambda x.F f x)$ where F is a value [12]. Moreover, if fix^L satisfies a suitable uniformity principle (cf. [17]), the uniformity of fix^V with respect to the rigid functionals [12] is validated by this interpretation. We expect that this extension does not break the full completeness, but this remains an open issue.

Another related issue we do not discuss here is the extension with *recursive types* which are extensively used in [3]. Again the type soundness and equational soundness are straightforward, but we do not know if there is a general criteria for ensuring the full completeness for such extensions with recursive types.

7   Classifying Effects via Linearity

One may wonder if we can also study the "non-linearly used effects" in this framework. In fact this is the case for some interesting ones, including the usual (non-linearly used) continuations. The crucial point is that they can be derived from monads which are *not* strong – the typing of $(-)^*$ must be changed to $(\tau_1 \multimap T\tau_2) \to T\tau_1 \multimap T\tau_2$ (note the use of $\to$); this exactly amounts to have a limited form of strength whose parameter is restricted on objects of the form $!X$, also called *strength with respect to* $!$ in [8]. Prop. 1 can be strengthened as:

Proposition 8. *Given a model of intuitionistic linear type theory $\mathcal{D}$ with a monoidal comonad $!$ and a monad T on $\mathcal{D}$ with a strength w.r.t. $!$, the induced monad on $\mathcal{D}_!$ is a strong monad.*   □

This ensures that our derivation of monadic transformations for strong monads is also applicable without any change for monads which are strong w.r.t. $!$. For instance, a triple $T\tau = (\tau \multimap o) \to o$, $\eta = \lambda x.\lambda k.k\, x$ and $f^* = \lambda h.\lambda k.h\,(\lambda x.f\, x\, k)$ forms such a monad which is strong w.r.t. $!$, from which we obtain the standard continuation monad $T!\tau = (\tau \to o) \to o$ and the CPS transformation.

Yet not all the strong monads on $\mathcal{D}_!$ arise from such monads on $\mathcal{D}$ in this way. It seems that there exists an interesting classification of computational effects: *linearly used effects* (for linearly strong monads on $\mathcal{D}$), *linearly definable effects* (for monads on $\mathcal{D}$ with strength w.r.t. $!$) and more general effects (for general strong monads on $\mathcal{D}_!$). We hope to report the detail of this classification and its implications elsewhere.

8   Concluding Remarks

In this paper we have proposed a framework for describing "linearly used effects" in terms of strong monads on models of intuitionistic linear type theories, and derived the monadic transformations from the computational lambda calculus into the linear lambda calculus. The case of CPS transformation, motivated by the work by Berdine et al. [3], is studied in some detail, and we have shown its full completeness. we believe that these preliminary results show that our framework is useful in capturing and generalizing the ideas proposed in *ibid.*: *linearity on the use of computational effects*.

However, there remain many open issues on this approach. Most importantly, we are yet to see if this approach is applicable to many interesting computational effects. In particular, in this paper we have considered only the pure computational lambda calculus as the source language. An obvious question is how to deal with extensions with several computational effects – we have only considered the core part of [3], and it is still open if several computational effects discussed in *ibid.* can be accommodated within our framework. More generally, we want to know a general characterization of effects which can be captured by strong monads on linear type theories (this is related to the consideration in Sec. 7).

There also remain several interesting issues related to the approach given here; we shall conclude this paper by giving remarks on some of them.

Linear Computational Lambda Calculus. Although in this paper we described our transformations as the translations from the computational lambda calculus to the linear lambda calculus, there is an obvious way to factor the transformations through yet another intermediate type theory: the *linear computational lambda calculus*, which is the !- (and ⊗-) fragment of intuitionistic linear logic enriched with computational function types (which should not be confused with linear or intuitionistic function types). While the semantics of this new calculus is easily described (as a symmetric monoidal category with a suitable monoidal comonad ! and Kleisli exponentials), we do not know if the calculus allows a reasonably simple axiomatization, which would be necessary for using the calculus in practice (e.g. as a foundation of "linearized" A-normal forms which could be used for the direct-style reasoning about linearly used effects).

Linearly Used Continuations vs. Linearly Used Global States. If we have chosen a *classical linear type theory* as the target language, the distinction between continuation-passing style and state-passing style no longer exists: since we have $\tau \simeq \tau^{\perp\perp}$ in classical linear logic (CLL), a linear continuation monad is isomorphic to a linear state monad: $(\tau \multimap o) \multimap o \simeq o^{\perp} \multimap (\tau \otimes o^{\perp})$. Thus there is no reason to deal with the effects induced by these monads separately, if we take the transformations into CLL as their semantics. In fact the usual (non-linear) state monad fits in this scheme, as we have $S \to (\tau \otimes !S) \simeq (\tau \multimap (!S)^{\perp}) \multimap (!S)^{\perp}$, so at least we can deal with global states as a special instance of linearly used continuations. Is this the case for the transformations into intuitionistic linear logic (as we considered in this paper) too?

We are currently studying these issues using a term calculus for CLL proposed in [11] as the target language of the transformations. In particular, if a conjecture on the fullness of CLL over ILL stated in *ibid.* is positively solved, it follows that the linear state-passing-style transformation (derived from the linear state monad) is also fully complete, by applying the correspondence between linear continuation monads and linear state monads as noted above.

Full Abstraction Result of Berger, Honda and Yoshida. In a recent work [5], Berger, Honda and Yoshida have shown that the translation from PCF into a linearly typed π-calculus is fully abstract. Since the translation ("functions as processes" [13]) can be seen a variant of the CPS transform (as emphasized by Thielecke) and the linear typing is used for capturing the linear usage of continuations, it should be possible to identify the common semantic structure behind their work and our approach.

Lily. The Lily project [7] considers the theory of polymorphic linear lambda calculi and their use as appropriate typed intermediate languages for compilers. It would be fruitful to combine their ideas and results with ours.

Acknowledgements

I thank Josh Berdine, Peter O'Hearn, Uday Reddy, Hayo Thielecke and Hongseok Yang for helpful discussions, and Jacques Garrigue and Susumu Nishimura for comments on an early version. Thanks also to anonymous reviewers for helpful comments. Part of this work was carried out while the author was visiting Laboratory for Foundations of Computer Science, University of Edinburgh.

References

[1] Barber, A. and Plotkin, G. (1997) Dual intuitionistic linear logic. Submitted. An earlier version available as Technical Report ECS-LFCS-96-347, LFCS, University of Edinburgh. 167, 171, 173, 174

[2] Benton, N. and Wadler, P. (1996) Linear logic, monads, and the lambda calculus. In *Proc. 11th Annual Symposium on Logic in Computer Science*, pp. 420–431. 169, 170

[3] Berdine, J., O'Hearn, P. W., Reddy, U. S. and Thielecke, H. (2001) Linearly used continuations. In *Proc. ACM SIGPLAN Workshop on Continuations (CW'01)*, Technical Report No. 545, Computer Science Department, Indiana University. 167, 171, 178, 179

[4] Berdine, J., O'Hearn, P. W. and Thielecke, H. (2000) On affine typing and completeness of CPS. Manuscript. 169, 171, 176

[5] Berger, M., Honda, K. and Yoshida, N. (2001) Sequentiality for the π-calculus. In *Proc. Typed Lambda Calculi and Applications (TLCA 2001)*, Springer Lecture Notes in Computer Science **2044**, pp. 29–45. 180

[6] Bierman, G. M. (1995) What is a categorical model of intuitionistic linear logic? In *Proc. Typed Lambda Calculi and Applications (TLCA'95)*, Springer Lecture Notes in Computer Science **902**, pp. 78–93. 169

[7] Bierman, G. M., Pitts, A. M. and Russo, C. V. (2000) Operational properties of Lily, a polymorphic linear lambda calculus with recursion. In *Proc. Higher Order Operational Techniques in Semantics (HOOTS 2000)*, Electronic Notes in Theoretical Computer Science **41**. 180

[8] Blute, R., Cockett, J. R. B. and Seely, R. A. G. (1996) ! and ? - Storage as tensorial strength. *Math. Structures Comput. Sci.* **6**(4), 313–351. 178

[9] Girard, J.-Y. (1987) Linear logic. *Theoret. Comp. Sci.* **50**, 1–102. 167

[10] Hasegawa, M. (2000) Girard translation and logical predicates. *J. Functional Programming* **10**(1), 77–89. 176

[11] Hasegawa, M. (2002) Classical linear logic of implications. In *Proc. Computer Science Logic (CSL'02)*, Springer Lecture Notes in Computer Science. 179

[12] Hasegawa, M. and Kakutani, Y. (2001) Axioms for recursion in call-by-value (extended abstract). In *Proc. Foundations of Software Science and Computation Structures (FoSSaCS 2001)*, Springer Lecture Notes in Computer Science **2030**, pp. 246–260. 177, 178

[13] Milner, R. (1992) Functions as processes. *Math. Structures Compt. Sci.* **2**(2), 119–141. 180

[14] Moggi, E. (1989) Computational lambda-calculus and monads. In *Proc. 4th Annual Symposium on Logic in Computer Science*, pp. 14–23; a different version available as Technical Report ECS-LFCS-88-86, University of Edinburgh, 1988. 168, 169, 171

[15] Plotkin, G. D. (1975) Call-by-name, call-by-value, and the λ-calculus. *Theoret. Comput. Sci.* **1**(1), 125–159. 171, 175

[16] Sabry, A. and Felleisen, M. (1992) Reasoning about programs in continuation-passing style. In *Proc. ACM Conference on Lisp and Functional Programming*, pp. 288–298; extended version in *Lisp and Symbolic Comput.* **6**(3/4), 289–360, 1993. 168, 171, 176

[17] Simpson, A. K. and Plotkin, G. D. (2000) Complete axioms for categorical fixed-point operators. In *Proc. 15th Annual Symposium on Logic in Computer Science (LICS 2000)*, pp. 30–41. 178

A   The Inversion Function

Answers : $\Gamma^\circ \; ; \; k : \theta^\circ \to o \vdash A : o \implies \Gamma \vdash A^* : \theta$

$$\frac{\overline{\Gamma^\circ \; ; \; k : \theta^\circ \to o \vdash k : \theta^\circ \to o} \quad \vdots \atop \Gamma^\circ \; ; \; \emptyset \vdash V : \theta^\circ}{\Gamma^\circ \; ; \; k : \theta^\circ \to o \vdash k \, @ \, V : o} \qquad \mapsto \qquad \begin{matrix} \vdots \\ \Gamma \vdash V^* : \theta \end{matrix}$$

$$\frac{\vdots \atop \Gamma^\circ \; ; \; \emptyset \vdash P : (\sigma_2^\circ \to o) \multimap o \quad \vdots \atop \Gamma^\circ \; ; \; k : \theta^\circ \to o \vdash C : \sigma_2^\circ \to o}{\Gamma^\circ \; ; \; k : \theta^\circ \to o \vdash P \, C : o}$$

$$\mapsto \qquad \frac{\begin{matrix} \vdots \\ \Gamma \vdash C^* : \sigma_2 \to \theta \end{matrix} \quad \begin{matrix} \vdots \\ \Gamma \vdash P^* : \sigma_2 \end{matrix}}{\Gamma \vdash C^* \, P^* : \theta}$$

where $\Gamma = \Gamma_1, x : \sigma_1 \to \sigma_2, \Gamma_2$ and $P = x \, @ \, V$ with $\Gamma^\circ \; ; \; \emptyset \vdash V : \sigma_1^\circ$
(see the last case of **Programs**)

Values : $\Gamma^\circ \; ; \; \emptyset \vdash V : \sigma^\circ \implies \Gamma \vdash V^* : \sigma$

$$\overline{\Gamma_1^\circ, x : \sigma^\circ, \Gamma_2^\circ \; ; \; \emptyset \vdash x : \sigma^\circ} \qquad \mapsto \qquad \overline{\Gamma_1, x : \sigma, \Gamma_2 \vdash x : \sigma}$$

$$\frac{\vdots \atop \Gamma^\circ, x : \sigma_1^\circ \; ; \; \emptyset \vdash P : (\sigma_2^\circ \to o) \multimap o}{\Gamma^\circ \; ; \; \emptyset \vdash \boldsymbol{\lambda} x^{\sigma_1^\circ}.P : (\sigma_1 \to \sigma_2)^\circ} \qquad \mapsto \qquad \frac{\vdots \atop \Gamma, x : \sigma_1 \vdash P^* : \sigma_2}{\Gamma \vdash \lambda x^{\sigma_1}.P^* : \sigma_1 \to \sigma_2}$$

Continuations : $\Gamma^\circ \; ; \; k : \theta^\circ \to o \vdash C : \sigma^\circ \to o \implies \Gamma \vdash C^* : \sigma \to \theta$

$$\overline{\Gamma^\circ \; ; \; k : \theta^\circ \to o \vdash k : \theta^\circ \to o} \qquad \mapsto \qquad \frac{\overline{\Gamma, x : \theta \vdash x : \theta}}{\Gamma \vdash \lambda x^\theta.x : \theta \to \theta}$$

$$\frac{\vdots \atop \Gamma^\circ, x : \sigma^\circ \; ; \; k : \theta^\circ \to o \vdash A : o}{\Gamma^\circ \; ; \; k : \theta^\circ \to o \vdash \boldsymbol{\lambda} x^{\sigma^\circ}.A : \sigma^\circ \to o} \qquad \mapsto \qquad \frac{\vdots \atop \Gamma, x : \sigma \vdash A^* : \theta}{\Gamma \vdash \lambda x^\sigma.A^* : \sigma \to \theta}$$

Programs : $\Gamma^\circ \; ; \; \emptyset \vdash P : (\sigma^\circ \to o) \multimap o \implies \Gamma \vdash P^* : \sigma$

$$\frac{\vdots \atop \Gamma^\circ \; ; \; k : \theta^\circ \to o \vdash A : o}{\Gamma^\circ \; ; \; \emptyset \vdash \lambda k^{\theta^\circ \to o}.A : (\theta^\circ \to o) \multimap o} \qquad \mapsto \qquad \begin{matrix} \vdots \\ \Gamma \vdash A^* : \theta \end{matrix}$$

$$\frac{\overline{\Gamma^\circ \; ; \; \emptyset \vdash x : (\sigma_1 \to \sigma_2)^\circ} \quad \vdots \atop \Gamma^\circ \; ; \; \emptyset \vdash V : \sigma_1^\circ}{\Gamma^\circ \; ; \; \emptyset \vdash x \, @ \, V : (\sigma_2^\circ \to o) \multimap o} \qquad \mapsto \qquad \frac{\overline{\Gamma \vdash x : \sigma_1 \to \sigma_2} \quad \begin{matrix} \vdots \\ \Gamma \vdash V^* : \sigma_1 \end{matrix}}{\Gamma \vdash x \, V^* : \sigma_2}$$

where $\Gamma = \Gamma_1, x : \sigma_1 \to \sigma_2, \Gamma_2$

Coinductive Interpreters for Process Calculi

Luís Soares Barbosa and José Nuno Oliveira

Departamento de Informática, Universidade do Minho, Braga, Portugal
{lsb,jno}@di.uminho.pt

Abstract. This paper suggests *functional programming* languages with coinductive types as suitable devices for prototyping *process calculi*. The proposed approach is independent of any particular process calculus and makes explicit the different ingredients present in the design of any such calculi. In particular structural aspects of the underlying *behaviour model* become clearly separated from the *interaction* structure which defines the synchronisation discipline. The approach is illustrated by the detailed development in CHARITY of an interpreter for a family of process languages.

Keywords: functional programming, applications, coinductive types.

1 Introduction

The essence of *concurrent* computation lies in the fact that a transition in a system may *interact* with, or depend upon, another transition occurring in a different system executing alongside. Since this was observed by C. A. Petri, in the early sixties, several process calculi have been proposed to specify and reason about concurrent and communicating systems.

This paper argues that *functional programming* may provide a suitable vehicle for prototyping such calculi and assess alternative design decisions. Such a role for functional languages has long been established in the formal methods community. However, only static, data-oriented, aspects of computational systems are usually considered there.

Our starting point is the well known fact that *initial* algebras and *final* coalgebras, underlying *inductive* and *coinductive* types, provide abstract descriptions of a variety of phenomena in programming, namely of *data* and *behavioural* structures, respectively. Initiality and finality, as (categorical) universal properties, entail definitional as well as proof principles, *i.e.*, a basis for the development of program calculi directly based on (*i.e.*, actually driven by) type specifications. Moreover, such properties can be turned into programming *combinators* which are parametric on the *shape* of the type structure, captured by a signature of operations encoded in a suitable functor. These can be used, not only to reason about programs, but also to program with. In fact, such combinators have been incorporated in real programming languages as *polytypic* functionals, generalising well-known `map`, `fold` and `unfold` constructs (see, *e.g.*, [3, 8]).

In this paper we resort to the experimental programming language CHARITY [4] to prototype process calculi and quickly implement simple interpreters for

Z. Hu and M. Rodríguez-Artalejo (Eds.): FLOPS 2002, LNCS 2441, pp. 183–197, 2002.

the corresponding process languages. As a programming language, CHARITY is based on the term logic of distributive categories and provides a definitional mechanism for categorical datatypes *i.e.*, for both initial algebras and final coalgebras. Processes can therefore be directly represented as inhabitants of coinductive types, *i.e.*, of the carriers of final coalgebras for suitable Set endofunctors.

We believe this approach has a number of advantages:

- First of all, it provides a *uniform* treatment of processes and other computational structures, *e.g.*, data structures, both represented as categorical types for functors capturing signatures of, respectively, observers and constructors. Placing data and behaviour at a similar level conveys the idea that process models can be chosen and specified according to a given application area, in the same way that a suitable data structure is defined to meet a particular engineering problem. As a prototyping platform, CHARITY is a sober tool in which different process combinators can be defined, interpreters for the associated languages quickly developed and the expressiveness of different calculi compared with respect to the intended applications. We believe that prototyping has an important role in any specification method, as it supports stepwise development. In particular, it allows each design stage to be immediately animated and quick feedback about its behaviour gathered.
- The approach is independent of any particular process calculus and makes explicit the different ingredients present in the design of any such calculi. In particular structural aspects of the underlying *behaviour model* (*e.g.*, the dichotomies such as active *vs* reactive, deterministic *vs* non-deterministic) become clearly separated from the *interaction* structure which defines the synchronisation discipline.
- Finally, as discussed in [2], proofs of process properties can be done in a calculational (basically *equational* and *pointfree*) style, therefore circumventing the explicit construction of bisimulations typical of most of the literature on process calculi.

2   Preliminaries

It is well known that the signature of a data type, *i.e.*, its contractual interface, may be captured by a *functor*, say T, and that a canonical representative of the envisaged structure arises as a solution, *i.e.*, as fixed point, of the equation $X \cong T\, X$. In fact, an abstract data structure is defined as a T-*algebra*, *i.e.*, a map $t : T\, D \longrightarrow D$ which specifies how values of D are built using a collection of constructors, recorded in T. The canonical representative of such T-algebras is the (initial) term algebra.

There are, however, several phenomena in computing which are hardly definable (or even simply not definable) in terms of a complete set of constructors. This leads to *coalgebra* theory [16]. While in algebra data entities are built by constructors and regarded as different if 'differently constructed', coalgebras deal with entities that are observed, or decomposed, by observers and whose internal configurations are identified if not distinguishable by observation. Given an endofunctor T, a T-coalgebra is simply a map $p : U \longrightarrow T\ U$ which may be thought of as a transition structure, of *shape* T, on a set U, usually referred to as the *carrier* or the *state space*. The shape of T reflects the way the state is (partially) accessed, through *observers*, and how it evolves, through *actions*. As a consequence, equality has to be replaced by *bisimilarity* (*i.e.*, equality with respect to the observation structure provided by T) and coinduction replaces induction as a proof principle. For a given T, the final coalgebra consists of all possible behaviours up to bisimilarity, in the same sense that an initial algebra collects all terms up to isomorphism. This is also a fixpoint of a functor equation and provides a suitable universe for reasoning about behavioural issues. This has lead to some terminology for final coalgebras: *coinductive* or *left datatypes* in [6] or [5], *codata* and *codatatypes* [9], *final systems* in [16] or *object types* in [7].

A T-coalgebra *morphism* between two T-coalgebras, p and q, is a map h between their carriers such that $T\ h \cdot p = q \cdot h$. The *unique* such morphism to the final coalgebra $\omega_T : \nu_T \longrightarrow T\ \nu_T$ from any other coalgebra $\langle U, p \rangle$ is called a T-*anamorphism* [13], or the *coinductive extension* of p [17]. It is written $[\![p]\!]_T$ or, simply, $[\![p]\!]$, and satisfies the following universal property,

$$k = [\![p]\!]_T \;\; \Leftrightarrow \;\; \omega_T \cdot k = T\ k \cdot p$$

being unique up to isomorphism. Its dual, in the algebraic side, is the unique arrow $(\![d]\!)_T$, or simply $(\![d]\!)$, from the initial T-algebra to any other algebra d, known as a *catamorphism*. Both d here and p above are referred in the sequel as the catamorphism (resp., anamorphism) *gene*.

CHARITY provides direct support for both initial algebras and final coalgebras for strong functors. The *strong* qualification means that the underlying functor T possess a *strength* [10, 5], *i.e.*, a natural transformation $\tau_r^T : T \times - \implies T(\mathsf{Id} \times -)$ subject to certain conditions. Its effect is to *distribute* context along functor T. When types are modeled in such a setting, the universal combinators (as, *e.g.*, cata and anamorphisms) will possess a somewhat more general shape, able to deal with the presence of extra parameters in the functions being defined. This holds, of course, even when the underlying category is not cartesian closed (and therefore *currying* is not available).

3   Processes and Combinators

3.1   Processes

The operational semantics of a process calculus is usually given in terms of a transition relation $\xrightarrow{a}$ over processes, indexed by a set *Act* of actions, in which a process gets committed, and the resulting 'continuations', *i.e.*, the behaviours subsequently exhibited. A first, basic design decision concerns the definition of what should be understood by such a collection. As a rule, it is defined as a *set*, in order to express non-determinism. Other, more restrictive, possibilities consider a sequence or even just a single continuation, modelling, respectively, 'ordered' non-determinism or determinism. In general, this underlying behaviour model can be represented by a functor B.

An orthogonal decision concerns the intended interpretation of the transition relation, which is usually left implicit or underspecified in process calculi. We may, however, distinguish between

- An 'active' interpretation, in which a transition $p \xrightarrow{a} q$ is informally characterised as 'p evolves to q by performing an action a', both q and a being solely determined by p.
- A 'reactive' interpretation, informally reading 'p reacts to an external stimulus a by evolving to q'.

Processes will then be taken as inhabitants of the carrier of the final coalgebra $\omega : \nu \longrightarrow \mathsf{T}\,\nu$, with T defined as $\mathsf{B}\,(Act \times \mathsf{Id})$, in the first case, and $(\mathsf{B}\,\mathsf{Id})^{Act}$, in the second. To illustrate our approach, we shall focus on the particular case where B is the finite powerset functor and the 'active' interpretation is adopted. The transition relation, for this case, is given by $p \xrightarrow{a} q$ iff $\langle a, q \rangle \in \omega\,p$.

The restriction to the finite powerset avoids cardinality problems and assures the existence in Set of a final coalgebra for T. This restricts us to *image-finite* processes, a not too severe restriction in practice which may be partially circumvented by a suitable definition of the structure of *Act*. For instance, by taking *Act* as *channel* names through which data flows. This corresponds closely to 'Ccs with value passing' [14]. Therefore, only the set of channels, and not the messages (seen as pairs channel/data), must remain finite. In fact, as detailed below, an algebraic structure should be imposed upon the set *Act* of actions in order to capture different interaction disciplines. This will be called an *interaction structure* in the sequel.

Down to the prototype level, we will start by declaring a process space as the coinductive type `Pr(A)`, parametrized by a specification A of the interaction structure:

```
data C -> Pr(A) = bh: C -> set(A * C).
```

where `set` stands for a suitable implementation of (finite) sets.

3.2 Interaction

We first assume that actions are generated from a set L of *labels*, *i.e.*, a set of formal names. Then, an *interaction structure* is defined as an Abelian positive monoid $\langle Act; \theta, 1 \rangle$ with a zero element 0. It is assumed that neither 0 nor 1 belong to the set L of labels. The intuition is that θ determines the interaction discipline whereas 0 represents the absence of interaction: for all $a \in Act$, $a\theta 0 = 0$. On the other hand, the monoid being positive implies $a\theta a' = 1$ iff $a = a' = 1$. Notice that the role of both 0 and 1 is essentially technical in the description of the interaction discipline. In some situations, 1 may be seen as an *idle* action, but its role, in the general case, is to equip the behaviour functor with a *monadic* structure, which would not be the case if *Act* were defined simply as an Abelian semigroup.

Let us consider two examples of interaction structures. For each process calculus, actions over L are introduced as an inductive type Ac(L) upon which an equality function and a product θ are defined.

Co-occurrence. A basic example of an interaction structure captures action co-occurrence: θ is defined as $a\theta b = \langle a, b \rangle$, for all $a, b \in Act$ different from 0 and 1. The corresponding type, parametric on the set L labels, is therefore defined inductively as follows

```
data Ac(L) -> A =
    act: L -> A | syn: A * A -> A | nop: 1 -> A | idle: 1 -> A.
```

The embedding of labels into actions is explicitly represented by the constructor act. The distinguished actions 0 and 1 are denoted by nop and idle, respectively. Action co-occurrence, for any actions a and b different from 0 and 1, is represented by syn(a,b). The specification is complete with a definition of action product θ, encoded here as the function prodAc, and an equality predicate eqA on actions, both parametric on L. The actual CHARITY code for θ is as follows,

```
def prodAc : Ac(L) * Ac(L) -> Ac(L)
    = (nop, _ ) => nop  | ( _ ,nop) => nop | (idle, x) => x
    | (x ,idle) => x    | ( a1, a2) => syn( a1, a2).
```

The CCS case. CCS [14] synchronisation discipline provides another example. In this case the set L of labels carries an involutive operation represented by an horizontal bar as in $\bar{a}$, for $a \in L$. Any two actions a and $\bar{a}$ are called complementary. A special action $\tau \notin L$ is introduced to represent the result of a synchronisation between a pair of complementary actions. Therefore, the result of θ is τ whenever applied to a pair of complementary actions and 0 in all other cases, except, obviously, if one of the arguments is 1.

We first introduce the involutive complement operation on labels by replacing L by the parametric type Lb(N) and defining a label equality function eqL.

```
data Lb(N) -> I = name: N -> I | inv: I -> I.
```

Then the interaction structure is defined by Ac(L) as above, together with action equality and product:

```
def prodAc{eqL: Lb(N) * Lb(N) -> bool} :
        Ac(Lb(N)) * Ac(Lb(N)) -> Ac(Lb(N))
    = (act(l),act(k)) | or(eqL(l,inv(k)),eqL(inv(l),k) => tau
                      |  ..    => nop
    | (idle, x) => x  | (x ,idle) => x  |  _        => nop.
```

3.3   Dynamic Combinators

The usual CCS dynamic combinators — *i.e.*, *inaction*, *prefix* and non-deterministic *choice* — are defined as operators on the final universe of processes. Being no recursive, they have a direct (coinductive) definition which depends solely on the chosen process structure. Therefore, the *inactive process* is represented as a constant $\mathsf{nil} : 1 \longrightarrow \nu$ upon which no relevant observation can be made. *Prefix* gives rise to an *Act*-indexed family of operators $a. : \nu \longrightarrow \nu$, with $a \in Act$. Finally, the possible actions of the *non-deterministic choice* of two processes p and q corresponds to the collection of all actions allowed for p and q. Therefore, the operator $+ : \nu \times \nu \longrightarrow \nu$ can only be defined over a process structure in which observations form a collection. Formally,

$$
\begin{array}{rl}
\text{inaction} & \omega \cdot \mathsf{nil} = \underline{\emptyset} \\
\text{choice} & \omega \cdot + = \cup \cdot (\omega \times \omega) \\
\text{prefix} & \omega \cdot a. = \mathsf{sing} \cdot \mathsf{label}_a
\end{array}
$$

where $\mathsf{sing} = \lambda x. \ \{x\}$ and $\mathsf{label}_a = \lambda x. \ \langle a, x \rangle$. These definitions are directly translated to CHARITY as functions `bnil`, `bpre` and `bcho`, respectively:

```
def bnil: 1 -> Pr(A)              def bpre: A * Pr(A) -> Pr(A)
    = () => (bh: empty).              = (a, t)  => (bh: sing(a,t)).

            def bcho: Pr(A) * Pr(A)  -> Pr(A)
                = (t1, t2) => (bh: union(bh t1, bh t2)).
```

3.4   Static Combinators

Persistence through action occurrence leads to the recursive definition of *static* combinators. This means they arise as anamorphisms generated by suitable 'gene' coalgebras. *Interleaving*, *restriction* and *renaming* are examples of *static* combinators, which, moreover, depend only on the process structure. On the other hand, *synchronous product* and *parallel composition* also rely on the interaction structure underlying the calculus. In each case, we give both a mathematical definition of the combinator and the corresponding CHARITY code. There is a direct correspondence between these two levels. Some 'housekeeping' morphisms, like the *diagonal* $\triangle$, used in the former are more conveniently handled by the CHARITY term logic.

Interleaving. Although *interleaving*, a binary operator $||| : \nu \times \nu \longrightarrow \nu$, is not considered as a combinator in most process calculi, it is the simplest form of 'parallel' aggregation in the sense that it is independent of any particular interaction discipline. The definition below captures the intuition that the observations over the interleaving of two processes correspond to all possible interleavings of the observations of its arguments. Thus, one defines $||| = [\![\alpha_{|||}]\!]$, where

$$\alpha_{|||} = \nu \times \nu \xrightarrow{\Delta} (\nu \times \nu) \times (\nu \times \nu)$$

$$\xrightarrow{(\omega \times \mathrm{id}) \times (\mathrm{id} \times \omega)} (\mathcal{P}(Act \times \nu) \times \nu) \times (\nu \times \mathcal{P}(Act \times \nu))$$

$$\xrightarrow{\tau_r \times \tau_l} \mathcal{P}(Act \times (\nu \times \nu)) \times \mathcal{P}(Act \times (\nu \times \nu)) \xrightarrow{\cup} \mathcal{P}(Act \times (\nu \times \nu))$$

The CHARITY code [1] for this

```
def bint: Pr(Ac(L)) * Pr(Ac(L))  -> Pr(Ac(L))
  = (t1, t2) =>
    (| (r1,r2) => bh: union(taur(bh r1, r2), taul(bh r2, r1)) |) (t1,t2).
```

Restriction and Renaming. The *restriction* combinator $\setminus_K$, for each subset $K \subseteq L$, forbids the occurrence of actions in K. Formally, $\setminus_K = [\![\alpha_{\setminus K}]\!]$ where

$$\alpha_{\setminus K} = \nu \xrightarrow{\omega} \mathcal{P}(Act \times \nu) \xrightarrow{\text{filter}_K} \mathcal{P}(Act \times \nu)$$

where $\text{filter}_K = \lambda s . \{t \in s \mid \pi_1 t \notin K\}$.

Once an interaction structure is fixed, any homomorphism $f : Act \longrightarrow Act$ lifts to a *renaming* combinator $[f]$ between processes defined as $[f] = [\![\alpha_{[f]}]\!]$, where

$$\alpha_{[f]} = \nu \xrightarrow{\omega} \mathcal{P}(Act \times \nu) \xrightarrow{\mathcal{P}(f \times \mathrm{id})} \mathcal{P}(Act \times \nu)$$

Let us consider the CHARITY encoding of *restriction*:

```
def bret{eqL: Lb(N) * Lb(N) -> bool}:
       Pr(Ac(Lb(N))) * set(Lb(N)) -> Pr(Ac(Lb(N)))

= (t, k) =>
  (| r => bh:
       filter{x => not member{eqA{eqL}}(p0 x, compret k)} (bh r) |) t.
```

Any restriction set K of labels will have to be extended to a set of actions, by application of the embedding **act**, before it can be used in **bret**. Additionally, it may be 'completed' in order to cope with some syntactic conventions appearing in particular calculi. For example, to model CCS, it becomes necessary to close K with respect to label complement (*i.e.*, the constructor **inv** in the CCS label algebra implementation given above). Both tasks are achieved by function **compret** below, which should be tuned according to the syntactic particularities of the calculus under consideration. In the case of CCS it will look like

---

[1] Notice morphisms $\tau_r : \mathcal{P}(Act \times X) \times C \longrightarrow \mathcal{P}(Act \times (X \times C))$ and $\tau_l : C \times \mathcal{P}(Act \times X) \longrightarrow \mathcal{P}(Act \times (C \times X))$ stand for, respectively, the right and left *strength* associated to functor $\mathcal{P}(Act \times \mathrm{Id})$. They are straightforwardly encoded in CHARITY, *e.g.*, `def taur = (s,t) => set{(a,x) => (a, (x,t))} s`.

```
def compret: set(Lb(N)) -> set(Ac(Lb(N)))
 = s => union( set{l => act(l)} s , set{l => act(inv(l)) } s).
```

Synchronous Product. This static operator models the simultaneous execution of its two arguments. At each step the resulting action is determined by the interaction structure for the calculus. Formally, $\otimes = [\![\alpha_\otimes]\!]$ where

$$\alpha_\otimes = \nu \times \nu \xrightarrow{(\omega \times \omega)} \mathcal{P}(Act \times \nu) \times \mathcal{P}(Act \times \nu)$$

$$\xrightarrow{\delta_r} \mathcal{P}(Act \times (\nu \times \nu)) \xrightarrow{\text{sel}} \mathcal{P}(Act \times (\nu \times \nu))$$

where $\text{sel} = \text{filter}_{\{0\}}$ filters out all synchronisation failures. Notice how interaction is catered by δ_r — the distributive law for the strong monad $\mathcal{P}(Act \times \text{Id})$. In fact, the monoidal structure in Act extends functor $\mathcal{P}(Act \times \text{Id})$ to a strong monad, δ_r being the Kleisli composition of the left and the right strengths. This, on its turn, involves the application of the monad multiplication to 'flatten' the result and this, for a monoid monad, requires the suitable application of the underlying monoidal operation. This, in our case, fixes the interaction discipline. Going pointwise:

$$\delta_r^{\mathcal{P}(Act \times \text{Id})} \langle c_1, c_2 \rangle = \{\langle a'\theta a, \langle p, p' \rangle\rangle | \langle a, p \rangle \in c_1 \wedge \langle a', p' \rangle \in c_2\}$$

In CHARITY,

```
def bsyn{eqL: Lb(N) * Lb(N) -> bool}:
      Pr(Ac(Lb(N))) * Pr(Ac(Lb(N))) -> Pr(Ac(Lb(N)))

= (t1, t2) =>
      (| (r1,r2) => bh:  sel{eqL} deltar{eqL} (bh r1, bh r2) |) (t1,t2).
```

where `deltar` and `sel` implement morphisms δ_r and `sel`, respectively.

Parallel Composition. *Parallel* composition arises as a combination of *interleaving* and *synchronous product*, in the sense that the evolution of $p \mid q$, for processes p and q, consists of all possible derivations of p and q plus the ones associated to the synchronisations allowed by the particular interaction structure for the calculus. This cannot be achieved by mere composition of the corresponding combinators ||| and $\otimes$: it has to be performed at the 'genes' level for ||| and $\otimes$. Formally, $\mid = [\![\alpha_\mid]\!]$, where

$$\alpha_\mid = \nu \times \nu \xrightarrow{\Delta} (\nu \times \nu) \times (\nu \times \nu)$$

$$\xrightarrow{(\alpha_{|||} \times \alpha_\otimes)} \mathcal{P}(Act \times (\nu \times \nu)) \times \mathcal{P}(Act \times (\nu \times \nu))$$

$$\xrightarrow{\cup} \mathcal{P}(Act \times (\nu \times \nu))$$

which is coded in CHARITY as

```
def bpar{eqL: Lb(N) * Lb(N) -> bool}:
       Pr(Ac(Lb(N))) * Pr(Ac(Lb(N))) -> Pr(Ac(Lb(N)))

= (t1, t2) =>
   (| (r1,r2) => bh: union(
                  sel{eqL} deltar{eqL} (bh r1, bh r2),
                  union(taur(bh r1, r2), taul(bh r2, r1)))
   |) (t1,t2).
```

4   A Process Language

There is so far no place for *recursive* processes in the approach we have been discussing. The possibility of supplying the dynamics of each particular example as a particular 'gene' coalgebra, is unsatisfactory in this respect. Instead, the obvious way to deal with *recursive* processes in general consists of defining a *language* whose terms stand for process expressions, including a construction involving process *variables* as valid terms. Such variables should be bound, in whatever we understand as the interpreter *environment*, by process equations of the form $v = exp$, where v is a variable and exp a process expression. We have, however, to proceed with some care as it is well-known that not all defining equations determine process behaviour in an unique way. For example, not only any process is a solution to $v = v$, but also equations like $v = v|v$ admit different, no bisimilar, solutions. One way of ensuring the existence of unique solutions, is to require that all variables occurring on the right hand side of an equation are guarded, in the sense that they are bounded by a prefix combinator. This has been proved in [14] as a sound criteria for the existence of unique solutions to what is called there *strict bisimulation equations* which, recall, correspond to equality in the final coalgebra. In fact, in [14], guardedness is only required for variables wrt expressions in which they occurr. The extension, assumed here, of this requirement to all variables in an expression facilitates the development of the interpreter and does not appear to be a major restriction. Therefore, our process language will include a prefix-like construction — pvar — to introduce (guarded) variables in an expression.

Summing up, we are left with the tasks of defining a term language for processes, its interpretation in the (final) semantic model and a suitable model for the environment collecting the relevant process defining equations. Let us tackle them, one at a time.

The Language. As expected, a term language for processes, over a set L of labels, will be defined as an inductive type. The CHARITY declaration below introduces Ln(L) as the initial algebra for a functor Σ induced by the following BNF description:

$$\langle P \rangle ::= \texttt{pnil} \qquad | \ \texttt{ppre}(a, \langle P \rangle) \ | \ \texttt{pcho}(\langle P \rangle, \langle P \rangle) \ |$$
$$\texttt{pint}(\langle P \rangle, \langle P \rangle) \ | \ \texttt{psyn}(\langle P \rangle, \langle P \rangle) \ | \ \texttt{ppar}(\langle P \rangle, \langle P \rangle) \ |$$
$$\texttt{pret}(\langle P \rangle, K) \ | \ \texttt{pren}(\langle P \rangle, f) \ | \ \texttt{pvar}(a, i)$$

where $a \in \text{Ac(L)}$, $K \subseteq \text{L}$, i is a process variable and f a renaming Ac(L) homomorphism. Constructors pnil, ppre, pcho, pint, psyn, ppar, pret and pren correspond to the different process combinators. The only exception is pvar, which builds a new process given an action and a process variable. Its semantics is defined similarly to the one of the prefix combinator, according to the discussion above.

The equivalent CHARITY declaration follows. Note the definition is sufficiently generic, as it is parametric on L and resorts to whatever interaction structure is provided for Ac(L):

```
data Ln(L) -> P =
    pnil: 1 -> P | ppre: Ac(L) * P -> P |
    pcho: P * P -> P | pint: P * P -> P |
    psyn: P * P -> P | ppar: P * P -> P |
    pret: P * set(L) -> P |
    pren : P * map(Ac(L), Ac(L)) -> P |
    pvar: Ac(L) * string -> P.
```

The Interpreter. How can Ln(L) expressions be interpreted as processes? Within the initial algebra approach to semantics, once the syntax is fixed, a semantic Σ-algebra would be produced and the interpretation defined as the associated catamorphism. Our semantic universe, however, is the final coalgebra for functor $\mathcal{P}(\text{Ac(L)} \times \text{Id})$, and, therefore, the dual final semantics approach will be followed up. What has to be done is to cast the syntax, *i.e.*, the set of terms Ln(L), into a $\mathcal{P}(\text{Ac(L)} \times \text{Id})$-coalgebra. The interpreter will follow as the associated *anamorphism*.

Let function $\text{sem} : \text{Ln(L)} \longrightarrow \text{Pr(Ac(L))}$ stand for the desired interpreter. The 'gene' for this anamorphism is a 'syntactic' coalgebra $\text{syn} : \text{Ln(L)} \longrightarrow \mathcal{P}(\text{Ac(L)} \times \text{Ln(L)})$ which computes the 'syntactical' derivations of process terms. Observe, now, that the 'canonical' way to define syn is as a Σ-catamorphism. Its 'gene' is denoted by α_{syn} in the sequel. The diagram below contains the 'full' picture, where α_{syn} is actually the *only* function to be supplied by the programmer:

$$
\begin{array}{ccc}
\text{Pr(Ac(L))} & \overset{\omega}{\longrightarrow} & \mathcal{P}(\text{Ac(L)} \times \text{Pr(Ac(L))}) \\
\scriptstyle{\text{sem}} \big\uparrow & & \big\uparrow \scriptstyle{\mathcal{P}(\text{id} \times \text{sem})} \\
\text{Ln(L)} & \overset{\text{syn}}{\longrightarrow} & \mathcal{P}(\text{Ac(L)} \times \text{Ln(L)}) \\
\scriptstyle{\alpha} \big\uparrow & & \big\uparrow \scriptstyle{\alpha_{\text{syn}}} \\
\Sigma\,\text{Ln(L)} & \overset{\Sigma\,\text{syn}}{\longrightarrow} & \Sigma\,\mathcal{P}(\text{Ac(L)} \times \text{Ln(L)})
\end{array}
$$

Then, we get for free

$$\text{syn} = (\![\alpha_{\text{syn}}]\!)_{\Sigma}$$

and

$$\text{sem} = [\![\text{syn}]\!]_{\mathcal{P}(\text{Ac(L)} \times \text{Id})}$$

where ω and α are, respectively, the final $\mathcal{P}(\texttt{Ac(L)} \times \textsf{Id})$-coalgebra and the initial Σ-algebra.

Environment. Our last concern is the introduction of an environment to the interpreter in order to collect all the process defining equations relevant to conduct experiments on a particular network of processes. Such an environment E can be thought of as mapping assigning to each process variable an expression in $\texttt{Ln(L)}$. Assuming variable identifiers are modeled by strings, E will be typed in CHARITY as $\texttt{map(string, Ln(L))}$. Clearly, E acts as a supplier of context information to the interpretation function $\texttt{sem}$, whose type is

$$\texttt{sem} : \texttt{Ln(L)} \times E \longrightarrow \texttt{Pr(Ac(L))}$$

All types in CHARITY are *strong* and, therefore, this extra parameter is smoothly accommodated in our framework. In fact, both $\texttt{sem}$ and $\texttt{syn}$ become defined as, respectively, a *strong anamorphism* for $\mathcal{P}(\texttt{Ac(L)} \times \textsf{Id})$ and a *strong catamorphism* for Σ. The diagram above remains valid, but it has to be interpreted in the Kleisli category for the product comonad. Its interpretation in the original category is depicted in the diagram below, which makes explicit the structure involved by including dotted lines to correctly type an arrow in the Kleisli as an arrow in the original category. Symbols ω' and α' denote, respectively, the corresponding final coalgebra and initial algebra in the Kleisli, defined simply as $\omega \cdot \pi_1$ and $\alpha \cdot \pi_1$ (*cf.*, proposition 4.3 in [5]). Thus,

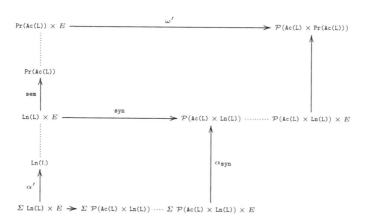

Fig. 1. The overall interpreter diagram

Formally, the interpretation function arises as

$$\texttt{sem} \;=\; \texttt{unfold}_{\mathcal{P}(\texttt{Ac(L)} \times \textsf{Id})} \; \texttt{syn}$$

where

$$\mathsf{syn} \;=\; \mathsf{fold}_{\varSigma}\, \alpha_{\mathsf{syn}}$$

and unfold /fold stand, respectively, for the strong anamorphism and catamorphism combinator.

The actual picture is slightly more complex, however, as the definition of syn is made in terms of both the computations on the substructures of its argument and these substructures themselves. To be precise, it arises as a *strong paramorphism*. *Paramorphisms* [12] generalise catamorphisms in order to deal with cases in which the result of a recursive function depends not only on computations in substructures of its argument, but also on the substructures themselves. The recursion pattern it entails, in the particular case of $\mathbb{N}$, is known as *primitive recursion*.

In the general case, a *paramorphism* is defined as the unique arrow making the following diagram to commute.

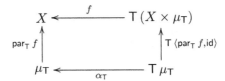

Notice the domain of the 'target algebra' is now the T image of its carrier with the inductive type itself. Paramorphisms have no direct implementation in CHARITY, but we can program their transformation to catamorphisms captured by law

$$\mathsf{par}_{\mathsf{T}}\, f \;=\; \pi_1 \cdot (\!|\langle f, \alpha_{\mathsf{T}} \cdot \mathsf{T}\, \pi_2 \rangle|\!)_{\mathsf{T}}$$

The language, however, provides an easier way of dealing with functions defined as paramorphisms, by using '#'s. Inside a fold, # stands for the value being currently analysed, *before* the recursive application. This is exactly what is done in the interpreter sem presented in Appendix A. Not much remains to be said about this definition as the encoding of each process combinator has already been detailed in the previous section. Just note the interpretation of the new construction pvar(a,i) is as expected: the continuation process arises as the interpretation of the process expression associated to variable i, if i is collected in the environment, or pnil otherwise.

To fully understand the definition, observe that the derivations of a process expression are (a set of pairs of actions and) *process expressions*, whereas, in the previous definition of 'stand-alone' combinators they were defined in terms of *processes* themselves. As an illustration, compare the entry corresponding to renaming in the 'gene' of syn with the definition of bren in the previous section. This same observation justifies the auxiliary definitions of stau1, stau2, ssel, sdelta1 and sdelta2, whose role is similar to the original taur, sel and deltar.

5   Conclusions

This paper specifies process combinators in a way which is directly translatable into the CHARITY programming language. In this way, a functional implementation of a (family of) of calculi becomes available in which experiments can be carried out. By experiments one means that a process expression is supplied to the system and its evolution traced. In fact, all the allowed derivations are computed step by step, resorting to the CHARITY evaluation mechanism for coinductive types. Experimenting with process prototypes is not essentially different from animating data oriented specifications in any of the rapid prototyping systems popular among the formal methods community. The difference lies in the underlying shift towards coinduction, namely final semantics for processes, an active research area triggered by Aczel's landmark paper [1]. Other recent contributions include, for example, references [18] and [11] on model theory for CSP and π-calculus, respectively. Our approach is certainly more programming oriented. Rather than foundational, it favours both *calculation* [2] and animation. Current work includes the full development of a prototyping kernel for this kind of calculi specifications, incorporating an interface layer to provide a more adequate user interface for prototype testing. We feel challenged by *mobility* [15], whose extension in this framework should incorporate variable binding and dynamically generated names and localities.

Although we have illustrated our approach to process prototyping going through, in some detail, a particularly well known family of such calculi in the CCS tradition, we would like to stress its *genericity* at two distinct levels.

First of all, the *behaviour model* is a parameter of the calculus (and of its interpreter). Recall that processes were defined as inhabitants of the carrier of the final coalgebra for $T = B \, (Act \times Id)$, for B the finite powerset functor. We have shown that, assuming a commutative monoidal structure over Act, the behaviour model captured by $\mathcal{P}(Act \times Id)$ is a *strong Abelian monad*. The proposed constructions remain valid for any instantiation of B by such a monad. For example, taking B the identity monad (B = Id), leads to a calculus of *deterministic* (and perpetual) processes. A further elaboration of this would replace Id by Id + 1, entailing a calculus for deterministic, but *partial* processes in the sense that the derivation of a 'dead' state is always possible. Such a calculus is far less expressive than the one dealt with in this paper. In fact, derivations do not form any kind of *collection* and, thus, non-determinism is ruled out. Therefore, combinators which explore non-determinism, lack a counterpart here. Such is the case of *choice, interleaving* and *parallel*. On the other hand, the composition of Id + 1 with the monoidal monad generated by Act is still a strong Abelian monad, and therefore *synchronous product* is still definable.

A second source of genericity, orthogonal to the one above, is the separate specification of an *interaction structure*. Note that all the process combinators introduced in this paper are either *independent* of any particular interaction discipline or *parametrized* by it.

Acknowledgement

The authors wish to thank the *Logic and Formal Methods* group at Minho for the smooth working environment they had the chance to benefit from. Comments by Jan Rutten and Luis Monteiro about research described in this paper are gratefully acknowledged.

References

[1] P. Aczel. Final universes of processes. In Brooks et al, editor, *Proc. Math. Foundations of Programming Semantics*. Springer Lect. Notes Comp. Sci. (802), 1993. 195

[2] L. S. Barbosa. Process calculi à la Bird-Meertens. In *CMCS'01 - Workshop on Coalgebraic Methods in Computer Science*, pages 47–66, Genova, April 2001. ENTCS, volume 44.4, Elsevier. 184, 195

[3] R. Bird and O. Moor. *The Algebra of Programming*. Series in Computer Science. Prentice-Hall International, 1997. 183

[4] R. Cockett and T. Fukushima. About Charity. Yellow Series Report No. 92/480/18, Dep. Computer Science, University of Calgary, June 1992. 183

[5] R. Cockett and D. Spencer. Strong categorical datatypes I. In R. A. G. Seely, editor, *Proceedings of Int. Summer Category Theory Meeting, Montréal, Québec, 23-30 June 1991*, pages 141–169. AMS, CMS Conf. Proceedings 13, 1992. 185, 193

[6] T. Hagino. A typed lambda calculus with categorical type constructors. In D. H. Pitt, A. Poigné, and D. E. Rydeheard, editors, *Category Theory and Computer Science*, pages 140–157. Springer Lect. Notes Comp. Sci. (283), 1987. 185

[7] B. Jacobs. Objects and classes, co-algebraically. In C. Lengauer B. Freitag, C. B. Jones and H.-J. Schek, editors, *Object-Orientation with Parallelism and Persistence*, pages 83–103. Kluwer Academic Publishers, 1996. 185

[8] P. Jansson and J. Jeuring. POLYP - a polytypic programming language extension. In *POPL'97: The 24th ACM SIGPLAN-SIGACT Symposium on Principles of Programming Languages*, pages 470–482. ACM Press, 1997. 183

[9] R. B. Kieburtz. Codata and comonads in HASKELL. Unpublished manuscript, 1998. 185

[10] A. Kock. Strong functors and monoidal monads. *Archiv für Mathematik*, 23:113–120, 1972. 185

[11] M. Lenisa. *Themes in Final Semantics*. PhD thesis, Universita de Pisa-Udine, 1998. 195

[12] L. Meertens. Paramorphisms. *Formal Aspects of Computing*, 4(5):413–425, 1992. 194

[13] E. Meijer, M. Fokkinga, and R. Paterson. Functional programming with bananas, lenses, envelopes and barbed wire. In J. Hughes, editor, *Proceedings of the 1991 ACM Conference on Functional Programming Languages and Computer Architecture*, pages 124–144. Springer Lect. Notes Comp. Sci. (523), 1991. 185

[14] R. Milner. *Communication and Concurrency*. Series in Computer Science. Prentice-Hall International, 1989. 186, 187, 191

[15] R. Milner, J. Parrow, and D. Walker. A calculus of mobile processes (parts I and II). *Information and Computation*, 100(1):1–77, 1992. 195

[16] J. Rutten. Universal coalgebra: A theory of systems. *Theor. Comp. Sci.*, 249(1):3–80, 2000. (Revised version of CWI Techn. Rep. CS-R9652, 1996). 184, 185

[17] D. Turi and J. Rutten. On the foundations of final coalgebra semantics: non-well-founded sets, partial orders, metric spaces. *Mathematical Structures in Computer Science*, 8(5):481–540, 1998. 185

[18] U. Wolter. A coalgebraic introduction to CSP. In *II Workshop on Coalgebraic Methods in Computer Science*. ENTCS, volume 19, Elsevier, 1999. 195

A   The Interpreter

```
def sem{eqL: Lb(N) * Lb(N) -> bool}:
    Ln(Lb(N)) * map(string, Ln(Lb(N)))  -> Pr(Ac(Lb(N)))

  = (exp,m)  => (| e => bh: syn{eqL}(e,m) |) exp.


def syn{eqL: Lb(N) * Lb(N) -> bool}:
    Ln(Lb(N)) * map(string, Ln(Lb(N)))
    ->  set(Ac(Lb(N)) * Ln(Lb(N)))

 = (pr,m) =>
   {| pnil: ()       => empty
    | ppre: (a,l)    => sing(a, p1 #)
    | pvar: (a,s)    => { ss(p) => sing(a, p)
                        | ff     => empty
                        } app{eq_string}(m,s)
    | pcho: (lp,lq) => union(lp, lq)
    | pint: (lp,lq) => union(stau1(lp, p1 #), stau1(lq,  p0 #))
    | psyn: (lp,lq) => ssel{eqL} sdelta1{eqL} (lp,lq)
    | ppar: (lp,lq) => union(union(stau2(lp, p1 #), stau2(lq,  p0 #)),
                            ssel{eqL} sdelta2{eqL} (lp,lq))
    | pret: (l,k)   => set{x => (p0 x, pret(p1 x, k))}
               filter{x => not member{eqA{eqL}}(p0 x, compren k)} l
    | pren: (l,h)   => set{x => { ff     => (p0 x,  pren(p1 x, h))
                               | ss a~=> (a, pren(p1 x, h))
                               } app{eqA{eqL}}(compret h, p0 x) } l
   |} pr.
```

where

```
def stau1: set(Ac(L) * Ln(L)) * Ln(L) -> set(Ac(L) * Ln(L))
   = (s,p) => set{(a,x) => (a, pint(x,p))} s.

def ssel{eql: L * L -> bool}: set(Ac(L) * B)  -> set(Ac(L) * B)
   = s => filter{x => not eqA{eql}(p0 x, nop)} s.
```

Descendants and Head Normalization of Higher-Order Rewrite Systems

Hideto Kasuya[1], Masahiko Sakai[2], and Kiyoshi Agusa[2]

[1] Faculty of Information Science and Technology, Aichi Prefectural University
1522–3 Ibaragabasama, Kumabari Nagakute-cho, Aichi, 480–1198 Japan
[2] Department of Information Engineering, Nagoya University
Furo-cho, Chikusa-ku Nagoya, 464–8603 Japan

Abstract. This paper describes an extension of head-needed rewriting on term rewriting systems to higher-order rewrite systems. The main difficulty of this extension is caused by the β-reductions induced from the higher-order reductions. In order to overcome this difficulty, we define a new descendant of higher-order rewrite systems. This paper shows the new definition of descendant, its properties and head normalization of head-needed rewriting on orthogonal higher-order rewrite systems.

1 Introduction

Higher-order rewrite systems (HRSs), an extension of term rewriting systems (TRSs) to higher-order terms, are used in functional programming, logic programming, and theorem proving as a model that contains the notion of λ-calculus. Properties of HRSs such as termination and confluence have been studied [11, 4, 5, 6, 9, 10]. On the other hand, there are a lot of works on reduction strategies of TRSs. Huet and Lévy show the following theorem on optimal normalizing strategy of orthogonal TRS [3]: a reducible term having a normal form contains at least one needed-redex to be reduced in every reduction sequence to a normal form. They also show that we always obtain a normal form of a given term by repeated reduction of the needed redex. Middeldorp generalized this result to head-needed reduction which computes head normal forms of terms [7].

In this paper, we discuss about head-needed reduction of HRSs. Since β-reductions induced by substitutions to higher-order variables change the structure of the higher-order term, the definition of descendant for TRSs [3, 2] works correctly no more. We give a definition of descendants on higher-order reduction, which represents where a redex is transferred to by a reduction. We prove that the strategy that reduces a head-needed redex is a head normalizing strategy in a higher-order setting.

Z. Hu and M. Rodríguez-Artalejo (Eds.): FLOPS 2002, LNCS 2441, pp. 198–211, 2002.

2   Preliminaries

Let S be a set of basic types. The set τ_s of types is generated from S by the function space constructor $\rightarrow$ as follows:

$$\tau_s \supseteq S$$
$$\tau_s \supseteq \{\alpha \rightarrow \alpha' | \alpha, \alpha' \in \tau_s\}$$

Let $\mathcal{X}_\alpha$ be a set of variables with type α and $\mathcal{F}_\alpha$ be a set of function symbols with type α. The set of all variables with types is denoted by $\mathcal{X} = \bigcup_{\alpha \in \tau_s} \mathcal{X}_\alpha$, and the set of all function symbols with types is denoted by $\mathcal{F} = \bigcup_{\alpha \in \tau_s} \mathcal{F}_\alpha$. Simply typed λ-terms are defined by following inference rules:

$$\frac{x \in \mathcal{X}_\alpha}{x : \alpha} \quad \frac{f \in \mathcal{F}_\alpha}{f : \alpha} \quad \frac{s : \alpha \rightarrow \alpha' \ t : \alpha}{(st) : \alpha'} \quad \frac{x : \alpha \ s : \alpha'}{(\lambda x.s) : \alpha \rightarrow \alpha'}$$

If $t : \alpha$ is inferred from the rules then t is a simply typed λ-term with type α denoted by $\mathcal{T}_\alpha$. The set $\bigcup_{\alpha \in \tau_s} \mathcal{T}_\alpha$ of all λ-terms is denoted by $\mathcal{T}$. A simply typed λ-term is called a higher-order term or a term. We use well-known notion of bound variables and free variables. The sets of bound and free variables occurring in a term t are denoted by $BV(t)$ and $FV(t)$, respectively. The set $FV(t) \cup BV(t)$ is denoted by $Var(t)$. A higher-order term without free variables is called a ground term. If a term s is generated by renaming bound variables in a term t then s and t are equivalent and denoted by $s \equiv t$. We use X, Y and Z for free variables, and x, y and z for bound variables unless it is known to be free or bound from other conditions. We sometimes write $\boldsymbol{x}$ for a sequence $x_1 x_2 \cdots x_m$ $(m \geq 0)$.

A mapping $\sigma : \mathcal{X} \mapsto \mathcal{T}$ from variables to higher-order terms of the same type is called substitution, if the domain $Dom(\sigma) = \{X | X \neq \sigma(X)\}$ is finite. If $Dom(\sigma) = \{X_1, \ldots, X_n\}$ and $\sigma(X_i) = t_i$, we also write it as $\sigma = \{X_1 \mapsto t_1, \ldots, X_n \mapsto t_n\}$. Let W be a set of variables and σ be a substitution. We write $\sigma|_W$ for a substitution generated by restricting the domain of σ to W. The set of free variables of σ is defined by $FV(\sigma) = \bigcup_{X \in Dom(\sigma)} FV(\sigma(X))$. Substitutions are extended to mappings σ' from higher-order terms to higher-order terms as follows:

$$\begin{array}{ll} \sigma'(X) \equiv \sigma(X) & \text{if } X \in \mathcal{X} \\ \sigma'(f) \equiv f & \text{if } f \in \mathcal{F} \\ \sigma'((t_1 t_2)) \equiv (\sigma'(t_1)\sigma'(t_2)) & \text{if } t \equiv (t_1 t_2) \\ \sigma'(\lambda x.t_1) \equiv \lambda x.\sigma'|_{\overline{\{x\}}}(t_1) & \text{if } t \equiv \lambda x.t_1 \text{ and } x \notin FV(\sigma) \end{array}$$

where $\overline{W}$ denotes the complement $\mathcal{X} - W$ of the set W of variables. We identify σ' with σ, and write $t\sigma$ instead of $\sigma'(t)$.

β-reduction is the operation that replaces $(\lambda x.s)t$ by $s\{x \mapsto t\}$. Let s be a term with type $\alpha \rightarrow \alpha'$, and $x \notin Var(s)$ be a variable with type α. Then, η-expansion is an operation that replaces s by $\lambda x.(sx)$. We say a term is η-long, if it is in normal form with respect to η-expansion. We also say a term is normalized if it is in β η-long normal form. A normalized term of t is denoted by $t\downarrow$. It is known that every higher-order term has a unique normalized term [5]. We say a substitution σ is normalized if $\sigma(X)$ is normalized for all $X \in Dom(\sigma)$.

Every normalized term can be represented by the form $\lambda x_1 \cdots x_m.$ $(\cdots(at_1)\cdots t_n)$ where $m, n \geq 0$, $a \in \mathcal{F} \cup \mathcal{X}$ and $(\cdots(at_1)\cdots t_n)$ is basic type [5]. In this paper, we represent this term t by $\lambda x_1 \cdots x_m.a(t_1,\ldots,t_n)$. Note that $a(t_1,\ldots,t_n)$ is basic type. The top symbol of t is defined as $top(t) \equiv a$.

We define the position of a normalized term based on the form of $\lambda x_1 \cdots x_m.a(t_1,\ldots,t_n)$. In order to simplify the definition of descendants in the following section, we consider $\lambda \boldsymbol{x}.a$ in $\lambda \boldsymbol{x}.a(t)$ single symbol when defining positions. A position of a normalized term is a sequence of natural numbers. The set of positions in $t \equiv \lambda \boldsymbol{x}.a(t_1,\ldots,t_n)$ is defined by $Pos(t) = \{\varepsilon\} \cup \{i \cdot p \mid 1 \leq i \leq n, p \in Pos(t_i)\}$. Let p, q and r be positions. We write $p \leq r$ if $pq = r$. Moreover, if $q \neq \varepsilon$ that is $p \neq r$, we write $p < r$. If $p \not\leq r$ and $p \not\geq r$, we write $p|r$.

$$(\lambda \boldsymbol{x}.a(t_1,\ldots,t_n))|_p \equiv \begin{cases} a(t_1,\ldots,t_n) & \text{if } p = \varepsilon \\ t_i|_q & \text{if } p = iq \end{cases}$$

$Pos_{\mathcal{X}}(t)$ indicates the set of positions $p \in Pos(t)$ such that $t|_p$ is a free variable in a normalized term t. $t[u]_p$ represents the term obtained by replacing $t|_p$ in a normalized term t by normalized term u having the same basic type as $t|_p$. This is defined as follows:

$$(\lambda \boldsymbol{x}.a(t_1,\ldots,t_n))[u]_p \equiv \begin{cases} \lambda \boldsymbol{x}.u & \text{if } p = \varepsilon \\ \lambda \boldsymbol{x}.a(\ldots,t_i[u]_q,\ldots) & \text{if } p = iq \end{cases}$$

$BV_p(t)$ that indicates the set of the positions $p \in Pos(t)$ of bound variables in normalized term t is defined as follows:

$$BV_p(\lambda x_1 \cdots x_m.a(t_1,\ldots,t_n)) \equiv \begin{cases} \emptyset & \text{if } p = \varepsilon \\ \{x_1,\ldots,x_m\} \cup BV_q(t_i) & \text{if } p = iq \end{cases}$$

Let t be a normalized term whose η-normal form is not a variable. We say t is a pattern if $u_1\downarrow_\eta,\ldots,u_n\downarrow_\eta$ are different bound variables for any subterm $F(u_1,\ldots,u_n)$ of t such that $F \in FV(t)$ [8]. Let α be a basic type, $l : \alpha$ be a pattern and $r : \alpha$ be a normalized term such that $FV(l) \supseteq FV(r)$. Then, $l \rhd r : \alpha$ is called a higher-order rewrite rule of type α. A higher-order rewrite system (HRS) is a set of higher-order rewrite rules.

Let $\mathcal{R}$ be a HRS, $l \rhd r$ be a rewrite rule of $\mathcal{R}$ and σ be a substitution. Then, we say $l\sigma\downarrow$ is a redex. If p is a position such that $s \equiv s[l\sigma\downarrow]_p$ and $t \equiv s[r\sigma\downarrow]_p$ then s is reduced to t, denoted by $s \rightarrow_R t$ or simply $s \rightarrow t$. In case of $p = \varepsilon$, the reduction is denoted by $s \xrightarrow{\varepsilon} t$. In case of $p > \varepsilon$, it is denoted by $s \xrightarrow{>\varepsilon} t$. Since all rewrite rules are with basic type, t is normalized if s is so[5].

The reflexive transitive closure of the reduction relation $\rightarrow$ is denoted by $\rightarrow^*$. If there exists an infinite reduction sequence $t \equiv t_0 \rightarrow t_1 \rightarrow \cdots$ from t, we say t has an infinite reduction sequence. If there exists no term which has

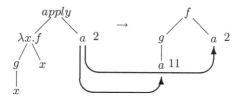

Fig. 1. Descendants

an infinite reduction sequence, we say $\rightarrow$ is terminating. If $\rightarrow_R$ is terminating, we also say HRS $\mathcal{R}$ is terminating. We sometimes refer the reduction sequence $A : t_0 \rightarrow t_1 \rightarrow \cdots \rightarrow t_n$ by attaching label A.

Let $l \rhd r$ and $l' \rhd r'$ be rewrite rules. If there exist substitutions σ, σ' and a position $p \in Pos_{\mathcal{X}}(l')$ such that $l\sigma{\downarrow} \equiv l'|_p(\sigma'|_{\overline{BV_p(l')}}){\downarrow}$, then we say these rewrite rules overlap[1]. If HRS $\mathcal{R}$ has overlapping rules, we say $\mathcal{R}$ is overlapping. When $\mathcal{R}$ is not overlapping and every rule of $\mathcal{R}$ is left-liner, we say it is orthogonal.

3   Descendant

Considering a reduction $s \rightarrow t$, t is obtained by replacing a redex in s by a term. Since the other redexes in s may appear in possibly different positions in t, we must follow the redex positions in order to argue the needed-redex. Thus, the notion of descendants was proposed[3]. From now, we extend the definition of descendants on TRSs to that on HRSs.

In TRSs, it is easy to follow descendants of redexes. However, it is not easy in HRSs because the positions of redexes move considerably by β-reductions taken in a reduction as the following shows.

Example 1. Consider the following HRS $\mathcal{R}_1$,

$$\mathcal{R}_1 = \begin{cases} apply(\lambda x.F(x), X) \rhd F(X) \\ a \rhd b, \end{cases}$$

and a reduction $A_1 : t \equiv apply(\lambda x.f(g(x), x), a) \rightarrow f(g(a), a) \equiv s$. Descendants of a redex position a that occurs at position 2 of t are positions 2 and 11 of s as shown in Fig. 1.

In order to follow positions of redexes correctly, we give mutually recursive functions PV and PT each of which returns a set of positions. The function PV that takes a term t, a substitution σ, a variable F and a position p as arguments computes the set of positions of $(F\sigma)|_p$ that occurs in $t\sigma{\downarrow}$. The function PT

---

[1] The original definition of overlapping [9] is formal but complicated because $\overline{x_k}$ lifter is used to prohibit the substitution to free variables in a subterm that is bound in the original term.

that takes a term t, a substitution σ and a position p as arguments computes the set of positions of a $t|_p$ that occurs in $t\sigma\downarrow$. In the previous example, we have $PV(F(X), \{F \mapsto \lambda x.f(g(x), x), X \mapsto a\}, X, \varepsilon) = \{11, 2\}$.

Definition 1 (PV). *Let t be a normalized term, σ be a normalized substitution, F be a variable and $p \in Pos(F\sigma)$ be a position.*
$PV(t, \sigma, F, p) =$

$$
\begin{cases}
\{p\} & \text{if } t \equiv F & (1) \\
\{iq \mid q \in PV(t_i, \sigma, F, p)\} & \text{if } t \equiv f(t_1, \ldots, t_n) \text{ and } n > 0 & (2) \\
PV(t', \sigma|_{\overline{\{x_1,\ldots,x_n\}}}, F, p) & \text{if } t \equiv \lambda x_1 \cdots x_n.t' \text{ and } n > 0 & (3) \\
\bigcup_i \bigcup_{q \in PV(t_i, \sigma, F, p)} PV(t', \sigma', y_i, q) & \text{if } t \equiv G(t_1, \ldots, t_n), n > 0 \text{ and } F \neq G & \\
& \text{where } G\sigma \equiv \lambda y_1 \ldots y_n.t' & \\
& \text{s.t. } \sigma' = \{y_1 \mapsto t_1\sigma\downarrow, \ldots, y_n \mapsto t_n\sigma\downarrow\} & (4) \\
(\bigcup_i \bigcup_{q \in PV(t_i, \sigma, F, p)} PV(t', \sigma', y_i, q)) \cup PT(t', \sigma', p) & \\
& \text{if } t \equiv F(t_1, \ldots, t_n) \text{ and } n > 0 & \\
& \text{where } F\sigma \equiv \lambda y_1 \ldots y_n.t' & \\
& \text{s.t. } \sigma' = \{y_1 \mapsto t_1\sigma\downarrow, \ldots, y_n \mapsto t_n\sigma\downarrow\} & (5) \\
\emptyset & \text{otherwise} & (6)
\end{cases}
$$

Definition 2 (PT). *Let t be a normalized term, σ be a normalized substitution, F be a variable and $p \in Pos(t)$ be a position.*
$PT(t, \sigma, p) =$

$$
\begin{cases}
\{\varepsilon\} & \text{if } p = \varepsilon & (1) \\
\{iq \mid q \in PT(t_i, \sigma, p')\} & \text{if } t \equiv f(t_1, \ldots, t_n), n > 0 \text{ and } p = ip' & (2) \\
\bigcup_{q \in PT(t_i, \sigma, p')} PV(t', \sigma', y_i, q) & \text{if } t \equiv G(t_1, \ldots, t_n), n > 0 \text{ and } p = ip' & \\
& \text{where } G\sigma \equiv \lambda y_1 \ldots y_n.t' & \\
& \text{s.t. } \sigma' = \{y_1 \mapsto t_1\sigma\downarrow, \ldots, y_n \mapsto t_n\sigma\downarrow\} & (3)
\end{cases}
$$

Example 2. Followings are examples of PV and PT.

1. $PT(f(y), \sigma, \varepsilon) = \{\varepsilon\}$ for any σ by the definition of PT (1).
2. $PV(f(y), \sigma, y, 11)$ for any σ,
   $= \{1q \mid q \in PV(y, \sigma, y, 11)\}$ by $PV(2)$,
   $= \{111\}$.
3. $PV(F(x), \sigma, F, \varepsilon)$ where $\sigma = \{F \mapsto \lambda y.f(y)\}$,
   $= (\bigcup_{q \in PV(x, \sigma, F, \varepsilon)} PV(f(y), \sigma', y, q)) \cup PT(f(y), \sigma', \varepsilon)$ where $\sigma' = \{y \mapsto x\}$
   by PV (5),
   $= (\bigcup_{q \in \emptyset} PV(f(y), \sigma', y, q)) \cup \{\varepsilon\}$ by PV (6) and from 1 of this example,
   $= \{\varepsilon\}$.
4. $PV(g(\lambda x.h(F(x))), \sigma, F, \varepsilon)$ where $\sigma = \{F \mapsto \lambda y.f(y)\}$,
   $= \{1q \mid q \in PV(\lambda x.h(F(x)), \sigma, F, \varepsilon)\}$ by PV (2),
   $= \{1q \mid q \in PV(h(F(x)), \sigma, F, \varepsilon)\}$ by PV (3),
   $= \{11q \mid q \in PV(F(x), \sigma, F, \varepsilon)\}$ by PV (2),
   $= \{11\}$ from 3 of this example.
5. $PV(F(g(\lambda x.h(F(x)))), \sigma, F, \varepsilon)$ where $\sigma = \{F \mapsto \lambda y.f(y)\}$,
   $= (\bigcup_{q \in PV(g(\lambda x.h(F(x))), \sigma, F, \varepsilon)} PV(f(y), \sigma', y, q)) \cup PT(f(y), \sigma', \varepsilon)$ where $\sigma' =$

$\{y \mapsto g(\lambda x.h(f(x)))\}$ by PV (5),
$= PV(f(y), \sigma', y, 11) \cup PT(f(y), \sigma', \varepsilon)$ from 4 of this example,
$= \{111, \varepsilon\}$ from 1 and 2 of this example.

Definition 3 (descendants of HRSs). *Let $A : s[l\sigma \downarrow]_u \to_{l \rhd r} s[r\sigma \downarrow]_u$ be a reduction for a rewrite rule $l \rhd r \in \mathcal{R}$, a substitution σ, a term s and positions u, v in s. Then, the set of descendants of v by A is defined as follows:*

$$v \backslash A = \begin{cases} \{v\} & \text{if } v \mid u \text{ or } v \prec u \\ \{up_3 \mid p_3 \in PV(r, \sigma, top(l|_{p_1}), p_2)\} & \text{if } v = up_1p_2 \text{ and } p_1 \in Pos_v(l) \\ \emptyset & \text{otherwise.} \end{cases}$$

For a set D of positions, $D \backslash A$ denotes the set $\bigcup_{v \in D} v \backslash A$. For a reduction sequence $B : s \to^* t$, $D \backslash B$ is naturally extended from $D \backslash A$.

Example 3. Consider the HRS $\mathcal{R}_1$ and the reduction sequence A_1 in Example 1. The descendants $2 \backslash A_1$ of redex position 2 of t are following:

$2 \backslash A_1 = PV(F(X), \{F \mapsto \lambda x.f(g(x), x), X \mapsto a\}, X, \varepsilon)$
$= \bigcup_{q \in PV(X, \{F \mapsto \lambda x.f(g(x),x), X \mapsto a\}, X, \varepsilon)} PV(f(g(x), x), \{x \mapsto a\}, x, q)$ by PV (4)
$= PV(f(g(x), x), \{x \mapsto a\}, x, \varepsilon)$ by PV (1)
$= \{1q' \mid q' \in PV(g(x), \{x \mapsto a\}, x, \varepsilon)\} \cup \{2q'' \mid q'' \in PV(x, \{x \mapsto a\}, x, \varepsilon)\}$ by PV (2)
$= \{11q''' \mid q''' \in PV(x, \{x \mapsto a\}, x, \varepsilon)\} \cup \{2\}$ by PV (1) and (2)
$= \{11, 2\}$ by PV (1)

Example 4. Consider the following HRS $\mathcal{R}_2$, a substitution σ and a reduction sequence A:

$$\mathcal{R}_2 = \{f(g(\lambda x.F(x))) \rhd F(g(\lambda x.h(F(x))))\},$$

$$\sigma = \{F \mapsto \lambda y.f(y)\},$$

$$A : f(g(\lambda x.f(x))) \equiv f(g(\lambda x.F(x)))\sigma \downarrow \to F(g(\lambda x.h(F(x))))\sigma \downarrow \equiv f(g(\lambda x.h(f(x)))).$$

The descendants $11 \backslash A$ of position 11 by the reduction sequence A are following:

$$11 \backslash A = PV(F(g(\lambda x.h(F(x)))), \sigma, F, \varepsilon)$$ by Definition 3.

From Example 2,

$$11 \backslash A = \{111, \varepsilon\}.$$

In the following we are only interested in descendants of redex positions. For convenience we identify redex positions with redexes. We show the property that descendants of a redex are redexes.

Lemma 1. *Descendants are well-defined.*

Proof. We define a measurement of $PT(t, \sigma, p)$ and $PV(t, \sigma, F, p)$ by the term $t\sigma$ and the order $>_{def}$ defined as follows:

$$s >_{def} s' \Leftrightarrow \begin{array}{l} |s\!\downarrow| > |s'\!\downarrow|, \text{ or,} \\ |s\!\downarrow| \geq |s'\!\downarrow| \ \wedge \ min\beta(s) > min\beta(s'), \end{array}$$

where $min\beta(s)$ is the minimum steps m such that $s \xrightarrow{m}_\beta s\!\downarrow$.

We can prove that PV or PT recursively called in the right-hand side of their definition is smaller than that in the left-hand side by this measurement. Here, we show this only in the case (4) of Definition 1 of PV by comparing $t\sigma$ in $PV(t, \sigma, F, p)$ with $t'\sigma'$ in $PV(t', \sigma', y_i, q)$ by $>_{def}$. Since $t\sigma \equiv (G(t_1, \ldots, t_n)\sigma) \rightarrow^*_\beta ((\lambda y_1 \cdots y_n.t')(t_1\sigma \downarrow, \ldots, t_n\sigma \downarrow)) \rightarrow_\beta (t'\{y_1 \mapsto t_1\sigma\downarrow, \ldots, y_n \mapsto t_n\sigma\downarrow\}) \equiv t'\sigma'$, we have $t\sigma\!\downarrow \equiv t'\sigma'\!\downarrow$ and $min\beta(t\sigma) > min\beta(t'\sigma')$. Hence, we have $t\sigma >_{def} t'\sigma'$. Since we can show the claim in all other cases similarly to the above case, PV and PT are well-defined. Therefore, descendants are well-defined. □

Lemma 2 (redex preservation on PV and PT). *Let t be a normalized term, σ be a normalized substitution and F be a variable.*

(a) *Let $F\sigma|_p$ be a redex for a position $p \in Pos(F\sigma)$. Then, for any $q \in PV(t, \sigma, F, p)$ there exists a substitution θ such that $(t\sigma\!\downarrow)|_q \equiv ((F\sigma)|_p \cdot \theta)\!\downarrow$. Hence, $(t\sigma\!\downarrow)|_q$ is a redex.*

(b) *Let $t|_p$ be a redex for a position $p \in Pos(t)$. Then, for any $q \in PT(t, \sigma, p)$ there exists a substitution θ such that $(t\sigma\!\downarrow)|_q \equiv (t|_p \cdot \theta)\!\downarrow$. Hence, $(t\sigma\!\downarrow)|_q$ is a redex.* □

The proof of Lemma 2 is found in the appendix.

Theorem 1 (redex preservation of descendants). *Let $A : s \rightarrow t$. If $s|_v$ is a redex then $t|_p$ are also redexes for all $p \in v\backslash A$.*

Proof. This is trivial from Lemma 2. □

From the above, we can say that the definition of descendants is well-defined and descendants of redexes are also redexes.

4   Head Normalization

We discuss an extension of head normalization on TRSs to that on HRSs.

4.1   Head-Needed Redex

Definition 4 (head normal form). *Let $\mathcal{R}$ be an HRS. A term that cannot be reduced to any redex is said to be in head normal form.*

Lemma 3. *Let $\mathcal{R}$ be an HRS and a term s be in head normal form. If there exists a reduction sequence $s \rightarrow^* t$ then t is in head normal form.* □

This lemma trivially holds.

Lemma 4. *Let $\mathcal{R}$ be an orthogonal HRS and a term t be in head normal form. If there exists a reduction sequence $s \xrightarrow{\geq \varepsilon} {}^* t$, s is in head normal form.*

Proof. Assume that s is not in head normal form, then there exists a redex s' such that $s \xrightarrow{\geq \varepsilon} {}^* s'$. Since it is easy to see $\xrightarrow{\geq \varepsilon}$ is confluent, we have $s' \xrightarrow{\geq \varepsilon} {}^* t'$ and $t \xrightarrow{\geq \varepsilon} {}^* t'$. Since $s' \xrightarrow{\geq \varepsilon} {}^* t$ and s' is redex, t' is also redex from orthogonality. It is a contradiction to the fact that t' is in head normal form by Lemma 3.   □

Definition 5 (head-needed redex). *Let $\mathcal{R}$ be an HRS. A redex r in a term t is head-needed, if in every reduction sequence from t to a head normal form a descendant of r is reduced.*

Lemma 5. *Let $\mathcal{R}$ be an orthogonal HRS and t be not in head normal form. Then the pattern of the first redex, which appears in every reduction sequence from t to a redex, is unique.*

Proof. From orthogonality.   □

Theorem 2. *Let $\mathcal{R}$ be an orthogonal HRS. Every term that is not in head normal form contains a head-needed redex.*

Proof. In similar to the proof of Theorem 4.3 in [7], it is proved by Lemma 5.   □

4.2   Head Normalizing Strategy

The development $\multimap^D$ is defined by the following inference rules:

$$\frac{s_i \multimap^{D_i} t_i \ (i=1,\dots,n)}{a(\overline{s_n}) \multimap^D a(\overline{t_n})} \quad D = \{ip|p \in D_i\} \tag{A}$$

$$\frac{s \multimap^D t}{\lambda x.s \multimap^D \lambda x.t} \tag{L}$$

$$\frac{s_i \multimap^{D_i} t_i \ (i=1,\dots,n) \quad c(\overline{s_n})=l\theta' \quad c(\overline{t_n})=l\theta \ (l \triangleright r) \in R}{c(\overline{s_n}) \multimap^D r\theta} \quad D = \{\varepsilon\} \cup \{ip|p \in D_i\} \tag{R}$$

where D is a set of redex positions.

Proposition 1 (development sequence). *If $p_i \not\prec p_j$ for any $i < j$ then the following holds: $\multimap^{\{p_1 \cdots p_n\}} = \multimap^{p_1} \cdot \multimap^{p_2} \cdots \multimap^{p_n}$.*

Let A and B be developments such that $A : s \multimap t_1$ and $B : s \multimap t_2$. Let D be the set of positions of the redexes contracted in A. The development starting from t_2 in which all redexes at positions $D \backslash B$ are contracted is denoted by $A \backslash B$.

Let A and B be development sequences such that $A : s_1 \twoheadrightarrow^* s_2$ and $B :$ $t_1 \twoheadrightarrow^* t_2$. We say A and B are *permutation equivalent* denoted by $A \simeq B$, if $s_1 \equiv t_1$, $s_2 \equiv t_2$ and $p\backslash A = p\backslash B$ for all redex positions p in s_1. $A; B$ denotes the concatenation of the development sequences A and B. The following lemma corresponds to Lemma 2.4 in [3].

Lemma 6. *Let $\mathcal{R}$ be an orthogonal HRS. If A and B are developments starting from the same term then $A; (B\backslash A) \simeq B; (A\backslash B)$.* □

Definition 6 (∇ and Δ). *Let B and D be sets of positions. If $\forall p \in D, \exists q \in B, q \prec p$ then we denote $D_{\nabla B}$ for D. If $\forall p \in D, \forall q \in B, q \npreceq p$ then we denote $D_{\Delta B}$ for D.*

We sometimes write $\twoheadrightarrow^{\nabla}$ and $\twoheadrightarrow^{\Delta}$ for $\twoheadrightarrow^{D_{\nabla B}}$ and $\twoheadrightarrow^{D_{\Delta B}}$, respectively.

Lemma 7. *Let B, D and D' be sets of redex positions of term t such that $D_{\nabla B}$ and $D'_{\Delta B}$. Let $A_1 : t \twoheadrightarrow^{D_{\nabla B}} t_1$ and $A_2 : t_1 \twoheadrightarrow^{D'_{\Delta B}} t_2$ be developments. Then, there exists developments $A_3 : t \twoheadrightarrow^{D'_{\Delta B}} t_3$ and $A_4 : t_3 \twoheadrightarrow^{(D\backslash A_3)_{\nabla (B\backslash A_3)}} t_2$ for some t_3.* □

The proof of Lemma 7 is found in the appendix.
We define an order on development sequences with the same length.

Definition 7. *Let $A = A_1; A_2; \cdots; A_n$ and $B = B_1; B_2; \cdots; B_n$ be development sequences with length n. We write $A > B$ if there exists an $i \in \{1, \ldots, n\}$ such that $|A_i| > |B_i|$ and $|A_j| = |B_j|$ for every $i < j \leq n$. We also write $A \geq B$ if $A > B$ or $|A_j| = |B_j|$ for every $1 \leq j \leq n$.*

Definition 8. *Let A be a development sequence and B be a development starting from the same term. We write $B \bot A$ if any descendant of redexes reduced in B is not reduced in A.*

The following two lemmas actually correspond to Lemma 5.4 and 5.5 introduced in [7]. These two lemmas can be proved in the similar way as [7].

Lemma 8. *Let $A : s \twoheadrightarrow^* s_n$ and $B : s \twoheadrightarrow t$ be such that $B \bot A$. If s_n is in head normal form then there exists a $C : t \twoheadrightarrow^* t_n$ such that $A \geq C$ and t_n is in head normal form.*

Proof. This lemma is proved by using Lemma 6 and Lemma 7. □

Lemma 9. *Let $A : s \twoheadrightarrow^* s_n$ and $B : s \twoheadrightarrow t$ be such that $B \not\bot A$. If s_n is in head normal form then there exists a $C : t \twoheadrightarrow^* t_n$ such that $A > C$ and t_n is in head normal form.*

Proof. This lemma is proved by using Lemma 6 and Lemma 8. □

Theorem 3. *Let $\mathcal{R}$ be an orthogonal HRS. Let t be a term that has a head normalizing reduction. There is no development sequence starting from t that contains infinitely many head-needed rewriting steps.*

Proof. By using Lemma 8 and Lemma 9, this lemma is proved in the same way as [7]. □

From above, head-needed rewritings are head normalizing strategy in HRS. In other words, we can obtain a head normal form by rewriting head-needed redexes.

Acknowledgement

We thank Prof. Toshiki Sakabe for discussion. This work is partly supported by Grants from Ministry of Education, Science and Culture of Japan #11680352.

References

[1] F. Baader and T. Nipkow. Term Rewriting and All That. Cambridge University Press (1998)

[2] I. Durand and A. Middeldorp: Decidable Call by Need Computations in Term Rewriting (Extended Abstract). Proc. 14th CADE, LNAI **1249** (1997) 4–18 198

[3] G. Huet and J.-J. Lévy: Computations in Orthogonal Rewriting Systems, I and II. Computational Logic, Essays in Honor of Alan Robinson, The MIT Press (1991) 396–443 198, 201, 206

[4] M. Iwami and Y. Toyama: Simplification Ordering for Higher-order Rewrite systems. IPSJ Trans. on Programming **40** SIG 4 (PRO 3) (1999) 1–10 198

[5] J.-P. Jouannaud and A. Rubio: Rewrite Orderings for Higher-order Terms in η-long β-normal Form and the Recursive Path Ordering. Theoretical Computer Science **208** (1998) 33–58 198, 200

[6] R. Mayr and T. Nipkow: Higher-order Rewrite Systems and their Confluence. Theoretical Computer Science **192** (1998) 3–29 198

[7] A. Middeldorp: Call by Need Computations to Root-Stable Form. Proc. 24th POPL (1997) 94–105 198, 205, 206, 207

[8] D. Miller: A Logic Programming Language with Lambda-Abstraction, Function Variables, and Simple Unification. Journal of Symbolic Logic **1** 4 (1991) 497–536 200

[9] T. Nipkow: Higher-Order Critical Pairs. Proc. 6th IEEE Symp. Logic in Computer Science (1991) 342–349 198, 201

[10] T. Nipkow: Orthogonal Higher-Order Rewrite Systems are Confluent. Proc. Int. Conf. Typed Lambda Calculi and Applications, LNCS **664** (1993) 306–317 198

[11] V. van Oostrom: Confluence for Abstract and Higher-Order Rewriting. PhD thesis, Vrije Universiteit, Amsterdam, (1994) 198

[12] C. Talcott: A Theory of Binding Structures and Applications to Rewriting. Theoretical Computer Science **112** (1993) 99–143

A   Proof of Lemma 2

Lemma 2. *Let t be a normalized term, σ be a normalized substitution and F be a variable.*

(a) *Let $F\sigma|_p$ be a redex for a position $p \in Pos(F\sigma)$. Then, for any $q \in PV(t,\sigma,F,p)$ there exists a substitution θ such that $(t\sigma{\downarrow})|_q \equiv ((F\sigma)|_p \cdot \theta){\downarrow}$. Hence, $(t\sigma{\downarrow})|_q$ is a redex.*

(b) *Let $t|_p$ be a redex for a position $p \in Pos(t)$. Then, for any $q \in PT(t,\sigma,p)$ there exists a substitution θ such that $(t\sigma{\downarrow})|_q \equiv (t|_p \cdot \theta){\downarrow}$. Hence, $(t\sigma{\downarrow})|_q$ is a redex.*

Proof. We prove by mutual induction on the structure of $t\sigma$ with $>_{def}$.

(a) Let $F\sigma|_p$ be a redex and q be a position such that $q \in PV(t,\sigma,F,p)$. We show $(t\sigma{\downarrow})|_q \equiv ((F\sigma)|_p)\theta{\downarrow}$ for some substitution θ.

(1) If $t \equiv F$ then $q = p$. Since σ is a normalized substitution, $(t\sigma{\downarrow})|_q \equiv (F\sigma{\downarrow})|_p \equiv (F\sigma)|_p \equiv ((F\sigma)|_p){\downarrow}$ holds.

(2) If $t \equiv f(t_1,\ldots,t_n)$, there exists q' such that $q = iq'$ and $q' \in PV(t_i,\sigma,F,p)$. Since $t\sigma >_{def} t_i\sigma$, there exists θ' such that $(t_i\sigma{\downarrow})|_{q'} \equiv ((F\sigma)|_p)\theta'{\downarrow}$ by induction hypothesis. Then, $(t\sigma{\downarrow})|_q \equiv (f(t_1,\ldots,t_n)\sigma{\downarrow})|_{i\cdot q'} \equiv (t_i\sigma{\downarrow})|_{q'} \equiv ((F\sigma)|_p)\theta'{\downarrow}$ holds.

(3) If $t \equiv \lambda x_1 \cdots x_n.t'$ then $q \in PV(t',\sigma',F,p)$ where $\sigma' = \sigma|_{\overline{\{x_1,\ldots,x_n\}}}$. Since $t\sigma >_{def} t'\sigma'$, there exists θ' such that $(t'\sigma'{\downarrow})|_q \equiv ((F\sigma)|_p)\theta'{\downarrow}$ by induction hypothesis. Then, $(t\sigma{\downarrow})|_q \equiv ((F\sigma)|_p)\theta'{\downarrow}$ holds from $(t\sigma{\downarrow})|_q \equiv (t'\sigma'{\downarrow})|_q$.

(4) If $t \equiv G(t_1,\ldots,t_n)$ and $F \neq G$, there exist i and $q' \in PV(t_i,\sigma,F,p)$ such that $q \in PV(t',\sigma',y_i,q')$ where $\sigma' = \{y_1 \mapsto t_1\sigma{\downarrow},\ldots,y_n \mapsto t_n\sigma{\downarrow}\}$ and $G\sigma \equiv \lambda y_1 \cdots y_n.t'$. Since $t\sigma >_{def} t'\sigma'$, there exists θ' such that $(t'\sigma'{\downarrow})|_q \equiv ((y_i\sigma')|_{q'})\theta'{\downarrow}$ by induction hypothesis. Then, $(t\sigma{\downarrow})|_q \equiv (t'\sigma'{\downarrow})|_q \equiv ((y_i\sigma')|_{q'})\theta'{\downarrow} \equiv ((t_i\sigma{\downarrow})|_{q'})\theta'{\downarrow}$ holds. Since $t\sigma >_{def} t_i\sigma$, there exists θ'' such that $(t_i\sigma{\downarrow})|_{q'} \equiv ((F\sigma)|_p)\theta''{\downarrow}$ by induction hypothesis. Then, $(t\sigma{\downarrow})|_q \equiv ((F\sigma)|_p)\theta''{\downarrow}\,\theta'{\downarrow} \equiv ((F\sigma)|_p)\theta''\theta'{\downarrow}$ holds.

(5) If $t \equiv F(t_1,\ldots,t_n)$, there exist i and $q' \in PV(t_i,\sigma,F,p)$ such that $q \in PV(t',\sigma',y_i,q')$ or $q \in PT(t',\sigma',p)$ where $\sigma' = \{y_1 \mapsto t_1\sigma{\downarrow},\ldots,y_n \mapsto t_n\sigma{\downarrow}\}$ and $F\sigma \equiv \lambda y_1 \cdots y_n.t'$. The former case can be shown as (4). Considering the latter case, since $t\sigma >_{def} t'\sigma'$, there exists θ such that $(t'\sigma'{\downarrow})|_q \equiv (t'|_p)\theta{\downarrow}$. Then, $(t\sigma{\downarrow})|_q \equiv (t'\sigma'{\downarrow})|_q \equiv (t'|_p)\theta{\downarrow} \equiv ((\lambda y_1 \cdots y_n.t')|_p)\theta{\downarrow} \equiv ((F\sigma)|_p)\theta{\downarrow}$ holds.

(6) Otherwise, it is obvious from $PV(t,\sigma,F,p) = \emptyset$.

(b) Let $t|_p$ be a redex and q be a position such that $q \in PT(t,\sigma,p)$. We show $(t\sigma{\downarrow})|_q = (t|_p)\theta{\downarrow}$ for some substitution θ.

(1) If $p = \varepsilon$ then $q = \varepsilon$ follows from $PT(t,\sigma,\varepsilon) = \{\varepsilon\}$. Thus, we have $(t\sigma{\downarrow})|_q \equiv t\sigma{\downarrow} \equiv (t|_p)\sigma{\downarrow}$.

(2) If $t \equiv f(t_1,\ldots,t_n)$ and $p = ip'$, there exists q' such that $q = iq'$ and $q' \in PT(t_i,\sigma,p')$. Since $t|_p \equiv t_i|_{p'}$, $t_i|_{p'}$ is a redex. It follows from $t >_{def} t_i$ and induction hypothesis that $(t_i\sigma{\downarrow})|_{q'} \equiv (t_i|_{p'})\theta{\downarrow}$ for some θ. Thus, $(t\sigma{\downarrow})|_q \equiv f(t_1\sigma{\downarrow},\ldots,t_n\sigma{\downarrow})|_{iq'} \equiv (t_i\sigma{\downarrow})|_{q'} \equiv (t_i|_{p'})\theta{\downarrow} \equiv (f(t_1,\ldots,t_n)|_{ip'})\theta{\downarrow} \equiv (t|_p)\theta{\downarrow}$.

(3) If $t \equiv G(t_1, \ldots, t_n)$ and $p = ip'$, there exists $q' \in PT(t_i, \sigma, p')$ such that $q \in PV(t', \sigma', y_i, q')$ where $\sigma' = \{y_1 \mapsto t_1\sigma \downarrow, \ldots, y_n \mapsto t_n\sigma \downarrow\}$ and $G\sigma \equiv \lambda y_1 \cdots y_n.t'$. Since $t\sigma >_{def} t'\sigma'$, there exists θ' such that $(t'\sigma' \downarrow)|_q \equiv ((y_i\sigma')|_{q'})\theta' \downarrow$ by induction hypothesis. Thus, $(t\sigma)|_q \equiv (t'\sigma' \downarrow)|_q \equiv ((y_i\sigma')|_{q'})\theta' \downarrow \equiv ((t_i\sigma \downarrow)|_{q'})\theta' \downarrow$ holds. Moreover, since $t\sigma >_{def} t_i\sigma$, there exists a position θ'' such that $(t_i\sigma \downarrow)|_{q'} \equiv ((t_i|_{p'})\theta'' \downarrow)$. Therefore, $(t\sigma)|_q \equiv ((t_i|_{p'})\theta''\downarrow)\theta'\downarrow \equiv (G(t_1, \ldots, t_n)|_{ip'})\theta''\theta'\downarrow \equiv (t|_p)\theta''\theta'\downarrow$ holds.

$\square$

B   Proof of Lemma 7

Lemma 10. *Let F be a variable, σ be a substitution, and v and v' be positions such that $v' \prec v$. Then, the followings hold;*

(a) *If $F\sigma|_{v'}$ and $F\sigma|_v$ are redexes, then $\forall p \in PV(t, \sigma, F, v)$, $\exists p' \in PV(t, \sigma, F, v')$, $p' \prec p$.*

(b) *If $t|_{v'}$ and $t|_v$ are redexes, then $\forall p \in PT(t, \sigma, v)$, $\exists p' \in PT(t, \sigma, v')$, $p' \prec p$.*

Proof. We prove them by mutual induction on the structure of t with $>_{def}$. Firstly consider (a). Let $P = PV(t, \sigma, F, v)$ and $P' = PV(t, \sigma, F, v')$.

(1) In case of $t \equiv F$, we have $P = \{v\}$ and $P' = \{v'\}$. Hence, the claim holds.

(2) Consider the case that $t \equiv f(t_1, \ldots, t_n)$. Let $p \in P$. Then, we have $p = iq$ for some i and $q \in PV(t_i, \sigma, F, v)\}$. Since $t\sigma >_{def} t_i\sigma$, we have $q' \prec q$ for some $q' \in PV(t_i, \sigma, F, v')$ by induction hypothesis. Thus we have $iq' \prec iq = p$ and $iq' \in P'$.

(3) In case of $t \equiv \lambda x_1 \cdots x_n.t'$, we have $P = PV(t', \sigma', F, v)$ and $P' = PV(t', \sigma', F, v')$ where $\sigma' = \sigma|_{\overline{\{x_1, \ldots, x_n\}}}$. Since $t\sigma >_{def} t'\sigma'$, the claim follows from induction hypothesis.

(4) Consider the case that $t \equiv G(t_1, \ldots, t_n)$. Let $p \in P$, $Q = PV(t_i, \sigma, F, v)$ and $Q' = PV(t_i, \sigma, F, v')$. Then, $p \in PV(t', \sigma', y_i, q)$ for some $q \in Q$ and i, where $G\sigma \equiv \lambda y_1 \cdots y_n.t'$ and $\sigma' = \{y_1 \mapsto t_1\sigma \downarrow, \ldots, y_n \mapsto t_n\sigma \downarrow\}$. Since $t\sigma >_{def} t_i\sigma$, we have $q' \prec q$ for some $q' \in Q'$ by induction hypothesis. Since $t\sigma >_{def} t'\sigma'$, it follows from $q' \prec q$ by induction hypothesis that $p' \prec p$ for some $p' \in PV(t', \sigma', y_i, q') \subseteq P$.

(5) In case of $t \equiv F(t_1, \ldots, t_n)$, we only check the subcase that $p \in PT(t', \sigma', v)$ since the other case is proved in similar to the case (4). It follows from $t\sigma >_{def} t'\sigma'$ by induction hypothesis that $p' \prec p$ for some $p' \in PT(t', \sigma, v')$.

(6) In the other cases, that is $F \notin Var(t)$ or $P = P' = \emptyset$, it is obvious.

Next, consider (b). Let $P = PT(t, \sigma, v)$ and $P' = PT(t, \sigma, v')$.

(1) In case of $v' = \varepsilon$, we have $t \equiv f(t_1, \ldots, t_n)$ from the assumption that $t|_{v'}$ and $t|_v$ are redexes. Let $p \in P = PT(f(t_1, \ldots, t_n), \sigma, v)$. Then, we have $p \succ \varepsilon$ from the definition of PT. Thus, the claim follows from $P' = \{\varepsilon\}$.

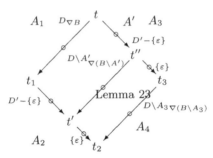

Fig. 2. The proof of Lemma 7

(2) In case of $t \equiv f(t_1, \ldots, t_n)$ and $v' = iw'$, we have $v = iw$ and $w' \prec w$ for some w. Let $p \in P$. Then, we have $p = iq$ for some $q \in PT(t_i, \sigma, w)$. Since $t\sigma >_{def} t_i\sigma$, we have $q' \prec q$ for some $q' \in PT(t_i, \sigma, w')$ by induction hypothesis. Thus, we have $iq' \prec iq = p$ and $iq' \in P'$.

(3) In case of $t \equiv G(t_1, \ldots, t_n)$ and $v' = iw'$, we have $v = iw$ and $w' \prec w$ for some w. Let $p \in P$. Then, we have $p \in PV(t', \sigma', y_i, q)$ for some $q \in PT(t_i, \sigma, w)$ where $\sigma' = \{y_1 \mapsto t_1\sigma\downarrow, \ldots, y_n \mapsto t_n\sigma\downarrow\}$ and $G\sigma \equiv \lambda y_1 \cdots y_n.t'$. Since $t\sigma >_{def} t_i\sigma$, we have $q' \prec q$ for some $q' \in PT(t_i, \sigma, w')$ by induction hypothesis. Since $t\sigma >_{def} t'\sigma'$, it follows from $q' \prec q$ and induction hypothesis that $p' \prec p$ for some $p' \in PV(t', \sigma', y_i, q')$.

$\square$

Lemma 11. *Let $A : t \twoheadrightarrow^{\{\varepsilon\}} t'$ be a development, B and D be sets of redex positions of t such that $D_{\nabla B}$. Then, $(D\backslash A)_{\nabla(B\backslash A)}$.*

Proof. Let $l \rhd r$ be a rewrite rule, σ be a substitution such that $t \equiv l\sigma\downarrow$ and $t' \equiv r\sigma\downarrow$. Without loss of generality, we can assume that $Dom(\sigma) = Var(l)$ and σ is idempotent, that is $Dom(\sigma) \cap \bigcup_{X \in Dom(\sigma)} Var(X\sigma) = \emptyset$.

Now we prove that $\forall p \in D\backslash A, \exists p' \in B\backslash A, p' \prec p$. Let $p \in D\backslash A$. Then, there exists $q \in D$ such that $p \in q\backslash A$. Since $q \in D_{\nabla B}$, there exists $q' \in B$ such that $q' \prec q$. On the other hand, there exists $p_1 \in Pos_v(l)$ such that $q' = p_1p_2$ and $q = p_1p_2p_2'$ from orthogonality. From the definition of descendants, we have

$$q'\backslash A = PV(r, \sigma, top(l|_{p_1}), p_2), \text{ and}$$
$$q\backslash A = PV(r, \sigma, top(l|_{p_1}), p_2p_2').$$

By Lemma 10 and the fact that $p \in q\backslash A$, we have $p' \prec p$ such that $p' \in q'\backslash A \subseteq B\backslash A$. Therefore, $(D\backslash A)_{\nabla(B\backslash A)}$ holds. $\square$

Lemma 7. *Let B, D and D' be sets of redex positions of term t such that $D_{\nabla B}$ and $D'_{\Delta B}$. Let $A_1 : t \twoheadrightarrow^{D_{\nabla B}} t_1$ and $A_2 : t_1 \twoheadrightarrow^{D'_{\Delta B}} t_2$ be developments. Then, there exists developments $A_3 : t \twoheadrightarrow^{D'_{\Delta B}} t_3$ and $A_4 : t_3 \twoheadrightarrow^{(D\backslash A_3)_{\nabla(B\backslash A_3)}} t_2$ for some t_3.*

Proof. It is not difficult to show that $A_3 : t \twoheadrightarrow^{D'_{\triangle B}} t_3$. We also have $A_4 : t_3 \twoheadrightarrow^{(D \backslash A_3)} t_2$ is from Lemma 6. Now, we prove $(D \backslash A_3)_{\nabla(B \backslash A_3)}$ by induction on the structure of term t.

Since $D_{\nabla B}$, we have $\varepsilon \notin D$. In case of $\varepsilon \in B$, we have $D = \emptyset$. Hence, the claim obviously holds. In case of $\varepsilon \notin B \wedge \varepsilon \notin D'$, the claim can be shown by using induction hypothesis. Thus, we consider the most interesting case $\varepsilon \notin D \wedge \varepsilon \in D'$.

From Proposition 1, A_2 and A_3 can be represented as $A_2 : t_1 \twoheadrightarrow^{D'-\{\varepsilon\}} t' \twoheadrightarrow^{\{\varepsilon\}} t_2$ and $A_3 : t \twoheadrightarrow^{D'-\{\varepsilon\}} t'' \twoheadrightarrow^{\{\varepsilon\}} t_3$, respectively. Let $A' : t \twoheadrightarrow^{D'-\{\varepsilon\}} t''$. We can show that $t'' \twoheadrightarrow^{(D \backslash A')_{\nabla(B \backslash A')}} t'$ in the same way as the case that $\varepsilon \notin D \wedge \varepsilon \notin D'$. We can complete the Fig. 2 by Lemma 11. $\square$

Narrowing Failure
in Functional Logic Programming

Francisco Javier López-Fraguas and Jaime Sánchez-Hernández

Dep. Sistemas Informáticos y Programación, Univ. Complutense de Madrid
{fraguas,jaime}@sip.ucm.es

Abstract. Negation as failure is an important language feature within the logic programming paradigm. The natural notion generalizing negation as failure in a functional logic setting is that of finite failure of reduction. In previous works we have shown the interest of using such programming construct when writing functional logic programs, and we have given a logical status to failure by means of proof calculi designed to deduce failures from programs. In this paper we address the problem of the operational mechanism for the execution of functional logic programs using failure. Our main contribution is the proposal of a narrowing relation able to deal with failures, which is constructive in the usual sense of the term in the context of negation, that is, narrowing is able to find substitutions for variables even in presence of failures. As main technical results, we prove correctness and completeness of the narrowing relation with respect to the proof-theoretic semantics.

1 Introduction

Motivation   Functional logic programming (*FLP* for short) tries to combine the nicest properties of functional and logic programming (see [9] for a now 'classical' survey on *FLP*). Theoretical aspects of *FLP* are well established (e.g. [8]) and there are also practical implementations such as *Curry* [10] or $\mathcal{TOY}$ [1, 11]. Disregarding syntax, both pure Prolog and (a wide subset of) Haskell are subsumed by those systems. The usual claim is then that by the use of an *FLP* system one can choose the style of programming better suited to each occasion.

There is nevertheless a very important feature in the logic programming (*LP* for short) paradigm, namely *negation as failure* [6], yet not available in *FLP* systems. Negation is a major issue in the *LP* field, both at the theoretical and the practical levels. There are hundreds of papers about negation in *LP* (see e.g. [4] for a survey), and almost all real Prolog programs use negation at some point.

This situation poses some problems to *FLP*, since logic programs using negation cannot be directly seen as *FLP* programs. This would be a not very serious inconvenience if other features of *FLP* could easily replace the use of failure. This happens in some cases, when the possibility of defining two-valued boolean functions is a good alternative to the use of negation in a logic program.

Z. Hu and M. Rodríguez-Artalejo (Eds.): FLOPS 2002, LNCS 2441, pp. 212–227, 2002.

But there are problems where the use of failure as a programming construct is a real aid to the writing of concise declarative programs. We give an example – to be used several times throughout the paper – of that situation in the context of *FLP*. Some other examples can be found in [15].

Example   Consider the problem of determining if there is a path connecting two nodes of an acyclic directed graph. A typical way of representing a graph in current *FLP* languages is by means of a non-deterministic function *next*, with rules of the form $next(N) \rightarrow N'$, indicating that there is an arc from N to N'. A concrete graph with nodes a, b, c and d could be given by the rules:

$$next(a) \rightarrow b \qquad next(b) \rightarrow c$$
$$next(a) \rightarrow c \qquad next(b) \rightarrow d$$

And to determine if there is a path from X to Y we can define:

$$path(X, Y) \rightarrow if\ eq(X, Y)\ then\ true\ else\ path(next(X), Y)$$

where *eq* stands for strict equality, which can be defined by the rules $eq(a, a) \rightarrow true$, $eq(a, b) \rightarrow false$ and so on.

Notice that *path* behaves as a semidecision procedure recognizing only the positive cases, and there is no clear way (in 'classical' *FLP*) of completing its definition with the negatives ones, unless we change from the scratch the representation of graphs. Therefore we cannot, for instance, program in a direct way a property like

$$safe(X) \Leftrightarrow X\ is\ not\ connected\ with\ d$$

To this purpose, something like negation as failure would be very useful. Since predicates can be programmed in *FLP* systems like *true*-valued functions, a natural *FLP* generalization of negation as failure is given by the notion of *failure of reduction to head normal form*. This could be expressed by means of a 'primitive' function *fails*, with the following intended behavior:

$$fails(e) ::= \begin{cases} true & \text{if } e \text{ fails to be reduced to hnf} \\ false & \text{otherwise} \end{cases}$$

Using this primitive it is now easy to define the property *safe*:

$$safe(X) \rightarrow fails(path(X, d))$$

With this definition and the previous graph, $safe(X)$ becomes *true* for $X = c$ and *false* for $X = a$, $X = b$ and $X = d$.

Previous and related work. Aim of the paper   In some previous works [12, 15, 13] we addressed the problem of failure within *FLP*, from the point of view of its semantic foundations. Our starting point was *CRWL* [7, 8], a general framework for *FLP*, based on a Constructor-based ReWriting Logic. From the point of view of programming, a fundamental notion of *CRWL* (as well as for existing *FLP* systems like *Curry* [10] or $\mathcal{TOY}$ [11, 1]) is that of non-strict non-deterministic function, for which *call-time choice semantics* is considered. Programs in $CRWL$ have a logical semantics given by the logical consequences of the program according to a proof calculus able to prove reduction statements of the form $e \rightarrow t$, meaning that one of the possible reductions of an expression e results in the (possibly partial) value t.

Our first step [12, 15] for dealing with failure in FLP, was to extend the rewriting logic $CRWL$ to $CRWLF$ ($CRWL$ "with failure"). The main insight was to replace statements $e \rightarrow t$ by statements $e \lhd C$, where C are sets of partial values (called *Sufficient Approximation Sets* or SAS's) corresponding to the different possibilities for reducing e. In [13] we realized the benefits of making more explicit the set nature of non deterministic functions, and therefore we reformulated $CRWLF$ by giving a set-oriented view of programs. This was done even at the syntactic level, by introducing classical mathematical set notation, like union or indexed unions; union is useful to transform programs to an inductively sequential format [2], and indexed unions turn to be useful for expressing call-time choice semantics and sharing.

One of the motivations for the set-oriented view adopted in [13] was our thought that such approach, by reflecting better the meaning of programs, would be an appropriate semantic basis upon which develop a suitable operational semantics for functional logic programs using failure. This is exactly the purpose of this paper. We propose an operational mechanism given by a narrowing relation which can operate with failure, that is, which is able to narrow expressions of the form *fails(e)*. Since we start from a precise semantic interpretation of failure, we are able to prove correctness and completeness of narrowing with respect to the semantics.

A major feature of our proposal is that the narrowing relation is *constructive* in the usual sense given to the term in the context of negation [5, 19, 20]: if an expression *fails(e)* contains variables, it can still be narrowed to obtain appropriate substitutions for them. For instance, in the example of the graph, our narrowing relation is able to narrow the expression *safe(X)* to obtain the value *true* together with the substitution $X = c$ and the value *false* together with the substitutions (corresponding to different computations) $X = a$, $X = b$ and $X = d$.

There are very few works about negation in FLP. In [16] the work of Stuckey about constructive negation [19, 20] is adapted to the case of FLP with strict functions and innermost narrowing as operational mechanism. In [17] a similar work is done for the case of non-strict functions and lazy narrowing. This approach, apart from being in the technical side very different from ours, does not take into account non-determinism of functions, an essential aspect in our work.

The organization of the paper is as follows: Section 2 contains some technical preliminaries. In Section 3 we present (a slight variant of) the set-oriented semantic framework for failure of [13], including the proof calculus, together with some new results which are needed for subsequent sections. Section 4 is the core of the paper, where we define the narrowing relation and prove the results of correctness and completeness with respect to the logical semantics. Finally, Section 5 summarizes some conclusions and hints for future work. Due to lack of space, proofs are omitted, but can be found in [14].

2   Technical Preliminaries

We assume a signature $\Sigma = DC_\Sigma \cup FS_\Sigma \cup \{fails\}$ where $DC_\Sigma = \bigcup_{n\in\mathbb{N}} DC_\Sigma^n$ is a set of *constructor* symbols containing at least the usual boolean ones *true* and *false*, $FS_\Sigma = \bigcup_{n\in\mathbb{N}} FS_\Sigma^n$ is a set of *function* symbols, all of them with associated arity and such that $DC_\Sigma \cap FS_\Sigma = \emptyset$, and $fails \notin DC \cup FS$ (with arity 1). We also assume a countable set $\mathcal{V}$ of *variable* symbols. We write $Term_\Sigma$ for the set of (total) *terms* (we say also *expressions*) built over Σ and $\mathcal{V}$ in the usual way, and we distinguish the subset $CTerm_\Sigma$ of (total) constructor terms or (total) *cterms*, which only make use of DC_Σ and $\mathcal{V}$. The subindex Σ will usually be omitted. Terms intend to represent possibly reducible expressions, while cterms represent data values, not further reducible.

The constant (0-arity constructor) symbol F is explicitly used in our terms, so we consider the signature $\Sigma_F = \Sigma \cup \{F\}$. This symbol F will be used to express failure of reduction. The sets $Term_F$ and $CTerm_F$ are defined in the natural way. The denotational semantics also uses the constant symbol $\bot$, that plays the role of the undefined value. We define $\Sigma_{\bot,F} = \Sigma \cup \{\bot, F\}$; the sets $Term_{\bot,F}$ and $CTerm_{\bot,F}$ of (partial) terms and (partial) cterms respectively, are defined in a natural way. Partial cterms represent the result of partially evaluated expressions; thus, they can be seen as approximations to the value of expressions in the denotational semantics.

As usual notations we will write $X, Y, Z, \ldots$ for variables, c, d for constructor symbols, f, g for functions, e for terms and s, t for cterms. In all cases, primes (') and subindices can be used.

The sets of substitutions $CSubst, CSubst_F$ and $CSubst_{\bot,F}$ are defined as applications from $\mathcal{V}$ into $CTerm, CTerm_F$ and $CTerm_{\bot,F}$ respectively. We will write θ, σ, μ for substitutions and ϵ for the identity substitution. The notation $\theta\sigma$ stands for the usual composition of substitutions. All the considered substitutions are idempotent ($\theta\theta = \theta$). We write $[X_1/t_1, \ldots, X_n/t_n]$ for the substitution that maps X_1 into $t_1, \ldots, X_n$ into t_n.

Given a set of constructor symbols D, we say that the terms t and t' have a D-*clash* if they have different constructor symbols of D at the same position. We say that two tuples of cterms $t_1, \ldots, t_n$ and $t'_1, \ldots, t'_n$ have a D-*clash* if for some $i \in \{1, \ldots, n\}$ the cterms t_i and t'_i have a D-*clash*.

A natural *approximation ordering* $\sqsubseteq$ over $Term_{\bot,F}$ can be defined as the least partial ordering over $Term_{\bot,F}$ satisfying the following properties:

- $\bot \sqsubseteq e$ for all $e \in Term_{\bot,F}$,
- $h(e_1, \ldots, e_n) \sqsubseteq h(e'_1, \ldots, e'_n)$, if $e_i \sqsubseteq e'_i$ for all $i \in \{1, \ldots, n\}$, $h \in DC \cup FS \cup \{fails\} \cup \{F\}$

The intended meaning of $e \sqsubseteq e'$ is that e is less defined or has less information than e'. Two expressions $e, e' \in Term_{\bot,F}$ are *consistent* if they can be refined to obtain the same information, i.e., if there exists $e'' \in Term_{\perp,\mathsf{F}}$ such that $e \sqsubseteq e''$ and $e' \sqsubseteq e''$. Notice that according to this F is maximal. This is reasonable from an intuitive point of view, since F represents 'failure of reduction' for an expression and this gives a no further refinable information about the result of the evaluation of such expression. This contrasts with the status given to failure in [17], where F is chosen to verify $\mathsf{F} \sqsubseteq t$ for any t different from $\perp$. We also use the relation $\sqsubseteq$ referred to substitutions: $\sigma \sqsubseteq \sigma'$ iff $X\sigma \sqsubseteq X\sigma'$ for all $X \in \mathcal{V}$. And for tuples of cterms: $\bar{t} \sqsubseteq \bar{t}'$ iff the ordering relation is pairwise satisfied.

Extending $\sqsubseteq$ to sets of terms results in the *Egli-Milner* preordering (see e.g. [18]): given $D, D' \subseteq CTerm_{\perp,\mathsf{F}}$ we say that D' is more refined than D and write $D \sqsubseteq D'$ iff for all $t \in D$ there exists $t' \in D'$ with $t \sqsubseteq t'$ and for all $t' \in D'$ there exists $t \in D$ with $t \sqsubseteq t'$. The sets D and D' are **consistent** iff there exists D'' such that $D \sqsubseteq D''$ and $D' \sqsubseteq D''$.

3   A Semantic Framework for *FLP* with Failure

3.1   Set Expressions

A set-expression is a syntactical construction designed for manipulating sets of values. A (total) set-expression $\mathcal{S}$ is defined as:

$$\mathcal{S} ::= \{t\} \mid f(\bar{t}) \mid fails(\mathcal{S}_1) \mid \bigcup_{X \in \mathcal{S}_1} \mathcal{S}_2 \mid \mathcal{S}_1 \cup \mathcal{S}_2$$

where $t \in CTerm_\mathsf{F}$, $\bar{t} \in CTerm_\mathsf{F} \times ... \times CTerm_\mathsf{F}$, $f \in FS^n$, and $\mathcal{S}_1, \mathcal{S}_2$ are set-expressions. We write $SetExp$ for the set of (total) set-expressions. The set $SetExp_\perp$ of *partial* set-expressions is analogous but $t, \bar{t}$ can contain $\perp$.

Indexed unions bind variables in a similar way to other more familiar constructs like first order quantifications or λ-abstraction. The set $PV(\mathcal{S})$ of bound or *produced variables* of a set-expression $\mathcal{S}$ can be formally defined as:

- $PV(\{t\}) = PV(f(\bar{t})) = \emptyset$ • $PV(\bigcup_{X \in \mathcal{S}_1} \mathcal{S}_2) = \{X\} \cup PV(\mathcal{S}_1) \cup PV(\mathcal{S}_2)$
- $PV(fails(\mathcal{S})) = PV(\mathcal{S})$ • $PV(\mathcal{S}_1 \cup \mathcal{S}_2) = PV(\mathcal{S}_1) \cup PV(\mathcal{S}_2)$

We can also define the set $FV(\mathcal{S})$ of *free variables* of a set-expression $\mathcal{S}$ as:

- $FV(\{t\}) = var(t)$ • $FV(f(\bar{t})) = var(\bar{t})$ • $FV(fails(\mathcal{S}_1)) = FV(\mathcal{S}_1)$
- $FV(\bigcup_{X \in \mathcal{S}_1} \mathcal{S}_2) = (FV(\mathcal{S}_2) - \{X\}) \cup FV(\mathcal{S}_1)$
- $FV(\mathcal{S}_1 \cup \mathcal{S}_2) = FV(\mathcal{S}_1) \cup FV(\mathcal{S}_2)$

In order to avoid variable renamings and simplify further definitions, we add an *admissibility condition* to set expressions: for $\bigcup_{X \in \mathcal{S}_1} \mathcal{S}_2$ we require $X \notin var(\mathcal{S}_1) \cup PV(\mathcal{S}_2)$ and $PV(\mathcal{S}_1) \cap PV(\mathcal{S}_2) = \emptyset$; and $\mathcal{S}_1 \cup \mathcal{S}_2$ must verify $PV(\mathcal{S}_1) \cap FV(\mathcal{S}_2) = \emptyset$ and $PV(\mathcal{S}_2) \cap FV(\mathcal{S}_1) = \emptyset$. Notice that with this conditions, the sets $PV(\mathcal{S})$ and $FV(\mathcal{S})$ define a partition over $var(\mathcal{S})$. In the following we always assume this admissibility condition over set-expressions.

As an example, if $f \in FS^2$ and $c \in DC^2$, then

$$\mathcal{S} = \bigcup_{A \in \bigcup_{B \in f(X,Y)} \{B\}} \{c(A, X)\} \cup \bigcup_{C \in \{X\}} f(C, Y)$$

is an admissible set-expression with $PV(\mathcal{S}) = \{A, B, C\}$ and $FV(\mathcal{S}) = \{X, Y\}$.

We assume also some admissibility conditions over substitutions: given a set-expression $\mathcal{S}$ we say that σ is an *admissible substitution for* $\mathcal{S}$, if $Dom(\sigma) \cap PV(\mathcal{S}) = \emptyset$ and $Ran(\sigma) \cap PV(\mathcal{S}) = \emptyset$. In such case, the set-expression $\mathcal{S}\sigma$ is naturally defined as:

- $\{t\}\sigma = \{t\sigma\}$
- $f(\bar{t})\sigma = f(\bar{t}\sigma)$
- $fails(\mathcal{S})\sigma = fails(\mathcal{S}\sigma)$
- $(\bigcup_{X \in \mathcal{S}_1)} \mathcal{S}_2)\sigma = \bigcup_{X \in \mathcal{S}_1\sigma} \mathcal{S}_2\sigma$
- $(\mathcal{S}_1 \cup \mathcal{S}_2)\sigma = \mathcal{S}_1\sigma \cup \mathcal{S}_2\sigma$

Notice that produced variables are not affected by the substitution due to the condition $Dom(\sigma) \cap PV(\mathcal{S}) = \emptyset$; and we avoid capture of produced variables with the condition $Ran(\sigma) \cap PV(\mathcal{S}) = \emptyset$. We will also use (admissible) *set-substitutions* for set-expressions: given a set $D = \{s_1, ..., s_n\} \subseteq CTerm_{\perp,\mathsf{F}}$ we write $\mathcal{S}[Y/D]$ as a shorthand for the distribution $\mathcal{S}[Y/s_1] \cup ... \cup \mathcal{S}[Y/s_n]$. Extending this notation, we also write $\mathcal{S}[X_1/D_1, ..., X_n/D_n]$ (where $D_1, ..., D_n \subseteq CTerm_{\perp,\mathsf{F}}$) as a shorthand for $(...(\mathcal{S}[X_1/D_1])...)[X_n/D_n]$. In the following all the substitutions we use are admissible.

The ordering $\sqsubseteq$ defined in Section 2 for terms and sets of terms can be extended also to set expressions: the relation $\sqsubseteq_{SetExp_\perp}$ is the least reflexive and transitive relation satisfying:

1. $\{\perp\} \sqsubseteq_{SetExp_\perp} \mathcal{S}$, for any $\mathcal{S} \in SetExp_\perp$
2. $\{t\} \sqsubseteq_{SetExp_\perp} \{t'\}$, if $t \sqsubseteq t'$
3. $f(\bar{t}) \sqsubseteq_{SetExp_\perp} f(\bar{t'})$, if $f(\bar{t}) \sqsubseteq f(\bar{t'})$
4. $fails(\mathcal{S}) \sqsubseteq_{SetExp_\perp} fails(\mathcal{S}')$, if $\mathcal{S} \sqsubseteq_{SetExp_\perp} \mathcal{S}'$
5. $\bigcup_{X \in \mathcal{S}_1} \mathcal{S}_2 \sqsubseteq_{SetExp_\perp} \bigcup_{X \in \mathcal{S}_1'} \mathcal{S}_2'$, if $\mathcal{S}_1 \sqsubseteq_{SetExp_\perp} \mathcal{S}_1'$ and $\mathcal{S}_2 \sqsubseteq_{SetExp_\perp} \mathcal{S}_2'$
6. $\mathcal{S}_1 \cup ... \cup \mathcal{S}_n \sqsubseteq_{SetExp_\perp} \mathcal{S}_1' \cup ... \cup \mathcal{S}_m'$, if for all $i \in \{1, ..., n\}$ there exists some $j \in \{1, ..., m\}$ such that $\mathcal{S}_i \sqsubseteq \mathcal{S}_j'$ and conversely, for all $j \in \{1, ..., m\}$ there exists some $i \in \{1, ..., n\}$ such that $\mathcal{S}_i \sqsubseteq \mathcal{S}_j'$

In the following the subindex of $\sqsubseteq_{SetExp_\perp}$ will be omitted.

3.2   Programs

A program is a set of rules of the form: $f(t_1, \ldots, t_n) \twoheadrightarrow \mathcal{S}$, where $f \in FS^n$, $t_i \in CTerm$, the tuple $(t_1, \ldots, t_n)$ is linear (each variable occurs only once), $\mathcal{S} \in SetExp$ and $FV(\mathcal{S}) \subseteq var((t_1, \ldots, t_n))$.

Notice that we allow F to appear in $\mathcal{S}$, but not in $t_1, \ldots, t_n$. This is not essential, and is done only for technical convenience. Notice also that known definitions which refer only to heads of rules, like that of *definitional tree* or *inductively sequential program* [2], can be applied also to our programs. Concretely, we are interested in the class of Complete Inductively Sequential Programs (*CIS*-programs for short), introduced in [2]. 'Complete' means that at every *case* distinction in the definitional tree of a function there is a branch for every constructor symbol from DC. By considering *CIS*-programs we ensure that, for any ground $t_1, \ldots, t_n \in CTerm$, exactly *one* program rule can be used to reduce a call $f(t_1, \ldots, t_n)$. And there is no loss of generality: in [3, 13] it is shown how to convert programs into *overlapping* inductively sequential programs, where several rules might have the same head; as mentioned in [13], by using $\cup$ it straightforward to achieve inductive sequentiality, just by merging with $\cup$ several body rules; in [13] it is also shown how to translate 'classical' syntax for expressions in bodies into set-oriented syntax; finally, to achieve completeness we only need to add, for every 'missing' constructor in a *case* distinction of a definitional tree, a rule with $\{\mathsf{F}\}$ as body.

As an example, the *CIS*-program corresponding to the program of Sect. 1 is:

$$next(a) \twoheadrightarrow \{b, c\} \qquad next(c) \twoheadrightarrow \{\mathsf{F}\}$$
$$next(b) \twoheadrightarrow \{c, d\} \qquad next(d) \twoheadrightarrow \{\mathsf{F}\}$$
$$path(X, Y) \twoheadrightarrow \bigcup\nolimits_{A \in eq(X,Y)} \bigcup\nolimits_{B \in \bigcup_{C \in next(X)} path(C,Y)} ifThenElse(A, true, B)$$
$$safe(X) \twoheadrightarrow fails(\bigcup\nolimits_{A \in eq(X,d)} \bigcup\nolimits_{B \in \bigcup_{C \in next(X)} path(C,d)} ifThenElse(A, true, B))$$

In practice, this syntax can be obtained by automating the translation.

3.3   Proof Calculus for Programs and Set-Expressions

Table 1 shows the *Set Reduction Logic* that determines the semantics of set-expressions with respect to *CIS*-programs, by defining the provability relation $\mathcal{S} \lhd \mathcal{C}$ between set-expressions $\mathcal{S}$ and sets $\mathcal{C}$ of partial cterms. When $\mathcal{S} \lhd \mathcal{C}$ is provable we say that $\mathcal{C}$ is a *sufficient approximation set (SAS)* for $\mathcal{S}$.

Rules 1 to 4 are "classical" in *CRWL(F)* [8, 13, 12]. Rule 4 uses a c-instance of a program rule; the set of such c-instances is defined as: $[\mathcal{P}]_{\perp,\mathsf{F}} = \{R\theta \mid R = (f(\bar{t}) \twoheadrightarrow \mathcal{S}) \in \mathcal{P}, \theta \in CSubst_{\perp,\mathsf{F}}\}$. Notice that this c-instance is unique if it exists (due to the non-overlapping condition imposed to programs). If such c-instance does not exist then, by rule 5, the corresponding set-expression reduces to $\{\mathsf{F}\}$.

Rules 6 and 7 establish the meaning of the function $fails(\mathcal{S})$: we must reduce $\mathcal{S}$; if we achieve $\{\mathsf{F}\}$ as a *SAS* for it, this means that any attempt to reduce $\mathcal{S}$ effectively fails. On the other hand, if we obtain a *SAS* with a cterm of the form $c(...)$ or X, then there is a possible reduction of $\mathcal{S}$ to a cterm. This is a "constructive" way of proving failure. Moreover, the only *SAS*'s for $\mathcal{S}$ that do not provide enough information for reducing $fails(\mathcal{S})$ are $\{\perp\}$ or $\{\perp, \mathsf{F}\}$. Finally, rules 8 and 9 have a natural set-theoretic reading.

Given a program $\mathcal{P}$ and $\mathcal{S} \in SetExp$ we write $\mathcal{P} \vdash_{SRL} \mathcal{S} \lhd \mathcal{C}$ if the relation $\mathcal{S} \lhd \mathcal{C}$ is provable with respect to *SRL* and the program $\mathcal{P}$. The *denotation* of $\mathcal{S}$ is defined as $[\![\mathcal{S}]\!] = \{\mathcal{C} \mid \mathcal{S} \lhd \mathcal{C}\}$. Then the denotation of a set-expression is a set of sets of (possible partial) cterms.

It is easy to check that the symbol $\cup$ is associative and commutative, i.e., $[\![(\mathcal{S}_1 \cup \mathcal{S}_2) \cup \mathcal{S}_3]\!] = [\![\mathcal{S}_1 \cup (\mathcal{S}_2 \cup \mathcal{S}_3)]\!]$ and $[\![\mathcal{S}_1 \cup \mathcal{S}_2]\!] = [\![\mathcal{S}_2 \cup \mathcal{S}_1]\!]$. So, in the following we avoid unnecessary parentheses and consider the expression $\mathcal{S}_1 \cup ... \cup \mathcal{S}_n$ as equivalent to $\mathcal{S}_{i_1} \cup ... \cup \mathcal{S}_{i_n}$, where $(i_1, ..., i_n)$ is any permutation of $(1, ..., n)$. Moreover, $\mathcal{S}_1 \cup ... \cup \mathcal{S}_n \lhd \mathcal{C}$ iff $\mathcal{S}_1 \lhd \mathcal{C}_1, ..., \mathcal{S}_n \lhd \mathcal{C}_n$, where $\mathcal{C} = \mathcal{C}_1 \cup ... \cup \mathcal{C}_n$.

In order to prove the results of Section 4 we have needed to generalize some results of [13] and to prove new ones. In particular, Theorem 1 below is a key technical result about the *SRL* calculus.

Lemma 1 (Lifting). *Let* $\sigma, \sigma' \in CSubst_{\perp,F}$ *with* $\sigma \sqsubseteq \sigma'$. *If* $\mathcal{S}\sigma \lhd \mathcal{C}$ *then there exist a proof in SRL for* $\mathcal{S}\sigma' \lhd \mathcal{C}$ *with the same length and structure.*

Theorem 1 (Refinement). *Let* $\mathcal{S}_1, ..., \mathcal{S}_n, \mathcal{S}$ *be set-expressions such that* $\mathcal{S}_1 \sqsubseteq \mathcal{S}, ..., \mathcal{S}_n \sqsubseteq \mathcal{S}$. *Then*

$$\mathcal{S}_1 \lhd \mathcal{C}_1, ..., \mathcal{S}_n \lhd \mathcal{C}_n \Rightarrow \mathcal{S} \lhd \mathcal{C}$$

for some $\mathcal{C}$ *such that* $\mathcal{C}_1 \sqsubseteq \mathcal{C}, ..., \mathcal{C}_n \sqsubseteq \mathcal{C}$.

The next two properties can be easily proved from the previous theorem.

Proposition 1 (Consistency). *If* $\mathcal{S}$ *and* $\mathcal{S}'$ *are consistent and* $\mathcal{S} \lhd \mathcal{C}$, $\mathcal{S}' \lhd \mathcal{C}'$, *then* $\mathcal{C}$ *and* $\mathcal{C}'$ *are also consistent.*

As a consequence of this property we have consistency of failure: if $\mathcal{S} \lhd \{F\}$, then $[\![\mathcal{S}]\!] = \{\{\perp\}, \{F\}\}$.

Proposition 2 (Monotonicity). *If* $\mathcal{S} \sqsubseteq \mathcal{S}'$ *and* $\mathcal{S} \lhd \mathcal{C}$, *then* $\mathcal{S}' \lhd \mathcal{C}'$ *for some* $\mathcal{C}'$ *with* $\mathcal{C} \sqsubseteq \mathcal{C}'$.

4   Operational Semantics

The narrowing relation to be defined in 4.2 makes an extensive use of a particular notion of *context*. The next section is devoted to formalize contexts in our framework and some other related aspects.

Table 1. Rules for *SRL*-provability

$$(1) \quad \frac{}{\mathcal{S} \lhd \{\perp\}} \quad \mathcal{S} \in SetExp_\perp \qquad (2) \quad \frac{}{\{X\} \lhd \{X\}} \quad X \in \mathcal{V}$$

$$(3) \quad \frac{\{t_1\} \lhd \mathcal{C}_1 \quad \{t_n\} \lhd \mathcal{C}_n}{\{c(t_1, ..., t_n)\} \lhd \{c(\overline{t'}) \mid \overline{t'} \in \mathcal{C}_1 \times ... \times \mathcal{C}_n\}} \quad c \in DC \cup \{F\}$$

$$(4) \quad \frac{\mathcal{S} \lhd \mathcal{C}}{f(\overline{t}) \lhd \mathcal{C}} \quad (f(\overline{t}) \twoheadrightarrow \mathcal{S}) \in [\mathcal{P}]_{\perp,F}$$

$$(5) \quad \frac{}{f(\overline{t}) \lhd \{F\}} \quad \begin{array}{l} \text{for all } (f(\overline{s}) \twoheadrightarrow \mathcal{S}') \in \mathcal{P}, \\ \overline{t} \text{ and } \overline{s} \text{ have a } DC \cup \{F\}\text{-clash} \end{array}$$

$$(6) \quad \frac{\mathcal{S} \lhd \{F\}}{fails(\mathcal{S}) \lhd \{true\}}$$

$$(7) \quad \frac{\mathcal{S} \lhd \mathcal{C}}{fails(\mathcal{S}) \lhd \{false\}} \quad \text{there is some } t \in \mathcal{C}, t \neq \perp, t \neq F$$

$$(8) \quad \frac{\mathcal{S}_1 \lhd \mathcal{C}_1 \quad \mathcal{S}_2[X/\mathcal{C}_1] \lhd \mathcal{C}}{\bigcup_{X \in \mathcal{S}_1} \mathcal{S}_2 \lhd \mathcal{C}} \qquad (9) \quad \frac{\mathcal{S}_1 \lhd \mathcal{C}_1 \quad \mathcal{S}_2 \lhd \mathcal{C}_2}{\mathcal{S}_1 \cup \mathcal{S}_2 \lhd \mathcal{C}_1 \cup \mathcal{C}_2}$$

4.1   Contexts

A *context* is a set-expression with some holes in the places of subexpressions. Syntactically a context is:

$$C ::= \mathcal{S} \mid [\,] \mid fails(C_1) \mid \bigcup_{X \in C_1} C_2 \mid C_1 \cup C_2$$

where $\mathcal{S}$ is a set-expression, and C_1 and C_2 are contexts. A *principal context* is:

$$C ::= f(\bar{t}) \mid [\,] \mid fails(\mathcal{S}) \mid \bigcup_{X \in \mathcal{S}} C_1 \mid C_1 \cup C_2$$

where $\mathcal{S}$ is a set-expression, and C_1 and C_2 are principal contexts. Intuitively, a principal context is a context without indexed holes, i.e., it has all its holes at the highest level.

Analogous to the case of set-expressions, we consider both *total (principal) contexts* when $\mathcal{S} \in SetExp$ and *partial (principal) contexts* if $\mathcal{S} \in SetExp_\perp$. From the definitions of produced variables and free variables of a set-expression it is direct to define *produced variables* $PV(C)$ and *free variables* $FV(C)$ of a context C. As in the case of set-expressions, for contexts we also impose *admissibility conditions*: contexts of the form $\bigcup_{X \in C_1} C_2$ must satisfy $X \notin var(C_1) \cup PV(C_2)$ and $PV(C_1) \cap PV(C_2) = \emptyset$; and contexts of the form $C_1 \cup C_2$ must satisfy $PV(C_1) \cap FV(C_2) = \emptyset$ and $PV(C_2) \cap FV(C_1) = \emptyset$. How to apply substitutions to contexts is defined in a natural way.

The *arity* of a context C, written $|C|$, is the number of its holes. A context C of arity n can be understood as a function that takes n contexts $C_1, ..., C_n$ as arguments and returns another context resulting of fulfilling the holes with the contexts of the arguments. Formally, the *application of a context* C to the tuple of arguments $C_1, ..., C_n$, notated as $C\,[C_1, ..., C_n]$, is defined as:

- $[\,]\,[C] = C$
- $fails(C)\,[C_1, ..., C_n] = fails(C\,[C_1, ..., C_n])$
- $(\bigcup_{X \in C} C')\,[C_1, ..., C_n, C'_1, ..., C'_m] = \bigcup_{X \in C\,[C_1,...,C_n]} C'\,[C'_1, ..., C'_n]$, where $|C| = n$ and $|C'| = m$
- $(C \cup C')\,[C_1, ..., C_n, C'_1, ..., C'_m] = (C\,[C_1, ..., C_n]) \cup (C'\,[C'_1, ..., C'_m])$, where $|C| = n$ and $|C'| = m$

In the rest of the paper all context applications are done in such a way that admissibility conditions are satisfied by the resulting context.

Notice that the application of a context C of arity n to a tuple of contexts $C_1, ..., C_n$ of arities $m_1, ..., m_n$ results in another context of arity $m_1 + ... + m_n$. And of course, if we apply this context C to a tuple of set-expressions (contexts with arity 0) the resulting context has arity 0, that is, a set-expression. With respect to substitutions its is easy to check that for any $\sigma \in CSubst_{\perp,\mathsf{F}}$ we have $(C\,[\mathcal{S}_1, ..., \mathcal{S}_n])\sigma = C\sigma\,[\mathcal{S}_1\sigma, ..., \mathcal{S}_n\sigma]$.

Given a set-expression $\mathcal{S}$, it is possible to determine a principal context $C_\mathcal{S}$ and a tuple of cterms $t_1, ..., t_n$ such that $\mathcal{S} = C_\mathcal{S}\,[\{t_1\}, ..., \{t_n\}]$. We can see it reasoning on the structure of $\mathcal{S}$:

- if $\mathcal{S} = \{t\}$, then clearly $\mathcal{S} = [\,]\,[\{t\}]$
- if $\mathcal{S} = f(\bar{t})$ or $\mathcal{S} = fails(\mathcal{S}')$, then $C_\mathcal{S} = \mathcal{S}$ (a 0-arity principal context) and the tuple of arguments is empty.

- if $\mathcal{S} = \bigcup_{X \in \mathcal{S}_1} \mathcal{S}_2$, we can assume, inductively, that $\mathcal{S}_2$ is of the form $C_{\mathcal{S}_2}\ [\{t_1\}, ..., \{t_n\}]$ (where $C_{\mathcal{S}_2}$ is a principal context). Then, clearly $\mathcal{S} = (\bigcup_{X \in \mathcal{S}_1} C_{\mathcal{S}_2})\ [\{t_1\}, ..., \{t_n\}]$, and $(\bigcup_{X \in \mathcal{S}_1} C_{\mathcal{S}_2})$ is a principal context.
- if $\mathcal{S} = \mathcal{S}_1 \cup \mathcal{S}_2$, then if $\mathcal{S}_1 = C_{\mathcal{S}_1}\ [\{t_1\}, ..., \{t_n\}]$ and $\mathcal{S}_2 = C_{\mathcal{S}_2}\ [\{s_1\}, ..., \{s_m\}]$, we have $\mathcal{S} = (C_{\mathcal{S}_1} \cup C_{\mathcal{S}_2})\ [\{t_1\}, ..., \{t_n\}, \{s_1\}, ..., \{s_m\}]$.

We say that $C_{\mathcal{S}}\ [\{t_1\}, ..., \{t_n\}]$ is the *principal contextual form* (in short p.c.f) of $\mathcal{S}$. In the following, we frequently refer to a set-expression by its p.c.f. Moreover, as an abuse of notation we will omit the braces '{', '}' and write $C_{\mathcal{S}}\ [t_1, ..., t_n]$ or simply $C_{\mathcal{S}}\ [\bar{t}]$.

Notice that the equality $\mathcal{S} = C_{\mathcal{S}}[t_1, ..., t_n]$, viewed as a context application, is a trivial identity. The important point of such format is that the cterms $t_1, ..., t_n$ reflect the skeleton or constructed part of the set-expression. With this idea, if $C_{\mathcal{S}}[t_1, ..., t_n]$ is the p.c.f. for $\mathcal{S}$, the *information set* $\mathcal{S}^*$ of $\mathcal{S}$ is defined as:

- $\{\bot\}$ if $n = 0$;
- $\{t_1\tau, ..., t_n\tau\}$ if $n > 0$, where $X\tau = \bot$ if $X \in PV(\mathcal{S})$ and $X\tau = X$ otherwise

For example, consider the set-expression introduced in Sect. 3

$$\mathcal{S} = \bigcup_{A \in \bigcup_{B \in f(X,Y)} \{B\}} \{c(A, X)\} \cup \bigcup_{C \in \{X\}} f(C, Y)$$

The context $C_{\mathcal{S}}$ of the p.c.f. has only a hole in the place of $\{c(A, X)\}$, which is the only argument of the p.c.f., that is:

$$\left(\bigcup_{A \in \bigcup_{B \in f(X,Y)} \{B\}}\ [\ ] \cup \bigcup_{C \in \{X\}} f(C, Y)\right)\ [c(A, X)]$$

In this case $\mathcal{S}^* = \{c(\bot, X)\}$ (obtained by replacing the variable A by $\bot$).

Proposition 3. *The information set of a set-expression is a SAS for $\mathcal{S}$, i.e., $\mathcal{S} \triangleleft \mathcal{S}^*$. Moreover, this SAS can be obtained by using rules 1, 2, 3, 8 and 9 of SRL (in other words, no function rule is needed to obtain $\mathcal{S}^*$).*

4.2   A Narrowing Relation for Set-Expressions

The rewriting logic *SRL* showed in Sect. 3 fixes the denotational semantics of set-expressions. Now we are interested in a operational mechanism for narrowing set-expressions into simplified or normal forms, while finding appropriate values for the variables of the expressions.

The syntactic structure of a *normal form* is: $\{t_1\} \cup ... \cup \{t_n\}$, with $t_1, ..., t_n \in CTerm_F$. According to this, $\{F\}$ is a normal form itself. Notice also that a normal form cannot contain any function symbol or indexed union. On the other hand, the undefined value $\bot$ has not any sense in the operational mechanism that deals only with total set-expressions.

One-Narrowing-Step Relation: Given a program $\mathcal{P}$, two set-expressions $\mathcal{S}, \mathcal{S}' \in SetExp$, $\theta \in CSubst_F$ and $\Gamma \subseteq \mathcal{V}$, a narrowing step is expressed as: $\mathcal{S} \overset{\Gamma}{\underset{\theta}{\rightsquigarrow}} \mathcal{S}'$ where the relation $\mathcal{S} \overset{\Gamma}{\underset{\theta}{\rightsquigarrow}} \mathcal{S}'$ is defined in the Table 2. The set Γ is the *set of protected variables*: produced variables of the external scope are stored into Γ in order to avoid to apply substitutions for them. For narrowing

Table 2. *SNarr* relation

Cntx	$C\ [\mathcal{S}] \overset{\Gamma}{\underset{\theta}{\leadsto}} C\theta\ [\mathcal{S}']$	if $\mathcal{S} \overset{\Gamma \cup PV(C)}{\underset{\theta}{\leadsto}} \mathcal{S}'$
Nrrw$_1$	$f(\bar{t}) \overset{\Gamma}{\underset{\theta\vert_{var(\bar{t})}}{\leadsto}} \mathcal{S}\theta$	if $(f(\bar{s}) \twoheadrightarrow \mathcal{S}) \in \mathcal{P}$, $\theta \in CSubst_{\text{F}}$ is a m.g.u. for $\bar{s}$ and $\bar{t}$ with $Dom(\theta) \cap \Gamma = \emptyset$
Nrrw$_2$	$f(\bar{t}) \overset{\Gamma}{\underset{\epsilon}{\leadsto}} \{\text{F}\}$	if for every rule $(f(\bar{s}) \twoheadrightarrow \mathcal{S}_1) \in \mathcal{P}$, $\bar{s}$ and $\bar{t}$ have a $DC \cup \{\text{F}\}$-clash
Fail$_1$	$fails(\mathcal{S}) \overset{\Gamma}{\underset{\epsilon}{\leadsto}} \{true\}$	if $\mathcal{S}^* = \{\text{F}\}$
Fail$_2$	$fails(\mathcal{S}) \overset{\Gamma}{\underset{\epsilon}{\leadsto}} \{false\}$	if $\exists t \in \mathcal{S}^*\ t \neq \bot, t \neq \text{F}$
Flat	$\bigcup_{X \in \bigcup_{Y \in \mathcal{S}_1} \mathcal{S}_2} \mathcal{S}_3 \overset{\Gamma}{\underset{\epsilon}{\leadsto}} \bigcup_{Y \in \mathcal{S}_1} \bigcup_{X \in \mathcal{S}_2} \mathcal{S}_3$	
Dist	$\bigcup_{X \in \mathcal{S}_1 \cup \mathcal{S}_2} \mathcal{S}_3 \overset{\Gamma}{\underset{\epsilon}{\leadsto}} \bigcup_{X \in \mathcal{S}_1} \mathcal{S}_3 \cup \bigcup_{X \in \mathcal{S}_2} \mathcal{S}_3$	
Bind	$\bigcup_{X \in \{t\}} \mathcal{S} \overset{\Gamma}{\underset{\epsilon}{\leadsto}} \mathcal{S}[X/t]$	
Elim	$\bigcup_{X \in \mathcal{S}'} \mathcal{S} \overset{\Gamma}{\underset{\epsilon}{\leadsto}} \mathcal{S}$	if $X \notin FV(\mathcal{S})$

a set-expression $\mathcal{S}$ we must take Γ such that $\Gamma \cap FV(\mathcal{S}) = \emptyset$; in fact, the simplest choice is $\Gamma = \emptyset$. The calculus itself will protect the appropriate variables in derivations. In the following we use *SNarr* as a name for this narrowing relation, and refer to it as *set-narrowing*.

Some comments about the rules in Table 2:

- **Cntx** performs a sub-derivation on a sub-set-expression and then replaces the original by the resulting one. Notice that it ensures the protection of produced variables of the context by adding them to Γ.
- The rule **Nrrw$_1$** narrows a function call $f(\bar{t})$ using a rule of the program. The m.g.u. θ used for the parameter passing is not allowed to affect to protected variables due to the condition $Dom(\theta) \cap \Gamma = \emptyset$. It is also clear that $Ran(\theta) \cap \Gamma = \emptyset$ because the variables of the rule are fresh variables. Notice also that, for technical convenience, the substitution θ is projected over the variables of the narrowed expression. Notice finally that this is *the* rule which really binds variables, since **Cntx** is merely a contextual rule and the rest produce an empty substitution.
- **Nrrw$_2$** operates only in the case that **Nrrw$_1$** cannot find an applicable rule of the program, i.e., all of them have a clash. As our programs are *DC-complete* this situation is only possible if the call $f(\bar{t})$ has F at a position in which the heads of program rules have a constructor symbol $c \in DC$ (the transformation to *CIS-programs* does not introduce F in heads).
- Rules **Fail$_1$** and **Fail$_2$** are direct counterpart of rules 6 and 7 of *SRL*.

- Rules **Flat**, **Dist**, **Bind** and **Elim** directly reflect some properties of sets in the mathematical sense. From an intuitive point of view, they all reduce the structural complexity of the set-expression.

The closure $S \leadsto_{\theta}^{\Gamma *} S'$ is defined in the usual way:

$$S = S_0 \underset{\theta_1}{\overset{\Gamma}{\leadsto}} S_1 \underset{\theta_2}{\overset{\Gamma}{\leadsto}} \ldots \underset{\theta_n}{\overset{\Gamma}{\leadsto}} S_n = S', \quad \text{with } \theta = \theta_1\theta_2\ldots\theta_n$$

It is easy to see that at any step $S_i\theta_i = S_i$ and also $S'\theta = S'$.

Example   Consider the *CIS*-program of graphs of Sect. 3. The node c is safe according to definitions, so *SNarr* must be able to narrow the expression $safe(X)$ to *true* with the substitution $X = c$. Table 3 shows the steps of such derivation; we underline the redex at each step and annotate the rule of *SNarr* applied. The applications of **Cntx** are omitted for simplicity. We assume the function *ifThenElse* defined by the natural rules, and we shorten *ifThenElse* by *iTe*. We recall that the function *eq* is defined by the rules $eq(a, a) \twoheadrightarrow \{true\}$, $eq(a, b) \twoheadrightarrow \{false\}$ and so on. The answer substitution $[X/c]$ is found in the third step by **Nrrw**$_1$ applied to the expression $eq(X, d)$.

This derivation has been performed by a little prototype that implements the relation *SNarr* with an appropriate criterion for selecting the redex. In fact this prototype provides four possible reductions for the expression $safe(X)$: *false* with $[X/a]$; *false* with $[X/b]$; *true* with $[X/c]$ and *false* with $[X/d]$.

4.3   Correctness and Completeness of *Snarr*

A desirable property is the preservation of semantics under context application: consider two set-expressions S and S' with $[\![S]\!] = [\![S']\!]$ and a 1-arity context C; then, we would like $[\![C\,[S]]\!] = [\![C\,[S']]\!]$. But this is not true in general. For example, assume the rules $f(z) \twoheadrightarrow \{z\}$ and $g(z) \twoheadrightarrow \{s(z)\}$. Then, for the set-expressions $f(X)$ and $g(X)$, $[\![g(X)]\!] = [\![f(X)]\!] = \{\bot\}$. But if we consider $C = \bigcup_{X \in \{z\}}[\,]$ then $C\,[f(X)] = \bigcup_{X \in \{z\}} f(X)$ and $C\,[g(X)] = \bigcup_{X \in \{z\}} g(X)$, whose denotations are $\{\{\bot\}, \{z\}\}$ and $\{\{\bot\}, \{s(z)\}\}$ resp. What is true is:

Lemma 2. *Let S and S' be set-expressions such that $[\![S\sigma]\!] = [\![S'\sigma]\!]$ for any $\sigma \in CSubst_{\bot,F}$ admissible for S and S'. Then $[\![(C\,[S])\sigma']\!] = [\![(C\,[S'])\sigma']\!]$, for any context C of arity 1 and any $\sigma' \in CSubst_{\bot,F}$ admissible for $C\,[S]$ and $C\,[S']$.*

Notice that in the example above, the hypothesis $[\![g(X)\theta]\!] = [\![f(X)\theta]\!]$ does not hold, for instance taking $\theta = [X/z]$. This lemma is used for proving correctness:

Theorem 2 (Correctness of *SNarr*). *Let S, $S' \in SetExp$, $\theta \in CSubst_F$, $\Gamma \subseteq V$ any set of variables, and $\sigma \in CSubst_{\bot,F}$ any admissible substitution for $S\theta$ and S'. Then: $S \leadsto_{\theta}^{\Gamma *} S' \Rightarrow [\![S\theta\sigma]\!] = [\![S'\sigma]\!]$. In particular, taking $\sigma = \epsilon$ we have: $S \leadsto_{\theta}^{\Gamma *} S' \Rightarrow [\![S\theta]\!] = [\![S']\!]$*

Table 3. A narrowing derivation for $safe(X)$

$safe(\underline{X})$	$(Nrrw_1)$
$fails(\underline{path(X,d)})$	$(Nrrw_1)$
$fails(\bigcup_{A\in \underline{eq(X,d)}}\bigcup_{B\in\bigcup_{C\in next(X)} path(C,d)} iTe(A,true,B))$ $\boxed{X/c}$	$(Nrrw_1)$
$fails(\bigcup_{A\in \{false\}}\bigcup_{B\in\bigcup_{C\in next(c)} path(C,d)} iTe(A,true,B))$	$(Bind)$
$fails(\bigcup_{B\in\bigcup_{C\in next(c)} path(C,d)} \underline{iTe(false,true,B)})$	$(Nrrw_1)$
$fails(\bigcup_{B\in\bigcup_{C\in next(c)} path(C,d)}\{B\})$	$(Flat)$
$fails(\bigcup_{C\in next(c)}\bigcup_{B\in \underline{path(C,d)}}\{B\})$	$(Nrrw_1)$
$fails(\bigcup_{C\in next(c)}\bigcup_{B\in\bigcup_{D\in eq(C,d)}\bigcup_{E\in\bigcup_{F\in next(C)} path(F,d)} iTe(D,true,E)}\{B\})$	$(Flat)$
$fails(\bigcup_{C\in next(c)}\bigcup_{D\in eq(C,d)}\bigcup_{B\in\bigcup_{E\in\bigcup_{F\in next(C)} path(F,d)} iTe(D,true,E)}\{B\})$	$(Flat)$
$fails(\bigcup_{C\in \underline{next(c)}}\bigcup_{D\in eq(C,d)}\bigcup_{E\in\bigcup_{F\in next(C)} path(F,d)}\bigcup_{B\in iTe(D,true,E)}\{B\})$	$(Nrrw_2)$
$fails(\bigcup_{C\in \{F\}}\bigcup_{D\in eq(C,d)}\bigcup_{E\in\bigcup_{F\in next(C)} path(F,d)}\bigcup_{B\in iTe(D,true,E)}\{B\})$	$(Bind)$
$fails(\bigcup_{D\in \underline{eq(F,d)}}\bigcup_{E\in\bigcup_{F\in next(F)} path(F,d)}\bigcup_{B\in iTe(D,true,E)}\{B\})$	$(Nrrw_2)$
$fails(\bigcup_{D\in \{F\}}\bigcup_{E\in\bigcup_{F\in next(F)} path(F,d)}\bigcup_{B\in iTe(D,true,E)}\{B\})$	$(Bind)$
$fails(\bigcup_{E\in\bigcup_{F\in next(F)} path(F,d)}\bigcup_{B\in \underline{iTe(F,true,E)}}\{B\})$	$(Nrrw_2)$
$fails(\bigcup_{E\in\bigcup_{F\in next(F)} path(F,d)}\bigcup_{B\in \{F\}}\{B\})$	$(Elim)$
$fails(\bigcup_{B\in \{F\}}\{B\})$	$(Bind)$
$fails(\underline{\{F\}})$	$(Fail_1)$
$\{true\}$	

We split completeness in two simpler lemmas. First, the relation $SNarr$ can refine the information of any SAS obtained by SRL.

Lemma 3 (Completeness I). *If $\mathcal{P} \vdash_{SRL} \mathcal{S} \lhd \mathcal{C}$ then for any Γ with $\Gamma \cap FV(\mathcal{S}) = \emptyset$ we can derive $\mathcal{S} \overset{\Gamma}{\underset{\epsilon}{\rightsquigarrow}}{}^{*} \mathcal{S}'$ such that $\mathcal{C} \sqsubseteq (\mathcal{S}')^{*}$*

Here we see the relation $SNarr$ as a pure rewriting relation: the answer substitution is ϵ. Lemma 4 shows that any substitution θ making reducible a set-expression $\mathcal{S}$ is captured or generalized by a narrowing derivation from $\mathcal{S}$. For example, for the rule $f(z) \twoheadrightarrow \{s(z)\}$, $SNarr$ can derive $f(z) \overset{\Gamma}{\underset{\epsilon}{\rightsquigarrow}}{}^{*} \{s(z)\}$. Then, there is a derivation $f(X) \overset{\Gamma}{\underset{[X/z]}{\rightsquigarrow}}{}^{*} \{s(z)\}$, i.e., the value z for X can be found.

Lemma 4 (Completeness II). *Let* $S \in SetExp$, $\theta \in CSubst$ *and* Γ *such that* $\Gamma \cap PV(S) = \emptyset$. *If* $S\theta \overset{\Gamma}{\underset{\epsilon}{\rightsquigarrow}}{}^{*} S'$ *then there exists* $\theta', \mu \in CSubst$, *with* $\theta = \theta'\mu$, *such that* $S \overset{\Gamma}{\underset{\theta'}{\rightsquigarrow}}{}^{*} S''$ *with* $S' = S''\mu$.

Theorem 3 (Completeness). *If* $\mathcal{P} \vdash_{SRL} S\theta \lhd \mathcal{C}$ *and* $\Gamma \cap FV(S) = \emptyset$, *then there exists a derivation* $S \overset{\Gamma}{\underset{\theta'}{\rightsquigarrow}}{}^{*} S'$ *such that, for some* μ, $\theta = \theta'\mu$ *(i.e.* θ' *is more general than* θ*) and* $\mathcal{C} \sqsubseteq (S'\mu)^{*}$.

Corollary 1. *If* $\mathcal{P} \vdash_{SRL} S\theta \lhd \{F\}$, *then* $S \overset{\emptyset}{\underset{\theta'}{\rightsquigarrow}}{}^{*} \{F\}$ *for some* θ' *more general than* θ.

This result shows that we have achieved our goal of devising an operational mechanism for failure, which is *constructive*, in the sense that in presence of variables is able to find appropriate substitutions for them.

5   Conclusions and Future Work

We have defined a narrowing relation for functional logic programs which can make use of failure as programming construct, by means of a function *fails(e)*, which is a computable approximation to the property ' *e cannot be reduced to head normal form'*. Programs are written in a set-oriented syntax where expressions can use unions and indexed unions. Thus the syntax directly reflects non-determinism of functions and call-time choice semantics in a suitable way as to facilitate the definition of narrowing of set-expressions.

The set-narrowing relation serves to the purpose of computing failures, since the failure of an expression e corresponds to the fact that the expression can be narrowed to the set $\{F\}$, where F is a constant introduced to represent failure. An important feature of our notion of narrowing is that it can operate to compute failures even in presence of variables, for which appropriate bindings are obtained. Using a frequent terminology in the context of logic programming and negation, our narrowing relation realizes *constructive failure* for functional logic programs. Nothing similar can be found in existing *FLP* systems like *Curry* or *TOY*.

The definition of set-narrowing is quite amenable for implementation, and we have indeed implemented a first prototype for it, with which the examples in the paper have been executed.

In this paper we have not addressed the issue of *strategies* for set-narrowing. Nevertheless, for the implementation we have used some kind of 'demand driven strategy' close to the usual one in existing systems. It this sense it is interesting to remark that, in contrast to other notions of narrowing proposed for non-determinism with call-time choice [7, 8], which has been criticized [3] as being too far from real computations, our definition of set-narrowing seems better suited to the adoption of strategies. Notice that, in particular, the rule **Nrrw**$_1$ performs exactly a narrowing step in the classical sense, just with some conditions imposed about what variables can be bound.

The theoretical investigation of set-narrowing strategies, as well as the integration of our implementation in the system $\mathcal{TOY}$ are the main subjects of future work.

References

[1] M. Abengózar-Carneros et al. $\mathcal{TOY}$: a multiparadigm declarative language, version 2.0. Technical report, Dep. SIP, UCM Madrid, January 2001. 212, 213

[2] S. Antoy. Definitional trees. In *Proc. ALP'92*, pages 143–157. Springer LNCS 632, 1992. 214, 217

[3] S. Antoy. Constructor-based conditional narrowing. In *Proc. PPDP'01*, pages 199–206. ACM Press, 2001. 217, 225

[4] K. R. Apt and R. Bol. Logic programming and negation: A survey. *Journal of Logic Programming*, 19&20:9–71, 1994. 212

[5] D. Chan. Constructive negation based on the completed database. In *Proc. ICSLP'88*, pages 111–125, 1988. 214

[6] K. L. Clark. Negation as failure. In H. Gallaire and J. Minker, editors, *Logic and Data Bases*, pages 293–322. Plenum Press, 1978. 212

[7] J. C. González-Moreno, T. Hortalá-González, F. J. López-Fraguas, and M. Rodríguez-Artalejo. A rewriting logic for declarative programming. In *Proc. ESOP'96*, pages 156–172. Springer LNCS 1058, 1996. 213, 225

[8] J. C. González-Moreno, T. Hortalá-González, F. J. López-Fraguas, and M. Rodríguez-Artalejo. An approach to declarative programming based on a rewriting logic. *Journal of Logic Programming*, 40(1):47–87, 1999. 212, 213, 218, 225

[9] M. Hanus. The integration of functions into logic programming: From theory to practice. *Journal of Logic Programming*, 19&20:583–628, 1994. 212

[10] M. Hanus (ed.). Curry: An integrated functional logic language. Available at `http://www-i2.informatik.rwth-aachen.de/~hanus/curry/report.html`, February 2000. 212, 213

[11] F. J. López-Fraguas and J. Sánchez-Hernández. $\mathcal{TOY}$: A multiparadigm declarative system. In *Proc. RTA'99*, Springer LNCS 1631, pages 244–247, 1999. 212, 213

[12] F. J. López-Fraguas and J. Sánchez-Hernández. Proving failure in functional logic programs. In *Proc. CL'00*, Springer LNAI 1861, pages 179–193, 2000. 213, 214, 218

[13] F. J. López-Fraguas and J. Sánchez-Hernández. Functional logic programming with failure: A set-oriented view. In *Proc. LPAR'01*, Springer LNAI 2250, pages 455–469, 2001. 213, 214, 217, 218

[14] F. J. López-Fraguas and J. Sánchez-Hernández. Narrowing failure in functional logic programming (long version). Available at `http://www.ucm.es/info/dsip/jaime/flopsExt.ps`, 2002. 215

[15] F. J. López-Fraguas and J. Sánchez-Hernández. A proof theoretic approach to failure in functional logic programming. Draft available at `http://www.ucm.es/info/dsip/jaime/tplp.ps`, 2002. 213, 214

[16] J. J. Moreno-Navarro. Default rules: An extension of constructive negation for narrowing-based languages. In *Proc. ICLP'94*, pages 535–549. MIT Press, 1994. 214

[17] J. J. Moreno-Navarro. Extending constructive negation for partial functions in lazy functional-logic languages. In *Proc. ELP'96*, pages 213–227. Springer LNAI 1050, 1996. 214, 216

[18] J. C. Reynolds. *Theories of Programing Languages*. Cambridge Univ. Press, 1998. 216

[19] P. J. Stuckey. Constructive negation for constraint logic programming. In *Proc. LICS'91*, pages 328–339, 1991. 214

[20] P. J. Stuckey. Negation and constraint logic programming. *Information and Computation*, 118:12–33, 1995. 214

The HiPE/x86 Erlang Compiler: System Description and Performance Evaluation

Mikael Pettersson, Konstantinos Sagonas, and Erik Johansson

Computing Science Department, Uppsala University, Sweden
{mikpe,kostis,happi}@csd.uu.se

Abstract. Erlang is a concurrent functional language, tailored for large-scale distributed and fault-tolerant control software. Its primary implementation is Ericsson's Erlang/OTP system, which is based on a virtual machine interpreter. HiPE (High-Performance Erlang) adds a native code execution mode to the Erlang/OTP system. This paper describes the x86 version of HiPE, including a detailed account of decisions and principles that guide the design of its compiler and runtime system. We also present a brief performance evaluation which indicates that HiPE/x86 delivers performance improvements on par with the more mature HiPE/SPARC system.

1 Introduction

Erlang is a functional programming language which supports concurrency, communication, distribution, fault-tolerance, automatic memory management, and on-line code updates [1]. It was designed for soft real-time control systems which are commonly developed by the telecommunications industry. Judging from commercial applications written in Erlang, the language is quite successful in this domain.

The most widely used implementation of Erlang, Ericsson's Erlang/OTP system, was until recently exclusively based on the BEAM virtual machine interpreter. This, and the fact that Erlang is a dynamically typed language requiring runtime type tests, made Erlang/OTP quite slow compared to implementations of other functional languages. The HiPE system [8, 9] was developed with the aim of significantly reducing this performance gap. HiPE achieves this by allowing flexible, user-controlled, just-in-time compilation of Erlang functions or modules to native machine code. As reported in [8], HiPE is currently the fastest Erlang implementation and offers performance which is competitive with implementations of other strict functional languages such as Scheme or SML/NJ. One drawback was that, until recently, HiPE only supported SPARC-based machines. To enable more widespread use of HiPE, we have developed an x86 version of the system. The result, HiPE/x86, is presented in this paper. Since October 2001, HiPE/x86 is included in the open source release of Erlang/OTP.[1]

---

[1] Available at www.erlang.org. See also www.csd.uu.se/projects/hipe.

Z. Hu and M. Rodríguez-Artalejo (Eds.): FLOPS 2002, LNCS 2441, pp. 228–244, 2002.

In this paper, we present a detailed account of the architecture of the HiPE/x86 compiler and runtime system, design decisions we made and their associated tradeoffs. The purpose of doing so is two-fold: First, we document our implementation in a form which is potentially more easy for other implementors to follow than HiPE's source code. Second, we believe that this information is applicable to other garbage-collected tail-recursive high-level languages and as such we hope that our experience will prove useful to anyone that gets involved in a similar project.

The paper begins with a brief overview of Erlang's characteristics (Sect. 2). After presenting the architecture of HiPE (Sect. 3), Sections 4–6 describe the HiPE/x86 system in detail. Some of its planned improvements are also discussed (Sect. 6). Section 7 contains a brief performance evaluation, Section 8 contrasts design decisions with those in related systems, and finally Section 9 ends with some concluding remarks.

2 The Erlang Language and Erlang/OTP

Erlang is a dynamically typed, strict, concurrent functional language. The basic data types include atoms, numbers, and process identifiers; compound data types are lists and tuples. There are no assignments or mutable data structures. Functions are defined as sets of guarded clauses, and clause selection is done by pattern matching. Iterations are expressed as tail-recursive function calls, and Erlang consequently requires tailcall optimisation. Erlang also has a catch/throw-style exception mechanism. Erlang processes are created dynamically, and applications tend to use many of them. Processes communicate through asynchronous message passing: each process has a *mailbox* in which incoming messages are stored, and messages are retrieved from the mailbox by pattern matching. Messages can be arbitrary Erlang values. Erlang implementations must provide automatic memory management, and the soft real-time nature of the language calls for bounded-time garbage collection techniques.

Erlang/OTP is the standard implementation of the language. It combines Erlang with the Open Telecom Platform (OTP) middleware [16], a library with standard components for telecommunications applications. Erlang/OTP is currently used industrially by Ericsson Telecom and other software and telecommunications companies around the world for the development of high-availability servers and networking equipment. Additional information about Erlang can be found at `www.erlang.org`.

3 HiPE: Brief System Overview

HiPE is included as an optional extension in the Open Source Erlang/OTP system. It consists of a compiler from BEAM virtual machine bytecode to native machine code (UltraSPARC or x86), and extensions to the runtime system to support mixing interpreted and native code execution, at the granularity of individual functions.

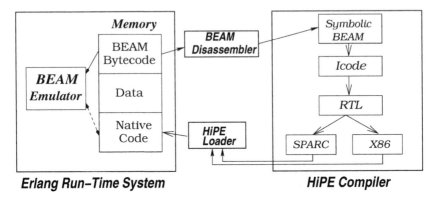

Fig. 1. Structure of a HiPE-enabled Erlang/OTP system

The overall structure of the HiPE system is shown in Fig. 1. This section briefly describes the generic parts of the compiler and runtime system. The specifics of HiPE/x86 are described in Sect. 4–6. A more detailed system description can be found in [8, 9].

BEAM. The BEAM intermediate representation is a symbolic version of the BEAM virtual machine bytecode, and is produced by disassembling the functions or module being compiled. BEAM operates on a largely implicit heap and call-stack, a set of global registers, and a set of slots in the current stack frame. BEAM is semi-functional: composite values are immutable, but registers and stack slots can be assigned freely.

BEAM to Icode. Icode is an idealised Erlang assembly language. The stack is implicit, any number of temporaries may be used, and temporaries survive function calls. Most computations are expressed as function calls. All bookkeeping operations, including memory management and process scheduling, are implicit.

BEAM is translated to Icode mostly one instruction at a time. However, function calls and the creation of tuples are sequences of instructions in BEAM but single instructions in Icode, requiring the translator to recognise those sequences.

The Icode form is then improved by application of constant propagation, constant folding, and dead-code elimination [12]. Temporaries are also renamed, to avoid false dependencies between different live ranges.

Icode to RTL. RTL is a generic three-address register transfer language. RTL itself is target-independent, but the code is target-specific, due to references to target-specific registers and primitive procedures. RTL has tagged registers for proper Erlang values, and untagged registers for arbitrary machine values. To simplify the garbage collector interface, function calls only preserve live tagged registers.

In the translation from Icode to RTL, many operations (e.g., arithmetic, data construction, or tests) are inlined. Data tagging operations [6, 13] are made explicit, data accesses and initialisations are turned into loads and stores, etc.

Icode-level switch instructions for switching on basic values are translated into code that implements the switches [2, 11]. Atoms are problematic since their runtime values differ between invocations of the runtime system, so switches on atoms are translated into semi-symbolic code which is finalised by the object code loader.

Optimisations applied to RTL include common subexpression elimination, constant propagation and folding, and merging of heap overflow tests.

The Runtime System. HiPE extends the standard Erlang/OTP runtime system to permit Erlang processes to execute both interpreted code and native machine code. [2]

Each process has two stacks, one for interpreted code and one for native code. This simplifies garbage collection and exception handling, since each stack contains only frames of a single type.

Control flow between interpreted and native code, e.g. at function calls and returns, is handled by a *mode-switch* interface. The implementation uses linker-generated *proxy code stubs* and *software trap return addresses* to trigger the appropriate mode-switches when invoked. Two important properties of the mode-switch interface are that it preserves tail-recursion (i.e., no sequence of consecutive mode-switching tailcalls grows either stack by more than a constant), and that it imposes no runtime overhead on same-mode calls and returns (i.e., from native to native or from BEAM to BEAM).

4   HiPE/x86 Runtime Architecture

In this section we describe the fundamental aspects of the HiPE/x86 runtime architecture. These are a prerequisite for the compiler's code generator, which is described in Sect. 5. The x86 is a family of CISC-style 32-bit processors. For a compiler writer, these are some of its most relevant properties:

- Arithmetic instructions are in 2-address form, i.e. `dst op= src`.
- It has only 8 general-purpose registers. Although memory operands are permitted in arithmetic instructions, instructions with register operands are faster to decode and execute with shorter latencies.
- Most high-performance implementations use pipelining and out-of-order and speculative execution. Branch-prediction misses are expensive.
- It has built-in support for a call stack, pointed to by the `%esp` general-purpose register, via the `call`, `ret`, `push`, and `pop` instructions.

---

[2] Very few FP language implementations provide support for mixing interpreted and native code.

- The branch-prediction hardware includes a circular return-stack buffer. A `call` instruction also pushes its return address on this buffer, and the predicted target of a `ret` instruction is popped off the buffer.
- For branch instructions with no history recorded in the branch prediction table, there is a static predictor that predicts forwards conditional branches as non-taken, and backwards conditional branches as taken.

Intel [7] in particular considers good branch prediction to be one of the most important factors in achieving high performance.

4.1   Register Usage

HiPE/x86 uses `%esp` as the current Erlang process' stack pointer, `%esi` as the current Erlang process' heap pointer, and `%ebp` as the pointer to the process control block (PCB) containing the current process' global state. The remaining 5 registers are used for function parameters and return values, and local caller-save[3] temporaries.

Using `%esp` as the Erlang stack pointer is beneficial since we avoid wasting a register for simulating a stack. It also allows us to use the processor's native support for function calls, although this is a mixed blessing; see Sect. 4.2 and Sect. 4.6.

Global state variables associated with an Erlang process, except for the heap and stack pointers, are accessed as memory operands indirectly via `%ebp`. The state variables frequently accessed this way include the heap and stack limits, and the time-slice counter. While not ideal, most x86 processors handle this fairly well.

4.2   Calling Convention

The HiPE/x86 calling convention was designed to meet two main goals: enabling tailcall optimisation (required in Erlang), and avoiding branch prediction misses at returns. To meet the latter goal, we must use the processor's `call` and `ret` instructions, and reserve the `%esp` register for the stack pointer.

Tailcall optimisation is implemented by having the caller *overwrite* its incoming parameter area on the stack with the new parameters for the callee, deallocate the remaining portion of its stack frame, and invoke the callee with a `jmp` instruction. When a function returns, it is also responsible for removing its parameters from the stack; to this end it uses the x86 `ret $n` instruction, which pops the return address, adds n to `%esp`, and then jumps to the return address.

Parameter passing is straightforward: the first 3 parameters are passed in registers, and the remaining ones are pushed on the stack in left-to-right order. A function puts its return value in the `%eax` register.

---

[3]   Callee-save registers complicate garbage collected implementations, see [4, Sec. 2.3].

Illustrating Calls and Tailcalls on x86. To illustrate how recursive calls and tailcalls are implemented by HiPE/x86, assume that f recursively calls g, g tailcalls h, and h finally returns to f. Figure 2 shows the stack layout changes in this process. State (a) shows the stack before f calls g. f evaluates the parameters to g, pushes them on the stack, and executes a `call` instruction which pushes a return address and jumps to g, leading to state (b). g allocates its frame (the dashed portion), evaluates the parameters to h, and shuffles the stack to overwrite the argument area and possibly parts of its frame with the new parameters, leading to state (c). Then g completes its tailcall to h by dropping its frame and jumping to h, leading to state (d). In state (d), the stack is exactly as if f had called h directly. Eventually h drops its frame, and executes a `ret $n` instruction, which pops the return address and stacked parameters and returns to f, leading to state (e). Register parameters are omitted from this description.

Figure 2 also illustrates why it is the callee which must deallocate the stacked parameters. In the presence of tailcalls, the caller (f above) does not know which function finally returns to it, and it does not know how many parameters there currently are on the stack. Therefore, the caller cannot deallocate the stacked parameters, but the returning function *can* since it knows how many parameters *it* takes. We point this out because this is the opposite of the calling convention normally used by C and Unix on x86.

A disadvantage of this calling convention is that the stack shuffle step during tailcalls must also consider the return address as a stacked parameter that will have to be moved to a different stack slot if the caller and callee (g and h above) have different numbers of stacked parameters. Passing parameters in registers reduces the number of calls with stacked parameters, alleviating this problem.

Tailcalls versus Branch Prediction. Our calling convention meets its goals of enabling both tailcall optimisation and the processor's return-stack branch predictor, with the downside of sometimes having to copy the return address from one stack slot to another.

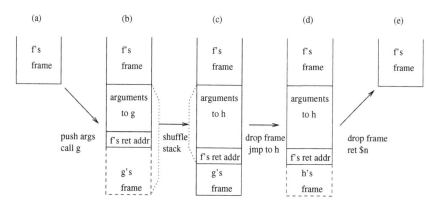

Fig. 2. Recursive calls and tailcalls on x86

An alternative calling convention is to push the return address (a code label) before the parameters are pushed, and then jmp to the callee. To return, the callee deallocates both its frame and the stacked parameters with a single add to the stack pointer, and then performs a simple ret or pops the return address into a register and performs an indirect jmp.[4] The advantage of this calling convention is that the compiler will never have to copy the return address at tailcalls, since it will always be in the slot just above the stacked parameters. However, the return stack branch predictor will not be effective, causing returns to be mispredicted at a higher rate.

As an experiment, we modified the HiPE/x86 assembler to replace call instructions with equivalent push;jmp sequences. The performance of our benchmark suite dropped by 9.2% overall, with several function call intensive programs losing 20–30%. While we did not utilise this change to improve the tailcall stack shuffle code, it does illustrate the significance of the return stack branch predictor.

Push Order. To simplify calling interpreted-mode closures from native code, parameters are pushed left-to-right. In a call to a closure, the closure itself is passed as the *last* parameter (this is the convention for both interpreted and native code), and every interpreted-mode closure has a native-code address which points to a native code stub procedure. Since the parameters are pushed left-to-right, the stub will always find the closure parameter just above the stack pointer, so a single stub can handle all native-code calls to BEAM-mode closures, regardless of how many parameters they take.

Since HiPE/x86 passes 3 parameters in registers, there are actually 4 stubs: three handles cases where the closure ends up as a register parameter, and the fourth handles all cases where the closure is pushed on the stack.

4.3   Stack Frames and Stack Descriptors

A function's stack frame is composed of two parts: a fixed-size part at the top for caller-save registers and spilled temporaries, and a variable-size part at the bottom for pushing the outgoing parameters in recursive calls.

On entry, the function first checks that enough stack space is available for the largest possible frame, calling a runtime system primitive if this is not the case. Then it allocates the fixed-size part by subtracting its size from %esp. On return, the function deallocates its frame by adding the frame size to %esp, and executing a ret $n instruction, which in turn empties the variable-sized part in the caller's frame.

The main benefit of fixed-size frames is their low maintenance cost. On the other hand, they may contain dead or uninitialised stack slots, which can increase their sizes and complicate garbage collection and exception handling.

---

[4] Some language implementations on x86 actually do this; see Sect. 8.

HiPE/x86 uses *stack descriptors* (also known as *stack maps*) to support exception handling and precise garbage collection. For each call site, the compiler constructs a stack descriptor describing that call site to the runtime system:

- the call site's return address (lookup key)
- the caller's frame size (excluding this call site's actual parameters)
- the caller's arity
- the caller's local exception handler, if present
- the live slots in the caller's frame

This data enables the runtime system to inspect stack frames and traverse call stacks.

A stack descriptor is represented by three-word header containing the return address, hash link, frame size, and arity, followed by a bitmask of the live stack slots. The exception handler is described by a single bit in the header; if set, the handler address is stored in the word immediately *before* the header. The memory overhead for the stack descriptors is currently about 35% of the code size. However, without stack descriptors additional code would have to be generated to remove or nullify dead stack slots.

There are techniques for compacting stack descriptor tables even further, e.g. [15]. However, they also tend to increase stack descriptor lookup costs, and we have found those costs to have a measurable performance impact in our system.

4.4   Garbage Collection and Generational Stack Scanning

HiPE/x86 uses a *safe points* garbage collection strategy: the compiler emits code to check for heap overflow and to call the collector in that case. These are normal recursive calls with associated stack descriptors. The garbage collector uses the stack descriptors to traverse the call stack and identify slots containing live Erlang values.

Repeated stack scanning can cause high runtime overheads in deeply recursive programs, so HiPE/x86 implements *generational stack scanning* [4]. Two pointers into the stack are maintained: a *gray* limit and a *black* limit. The black limit indicates how far the stack must be scanned at each minor collection, which corresponds to the boundary between new and old generation data. The gray limit separates frames touched since the previous collection from untouched frames, which corresponds to the boundary between young data and data in the new generation's aging buffer. After a minor collection, data in the aging buffer is promoted to the old generation, the gray limit becomes the black limit, and the gray limit is reset to the bottom of the stack.

To maintain the gray limit we *mark* the frame it points to, which involves saving its return address in the process' control block, and then replacing it with the address of a runtime system primitive. When the code returns to this frame, the runtime primitive moves the mark up a number of frames (currently 4), and then returns to the original return address. (The mark is also updated if an exception is thrown past it.) This implementation differs from [4] in that we never have more than one frame marked gray. Before each garbage collection, we check if the gray limit has passed the black limit, and update the black limit if this is the case. To keep overheads low in common cases, we avoid placing any mark on small stacks, currently stacks less than 512 bytes large. [5]

Generational stack scanning mainly benefits deeply recursive programs. One of our benchmark programs ran 6 times faster with generational stack scanning, and several others ran almost 2 times faster.

4.5   Exception Handling

When an exception is thrown, a runtime system primitive is called to find and invoke the handler for the most recently entered protected block. This is done by using the stack descriptors to unwind the stack until a frame with a local handler is found. The stack pointer is reset to the bottom of that frame, and the handler is invoked.

4.6   C and Unix Interface Issues

Calls between C and Erlang. As described previously, each Erlang process has its own %esp-based stack, so when the runtime system (written in C) starts or resumes an Erlang process executing native code, it performs a *stack switch*. Ignoring caching effects, a stack switch is very light-weight, requiring only two instructions to save %esp in the PCB and then load its new value.

The Erlang system comes with a large set of built-in functions, BIFs, implemented in C. However, there is no guarantee that the current Erlang process' x86 stack has room for executing a C function. Therefore, to call a BIF, a stack switch back to the standard C stack is made and the actual parameters are copied before the corresponding C function is called – the copy also compensates for differences in parameter passing conventions. After the call, the stacks are switched again and a return is made.

Unix Signal Handling. A Unix signal handler is typically invoked asynchronously on the current stack. This is problematic for HiPE/x86 since each Erlang process has its own stack. These stacks are initially very small, and grown only in response to explicit stack overflow checks emitted by the compiler. Execution of a signal handler could easily cause stack overflow and memory corruption.

To avoid this, we redirect all signal handlers to the Unix process' "alternate signal stack". Unfortunately, this redirection is optional and has to be requested as each handler is registered. Since we do not have full control of the entire system in which HiPE/x86 executes (the Erlang/OTP runtime system can be linked with foreign code and libraries), we enforce this by overriding the standard

---

[5] The tuning parameters mentioned here, 4 frames and 512 bytes, were derived from the results of extensive benchmarking.

sigaction() and signal() procedures with our own versions. This is highly system-dependent, which is why HiPE/x86 currently only supports Linux with glibc 2.1 or 2.2 libraries, and Solaris 8.

Some user-space threads implementations use over-sized stacks and write-protected guard pages. This is fine for systems supporting < 100 heavy-weight threads in a Unix address space, but an Erlang system is expected to support thousands of light-weight threads, so this solution is not an option for us.

Signals could be masked with sigprocmask() before running native code. However, that would increase context switching costs, increase the latency for detecting asynchronous events (such as I/O completion), and make some optimisations implemented in the BEAM interpreter (unmasking floating-point exceptions and catching SIGFPE instead of performing dynamic tests) impossible in HiPE/x86.

5 The HiPE/x86 Code Generator

5.1 Backend Intermediate Representation

The x86 intermediate representation is a simple abstract x86 assembly language. It differs from RTL in two major ways:

- Arithmetic operations are in two-address form, with the destination operand also being a source operand (i.e., x += y instead of x = x + y).
- Memory operands described by simple addressing modes (base register plus offset) are permitted in most operand positions.

To facilitate conversion to and from control-flow-graph (CFG) form, control-flow instructions with multiple possible successors (e.g., the jcc conditional jump instruction) are represented in a pseudo-x86 form with all successors listed explicitly – implicit fallthrough is not used until the final assembly phase.

The translation from RTL to x86 is mainly concerned with converting three-address instructions to two-address instructions, and converting recursive calls to push the actual parameters. The conversion from three-address to two-address form uses the following rules to minimise the the the number of new temporaries and moves:

- $x = x\ op\ y$ becomes $x\ op= y$
- $z = x\ op\ y$ becomes $z = x$; $z\ op= y$, if z is neither x nor y
- $y = x\ op\ y$ becomes $y\ op= x$, if $y \neq x$ and op commutes (e.g., integer $+$)
- $y = x\ op\ y$ becomes $t = x$; $t\ op= y$; $y = t$, if $y \neq x$ and op does not commute

Explicit memory operands are introduced in two cases. An RTL-level load instruction becomes a move with a memory operand as source; RTL stores are handled analogously. Some global variables located in the PCB are referenced as pseudo-registers at the RTL level, these include the stack limit, heap limit, and the time-slice counter. These pseudo-registers are turned into *offset*(%ebp) memory operands.

5.2   Register Allocation

Register allocation is applied to try to map temporaries to actual x86 registers. Spilled temporaries remain unallocated, and are mapped to stack slots in the subsequent frame management pass. The default register allocator is based on *linear scan* [14, 10] since it has low compile-time costs and is therefore suitable for JIT compilation, but at higher optimisation levels an *iterated register coalescing* [5] allocator is used.

Before register allocation, every temporary is semantically equivalent to a register, and any operand may be a temporary. After register allocation, any unallocated temporary is an implicit memory operand, but the x86 architecture places some restrictions on the use of memory operands. For example, in binary operations such as arithmetic and moves, either the source or the destination may be a memory operand, but not both. A "fixup" pass is run after register allocation to ensure that these conditions are met.

5.3   Frame Management

Stack frames are introduced to the code after register allocation, when the set of spilled temporaries is known. The frame management pass performs the following tasks:

- The register assignment map is applied, and temporaries are rewritten to other temporaries or physical registers.
- A map is built which maps each spilled temporary and stacked parameter to a stack slot. The mapping is given as an offset relative to a virtual frame pointer having the initial value of the stack pointer on entry to the function.
- The frame size and maximal stack usage for calls are computed, and code is added to the function prologue to check for stack overflow and set up the stack frame.
- All instructions are processed while recording the current stack depth (offset from the virtual frame pointer), and references to spilled temporaries are rewritten as memory operands using offsets from %esp.
- A stack descriptor is created for each call site, describing which stack slots are live (using the results of a liveness analysis) and whether the call is in the context of a local exception handler.
- At each tailcall, code is generated to copy the actual parameters to the initial portion of the stack frame. Actuals located in the destination area are first pushed at the end of the stack and rewritten as memory operands at those new locations. Then the actuals are moved to the destination area. The return address is treated like any other parameter.

5.4   Linearising the Code

During most parts of the compiler, the code is represented in a control-flow graph form. Before assembly, the CFG must be linearised by ordering the basic blocks and redirecting jump instructions accordingly.

It is important that this linearisation takes into account the likelihood of a conditional jump being taken or not, and the static branch prediction algorithm used in current x86 processors (forward conditional: not taken, backward conditional: taken). If this is not done, performance is likely to suffer due to mispredicted branches.

First, the HiPE compiler always annotates conditional jumps with taken/not-taken probabilities. These are usually accurate, since many conditionals are type safety checks and stack or heap overflow checks inserted by the compiler itself. Second, the x86 CFG module is careful to represent all conditional jumps as "unlikely". Third, the linearisation attempts to order blocks following the "likely" path. The net effect is that in most functions, the likely path is a straight sequence of instructions, with some forward conditional jumps to blocks implementing less likely special cases (such as non-fixnum arithmetic or calling the garbage collector on heap overflow).

5.5   Assembling the Code

The assembler converts the final symbolic x86 code to machine code, that is either loaded into the runtime system or saved in an object file. The main complication here is that branch instructions have both short and long forms, with the short forms being preferable for performance reasons but not always applicable. For this reason, assembly is divided into several passes: preliminary unoptimised assembly, rewriting branches to short form when possible, and then final generation of machine code.

6   Planned Future Improvements

Register Usage. HiPE/x86 currently passes 3 parameters in registers, but this does not improve performance much because of two limitations: calls clobber all non-reserved registers, and no live range splitting is performed. Since there are no real leaf functions (every function has conditional calls to runtime primitives to handle stack overflow and end of time slice), the parameter registers are always spilled immediately on entry to a function. To rectify this problem, we are planning to perform live-range splitting of temporaries live at function calls, similar to [3].

The frame management pass needs 2 scratch registers while performing the final translation of tailcalls. This is why only 3 parameter registers are used, even though 5 registers are non-reserved in the runtime architecture. To avoid wasting registers in the frame management pass, tailcalls will be reimplemented as parallel moves and expanded before register allocation. The linear scan register allocator also needs 2 scratch registers, but it is not yet known whether it can be fixed to avoid this.

We plan on using the %fs segment register instead of a general-purpose register to point to the current process' PCB. This would increase the number of non-reserved registers from 5 to 6. The operating-system support code is working on Linux and Solaris 8, but it is not yet known whether this can be made to work on Windows.

Leaf Functions. Every compiled function currently checks for stack overflow when called. By changing the compiler to guarantee that a larger minimum number of words is available on the stack at a call, we should be able to eliminate the stack overflow check from most leaf functions. HiPE/SPARC includes this feature.

Spill Slot Coalescing. The stack frame module maps each spilled temporary to its own stack slot. Since many temporaries are spilled on x86, it would be advantageous to coalesce spill slots when possible. This would help reduce the size of stack frames, improve cache utilisation, and reduce stack descriptor sizes and the overheads for parsing them.

7   Performance Evaluation

The performance of HiPE on SPARC, both compared with other Erlang systems and with other functional language implementations has been reported previously [8, 9]. Those results showed that HiPE significantly improves the performance of Erlang/OTP on SPARC, and reduces the gap to other functional language implementations. Here we measure the performance of HiPE/x86 vs. BEAM on a set of "standard" Erlang benchmarks, and compare the resulting speedups with those of HiPE/SPARC. The Erlang benchmark programs used are:

fib A recursive Fibonacci function. Calculates fib(30) 30 times.

tak Takeuchi function, uses recursion and integer arithmetic intensely. 1,000 repetitions of computing tak(18,12,6).

length A tail-recursive list length function finding the length of a 2,000 element list 50,000 times.

qsort Ordinary quicksort. Sorts a short list 100,000 times.

smith The Smith-Waterman DNA sequence matching algorithm. Matches a sequence against 100 others; all of length 32. This is done 30 times.

huff A Huffman encoder which encodes and decodes a 32,026 character string 5 times.

decode Part of a telecommunications protocol. 500,000 repetitions of decoding an incoming binary message. A medium-sized benchmark (≈ 400 lines).

ring A concurrent benchmark which creates a ring of 10 processes and sends 100,000 small messages.

life A concurrent benchmark executing 10,000 generations in Conway's game of life on a 10 by 10 board where each square is implemented as a process.

prettypr Formats a large source program for pretty-printing, repeated 4 times. Recurses very deeply. A medium-sized benchmark ($\approx 1,100$ lines).

Table 1. HiPE/x86 speedup compared with BEAM and HiPE/SPARC

| Benchmark | x86 | | | SPARC |
	BEAM	HiPE	speedup	speedup
fib	31230	7360	4.24	4.12
tak	31900	5570	5.73	5.68
length	20000	3540	5.65	9.30
qsort	16450	3630	4.53	4.14
smith	23830	4960	4.80	3.69
huff	24540	12220	2.01	3.14
decode	19410	5210	3.73	2.22
ring	18360	16840	1.09	0.99
life	25580	18690	1.37	1.30
prettypr	13830	4740	2.92	2.37
estone			2.25	2.31

estone Computes an Erlang system's Estone number by running a number of common Erlang tasks and reporting a weighted ranking of its performance on these tasks. This benchmark stresses all parts of an Erlang implementation, including its runtime system and concurrency primitives.

Table 1 shows execution times (in milliseconds) for running these benchmarks in Erlang/OTP R8 under BEAM and HiPE, and the speedup for HiPE over BEAM. For the **estone** benchmark, execution times are not shown as the benchmark contains artificial delays. Instead, the speedup is the relative improvement to the Estone-ranking for HiPE over BEAM. The performance evaluation was conducted on a Dell Inspiron 7000, with a 333 MHz Pentium-II processor, 128 MB memory, running Linux. For comparison, the last column shows the speedup of HiPE over BEAM on a Sun Enterprise 3000 with two 248 MHz UltraSPARC-II processors, 1.2 GB memory, running Solaris 7.

HiPE/x86 achieves speedups comparable to those of HiPE/SPARC, even though the x86 is a register-starved architecture. As explained in Sect. 6, HiPE/x86 currently spills the parameter registers on entry to a function. This hurts the **length** and **huff** benchmarks, since they frequently dereference pointer parameters to list cells on the heap. **fib** and **tak** are also function-call intensive, but suffer less since they operate on integer parameters that can be referenced directly as memory operands on the stack.

HiPE's modest speedup on **ring** and **life** is because they spend most of their time in the runtime system scheduling processes, and compute very little on their own.

8   Related Systems

We have investigated several other native x86 implementations of languages with similar requirements as Erlang, such as ML, Lisp, Scheme, Prolog, Clean,

Table 2. Feature summary of related language implementations on the x86

	call stack		argument
	native	simulated	registers
Objective Caml 3.04	X		6
Clean 2.0	X		4
CMU Common Lisp 20020228	X		3
Poplog V15.53	X		3
Poly/ML 4.1.2	X		2
Chalmers Haskell 0.9999.4	X		0
MLton 20011006		X	0
SML/NJ 110.35		X	1–5
MLKit 4.0		X	3
MIT Scheme 7.6.1		X	0
GNU Prolog 1.2.8		X	0

and Haskell. Our investigation focused on how these systems implement calls and returns, and how many registers are used for parameter passing. We found most systems to have inadequate documentation about their implementation (a tradition we intend to break with this paper), so we had to try to derive this information from their source code. This was not always successful, so the findings we report here are somewhat approximate, and we have excluded systems whose source code was too impenetrable.

Table 2 summarises our findings. The "native" column is checked for systems that use `call` and `ret` instructions on a normal `%esp`-based stack, which signifies that return-stack branch prediction is enabled. The "simulated" column is checked for systems that use direct and indirect `jmp` instructions for calls and returns, which signifies that returns risk causing branch prediction misses. The last column indicates how many registers are used for passing function parameters.

The three top-most systems listed (Objective Caml, Clean, CMU Common Lisp) are known to deliver relatively good performance, and it is interesting to note that all three use native call stacks and pass parameters in registers like HiPE/x86. MLKit and MIT Scheme use `%esp` as their stack pointer, but choose to simulate calls and returns, presumably in order to reduce the amount of stack rewriting at tailcalls.

SML/NJ uses a single argument register in its standard calling convention, since Standard ML functions always have exactly one formal parameter; multiple parameters are expressed as tuples or curried applications. Non-standard calling conventions can be used for local functions, and then up to 5 parameter registers may be available.

In MLton, `%esp` is the heap pointer and `%ebp` points to a simulated call stack. Using a different register than `%esp` to point to the stack is motivated [6] by two main reasons: the MLton stack grows towards higher addresses, which prohibits the use of `push`, `call`, and `ret`, and the compiler generates many accesses to

---

[6] Matthew Fluet, email correspondence, May 8, 2002.

variables in stack frame slots, but the instruction encoding when %esp is the base pointer is one byte longer than for other registers, leading to worse code density. Since %esp was not used for the stack, it was instead used as the heap pointer. sigaltstack() is used to redirect signal handlers, but this does not work on Windows, forcing MLton to ignore %esp and use another register as heap pointer on Windows.

Poly/ML also uses sigaltstack() to redirect signal handlers. Their workaround on Windows is to artificially enlarge the stack with a scratch area at the bottom.

9   Concluding Remarks

This paper has described the architecture and implementation of HiPE/x86, a publicly available native code compiler for Erlang. HiPE/x86 offers flexible, user-controlled integration of interpreted and native code, and allows significant performance improvements for Erlang applications on the widely available standard x86 platform.

Besides documenting our implementation choices, we believe that such information is potentially useful for anybody that is involved in the implementation of a tail-recursive high-level language that relies on precise garbage collection. As shown by the performance evaluation, the x86 port of HiPE manages to achieve performance improvements compared to interpreted BEAM code which are on par with the more mature HiPE/SPARC system. We believe that this validates our design choices, especially the function call and stack frame conventions which are surprisingly conventional compared to those in HiPE/SPARC.

Acknowledgement

This research has been supported in part by the ASTEC (Advanced Software Technology) competence center.

References

[1] J. Armstrong, R. Virding, C. Wikström, and M. Williams. *Concurrent Programming in Erlang*. Prentice-Hall, second edition, 1996. 228

[2] R. L. Bernstein. Producing good code for the case statement. *Software – Practice and Experience*, 15(10):1021–1024, Oct. 1985. 231

[3] R. G. Burger, O. Waddell, and R. K. Dybvig. Register allocation using lazy saves, eager restores, and greedy shuffling. In *Proceedings of the ACM SIGPLAN '95 Conference on Programming Language Design and Implementation*, pages 130–138. ACM Press, 1995. 239

[4] P. Cheng, R. Harper, and P. Lee. Generational stack collection and profile-driven pretenuring. In *Proceedings of the ACM SIGPLAN Conference on Programming Language Design and Implementation, PLDI'98*, pages 162–173. ACM Press, 1998. 232, 235, 236

[5] L. George and A. W. Appel. Iterated register coalescing. *ACM Trans. Prog. Lang. Syst.*, 18(3):300–324, May 1996. 238

[6] D. Gudeman. Representing type information in dynamically typed languages. Technical Report TR 93-27, University of Arizona, Department of Computer Science, Oct. 1993. 231

[7] Intel Corporation. *Intel Pentium 4 and Intel Xeon Processor Optimization Reference Manual*, 2002. Document number 248966-05. 232

[8] E. Johansson, M. Pettersson, and K. Sagonas. HiPE: A High Performance Erlang system. In *Proceedings of the ACM SIGPLAN Conference on Principles and Practice of Declarative Programming*, pages 32–43. ACM Press, Sept. 2000. 228, 230, 240

[9] E. Johansson, M. Pettersson, K. Sagonas, and T. Lindgren. The development of the HiPE system: Design and experience report. *Springer International Journal of Software Tools for Technology Transfer*, 2002. To appear. 228, 230, 240

[10] E. Johansson and K. Sagonas. Linear scan register allocation in a high performance Erlang compiler. In *Practical Applications of Declarative Languages: Proceedings of the PADL'2002 Symposium*, number 2257 in LNCS, pages 299–317. Springer, Jan. 2002. 238

[11] S. Kannan and T. A. Proebsting. Correction to "Producing good code for the case statement". *Software – Practice and Experience*, 24(2):233, Feb. 1994. 231

[12] S. S. Muchnick. *Advanced Compiler Design & Implementation*. Morgan Kaufman Publishers, San Fransisco, CA, 1997. 230

[13] M. Pettersson. A staged tag scheme for Erlang. Technical Report 029, Information Technology Department, Uppsala University, Nov. 2000. 231

[14] M. Poletto and V. Sarkar. Linear scan register allocation. *ACM Trans. Prog. Lang. Syst.*, 21(5):895–913, Sept. 1999. 238

[15] D. Tarditi. Compact garbage collection tables. In *Proceedings of the ACM SIGPLAN International Symposium on Memory Management*, pages 50–58. ACM Press, Oct. 2000. 235

[16] S. Torstendahl. Open Telecom Platform. *Ericsson Review*, 75(1):14–17, 1997. 229

Dynamic-Cut with Definitional Trees

Rafael Caballero and Francisco Javier López-Fraguas

Dpto. de Sistemas Informáticos y Programación, Universidad Complutense de Madrid
{rafa,fraguas}@sip.ucm.es

Abstract. The detection of deterministic computations at run-time can be used to introduce *dynamic cuts* pruning the search space and thus increasing the efficiency of Functional-Logic systems. This idea was introduced in an early work of R. Loogen and S. Winkler. However the proposal of these authors cannot be used in current implementations because it did not consider non-deterministic functions and was not oriented to the demand driven strategy. Our work adapts and extends the technique, both showing how to deal with non-deterministic computations and how definitional trees can be employed to locate the places where the cuts will be introduced. An implementation based on a Prolog-translation is proposed, making the technique easy to implement in current systems generating Prolog code. Some experiments showing the effectiveness of the cut are presented.

1 Introduction

Efficiency has been one of the major drawbacks associated to declarative languages. The problem becomes particularly severe in the case of Logic Programming (LP for short) and Functional-Logic Programming (FLP for short), where the introduction of non-deterministic computations often generates huge search spaces with their associated overheads both in terms of time and space.

In their work [8], Rita Loogen and Stephan Winkler presented a technique for the run-time detection of deterministic computations that can be used to safely prune the search space. This technique is known as *dynamic cut*. Unfortunately the programs considered in this work did not include non-deterministic functions, which are used extensively in FLP nowadays. Also the implementation (based on a modification of an abstract machine) did not follow the demand driven strategy [4, 9], which in the meantime has been adopted by all the current implementations of FLP languages.

Our proposal adapts the original idea to FLP languages with non-deterministic functions, which introduce some subtle changes in the conditions for the cut. These dynamic cuts can be easily introduced in a Prolog-based translation of FLP programs that uses definitional trees. This makes our technique easily adaptable to the current implementations of FLP languages based on translation into Prolog code. The result of implementing the dynamic cut are more efficient executions in the case of deterministic computations and with no serious

Z. Hu and M. Rodríguez-Artalejo (Eds.): FLOPS 2002, LNCS 2441, pp. 245–258, 2002.
© Springer-Verlag Berlin Heidelberg 2002

overhead in the case of non-deterministic ones, as shown in the runtime table of section 6.

The aim of this paper is eminently practical and the technique for introducing dynamic cuts is presented in a (hopefully) precise but no formal way.

In the following section we introduce some preliminaries. section 3 discusses several examples motivating the introduction of the dynamic cut in the implementation of FLP programs. The examples are written in the concrete syntax of the lazy FLP language Toy [10] but can be easily adapted to other languages such as Curry [7]. section 4 introduces more formally the key concept of deterministic function, while section 5 discusses an implementation of the technique. section 6 presents a table with the times obtained for the execution, with and without dynamic cut, of some examples. Finally section 7 presents some conclusions and future work.

2   Preliminaries

All the examples are written in the concrete syntax of the lazy FLP language $\mathcal{TOY}$ [10] but can be easily adapted to other FLP languages like Curry [7]. A $\mathcal{TOY}$ program is composed of data type declarations, type alias, infix operators, function type declarations and defining rules for functions symbols. Each defining rule for a function $f \in FS^n$ has a *left-hand side*, a *right-hand side* and an optional *condition*:

$$(R) \quad \underbrace{f\, t_1 \ldots t_n}_{\text{left-hand side}} \;\rightarrow\; \underbrace{r}_{\text{right-hand side}} \;\Leftarrow\; \underbrace{e_1, \ldots, e_k}_{\text{condition}}$$

where e_i and r are expressions (that can contain new extra variables) and each t_j is a pattern, with no variable occurring more than once in different t_k, t_l.

Each function is assumed to have a *definitional tree* [2, 9] with nodes *or, case* and *try*. However, in our setting we will not allow 'multiple tries', i.e. *try* nodes with several program rules, replacing them by nodes *or* with multiple *try* children nodes, one for each rule included in the initial multiple *try*. The tree obtained by this modification is obviously equivalent and will be more suitable for our purposes.

We consider goals as expressions e and *answers* as pairs (t, σ) where t is a pattern representing a result obtained by evaluating e, while σ is a substitution of patterns for variables such that $dom(\sigma) \subseteq vars(e)$. Notice that this notion of goal, suitable for this work, is compatible with usual goals in $\mathcal{TOY}$ which are of the form: $e_1 == e_1', \ldots, e_k == e_k'$, simply by assuming that an auxiliary function: main $R_1 \ldots R_n$ = true $\Leftarrow= e_1 == e_1', \ldots, e_k == e_k'$ is introduced with $\{R_1, \ldots R_n\} = vars(e_1) \cup vars(e_1') \cup \ldots \cup vars(e_k) \cup vars(e_k')$, and then evaluating the goal main $R_1 \ldots R_n$. The introduction of main is also helpful since it extends the application of dynamic cuts to goals, converted in this way to the general case of program functions. We assume that goals are solved by means of an operational mechanism based on needed narrowing with sharing [3, 4, 9], as well as a Prolog-based implementation as described in [9]. A main component of the operational mechanism is the computation of *head normal forms* (hnf) for expressions.

3   Motivating Examples

In this section we present examples showing informally the two situations where dynamic cut can be useful: the first one is associated to *or* nodes in the definitional trees of semantically deterministic functions, while the second one is associated to existential conditions in program rules. These examples as well as additional ones can be found at http://babel.dacya.ucm.es/cut.

Example 1: Parallel and

Figure 1 shows a correct way of defining the *and* connective in FLP programming, known as *parallel and*, together with its definitional tree.

A goal like false && false returns false as expected, but unnecessarily repeats the answer twice:

```
>false && false
false
more solutions? y
false
more solutions? y
no
```

Obviously the computation resulting in the second false was not needed and in this case could have been avoided. The definitional tree shows why: the *or* branch at the top of the tree means that the computations must try both alternatives. In spite of this *or* branch the function will be recognized in our proposal (as well as it was in [8]) as *semantically deterministic*, which means that if the first alternative of the *or* succeeds the other branch either fails or provides a repeated result. The dynamic cut will skip the second branch (under certain conditions) if

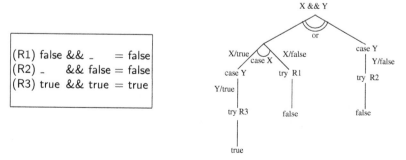

Fig. 1. The parallel and with its definitional tree

the first branch is successful, thus avoiding the waste of space and time required by the second computation.

However, as noticed in [8], the cut cannot be performed in all computations. For example, a goal like X && Y will return three different answers:

    X==false ⇒ false
    more solutions? y
    Y==false ⇒ false
    more solutions? y
    X==true, Y==true ⇒ true
    more solutions? y
    no

That is, the result is true if both X and Y are true and false if either X==false or Y==false. Here the second branch of the *or* node contributes to the answer by instantiating variable Y and hence should not be avoided. Therefore the dynamic cut must not be performed if the first successful computation binds any variable; in this case the second computation can eventually instantiate the variables in a different way, thus providing a different answer.

The situation complicates in a setting with non-deterministic functions. Consider for instance the function definition:

    maybe = true
    maybe = false

and the goal true && maybe. In this case no variable is bound during the first computation (the goal is ground) but the second computation is still necessary due to the second value returned by maybe

    true
    more solutions? y
    false
    more solutions? y
    no

Thus we shall extend the conditions for performing dynamic cuts, requiring not only that no variable has been bound but also that no non-deterministic function has been evaluated. As we will see, this introduces no serious overload in the implementation.

Example 2

The second example shows the second type of dynamic cut. The program in Figure 2 can be used to execute simple queries for finding substrings in a given text. A goal of the form matches (single S) Text succeeds if the string S is part of Text, failing otherwise. A goal matches (and S S') Text succeeds whenever both S and S' are part of Text, while matches (or S S') Text indicates that either S or S' (or both) are part of Text. Function matches relies on function part which checks if X is a substring of Y by looking for two existential variables U and V such that Y results of the concatenation of U, X and V. Function part is again semantically deterministic but will produce as many repeated results true as occurrences of X can be found. The dynamic cut can be introduced after the conditional part of the rule, since its re-evaluation cannot contribute to new results. Notice that in

```
infixr 50 ++
[] ++ Ys                    = Ys
[X|Xs] ++ Ys                = [X|Xs ++ Ys]

part X Y                    = true <==U ++ X ++ V == Y

data query = single [char] | and query query | or query query

matches (single S) Text  = true <== part S Text
matches (and S S') Text  = true <== matches S Text, matches S' Text
matches (or S S') Text   = true <== matches S Text
matches (or S S') Text   = true <== matches S' Text
```

Fig. 2. Simple Queries

this case the binding of U and V should not prevent the cut because they cannot contribute to the final substitution σ. In contrast a binding of X or Y will take part of the answer, avoiding the cut.

The effectiveness of the dynamic cut in part is still more noticeable because its effect over the function matches. Assume that there is no dynamic cut, and that we try a goal like

> matches (or (and (single "cut") (single "love")) (single "dynamic"))
> "Efficiency has been one of the ..."

where the text used as second argument is actually the whole introduction of this paper. Since the query is an *or* query, matches first tries the first alternative, (and (single "cut") (single "love")). Although "cut" is readily found there is no "love" in our introduction and part fails in a first attempt, after examining the whole text. Because of backtracking, a new occurrence of "cut" is sought and found (there are many occurrences of "cut" in the text), and then again part looks unsuccessfully for "love". The process repeats the examination of all the text looking for any occurrence of "love" as many times as occurrences of "cut" exist, therefore spending a huge amount of time before failing. Then the second alternative of the *or* query succeeds since "dynamic" appears in the text, and the query finally returns true (many times). With dynamic cut, the computation of the first alternative stops after the first fail of part "love" "..." and the query readily returns only one true, as expected.

Example 3

This last example combines both kinds of dynamic cuts presented above. Function palindrome detects when a string X is a palindrome, word detects strings built only from letters, and palinWord indicates if its argument W is both a palindrome and a word. Thus palinWord "refer" returns true, while palinWord "!!!" returns false repeated three times. In this case both the *or* branch of the

```
rev []        = []
rev [X|Xs]    = (rev Xs)+ + [X]

palindrome X = true <== Z ++ (rev Z) == X
palindrome X = true <== Z ++ [C] ++ (rev Z) == X

word []       = true
word [X|Xs]   = (isLetter X) && (word Xs)

isLetter X    = (ord(X)>=ord('a')) && (ord(X)<=ord('z'))

palinWord W = palindrome W && word W
```

Fig. 3. Palindrome Words

&& function and the (possibly) repeated existential search in *palindrome* contribute to decrease the efficiency of the program. Observe that the use of the parallel and (&&) in this example cannot be easily replaced by the usual *sequential and*:

    and true Y = Y
    and false Y = false

because this function requires the evaluation of the two boolean expressions, but palindrome either returns true or fails without returning false. Therefore a goal like palinWord "123" would fail with the sequential *and* but returns false when introducing the parallel *and*.

4   Detecting Deterministic Functions

As we have seen, one of the two types of dynamic cut is related to the existence of *or* nodes in definitional trees for semantically deterministic functions. Moreover, the deterministic nature of functions plays an important role when determining if a dynamic cut can be performed, as was illustrated in the examples above. We say that a function $f \in FS^n$ is *(semantically) deterministic* if for all ground terms $t_1 \ldots t_n$ the goal $f\ t_1 \ldots t_n$ cannot produce different (maybe partial) data values. The functions ++, &&, part, matches,rev, palindrome, isLetter and palinWord of section 3 are all deterministic, while the function maybe is not.

Now we introduce an adaptation of the non-ambiguity conditions in [8], which can serve as an easy mechanism for the effective recognition of deterministic functions. Despite their simplicity, they are enough in most practical cases, in particular for the examples of section 3.

Definition 1 (Non-ambiguous functions) *Let P be a program defining a set of functions G. We say that $F \subseteq G$ is a set of* non-ambiguous functions *if all $f \in F$ verifies:*

(i) *If $f(\bar{t}) = e \Leftarrow C$ is a defining rule for f, then $var(e) \subseteq var(\bar{t})$ and all function symbols in e belong to F (that is, extra variables and possibly non deterministic functions cannot occur in bodies).*

(ii) *For any pair of variants of defining rules for f, $f(\bar{t}) = e \Leftarrow C$, $f(\bar{t'}) = e' \Leftarrow C'$, one of the following two possibilities holds:*
    (a) *Heads do not overlap, that is, $f(\bar{t})$ and $f(\bar{t'})$ are not unifiable.*
    (b) *Right-hand sides can be fusioned, that is, if θ is a mgu of $f(\bar{t})$ and $f(\bar{t'})$, then $e\theta \equiv e'\theta$.*

The second part of the definition is equivalent to say that the set of unconditional parts of defining rules for functions $f \in F$ is a weakly orthogonal TRS [5].

Claim 1 *Non-ambiguous functions are semantically deterministic functions.*

Although the converse is not true, this is enough to ensure that the cuts will be safe. This claim is a well-known result about TRS, but in our case its validity depends on a suitable definition of the operational semantics of FLP languages which is not discussed here. A more detailed characterization of semantically deterministic functions will increase both the number of functions that can include dynamic cut and the number of cuts performed during the computations. The dynamic cut will be safe assuming the two following claims:

Claim 2 *Let G be goal, f a deterministic function and e an expression of the form $e \equiv f(e_1, \ldots, e_n)$. If a computation of a head normal form for e succeeds without:*

(i) *Binding any variable in e.*
(ii) *Computing a hnf for any expression $g(e'_1, \ldots, e'_m)$ where g is non-deterministic.*

Then any other alternative to the computation of this hnf for e can be discarded, since it cannot contribute to produce a different answer for the original goal.

Claim 3 *Let f be a function and $f(\bar{t}) = e \Leftarrow C$ is a defining rule for f used to compute a hnf of an expression $e \equiv f(e_1, \ldots, e_n)$. If the condition C is successfully computed without:*

(i) *Binding any variable in $e_1, \ldots, e_m$, r.*
(ii) *Computing a hnf for any expression $g(e'_1, \ldots, e'_m)$ where g is non-deterministic.*

Then no alternative re-evaluation of C is needed.

Although following these claims we could safely introduce dynamic cut associated to many evaluations of hnf, most of these cuts would be unnecessary. Instead, we will include code for dynamic cut only in the two situations presented in the examples of section 3 and described precisely in the code generation of the next section.

5   A Prolog Implementation of Dynamic Cut

We explain in this section how to accommodate dynamic cut into a translation scheme of the form $\mathcal{T} :$ **Source** $\rightarrow$ **Prolog** for the case of the FLP language $\mathcal{TOY}$, but we think that it is not difficult to extend the approach to other translations schemes.

5.1   The Translation Scheme

The translation scheme for $\mathcal{TOY}^1$, which can be found in [1], is the result of three stages:

(1) The source $\mathcal{TOY}$ program, which uses higher order syntax, is translated into $\mathcal{TOY}$-like programs written in first order syntax.

(2) The compiler introduces *suspensions* [6, 9] into first order $\mathcal{TOY}$ programs. The idea of *suspensions* is to replace each subexpression in right-hand sides of rules with the shape of a function call $f(e_1, \ldots, e_n)$ by a Prolog term of the form $susp(f(e_1, \ldots, e_n), R, S)$ (called a suspension) where R and S are initially (i.e, at the time of translation) new Prolog variables. During execution, parameter passing may produce many 'long distance' copies of a given suspension. If at some step of the execution the computation of a head normal form for $f(e_1, \ldots, e_n)$ is required, the variable R will be bound to the obtained value, and we say that the suspension has been evaluated. The argument S in a suspension is a flag to indicate if the suspension has been evaluated or not. Initially S is a variable (indicating a non-evaluated suspension), which is set to a concrete value, say hnf, once the suspension is evaluated.

(3) Finally the Prolog clauses which are the final result of the translation are generated, adding suitable code for *strict equality* and *hnf* (to compute head normal forms). To compute a hnf for an unevaluated suspension $susp(f(X_1, \ldots, X_n), R, S)$, a call $f(X_1, \ldots, X_n, H)$ is made to a specific predicate returning in H the desired head normal form. The set $Prolog_{FS}$ consists of the clauses for those predicates, which are exactly the predicates affected by the introduction of dynamic cut.

5.2   Generating Prolog Code

Next we explain in detail the third phase (code generation), taking into account dynamic cut. This is done regarding the definitional tree of the function, and will be represented as $prolog(f, dt(f))$ where the auxiliary function $prolog/2$ takes a definitional tree and a function symbol, possibly different to the function of the definitional tree (this is to introduce new auxiliary functions), returning as value a set of Prolog clauses.

The interesting cases for this paper are those when code for dynamic cut can be added. For this code we will use a pair of auxiliary predicates

---

[1] For the sake of simplicity, we consider here a simplified version of $\mathcal{TOY}$ not taking into account *disequality constraints*.

- *varlist(E, Vs)*, which returns in *Vs* the list of variables occurring in *E*, taking into account the following criterion for collecting variables inside suspensions:
(1) If *E* contains an unevaluated suspension $susp(f(e_1, \ldots, e_n), R, S)$ and *f* is a non-deterministic function then *R* must be added to *Vs*. This is essential for performing dynamic cut safely.
(2) If *E* contains an evaluated suspension $susp(f(e_1, \ldots, e_n), R, S)$, then we proceed recursively collecting variables in *R*.

- *checkvarlist(Vs)*, which checks that all elements in *Vs* are indeed different variables. This ensures that no variable in *Vs* was bound during the evaluation of *E*.

The combination of *varlist* and *checkvarlist* in a code sequence like

$$\text{varlist(E,Vs)}, <\text{compute something with } E >, \text{checkvarlist(Vs)}$$

is an easy way of controlling that no variables in *E* have been bound during the computation. In many practical cases *Vs* will be empty, and then *checkvarlist(Vs)* is a trivial test. The actual implementation of *varlist* and *checkvarlist* is a Prolog exercise and can be found at `http://babel.dacya.ucm.es/cut`.

The Prolog code $prolog(f, dt)$ is obtained by generating code corresponding to the root of the tree, and then descending recursively in the branches. We then distinguish cases according to the shape of the root of *dt*.

Case 1 (the root is a **case** node):

Assume $dt \equiv f(\overline{s}) \rightarrow \textbf{case } X \textbf{ of } \langle c_1 : dt_1 \ldots c_m : dt_m \rangle$

In this case different branches correspond to incompatible cases in a given position, and therefore there is nothing to prune. The generated code in this case is the same as if dynamic cut is not taken into account.

$$prolog(g, dt) = \{ \text{ g}(\overline{s},\text{H}) \text{ :- hnf(X,HX), g'}(\overline{s}\sigma,\text{H}).\} \ \cup$$
$$prolog(g', dt_1) \ \ldots \ \cup prolog(g', dt_m)$$

where $\sigma = $ X/HX and g' is a new function symbol.

Case 2 (the root is an **or** node):

Assume $dt \equiv f(\overline{s}) \rightarrow \textbf{or } \langle dt_1 \mid \ldots \mid dt_m \rangle$

In this case, some of the (head of) rules in different branches might overlap, maybe yielding to different computations with the same result. Code for dynamic cut at the root can be useful, but is safe only in case that the function defined by the tree is deterministic; otherwise, different branches, even overlapping, might produce different results and none of which should be pruned. To be precise: let *R* be the set of program rules in the leaves of *dt*. We consider two cases:

Case 2.1 If *R* define a non-deterministic function, then code for dynamic cut cannot be added:

$$prolog(g, dt) = \{ \text{ g}(\overline{s},\text{H}) \text{ :- g}_1(\overline{s},\text{H}).\} \ \cup \ \ldots \cup \ \{ \text{ g}(\overline{s},\text{H}) \text{ :- g}_m(\overline{s},\text{H}).\} \ \cup$$
$$prolog(g_1, dt_1) \ \cup \ \ldots \ \cup prolog(g_m, dt_m)$$

where $g_1, \ldots, g_m$ are new function symbols.

Case 2.2 If R define a deterministic function, then we add code for dynamic cut:

$$prolog(g, dt) = \{\ g(\overline{s}, H)\ \text{:-}\ \text{varlist}(\overline{s}, Vs),$$
$$g'(\overline{s}, H),$$
$$(\text{checkvarlist}(Vs),$$
$$!\ \% \ this\ is\ the\ dynamic\ cut$$
$$;$$
$$\text{true}).\ \}\ \cup$$
$$\{g'(\overline{s}, H)\ \text{:-}\ g_1(\overline{s}, H).\}\ \cup\ \ldots\ \cup\ \{g'(\overline{s}, H)\ \text{:-}\ g_m(\overline{s}, H).\}\ \cup$$
$$prolog(g_1, dt_1)\ \cup\ \ldots\ \cup\ prolog(g_m, dt_m)$$

where $g', g_1, \ldots, g_m$ are new function symbols. Observe that g' is defined as g in the case 2.1, that is, as g would be defined without dynamic cut. The behaviour of the clause for g is then clear: we collect the relevant variables of the call, and use g' to do the reduction; if after succeeding no relevant variable has been bound, we cut to prune other (useless) alternatives for g'.

Notice also that the condition required to add code for dynamic cut is *local* to the tree: only the rules in the tree are taken into account. This allows a 'fine tuning' of dynamic cut, which can be added to 'deterministic parts' of a function definition, even if the function is non-deterministic.

Case 3 (the tree is a leaf **try**):

Assume $dt \equiv \textbf{try}\ R$, where R is a program rule $f(\overline{s}) = e \Leftarrow C$. In this case it is always possible to add code for dynamic cut between the code for the conditions C and the code for the body e. Some care must be taken with extra variables in C, that is, variables in C not occurring in the head $f(\overline{s})$. If one of such variables does not occur in the body e, then it is an existential variable, whose only role is to witness the condition. The relevant fact is that if the conditions in C succeed with some bindings for existential variables, there is no need of finding alternative bindings for such variables. But if one extra variable in C occurs also in e, it might contribute to its value, and therefore to the value of $f(\overline{s})$; this means that bindings for such variables must inhibit the dynamic cut. To take this into account is quite easy: just add the variables in e to the list of variables relevant for dynamic cut.

$$prolog(g, dt) = \{\ g0(\overline{s}, H)\ \text{:-}$$
$$\text{varlist}((\overline{s}, e), Vs),\ \% \ notice\ the\ body\ e$$
$$\text{solve}(C),\ (\text{checkvarlist}(Vs),$$
$$!\ \% \ this\ is\ the\ dynamic\ cut$$
$$;\ \text{true}),$$
$$\text{hnf}(e, H).\ \}$$

We remark that this code is correct even if the body e is non-deterministic, because the cut is placed before evaluating the body, which implies that we only cut the re-evaluation of the conditional part of the rule.

5.3 Examples

Here we present a few examples of translations into Prolog following the ideas commented above. The complete generated code for the examples can be found at

http://babel.dacya.ucm.es/cut

It is worth noticing that the code found there is not *exactly* the code described in the paper: apart from typical optimizations, as the real code is going to be executed within $\mathcal{TOY}$, it must take into account disequality constraints, which are embedded in the system.

Parallel and Since the function && is deterministic and has an **or** node at the root of its definitional tree, dynamic cut code is added for it. Since the rules are unconditional, **try** nodes do not require dynamic cut. The Prolog code for && is then:

&&(X,Y,H) :- varlist((X,Y),Vs), &&'(X,Y,H), (checkvarlist(Vs), ! ; true).
. . . . . .

where the auxiliary predicate &&' is defined exactly as the predicate && would have been defined without dynamic cut in mind.

Simple queries In this example, the functions part and matches accept dynamic cut, the first because its rule has a condition with existential variables, and the second because it is deterministic and has an **or** node in its definitional tree. We write only the code for part:

part(X,Y,H) :- varlist((X,Y),Vs),
              equal(susp(++(U,susp(++(X,V),R,S)),R',S'), Y),
              (checkvarlist(Vs), !   % dynamic cut after the conditions
              ; true),
              hnf(true,H).

6 Experimental Results

Figure 4 presents some experimental results obtained with the system $\mathcal{TOY}^2$. The complete set of examples can be found at http://babel.dacya.ucm.es/cut. Additionally to the examples of section 3 we have used two examples:
- graph.toy: This program defines a graph with the shape of a grid, where each node is connected to its nearest right and down nodes. Also, a function to check whether two nodes are connected is defined. The natural coding of this function includes an existential condition in a program rule that will include code for the dynamic cut.

---

[2] Running on a PC under O.S. Linux with processor Intel Celeron at 600 MHZ and 128 Mb RAM.

- composed.toy: Program to check whether a number is composed, i.e. not prime. This is achieved by looking for two numbers whose product is the desired number, and this, again, is naturally represented in FLP languages by an existential search in the condition of a program rule. The dynamic cut will stop the computations after the first decomposition is found if the number is not prime.

In the following we describe briefly each goal.

- G_1 is false && (false && (.... (false && false) ...)) == true with 100000 false values.

- G_2 is (...((false && false) && false) && ...) && false == true with 5000 false values. In this case the cut cannot avoid the search of any *or* branch and the results are similar, with the code including cut slightly worse due to the run-time checking of bindings.

- G_3 is matches (or (and (single "cut") (single "love")) (single "dynamic")) intro where intro represents the text of the introduction of this paper.

- G_4 is matches (and (and (single "is") (single "this")) (single "love?")) intro.

- G_5 is matches (and (and (single "is") (single "a")) (single "love")). In this example notice that the goal fails due to the lack of "love" in the introduction, but both "a" and "is" occur many times in the text and therefore the search space is really huge.

- G_6 is palinWord "11...11" with "11..11" representing the string with 200 repetitions of digit 1 (which is obviously palindrome but not a word).

In the rest of the examples the goals have been forced to fail in order to check the time required to examine the whole search space. This is not as artificial as it could seem; on the contrary it happens whenever the goal is evaluated as part of a subcomputation that finally fails.

- G_7 looks for a path between the upper-left and the lower-right corner of a grid of 10×10 nodes. Without dynamic cut the backtracking will try all possible paths in the graph, but the dynamic cut stops after finding the first successful

Program	Goal	Without Dynamic Cut	Dynamic Cut
example1.toy	G1	23.4 sec	0 sec.
example1.toy	G2	105.2 sec.	119.8 sec.
example2.toy	G3	30.7 sec.	2.5 sec.
example2.toy	G4	327.3 sec.	2.3 sec.
example2.toy	G5	>5 hours	2.0 sec.
example3.toy	G6	33.5 sec.	4.8 sec.
graph.toy	G7	64.2 sec.	0 sec.
graph.toy	G8	>5 hours	0 sec.
graph.toy	G9	>5 hours	0.1 sec.
graph.toy	G10	66.7 sec.	70.6 sec.
composed.toy	G11	151.0 sec.	0.4 sec.
composed.toy	G12	>5 hours	4.0 sec.

Fig. 4. Runtime Table

path. G_8 and G_9 are analogous to the previous goal but for grids of 20×20 and 100×100, respectively.

- G_{10} looks for paths from the upper-left corner to a generic node represented as a variable N. In this case the cut takes no effect because variable N is bound during the computations and cutting would not be safe, and the times with and without dynamic cut are similar.

- G_{11} checks if number 1000 is not prime, while G_{12} is analogous but for number 10000.

7 Conclusions

This work presents a mechanism of *dynamic cut* for lazy FLP programs that can be easily introduced in a Prolog-based implementation. The technique requires a static analysis of determinism and the modification of the segment of the generated code where the cut is feasible (deterministic functions with *or* branches and rules with existential conditions).

By including dynamic cuts the efficiency of several computations both in terms of time and space is improved, often dramatically. This is done by avoiding redundant non-deterministic computations related to the evaluation of semantically deterministic functions. In contrast to Prolog cuts, the dynamic cut proposed here is transparent to the programmer (since it is automatically introduced by the system in the generated code) and safe.

The second consequence of the cut is that many repeated answers can be avoided. Also non-terminating computations become, in some cases, terminating. However, dynamic cut does not change the set of computed answers.

Because of these two benefits, functions that are usually avoided in FLP, like the *parallel and* presented in Figure 1, can be used now without decreasing the efficiency of the computations.

Compared to a previous work ([8]) on this subject our proposal present three major improvements:

• Non-deterministic functions are considered.

• The introduction of the dynamic cut is related to definitional trees allowing the integration of the technique into current systems based on demand driven strategies.

• We show how to incorporate the technique in systems that generate code by transforming FLP programs into Prolog-code. This, together with the two previous points, makes the technique fully applicable to several FLP implementations.

As future work we plan to fully integrate the optimization in the system $\mathcal{TOY}$ and to improve the implementation of the mechanism used to detect whether a relevant variable has been bound. In a different line, a deeper theoretical work would be desirable both extending the class of functions qualified as deterministic and providing an operational framework suitable to prove the properties of the technique.

References

[1] M. Abengózar-Carneros, P. Arenas-Sánchez, R. Caballero-Roldán, A. Gil-Luezas, J. C. González-Moreno, J. Leach-Albert, F. J. López-Fraguas, M. Rodríguez-Artalejo, J. J. Ruz-Ortiz and J. Sánchez-Hernández. *TOY: A Multiparadigm Declarative Language. Version 1.0.* Departamento de Sistemas Informáticos y Programación, Universidad Complutense de Madrid, Tech. Report SIP-119/00, February 2002. 252

[2] S. Antoy. *Definitional Trees.* Int. Conf. on Algebraic Logic Programming (ALP'92), LNCS 632, Springer Verlag 1992, 143-157. 246

[3] S. Antoy. *Constructed-based Conditional Narrowing.* PPDP'01, ACM Press 2001, 199-206. 246

[4] S. Antoy, R. Echahed, M. Hanus. *A Needed Narrowing Strategy.* Journal of the ACM Vol. 47, no. 4, pages 776-822, July 2000. 245, 246

[5] F. Baader and T. Nipkow. *Term Rewriting and All That.* Cambridge University Press, 1998. 251

[6] P. H. Cheong and L. Fribourg. *Implementation of narrowing: The Prolog-based approach.* In K. R. Apt, J. W. de Bakker, and J. J. M. M. Rutten, editors, Logic programming languages: constraints, functions, and objects, pages 1–20. MIT Press, 1993. 252

[7] M.Hanus. *Curry: An Integrated Functional Logic Language.* Version 0.7.1, June 2000. Available at http://www.informatik.uni-kiel.de/curry/report.html. 246

[8] R. Loogen, St. Winkler. *Dynamic Detection of Determinism in Functional-Logic Languages.* Int. Symp. on Programming Language Implementation and Logic Programming (PLILP'91), LNCS 528, Springer Verlag 1991, 335-346. 245, 247, 248, 250, 257

[9] R. Loogen, F. J. López-Fraguas, and M. Rodríguez-Artalejo. *A Demand Driven Computation Strategy for Lazy Narrowing.* Int. Symp. on Programming Language Implementation and Logic Programming (PLILP'93), LNCS 714, Springer Verlag 1993, 184-200. 245, 246, 247, 252

[10] F. J. López-Fraguas, and J. Sánchez-Hernández. *TOY a Multiparadigm Declarative System*, In Proc. RTA'99, LNCS 1631, Springer Verlag, 244-247, 1999. 246

The Head Condition and Polymorphic Recursion

Jan-Georg Smaus

Institut für Informatik, Universität Freiburg
Georges-Köhler-Allee 52, 79110 Freiburg, Germany
smaus@informatik.uni-freiburg.de

Abstract. In typed logic programming, the *head condition* states that for each clause defining a predicate p, the arguments of the clause head must have the declared type of p, rather than a proper polymorphic instance. In typed functional programming, *polymorphic recursion* means that in a recursive definition of a function f, the recursive call to f uses a type which is a proper instance of the declared type of f. We show that both notions are also meaningful in the respectively other paradigm. We observe a symmetry between the head condition and the "monomorphic recursion condition" (meaning absence of polymorphic recursion). We discuss arguments for and against each condition in both paradigms.

1 Introduction

Types are used frequently in functional programming (FP) but also in logic programming (LP). Typed LP languages include Gödel [10], HAL [5], and Mercury [24]; typed FP languages include Haskell [26], Miranda [25], and ML [19].

In typed LP, the *head condition* (HC) [8, 11, 15], also called *definitional genericity* [14], states that for each clause defining a predicate p, the vector of arguments of the clause head must have the declared type of p. An example of a violation of the HC is the following definition of a predicate wrap/2 specified as wrap(1,[]), wrap(2,[[]]), wrap(3,[[[]]]), ... :

```
wrap(1,[]).
wrap(N,[X]) <- N2 is N-1, wrap(N2,X).
```

If we assume that the declared type of wrap is $(\text{int}, \text{list}(U))$, then the argument vector of the head of the second clause has type $(\text{int}, \text{list}(\text{list}(U)))$.

In typed FP, *polymorphic recursion* (PR) [9, 12, 13] refers to the situation that in a recursive definition of a function f, the recursive call to f uses a type which is a proper polymorphic instance of the declared (generic) type of f. A (contrived) example is the following Miranda program defining list length:

```
len :: [*] -> num
len []    = 0
len (a:l) = 1 + len (lift l)
```

The first line is a type declaration stating that len is a function from the (built-in) parametric list type to the (built-in) type of numbers. The other two

Z. Hu and M. Rodríguez-Artalejo (Eds.): FLOPS 2002, LNCS 2441, pp. 259–274, 2002.

lines form a recursive definition. Here we assume that `lift` is the function that takes a list $[t_1, \ldots, t_n]$ and returns the list $[[t_1], \ldots, [t_n]]$. When `len` is called with the list, say, $[1, 2, 3]$ of type `[num]` (Miranda notation for a list of numbers), the recursive calls will be with types `[[num]]`, `[[[num]]]`, and `[[[[num]]]]`.

In this paper, we observe a close relationship between the HC and PR. Adjusting the terminology, one can speak of a symmetry: the HC is symmetric to *monomorphic* recursion, meaning absence of PR. The symmetry can be illustrated with the logic programs $P_{pr} = \{\text{p(X).}, \text{p(X)} \leftarrow \text{p([X]).}\}$ and $P_{hc} = \{\text{p([]).}, \text{p([X])} \leftarrow \text{p(X).}\}$. Letting `list(U)` be the declared type of `p`, P_{pr} uses PR, and P_{hc} violates the HC. The symmetry also shows up in the operational semantics: when P_{pr} is called with `p([])`, an infinite sequence of calls `p([])`, `p([[]])`, ... may arise, whereas P_{hc} has infinitely many computed answers `p([])`, `p([[]])`, ...

Both the HC and PR have been debated in the literature [6, 8, 9, 11, 12, 13, 14, 15, 16, 17, 18]. However, due to the fact that the former was mainly discussed in LP and the latter in FP, the formalisations of the type systems were quite different, and we are not aware that a symmetry has ever been observed. Our first contribution is to formalise the type systems in a uniform way.

This formalisation is the basis for two comparisons: first, we can compare the weight each argument of the debate carries for the two paradigms FP and LP. This comparison, to be found in Sections 3 and 4, is another contribution.

Secondly, we can compare the HC and PR. We discuss three aspects of this comparison: In Sec. 5.1, we give an example of a term language for which one finds that the HC and monomorphic recursion create (almost) unacceptable obstacles for programming. In Sec. 5.2, we show that violations of the HC, as well as PR, may be responsible for an infinite number of different types occurring in the semantics of a program. This phenomenon is undesirable in certain contexts of program analysis. We show under which conditions it can be avoided. In Sec. 5.3, we discuss the *magic set transformation*, which is a widespread technique for logic program analysis. For programming languages where the HC is enforced but PR is allowed, the magic transformation can transform a well-typed program into an ill-typed one. However, for programs meeting the HC and free from PR, the magic transformation of a program can be made well-typed.

2   Typed Logic and Functional Programming

We specify our type system by a set of rules for deriving type judgements. Any program element is well-typed iff an appropriate type judgement can be derived.

We start with some concepts common to both paradigms. The set of types $\mathcal{T}$ is given by the term structure based on a finite set of **type constructors** $\mathcal{K}$, where with each $K \in \mathcal{K}$ an arity $n \geq 0$ is associated (by writing K/n), and a denumerable set $\mathcal{U}$ of **parameters** (type variables). A **type substitution** is a mapping from parameters to types which is the identity almost everywhere.

We assume a denumerable set $\mathcal{V}$ of **variables**. A **variable typing** is a mapping from a finite subset of $\mathcal{V}$ to $\mathcal{T}$, written as $\{x_1 : \tau_1, \ldots, x_n : \tau_n\}$.

Table 1. Typing rules (Θ is a type substitution)

For logic and functional programs:

$(Var)\ \{x : \tau, \dots\} \vdash x : \tau$ $(Constr)\ \dfrac{\Gamma \vdash t_1:\tau_1\Theta \ \cdots\ \Gamma \vdash t_n:\tau_n\Theta}{\Gamma \vdash c_{\tau_1\dots\tau_n \to \tau}(t_1,\dots,t_n):\tau\Theta}$

For logic programs:

$(Atom)\ \dfrac{\Gamma \vdash t_1:\tau_1\Theta \ \cdots\ \Gamma \vdash t_n:\tau_n\Theta}{\Gamma \vdash p_{\tau_1\dots\tau_n}(t_1,\dots,t_n)\ Atom}$ $(Query)\ \dfrac{\Gamma \vdash a_1\ Atom \ \cdots\ \Gamma \vdash a_n\ Atom}{\Gamma \vdash a_1,\dots,a_n\ Query}$

$(Clause)\ \dfrac{\Gamma \vdash h\ Atom \qquad \Gamma \vdash Q\ Query}{\Gamma \vdash h \leftarrow Q\ Clause}$

For functional programs:

$(Func)\ \dfrac{\Gamma \vdash t_1:\tau_1\Theta \ \cdots\ \Gamma \vdash t_n:\tau_n\Theta}{\Gamma \vdash f_{\tau_1\dots\tau_n \to \tau}(t_1,\dots,t_n):\tau\Theta}$ $(Line^*)\ \dfrac{\Gamma \vdash f_{\tau_1\dots\tau_n \to \tau}(t_1,\dots,t_n):\tau\Theta \quad \Gamma \vdash t:\tau\Theta}{\Gamma \vdash f_{\tau_1\dots\tau_n \to \tau}(t_1,\dots,t_n)=t\ Line}$

We assume a set $\mathcal{C}$ of **term constructor** symbols, each with an arity n and a declared type (vector) $(\tau_1, \dots, \tau_n, \tau) \in \mathcal{T}^{n+1}$ associated with it, such that τ satisfies the *transparency condition* [11]: any parameter in $\tau_1, \dots, \tau_n$ also occurs in τ. We often indicate the declared type with subscripts, e.g., $c_{\tau_1\dots\tau_n \to \tau}$.

Constructor terms (in LP, these are the only terms) are built and assigned a type by the rules *(Var)* and *(Constr)* in Table 1. E.g., [7,2] is a constructor term.[1] Also for subsequent rules, all objects are defined relative to a variable typing Γ. The expressions of the form $\Gamma \vdash \dots$ are called **type judgements**. We write "$\_ \vdash$" for "there exists Γ such that $\Gamma \vdash$". We say that t **is of type** τ if τ is most general such that $\_ \vdash t : \tau$.

To simplify the notation, a vector such as $o_1, \dots, o_n$ is often denoted by $\bar{o}$.

Logic programs. We assume a finite set $\mathcal{P}$ of **predicate** symbols, each with an arity n and a declared type $(\tau_1, \dots, \tau_n) \in \mathcal{T}^n$ associated with it. The language of **atoms**, **queries** and **clauses** based on $\mathcal{K}$, $\mathcal{C}$, and $\mathcal{P}$ is defined by the rules for logic programs in Table 1.

Functional programs. Our formalisation of FP is simple and aimed at the analogy to LP: there is no Currying; there is no explicit use of **letrec** [13]; the type of every function is first-order, i.e., there are no functions as arguments.

We assume a finite set $\mathcal{F}$ of **function** symbols, each with an arity n and a declared type $(\tau_1, \dots, \tau_n, \tau) \in \mathcal{T}^{n+1}$ associated with it.

In FP, there is the additional rule *(Func)* for building terms. E.g., len([7]) is a term. We also have the rule *Line* to build a line of a function definition using

---

[1] Throughout this paper, we will assume that *lists*, defined in Ex. 1 but written using [_|_] where convenient, are included in the term languages we consider.

a **pattern** $(t_1, \ldots, t_n)$, with the following side condition:

$t_1 \ldots t_n$ are constructor terms, no variable occurs twice in $t_1 \ldots t_n$, and t contains only variables that also occur in $t_1 \ldots t_n$. $(*)$

Whichever the paradigm, we assume $\mathcal{K}$, $\mathcal{C}$, and $\mathcal{P}$, resp. $\mathcal{F}$, arbitrary but fixed. While we assume that the types in $\mathcal{C}$, and $\mathcal{P}$, resp. $\mathcal{F}$, are declared rather than inferred, we will also discuss different possible choices of declared types.

Example 1. Let $\mathcal{K} = \{\texttt{list}/1, \texttt{int}/0\}$, $\mathcal{C} = \{\texttt{nil}_{\rightarrow \texttt{list(U)}}, \texttt{cons}_{\texttt{U},\texttt{list(U)} \rightarrow \texttt{list(U)}},$ $0_{\rightarrow \texttt{int}}, \ldots\}$, $\mathcal{P} = \{\texttt{app}_{\texttt{list(U)},\texttt{list(U)},\texttt{list(U)}}\}$, $\mathcal{F} = \{\texttt{app}_{\texttt{list(U)},\texttt{list(U)} \rightarrow \texttt{list(U)}}\}$, and $\Gamma = \{\texttt{X} : \texttt{U}, \texttt{Xs} : \texttt{list(U)}, \texttt{Ys} : \texttt{list(U)}, \texttt{Zs} : \texttt{list(U)}\}$.

Consider first LP. We can derive the type judgement

$$\Gamma \vdash \texttt{app([X|Xs], Ys, [X|Zs])} \leftarrow \texttt{app(Xs, Ys, Zs)} \;\; \textit{Clause}$$

saying that the above is a well-typed clause.

Consider now FP. We can derive the type judgement

$$\Gamma \vdash \texttt{app([X|Xs], Ys)} = \texttt{[X|app(Xs, Ys)]} \;\; \textit{Line}$$

saying that the above is a well-typed "function definition line".

The typing rules *(Constr)* and *(Func)* are the same, but note that there is no transparency condition for functions; e.g., it is reasonable to have a function $\texttt{len}_{\texttt{list(U)} \rightarrow \texttt{int}}$. Transparency is crucial for unification and pattern matching.

We now define another FP concept: a *function definition*.

Definition 1. A **definition** of $f_{\tau_1 \ldots \tau_n \rightarrow \tau}$ is a sequence $\langle f(t_{1,1}, \ldots, t_{1,n}) = t_1,$ $\ldots, f(t_{m,1}, \ldots, t_{m,n}) = t_m \rangle$ such that $\_ \vdash f(t_{j,1}, \ldots, t_{j,n}) = t_j$ *Line* for all $j \in \{1, \ldots, m\}$.

Roughly, the usual semantics of a function definition is as follows: for a ground constructor term vector $(s_1, \ldots, s_n)$ of type $(\tau_1, \ldots, \tau_n)\Theta$ for some Θ, let j be the smallest number such that $(t_{j,1}, \ldots, t_{j,n})\theta = (s_1, \ldots, s_n)$ for some substitution θ; then , $f(s_1, \ldots, s_n)$ is defined as (the value of) $t_j\theta$; i.e., the first match counts. If no such j exists, $f(s_1, \ldots, s_n)$ is undefined; i.e., functions may be partial. Alternatively, one could require that for any $(s_1, \ldots, s_n)$ as above, *at most* one or *at least* one or *exactly* one $(t_{j,1}, \ldots, t_{j,n})$ matches.

A **program** P is specified by giving $\mathcal{K}$, $\mathcal{C}$, and $\mathcal{P}$, resp. $\mathcal{F}$ and a set of clauses, resp. function definitions. We write $C \in P$ if C is a program clause of P.

The following key definition is needed to formulate the HC and PR.

Definition 2. An application of rules *(Atom)* or *(Func)* is **generic** if the type substitution Θ is a mere parameter renaming [1].

3 The Head Condition

Definition 3. For LP, the **head condition** states that for each clause $h \leftarrow Q$ (so $\_ \vdash h \leftarrow Q$ *Clause*), the application of rule *(Atom)* to derive $\_ \vdash h$ *Atom* is generic.

For FP, the **head condition** states for each line $f_{\tau_1 \ldots \tau_n \to \tau}(t_1, \ldots, t_n) = t$ (so $\_ \vdash f_{\tau_1 \ldots \tau_n \to \tau}(t_1, \ldots, t_n) = t$ *Line*), the application of rule *(Func)* to derive $\_ \vdash f_{\tau_1 \ldots \tau_n \to \tau}(t_1, \ldots, t_n) : \tau\Theta$ is generic.

We first discuss LP. For example, given the $\mathtt{app}_{\mathtt{list(U),list(U),list(U)}}$ predicate above, the clause $\mathtt{app([1],[],[2])} \leftarrow$ would violate the HC. The HC is imposed in Gödel, HAL, and Mercury. We give two arguments in favour of it:

1. It is crucial for ensuring that logic programs have the *subject reduction* property, i.e., all queries in a derivation for a program are well-typed [6, 11].
2. It is an inherent characteristic of *generic* [15] (parametric) polymorphism: a polymorphic predicate must behave uniformly regardless of the type instance for which it is called. In FP, this principle is called *parametricity* [27].

We mention four arguments in *dis*favour of the HC:

3. It impedes *lemma construction*, which is an essential feature of LP [8]. For example, $\mathtt{app([1],[],[1])} \leftarrow$ could be a lemma that one might want to add to the usual $\mathtt{APPEND}$ program to improve efficiency.
4. It forbids *ad-hoc* polymorphism (overloading), meaning that a predicate "works in somewhat unrelated ways on several different types" [17].
5. It impedes higher-order programming, or rather, implementing higher-order constructs with a first-order definition. For example, one might define a parametric $\mathtt{quicksort}$ predicate, where the name of the ordering relation is passed as an argument. This program involves an $\mathtt{apply\_relation}_{\mathtt{string,U,U}}$ predicate defined by, say

$$\mathtt{apply\_relation("int\_order", X, Y)} \leftarrow \mathtt{int\_less}_{\mathtt{int,int}}(\mathtt{X, Y}).$$
$$\mathtt{apply\_relation("char\_order", X, Y)} \leftarrow \mathtt{char\_less}_{\mathtt{char,char}}(\mathtt{X, Y}).$$

which violates the HC.
6. For some term languages, the HC impedes writing programs using obvious algorithms (see Subsec. 5.1).

The HC is defined with respect to a declared type, but the interesting cases are those where the HC is violated for any choice of declared type, as for the clause $\mathtt{p([X])} \leftarrow \mathtt{p(X)} \in P_{hc}$ (see introduction). Whatever declared type we assume for $\mathtt{p}$, the argument of the clause head will have a type which is a proper instance of the declared type, or the clause will not be well-typed at all.

The disadvantages of the HC have led Nadathur and Pfenning to reject it and instead resort to runtime type checking [17] (see argument 1), whereas Louvet and Ridoux propose a type system where even ad-hoc polymorphism can be realised in a way that respects the HC [15].

The arguments against the HC can be found in the literature, but one can also give objections: (3) is somewhat contrived, since the obvious lemma one would add is $\mathtt{app([X],[],[X])} \leftarrow$; (4) ad-hoc polymorphism should be achieved by other means, e.g. type classes [7]; (5) primitives for higher-order programming should be provided in the language rather than being user-implemented.

We now discuss FP. Probably, argument 2 in favour of the HC is uncontested in the FP community. *Parametricity* can be seen as not just a principle of polymorphic typing, but rather a formal property [27]. For example, given a function $\mathtt{r}_{\mathtt{list(U) \to list(U)}}$, we know that for any $\mathtt{f}_{\mathtt{int \to char}}$, we have $(\mathtt{map\ f}) \circ \mathtt{r} = \mathtt{r} \circ (\mathtt{map\ f})$. Such parametricity results do not hold anymore if the HC is violated. To understand this on a more technical level, note that the semantics of pattern matching is commonly specified by a transformation to *case expressions* [20]. Such a transformation does not yield a well-typed expression if there are two definition lines with patterns of different types.

One could envisage a semantics of function definitions requiring that *exactly* one $(t_{j,1}, \ldots, t_{j,n})$ matches, so that functions are total and the order of definition lines is irrelevant (see Def. 1). It is hard to think of a realistic scenario where this requirement could be met while the HC is violated. For example, if we had a function $\mathtt{empty}_{\mathtt{U \to bool}}$ and definition lines $\mathtt{empty([]) = true}$ and $\mathtt{empty(leaf) =}$ $\mathtt{true}$, then we would have to add further lines so that for every constructor term in the term language, exactly one pattern matches. If the language was later extended, the code for $\mathtt{empty}$ would have to be extended, too. Actually, the reason why one might want to define $\mathtt{empty}$ this way is to realise *ad-hoc* polymorphism, but there are more appropriate means for this purpose [7].

On the other hand, argument 5 in disfavour of the HC is weaker for FP than for LP, since higher-order programming (passing functions/relations as arguments) is inherent in the paradigm, albeit not in the small fragment we consider here. In FP, it is straightforward to write a parametric $\mathtt{quicksort}$ function.

From the point of view usually taken in the FP literature, the head condition seems so "hard-wired" into the type system that the possibility of questioning it appears to be an artefact of our formalism using pattern matching.

4   Polymorphic Recursion

4.1   Digression: Polymorphic Recursion in the Usual FP Formalism

PR has mainly been studied for FP. We now recall PR as defined in [9, 13]. This digression helps to establish the link between FP and LP. For simple reference, we speak of *the type system of ML* [13].

In ML, a recursive function f of type $\sigma \equiv \tau \to \tau'$ is defined by an expression $M \equiv \lambda x.M'$, where f may occur in M', and applying a fixpoint constructor **fix** to it. The typing rule FIX is given in Table 2. It says: if under the assumption that f has the right type σ (one can think of σ as declared type) we can infer that the expression M defining f has type σ, then f has indeed type σ.

The absence or presence of PR is defined by the form that σ may take. One distinguishes between types as defined so far and *type schemes* [9], which are

Table 2. Some typing rules of ML

$$\text{FIX } \frac{\Gamma \cup \{f{:}\sigma\} \vdash M{:}\sigma}{\Gamma \vdash (\mathbf{fix}\ f\ M){:}\sigma} \qquad \text{APP } \frac{\Gamma \vdash M{:}\sigma \to \tau \quad \Gamma \vdash N{:}\sigma}{\Gamma \vdash (M\ N){:}\tau} \qquad \text{INST } \frac{\Gamma \vdash M{:}\forall u.\sigma}{\Gamma \vdash M{:}\sigma\{u/\tau\}}$$

types preceded by one or more quantifications of the form $\forall u$, where u is a parameter. This distinction cannot be understood in the type system of Table 1. Roughly speaking, the $\forall$-quantifier was implicit in our interpretation of types so far: to write $\mathtt{app}_{\mathtt{list(U),list(U)}\to\mathtt{list(U)}}$ meant that $\mathtt{app}$ could be applied to an argument of type $(\mathtt{list}(\tau), \mathtt{list}(\tau))$ for arbitrary τ. This is reflected in the fact that a type substitution could be applied in Rules *(Constr)*, *(Func)*, and *(Atom)*. In ML, this is different. Table 2 shows the rule APP, corresponding to our *(Func)*. Note that no type substitution is involved. On the other hand, there is a typing rule INST, and it is only here that type substitutions are applied.

If σ must be a *type* in rule FIX, we obtain a type system with *monomorphic* recursion, which is the usual ML. If σ may also be a type *scheme*, then we obtain a type system with PR, also called ML/1 [13].

As an example, consider the function $\mathtt{len}$. If Γ contains the appropriate typings for the if-then-else construct and functions $\mathtt{null}$ (returns $\mathbf{true}$ for the empty list) and $\mathtt{tail}$ (returns the tail of a list), we could derive in ML:

$$\Gamma \vdash (\mathbf{fix}\ \mathtt{len}\ \lambda\mathtt{x.if\ null\ x\ then}\ 0\ \mathbf{else}\ 1 + \mathtt{len}\ (\mathtt{tail}\ \mathtt{x})) : \mathtt{list(U)} \to \mathtt{int}.$$

In ML/1, if in addition we had function $\mathtt{lift} : \forall\mathtt{U.list(U)} \to \mathtt{list(list(U))}$ (see introduction), we could derive

$$\Gamma \vdash (\mathbf{fix}\ \mathtt{len}\ \lambda\mathtt{x.if\ null\ x\ then}\ 0\ \mathbf{else}\ 1 + \mathtt{len}\ \underline{(\mathtt{lift}\ (\mathtt{tail}\ \mathtt{x}))}) : \forall\mathtt{U.list(U)} \to \mathtt{int},$$

where the application of $\mathtt{len}$ in its own definition is to an argument (underlined) of type $\mathtt{list(list(U))}$. This is impossible in ML.

Note however that even with PR, it is only in *applied* occurrences (recursive calls) of the function that a polymorphic instance of the "declared" type may be used. This is reflected in the fact that in rule FIX, we must derive $M : \sigma$, and not $M : \sigma'$ for some instance σ' of σ. Thus for example if we attempted to define $\mathtt{len}$ by letting M be

$$\lambda\mathtt{x.if\ null\ x\ then}\ 0\ \mathbf{else}\ (\mathbf{if}\ \mathtt{x} = [1]\ \mathbf{then}\ 1\ \mathbf{else}\ 1 + \mathtt{len}\ (\mathtt{tail}\ \mathtt{x}))$$

then $\mathtt{x}$ would be constrained to be of type $\mathtt{list(int)}$, and so M could no longer be of type $\forall\mathtt{U.list(U)} \to \mathtt{int}$. If one translates this definition into our formalism, one sees that it would violate the HC.

This is important to stress since some sentences in the literature might be misunderstood as suggesting that PR allows for polymorphic uses of a function on *both* sides of its definition. We quote:

> Recursive definitions can be written as equations (i.e., in the form $f = \ldots f \ldots f \ldots$). The ML type discipline restricts all the occurrences of a

recursively defined function f on both sides of its definition to have the same type [13].

A peculiarity of the Damas-Milner Calculus [$= ML$] is that occurrences of a recursively defined function *inside* the body of its definition can only be used *monomorphically* [...], whereas occurrences *outside* its body can be used *polymorphically* [...] [9].

The truth is: even PR does not allow for polymorphic uses of a function on the *left* hand side of its definition.

4.2   Polymorphic Recursion in Our Formalism

To translate the above notion of PR into our formalism, we have to cater for three differences: we define functions using patterns rather than λ-expressions, our functions may take a tuple of arguments rather than just one argument, and our typing rule *(Func)* allows for the application of a type substitution.

To simplify the main technical arguments of this paper, we assume that programs do not use *mutual* recursion of predicates, respectively functions. We conjecture that adding mutual recursion would not pose any fundamental difficulties, since mutual recursion of two functions f and g can be simulated by defining a function that behaves like f or g depending on the value of some flag.

In the literature, the discussion is about *polymorphic* recursion. However, to obtain a symmetry with Def. 3, we define *monomorphic* recursion.

Definition 4. For FP, the **monomorphic recursion condition** (MRC) states that for each definition line $f_{\tau_1 \ldots \tau_n \to \tau}(t_1, \ldots, t_n) = t$, each application of rule *(Func)* for function $f_{\tau_1 \ldots \tau_n \to \tau}$ to derive $\_ \vdash t : \tau\Theta$ is generic.

For LP, the **monomorphic recursion condition** states that for each clause $p(\ldots) \leftarrow q_1(\ldots), \ldots, q_n(\ldots)$, for each $i \in \{1, \ldots, n\}$ with $q_i \equiv p$, the application of rule *(Atom)* to derive $\_ \vdash q_i(\ldots)$ *Atom* is generic.

An argument in favour of the MRC, or in disfavour of PR, is:

7. PR renders type inference undecidable [13].

While we assume here that types are declared, automatic type inference is a strong point of FP. In [14], automatic type inference is proposed for LP, excluding PR. In ML, polymorphic recursion is forbidden. In Miranda and Haskell, it is allowed provided that the type of the function is declared.

Henglein [9] gives the following argument in disfavour of the MRC, or in favour of PR:

8. Monomorphic recursion eliminates polymorphism from logic programs almost completely.

The problem lies with *mutual* recursion. We briefly explain this argument, although our formalisation does not consider mutual recursion. Without an analysis of the dependencies between the predicates of a program, one cannot be sure that two predicates are not mutually recursive, and hence one must assume that they are mutually recursive. But then the MRC applies to the entire program, so all occurrences of each predicate must be typed monomorphically.

Indeed, in the simplest setting, type inference algorithms rely on absence of mutual recursion. Type inference in the functional languages we mentioned, and also in [14], assumes that to infer the type of a function f (predicate p), we already know the types of all functions (predicates) used by f (p) in its definition. In ML, functions must be defined before they are used. In Haskell, a dependency analysis is performed by the type checker to order the functions accordingly [20], and the same has been proposed for Prolog [14].

Extensions to mutual recursion are possible in all languages mentioned above. ML provides special syntax for defining several functions simultaneously. In other languages, this is not even needed.

Henglein's argument hinges on the dislike of such a "data-flow" oriented analysis. However, his argument is not really limited to LP, and practical experience in FP shows that on the whole, it is not a very strong argument at all.

We mention another argument in disfavour of monomorphic recursion, related to argument 6 and discussed in Sec. 5.1.

9. There are some programs that need PR [6, 12, 16, 18].

While situations where PR is needed are rare, nothing seems to speak against the approach taken in Miranda and Haskell.

5   Relating the Two Conditions

Comparing Defs. 3 and 4, there is a clear symmetry between the two conditions. We now discuss some observations that initially pointed us to such a close relationship. The results of this section are formulated for LP. This is partly an arbitrary choice, partly related to the fact that we discuss aspects of LP semantics without obvious FP equivalent, and partly because we formulate results for LP for which related FP results have appeared previously [12].

5.1   A Special Kind of Term Language

We now discuss a term language for which the HC and MRC impedes writing programs using obvious algorithms.

Example 2. Let $\mathcal{K} = \{t/1\}$ and $\mathcal{C} = \{c_{\to t(U)}, g_{U \to t(U)}, f_{t(t(U)) \to t(U)}\}$. For all $i \geq 0$, $g^i(c)$ is of type $t^{i+1}(U)$ and $f^i(g^i(c))$ is of type $t(U)$. This means that there are infinitely many types that a subterm of a term of type $t(U)$ can have. This property of the type $t(U)$ is very unusual. Now consider the predicate $fgs_{int, t(U)}$ specified as $fgs(i, f^i(g^i(c)))$ ($i \in \mathbb{N}$).[2] When one tries to write a logic program defining this predicate, one finds that one has to violate at least one of our two conditions. Figure 1 presents three potential definitions of fgs.

---

[2] Assume that we add the integers to the term language.

```
fgs1(I,Y) <-           fgs2(I,Y) <-           fgs3(I,X) <-
   fs1(I,Y,I).            fs2(I,Y,I).            fgs3_aux(I,c,X).


fs1(I,f(X),J) <-       fs2(I,f(X),J) <-       fgs3_aux(I,X,f(Y)) <-
   I2 is I-1,             I2 is I-1,             I2 is I-1,
   fs1(I2,X,J).          fs2(I2,X,J).          fgs3_aux(I2,g(X),Y).
fs1(0,X,J) <-          fs2(0,X,J) <-          fgs3_aux(0,X,X).
   gs1(J,X).             gs2(J,X,c).


gs1(J,g(X)) <-         gs2(J,X,Y) <-
   J2 is J-1,             J2 is J-1,
   gs1(J2,X).            gs2(J2,X,g(Y)).
gs1(0,c).              gs2(0,X,X).
```

Fig. 1. Three potential solutions for Ex. 2

The first program builds the term $f^i(g^i(c))$ starting from the outside. Then, fs1 violates the MRC and gs1 violates the HC.

The second solution is to build the term $g^i(c)$ starting from the inside using an accumulator. This time the fact clause for gs2 violates the HC. Moreover, the recursive clauses for fs2 *and* gs2 violate the MRC.

The third solution is to build $f^i(\ldots)$ from the inside and $g^i(c)$ from the outside simultaneously. Here, fgs3_aux violates the MRC.

None of the above programs could be translated into ML, but the third program could be translated into Haskell or Miranda.

While it is generally accepted that any conceivable type system will forbid some useful programs, this fact is an argument in disfavour of type systems in general and of any restriction a type system imposes in particular. The problem of writing programs operating on term languages as seen above is an argument against the HC and the MRC alike.

Term languages where this problem occurs are rare but have been discussed in the literature. Kahrs has shown formally that a function very similar to the predicate fgs of the above example cannot be defined in ML, although the function could "soundly be given a type" [12]. The argument of the proof bears a strong resemblance with Theorem 2 below. He shows that a computation of the function in question would have to involve arbitrarily many different types, which is impossible for a program without PR.

5.2   Calls and Answers

In LP, it is common to distinguish *call* (*top-down*) semantics and *answer* (*bottom-up*) semantics. A definition of a top-down semantics for LP is as follows [1]:

Definition 5. A query Q' is **derived from** a query Q, denoted $Q \rightsquigarrow Q'$, if $Q \equiv a_1, \ldots, a_m$, $Q' \equiv (a_1, \ldots, a_{k-1}, B, a_{k+1}, \ldots, a_m)\theta$, and $h \leftarrow B$ is a clause (in a program clear from the context) such that h and a_k are unifiable with most general unifier (MGU) θ. A **derivation** $Q \leadsto^* Q'$ is defined in the usual way.

A definition of a bottom-up semantics (called *s-semantics* [2]) is as follows:

Definition 6. Given a logic program P, the **non-ground T_P-operator** is a function taking a set of atoms and returning a set of atoms, defined by[3]

$$T_P(I) = \{h\theta \mid C = h \leftarrow b_1, \ldots, b_n \in P, \langle a_1, \ldots, a_n \rangle \ll_C I,$$
$$\theta = MGU(\langle b_1, \ldots, b_n \rangle, \langle a_1, \ldots, a_n \rangle)\}.$$

We denote the least fixpoint of T_P by $[\![P]\!]_s$ and call it **answer semantics** of P.

Recall the programs P_{pr} and P_{hc} from the introduction. P_{pr} gives rise to a sequence of *calls* having infinitely many different types. P_{hc} gives rise to computed *answers* having infinitely many different types. Both phenomena are rare and would qualify P_{pr} and P_{hc} as bad programs, following the maxim "good programs have small types" [9].

Our motivation for studying the problem of finiteness was in the context of groundness analysis for logic programs [23]. There we assumed, as is common, that the HC is enforced but PR is allowed. We showed that the computed *answers* have only finitely many different types, which is essential for the termination of the analysis and hence a desirable property. This result had been stated previously, but without proof [22].

Lemma 1. [23] Let P be a typed logic program which meets the HC. For any atom $p_{\tau_1 \ldots \tau_n}(t_1, \ldots, t_n) \in [\![P]\!]_s$, we have $\_ \vdash (t_1, \ldots, t_n) : (\tau_1, \ldots, \tau_n)$.

One may expect a symmetric result for the calls: given a program meeting the MRC and a query, the atoms arising in any derivation have only finitely many different types. However, this is not true. For P_{hc} and the query $p(X), p(X)$, we obtain the derivation $p(X), p(X) \leadsto p(X'), p([X']) \leadsto p(X''), p([[X'']]) \ldots$. The reason for this asymmetry is that a clause head always consists of one atom, whereas a clause body (or query) may consist of several atoms.

We now show that if we enforce both conditions, then we also have a finiteness result for the calls. The result states that if we have a program and a predicate $p_{\bar{\tau}}$, then we can construct a finite set Σ of types that can play an active role in any derivation for $p_{\bar{\tau}}$. This means that for an initial query $p(\bar{t})$ where $\bar{t}$ is of type $\bar{\tau}\Theta$, the types occurring in the derivation are all contained in $\Sigma\Theta$. Intuitively, the computation does not look into the structure of Θ [27].

The idea of the formalisation (and the proof of the result) is that a typed program can be executed "abstractly" by replacing each term with its type [4].

Definition 7. For a well-typed clause $C \equiv p(\bar{t}) \leftarrow p_1(\bar{t}_1), \ldots, p_n(\bar{t}_n)$, consider the most general type vector $(\bar{\sigma}, \bar{\sigma}_1, \ldots, \bar{\sigma}_n)$ such that the type judgements $\Gamma \vdash \bar{t} :$

---

[3] $\langle a_1, \ldots, a_n \rangle \ll_C I$ denotes that $a_1, \ldots, a_n$ are elements of I renamed apart from C and from each other.

$\bar{\sigma}, \Gamma \vdash \bar{t}_1 : \bar{\sigma}_1, \dots, \Gamma \vdash \bar{t}_n : \bar{\sigma}_n$ are used in a derivation of the type judgement $\Gamma \vdash C$ *Clause*, for any choice of Γ [6]. We call $p(\bar{\sigma}) \leftarrow p_1(\bar{\sigma}_1), \dots, p_n(\bar{\sigma}_n)$ the **type clause corresponding** to C. In analogy, define the **type query** corresponding to a query and the **type atom** corresponding to an atom.

The type clause corresponding to a clause is unique up to renaming of parameters. We simply choose an arbitrary clause meeting the above definition.

We also need the following definition. Recall that we assume for simplicity that the program contains no mutual recursion.

Definition 8. Let P be a logic program. For a predicate p, define its degree $\mathcal{D}(p)$ as follows: if there exists no clause $p(\dots) \leftarrow \dots q(\dots) \dots$ in P with $p \not\equiv q$, then $\mathcal{D}(p) = 0$; otherwise, $\mathcal{D}(p) = 1 + \max\{\mathcal{D}(q) \mid p(\dots) \leftarrow \dots q(\dots) \cdots \in P\}$.

Without loss of generality, the following theorem is phrased for a one-atom query. The theorem subsumes the subject reduction property [11, Thm. 1.4.7], and this is naturally reflected in the proof.

Theorem 2. Let P be a typed logic program which meets the HC and MRC, and $p_{\bar{\tau}} \in \mathcal{P}$. Then there is a finite set Σ of type atoms such that for any type substitution Θ, for any $\bar{t}$ of type $\bar{\tau}\Theta$, for any derivation $p(\bar{t}) \rightsquigarrow^* Q$, for any $q(\bar{s})$ in Q, there is some $q(\bar{\sigma}) \in \Sigma$ such that $\Gamma \vdash \bar{s} : \bar{\sigma}\Theta$, where Γ is a variable typing such that $\Gamma \vdash Q$ *Query*.

Proof. We construct a set Σ fulfilling the statement inductively: Σ contains $p(\bar{\tau})$; moreover, if $a \in \Sigma$ and $h \leftarrow B$ is a type clause corresponding to some clause in P, and Θ is the MGU of a and h, then each atom in $B\Theta$ is in Σ.

We first show that Σ is finite. Consider a step in the construction of Σ, i.e., an atom $p'(\bar{\tau}') \in \Sigma$ and a type clause $p'(\bar{\sigma}) \leftarrow B$ corresponding to some clause in P. Due to the HC and the typing rules, $\bar{\sigma}$ is the declared type of p' and $\bar{\tau}'$ is an instance of it, so say $\bar{\sigma}\Theta' = \bar{\tau}'$. If B contains an atom whose predicate is p', then this must be $p'(\bar{\sigma})$, due to the MRC. Since $p'(\bar{\sigma}\Theta')$ is already in Σ, it is not added in this step. Therefore for any $q(\bar{\sigma}')$ added in this step, $\mathcal{D}(q) < \mathcal{D}(p)$. Since P contains only finitely many clauses and thus there are only finitely many corresponding type clauses, one can easily see that this construction terminates.

We next show by induction on the length of derivations that Σ fulfils the statement. For derivations of length 0, we have $Q = p(\bar{t})$ and since $\bar{t}$ is of type $\bar{\tau}\Theta$, there is a Γ such that $\Gamma \vdash \bar{t} : \bar{\tau}\Theta$ and so $\Gamma \vdash Q$ *Query*. Moreover, $p(\bar{\tau}) \in \Sigma$.

Now assume that the statement holds for a query $Q \equiv p_1(\bar{t}_1), \dots, p_n(\bar{t}_n)$ where $p(\bar{t}) \rightsquigarrow^* Q$, and consider a derivation step $Q \rightsquigarrow Q'$ using a clause $C \equiv p_i(\bar{s}) \leftarrow q_1(\bar{s}_1), \dots, q_m(\bar{s}_m)$. By the induction hypothesis, there exists a Γ such that $\Gamma \vdash Q$ *Query*, and for each $\bar{t}_j$ ($j \in \{1, \dots, n\}$), there is a $p_j(\bar{\tau}_j) \in \Sigma$ such that $\Gamma \vdash \bar{t}_j : \bar{\tau}_j\Theta$.

Let $p_i(\bar{\sigma}) \leftarrow q_1(\bar{\sigma}_1), \dots, q_m(\bar{\sigma}_m)$ be the type clause corresponding to C, and Γ_C the (most general, see Def. 7) variable typing such that $\Gamma_C \vdash \bar{s} : \bar{\sigma}$ and $\Gamma_C \vdash \bar{s}_j : \bar{\sigma}_j$ for all $j \in \{1, \dots, m\}$.

Let Θ' be the type substitution such that $\bar{\sigma}\Theta' = \bar{\tau}_i$ (which exists because $\bar{\sigma}$ must be the declared type of p_i). By the construction of Σ, for all $j \in \{1, \ldots, m\}$ we have $q_j(\bar{\sigma}_j\Theta') \in \Sigma$.

Let θ be the MGU of $p_i(\bar{t}_i)$ and $p_i(\bar{s})$. By some basic results about substitutions and type substitutions [6, 11], we have:

- $\Gamma_C\Theta'\Theta \cup \Gamma \vdash \bar{t}_j\theta : \bar{\tau}_j\Theta$ for all $j \in \{1, \ldots, n\}$;
- $\Gamma_C\Theta'\Theta\cup\Gamma \vdash \bar{s}\theta : \bar{\sigma}\Theta'\Theta$ and $\Gamma_C\Theta'\Theta\cup\Gamma \vdash \bar{s}_j\theta : \bar{\sigma}_j\Theta'\Theta$ for all $j \in \{1, \ldots, m\}$.

It thus follows that for the resolvent

$$Q' \equiv (p_1(\bar{t}_1), \ldots, p_{i-1}(\bar{t}_{i-1}), q_1(\bar{s}_1), \ldots, q_m(\bar{s}_m), p_{j+1}(\bar{t}_{i+1}), \ldots, p_n(\bar{t}_n))\theta$$

the claim in the statement holds. $\square$

We are confident that an equivalent of the above theorem for FP could be extracted from [12], but this is not entirely trivial.

5.3   The Magic Transformation

Above we observed a difference between calls and answers from the point of view of typing. The *magic (set) transformation* [3] is a widespread technique used in logic program analysis. It has the property that the answers (bottom-up semantics, T_P-operator [2]) of the transformed program capture both the calls and the answers of the original program. It is therefore not surprising that the same problems for typing also show up in the magic transformation of a program.

We define the magic transformation for the usual left-to-right selection rule.

Definition 9. Let $C = h \leftarrow b_1, \ldots, b_n$ be a clause. The **magic transformation** $C^{\mathcal{M}}$ is defined as follows:

$$C^{\mathcal{M}} = \{b_i^c \leftarrow h^c, b_1^a, \ldots, b_{i-1}^a \mid i \in \{1, \ldots, n\}\} \cup \{h^a \leftarrow h^c, b_1^a, \ldots, b_n^a\}$$

For a program P, the **magic transformation** $P^{\mathcal{M}}$ is $\cup_{C \in P} C^{\mathcal{M}}$.

The superscripts stand for *call* and *answer*. The magic transformation is usually considered together with an atom $p^c(\ldots)$ to model some initial query.

Example 3. Consider the program P_{pr} from the introduction.

$$P_{pr}^{\mathcal{M}} = \{\mathrm{p}^a(\mathrm{X}) \leftarrow \mathrm{p}^c(\mathrm{X})., \quad \mathrm{p}^c([\mathrm{X}]) \leftarrow \mathrm{p}^c(\mathrm{X})., \quad \mathrm{p}^a(\mathrm{X}) \leftarrow \mathrm{p}^c(\mathrm{X}), \mathrm{p}^a([\mathrm{X}]).\}.$$

$P_{pr}^{\mathcal{M}}$ contains information about the (left-to-right) execution of P_{pr}. For example, the clause $\mathrm{p}^a(\mathrm{X}) \leftarrow \mathrm{p}^c(\mathrm{X}), \mathrm{p}^a([\mathrm{X}])$ says: For $\mathrm{p}(\mathrm{X})$ to be answered, $\mathrm{p}(\mathrm{X})$ must be called and $\mathrm{p}^a([\mathrm{X}])$ must be answered.

One might say that the magic transformation turns clause heads into body atoms and vice versa. Thus it can happen that a program which meets the HC but uses polymorphic recursion is transformed into a program which does not meet the HC, as for the clause $\mathrm{p}^c([\mathrm{X}]) \leftarrow \mathrm{p}^c(\mathrm{X})$. For programming languages where the HC is enforced but PR is allowed, this means that the magic transformation can transform a well-typed program into an ill-typed one. This raises the question under which conditions this can be avoided.

It turns out that if P is a logic program which meets the HC and MRC, then $P^{\mathcal{M}}$ can be made well-typed. Technically, one first has to specialise the types of P such that any polymorphism used within P is eliminated. The underlying idea is the same as in Thm. 2. We do not develop the details here for lack of space, but the essence is this: for appropriate type declarations, possibly involving some code duplication, $P^{\mathcal{M}}$ is well-typed.

6   Conclusion

We have studied two conditions on type systems for FP and LP: the HC and the MRC. Previously, the HC had been mainly discussed in LP and the MRC in FP, but based on a uniform formalisation, we have shown that both conditions are meaningful in both paradigms, and that there is a symmetry between them.

For the sake of comparison, we had to adjust the terminology: we defined the *MRC*, meaning absence of PR. In the literature, saying *P uses PR* is preferred over saying *P violates the MRC*.

This is in line with the conclusion that emerged from our survey of different arguments for and against each condition, namely: the head condition is uncontested in FP and well-established in LP although there are reasonable arguments against it; the MRC is only relevant for type inference, and it is well understood how this problem can be overcome using explicit type declarations.

We have seen a term language for which obvious algorithms will violate one or both of those conditions, and it seems somewhat arbitrary which. The existence of such term languages is an argument against both conditions.

For program analysis, it is desirable that the semantics of the program should involve only finitely many types. We have seen that the two conditions ensure this property. For similar reasons, they also ensure a desirable behaviour of the magic transformation.

The interesting examples of violations of the two conditions are those where these violations are unavoidable, as seen in program P_{hc}. This is an aspect we found discussed only by Kahrs [12].

While we have no conclusive answer as to whether the two conditions should be enforced or not, we hope to have contributed some arguments to the debate.

Acknowledgement

The author thanks Achim Brucker, Stefan Friedrich, Stefan Kahrs and Erik Poll for sharing their expertise on functional programming, Michael Hanus for providing the example used in argument 5, and the anonymous referees for valuable comments. This paper is dedicated to the memory of Alessandro Baratta.

References

[1] K. R. Apt. *From Logic Programming to Prolog*. Prentice Hall, 1997. 262, 268

[2] A. Bossi, M. Gabbrielli, G. Levi, and M. Martelli. The *s*-semantics approach: theory and applications. *Journal of Logic Programming*, 19/20:149–197, 1994. 269, 271

[3] M. Codish. Efficient goal directed bottom-up evaluation of logic programs. *Journal of Logic Programming*, 38(3):355–370, 1999. 271

[4] P. Cousot and R. Cousot. Abstract interpretation: A unified lattice model for static analysis of programs by construction or approximation of fixpoints. In *Proceedings of the 4th Symposium on Principles of Programming Languages*, pages 238–252. ACM Press, 1977. 269

[5] B. Demoen, M. García de la Banda, W. Harvey, K. Marriott, and P. Stuckey. An overview of HAL. In J. Jaffar, editor, *Proc. of Principles and Practice of Constraint Programming*, volume 1713 of *LNCS*, pages 174–188. Springer-Verlag, 1999. 259

[6] P. Deransart and J.-G. Smaus. Subject reduction of logic programs as proof-theoretic property. *Journal of Functional and Logic Programming*, 2002(2), 2002. 260, 263, 267, 270, 271

[7] C. V. Hall, K. Hammond, S. L. Peyton Jones, and P. Wadler. Type classes in Haskell. *ACM Transactions on Programming Languages and Systems*, 18(2):109–138, 1996. 264

[8] M. Hanus. *Logic Programming with Type Specifications*, chapter 3, pages 91–140. 1992. In [21]. 259, 260, 263

[9] F. Henglein. Type inference with polymorphic recursion. *ACM Transactions on Programming Languages and Systems*, 15(2):253–289, 1993. 259, 260, 264, 266, 269

[10] P. M. Hill and J. W. Lloyd. *The Gödel Programming Language*. MIT Press, 1994. 259

[11] P. M. Hill and R. W. Topor. *A Semantics for Typed Logic Programs*, chapter 1, pages 1–61. 1992. In [21]. 259, 260, 261, 263, 270, 271

[12] S. Kahrs. Limits of ML-definability. In H. Kuchen and S. D. Swierstra, editors, *Proceedings of the 8th Symposium on Programming Language Implementations and Logic Programming*, volume 1140 of *LNCS*, pages 17–31. Springer-Verlag, 1996. 259, 260, 267, 268, 271, 272

[13] A. J. Kfoury, J. Tiuryn, and P. Urzyczyn. Type reconstruction in the presence of polymorphic recursion. *ACM Transactions on Programming Languages and Systems*, 15(2):290–311, 1993. Title wrongly given in table of contents: Type *recursion* in the presence of polymorphic recursion. 259, 260, 261, 264, 265, 266

[14] T. K. Lakshman and U. S. Reddy. Typed Prolog: A semantic reconstruction of the Mycroft-O'Keefe type system. In V. Saraswat and K. Ueda, editors, *Proceedings of the 1991 International Symposium on Logic Programming*, pages 202–217. MIT Press, 1991. 259, 260, 266, 267

[15] P. Louvet and O. Ridoux. Parametric polymorphism for Typed Prolog and λProlog. In H. Kuchen and S. D. Swierstra, editors, *Proceedings of the 8th Symposium on Programming Language Implementations and Logic Programming*, volume 1140 of *LNCS*, pages 47–61. Springer-Verlag, 1996. 259, 260, 263

[16] A. Mycroft. Polymorphic type schemes and recursive definitions. In M. Paul and B. Robinet, editors, *International Symposium on Programming*, volume 167 of *LNCS*, pages 217–228. Springer-Verlag, 1984. 260, 267

[17] G. Nadathur and F. Pfenning. *Types in Higher-Order Logic Programming*, chapter 9, pages 245–283. 1992. In [21]. 260, 263

[18] C. Okasaki. Catenable double-ended queues. In *Proceedings of the International Conference on Functional Programming*, volume 32(8) of *SIGPLAN Notices*, pages 66–74. ACM Press, 1997. 260, 267

[19] L. C. Paulson. *ML for the Working Programmer*. Cambridge University Press, 1996. 259

[20] S. Peyton Jones and J. Hughes (eds.). *Report on the Programming Language Haskell 98*, 1999. Available via http://www.haskell.org. 264, 267

[21] F. Pfenning, editor. *Types in Logic Programming*. MIT Press, 1992. 273, 274

[22] O. Ridoux and P. Boizumault. Typed static analysis: Application to the groundness analysis of Typed Prolog. *Journal of Functional and Logic Programming*, 2001(1), 2001. 269

[23] J.-G. Smaus. Analysis of polymorphically typed logic programs using ACI-unification. In R. Nieuwenhuis and A. Voronkov, editors, *Proceedings of the 8th International Conference on Logic for Programming, Artificial Intelligence and Reasoning*, volume 2250 of *LNAI*, pages 280–295. Springer-Verlag, 2001. 269

[24] Z. Somogyi, F. Henderson, and T. Conway. The execution algorithm of Mercury, an efficient purely declarative logic programming language. *Journal of Logic Programming*, 29(1–3):17–64, 1996. 259

[25] S. Thompson. *Miranda: The Craft of Functional Programming*. Addison-Wesley, 1995. 259

[26] S. Thompson. *Haskell: The Craft of Functional Programming*. Addison-Wesley, 1999. Second Edition. 259

[27] P. Wadler. Theorems for free! In *Proceedings of the 4th Conference on Functional Programming Languages and Computer Architecture*, pages 347–359. ACM, 1989. 263, 264, 269

Structural Abstraction and Application in Logic Programming

António Porto

Departamento de Informática, Faculdade de Ciências e Tecnologia
Universidade Nova de Lisboa
ap@di.fct.unl.pt

Abstract. This paper explores a seemingly very simple idea—an operation for extending a term with extra (start or end) arguments to yield a new term. This allows the definition a variety of structural operators that provide the power of functional composition and higher-order features on top of the non-directional and non-deterministic (relational) behavior of the underlying logic programming setting. Syntax alone is taken to be meaningless, semantics being associated to syntax *in context*. Multiple semantic views of each term are therefore possible, in different contexts. One such semantic view is structural, whereby any term is taken as an implicit abstraction of another term over some of its subterms. The standard operational semantics is extended with a rewrite step prior to each goal invocation, that appeals to a functional rewrite semantics to interpret certain terms as applications of implicit inner structural abstractions to inner arguments. The approach is first described through meta-level functional definitions, and then an implementation is shown through a collection of standard Prolog predicates. The powerful gain in expressiveness is thus achieved without any extension of the underlying machinery, much in the spirit of an old claim by D. H. Warren [5]. The scheme was motivated by the needs of a large real-world application [4] where it is now in use.

1 Introduction

In logic programming, data is passed around through the use of *explicit* place-holders—the logic variables. In functional programming, in contrast, intermediate data results are *implicit* in the syntax for function application and composition. A simple produce-and-consume task is logically written (in Prolog) as `(produce(X),consume(X))` and functionally (in ML) as `(consume produce)`. The latter is more compact, avoiding the proliferation of identifiers such as X. The former is semantically richer because of possible non-determinism and bi-directional data flow, and exhibits the property that the left-to-right (reading) order corresponds to the temporal execution order. The best of both worlds is achieved with the notation `(produce\consume)` in the logic programming setting, where \ is a structural operator meant to extend its argument terms with a common extra argument (a new variable) and glueing them conjunctively with (,). Such extensions of term arguments can be called explicitly, e.g.

Z. Hu and M. Rodríguez-Artalejo (Eds.): FLOPS 2002, LNCS 2441, pp. 275–289, 2002.

`name(abc)\:X` is equivalent to `name(abc,X)`. The advantage, of course, is to be able to use `T\:X` with a variable `T`, thereby obtaining straightforward higher-order functionality (think `T(X)`.) The catch is that `T` must be bound when the call is invoked, but this is the standard use in practice, and no higher-order unification is needed. This is the stance first expressed by D. H. Warren in [5], in contrast to the option taken by the authors of λ-Prolog [2, 3].

The terms to which "argument extension" operations are applied are not limited to be implicit abstractions of *atomic* goals, but also of generic goals, including application operations themselves.

In the following we detail a variety of structural operators, the underlying semantics, and examples of their use. The variety is mostly due to the multi-directional data flows obtained from unification, i.e. `append(X,Y,Z)` captures the operational flavor of producing `Z` from `X` and `Y`, but also `Y` from `X` and `Z` or `X` and `Y` from `Z`.

This research was motivated by practical requirements from a large ongoing project to build a comprehensive integrated information system for our Faculty based on Prolog technology [4], where it became essential to be able to construct and pass around abstractions for later application. The ideas described in this paper have been implemented and are being used in the current running system.

2   Syntax and Semantics

In many linguistic frameworks, semantics is directly associated to syntactic items of certain kinds. For example, in the predicate calculus there is a syntactic distinction between terms and predicate symbols, and a corresponding semantic characterization as denoting, respectively, domain elements and domain relations.

However, we find it much more useful and attractive to consider a meaningless but universal syntax, and semantic contexts where certain syntactic types are given meaning. I.e. we want a syntax capable of holding whatever information structures we might use, and define different semantics as particular ways to interpret syntax for certain effects.

Prolog is actually best understood in such terms, even though it departs from the standard first-order logic reading associated with logic programming. The term `X+Y` means nothing. If we invoke the goal (`A is X+Y`), *then* it is interpreted as denoting the sum of `X` and `Y`. If we invoke another goal `p(X+Y,A)` *then* it means whatever the author of predicate `p` has meant for the type of its first argument. We may also execute `X+Y` directly as a goal, when a predicate definition for binary `+` gives it yet another meaning. Notice that even the *term* (`A is X+Y`), by itself, means nothing. It is only in the context of being invoked as a goal that a particular semantic destiny falls upon it.

So we are interested in several semantics for terms, which are defined as (possibly partial) functions from terms to appropriate semantic domains. Henceforth we will use $[\![c]\!]$ to denote the semantic function associated with a given semantic context identified through the symbol c. To simplify the presentation we use the notation $t \overset{c}{\longmapsto} t'$ as an alternative to $[\![c]\!](t) = t'$.

3   Structural Abstraction

Consider the terms p, p(1), p(1,2), p(2,3) and p(1,2,3). There is a clear structural relationship among them, namely that all of them consist of the same constructor applied to a sequence of arguments which is a sub-sequence of 1,2,3. This suggests the following idea: to consider that any term consisting of a constructor and arguments can be obtained by "applying" extra arguments to a simpler term consisting of the same constructor and a sub-sequence of the arguments. For example p(1) results from applying 1 to p, and p(1,2,3) results from applying 3 "to the end" of p(1,2), or 1 "to the start" of p(2,3). This corresponds to viewing terms as implicit structural abstractions of extended terms.

This intuitive notion of structural abstraction can be made formal. We consider two semantic functions $[\![<]\!]$ and $[\![>]\!]$ through which terms are interpreted as abstractions of extended terms, respectively at the start or end:

$$ p(t_1, \ldots, t_n) \overset{<}{\longmapsto} \lambda t. \, p(t, t_1, \ldots, t_n) \, , $$

$$ p(t_1, \ldots, t_n) \overset{>}{\longmapsto} \lambda t. \, p(t_1, \ldots, t_n, t) \, . $$

In the sequel we will find it useful to consider alternative definitions of $[\![<]\!]$ and $[\![>]\!]$ for a special class of *application-specific* terms $\mathcal{T}^{\mathcal{A}}$, so we qualify the above definitions by the restriction that $p(t_1, \ldots, t_n) \notin \mathcal{T}^{\mathcal{A}}$.

We can abstract the structural mode ($<$ or $>$) and define a mode-parametric structural abstraction semantics $[\![\mathcal{A}]\!] \equiv \lambda m. \, [\![m]\!]$.

The functions $[\![<]\!]$ and $[\![>]\!]$ are partial, being only defined for non-variable terms. In practice this is not a significant restriction, meaning as it does that the power we get from them is "just" higher-order matching rather than unification. I.e., we agree with the arguments put forward by D. H. Warren in his early paper [5] and see no need for "real" higher-order logic programming as in [2, 3]. In our application [4] we do pass around (implicit) abstractions through variables, but these are always bound at application time.

A remark should be made on notation, to avoid confusion between literal and evaluated expressions. In the definition clauses for a given semantic function, as above, there generally appear expressions involving applications of other semantic functions, possibly in the scope of λ-abstractions, and usually mixed with object-level expressions. The defined value is taken to be the result of recursively evaluating all meta-level expressions (i.e. normalizing through β-reduction the initial right-hand side expression), while taking all object-level expressions as literal (unevaluated).

4   Structural Rewrite Semantics

The power of the structural abstraction semantics $\llbracket \mathcal{A} \rrbracket$ is explored by introducing, in the object language, a set of structural operators that use it for dynamic rewriting of terms to be executed as goals.

The idea is to extend the operational semantics with an implicit rewriting mechanism, so that every term invoked as a goal is recursively rewritten, according to the structural rewrite semantics of the term's main constructor, before applying the standard operational semantics. We will not define here the standard operational semantics,[1] but assuming it is $\llbracket \mathcal{O} \rrbracket$, what we propose is to replace it with another version $\llbracket \mathcal{O}' \rrbracket$ that appeals to the rewrite semantics $\llbracket \mathcal{R} \rrbracket$:

$$\llbracket \mathcal{O}' \rrbracket(t) = \begin{cases} \llbracket \mathcal{O}' \rrbracket(\llbracket \mathcal{R} \rrbracket(t)) & \text{if } t \in dom(\llbracket \mathcal{R} \rrbracket), \\ \llbracket \mathcal{O} \rrbracket(t) & \text{otherwise.} \end{cases}$$

$\llbracket \mathcal{R} \rrbracket$ will be such that the recursive definition of $\llbracket \mathcal{O}' \rrbracket$ is well-founded. It may happen, as we shall see, that $\llbracket \mathcal{R} \rrbracket(t)$ is not a regular object-level term but one wrapped by λ-abstractions. So we have to include in $\llbracket \mathcal{O} \rrbracket$ the operational semantics for such extended terms of the form $\lambda x_1. \ldots \lambda x_n. t$. These λ's are just meant for scoping. The variable environment is incremented with new unbound variables $v_1, \ldots, v_n$, and the term to which the standard operational semantics is applied is the normalization of $(\lambda x_1. \ldots \lambda x_n. t)(v_1, \ldots, v_n)$, i.e. t with the x's substituted by fresh v's. This is actually what happens when clauses of predicate definitions are invoked; we shall return later to this topic.

5   Structural Operators

5.1   Explicit Application

The simplest way to explore the structural rewrite semantics is by explicitly providing a missing argument to be added to a term (at the start or end). For this we reserve two infix operators ':\' and '\:' and define the corresponding rewrite semantics:

$$x :\backslash t \xrightarrow{\mathcal{R}} \llbracket < \rrbracket(t)(x) ,$$

$$t \backslash: x \xrightarrow{\mathcal{R}} \llbracket > \rrbracket(t)(x) .$$

It amounts to the explicit application of the implicit structural abstractions.

The real interest of these operators lies obviously in the fact that we can write code with calls of the form $(x :\backslash t)$ or $(t \backslash: x)$ where t is lexically a *variable*, meant to be dynamically bound prior to the execution of the calls. Thus we can write very generic procedures that incorporate, for example, parametric (variable t) formatting of values (x previously bound) or parametric (variable t) generation of values (x becomes bound upon execution). The chosen order of the

---

[1] It can be done in a fully compositional way, but that is the subject of a forthcoming paper.

arguments reflects these typical roles of x as "input" or "output", and so does the choice of structural mode. But note that there is really no corresponding fixed data flow as in functional programming, and in fact the consumption/generation nature the operation lies with the semantics of (extensions of) t rather than with the structural operators themselves.

We can notice that T\:X has the same flavor of T(X) as used in HiLog [1]. There are, however, two important advantages of our scheme. First, it does not require a change to the internal representation of terms, nor to the procedure for reading them. Second, calls of the form p(X)(Y) in HiLog can only match predicate definitions whose heads have the same syntactic form, whereas in our case all predicate definitions are kept standard and any defined predicates can be invoked via the structural operators.

The explicit application terms can themselves become the subject of an explicit application. For this we have to include them in the application-specific terms (i.e. consider them as $\mathcal{T}^{\mathcal{E}} \subset \mathcal{T}^{\mathcal{A}}$) and define the corresponding abstraction semantics, intuitively carried out over the term resulting from the explicit application:

$$t \xmapsto{\mathcal{A}} \lambda m.\, [\![\mathcal{A}]\!](m)(\ [\![\mathcal{R}]\!](t)\ ) \qquad \text{if}\ \ t \in \mathcal{T}^{\mathcal{E}}.$$

So we can use expressions such as X:\T\:Y (assume that ':\' binds tighter than '\:') and we can check that if X, T and Y are respectively bound to e.g. 1, p and 2 the term is rewritten as expected:

$$
\begin{aligned}
&[\![\mathcal{R}]\!](\, 1\!:\!\backslash p\backslash\!:\!2\,) \\
={}& [\![>]\!](\, 1\!:\!\backslash p\,)(\, 2\,) \\
={}& [\![>]\!](\, [\![\mathcal{R}]\!](\, 1\!:\!\backslash p\,)\,)(\, 2\,) \qquad [\, 1\!:\!\backslash p \in \mathcal{T}^{\mathcal{E}}\,] \\
={}& [\![>]\!](\, [\![<]\!](\, p\,)(\, 1\,)\,)(\, 2\,) \\
={}& [\![>]\!](\, p(\, 1\,)\,)(\, 2\,) \\
={}& p(\, 1,2\,)
\end{aligned}
$$

5.2   Implicit Application — Pipes

Now suppose we want to write a predicate to standardize a list in the sense of being sorted and without duplicate elements. The way to write it in Prolog is

```
standardize(L,N) :- remove_duplicates(L,R), sort(R,N).
```

The local variable R is introduced as a place holder for the "output" of remove_duplicates which is also the "input" of sort. The explicit mention of R can be avoided if we introduce a structural infix binary operator '\' expressing conjunctive composition with an implicit "output"-to-"input" link:

```
standardize(L,N) :- remove_duplicates(L)~sort(N).
```

The rewrite semantics for '\' is

$$A\backslash B \xmapsto{\mathcal{R}} \lambda x.\, (\ [\![>]\!](A)(x),\ [\![<]\!](B)(x)\ )$$

where the inner comma is the object-level conjunction symbol. Notice that this
is a case where $[\![\mathcal{R}]\!]$ returns a λ-wrapped term.

Let us work through the example, applying the definitions.

$$[\![\mathcal{O}']\!](\,\texttt{remove\_duplicates(L)\~sort(N)}\,)$$
$$= [\![\mathcal{O}']\!](\,\lambda x.(\,[\![>]\!](\,\texttt{remove\_duplicates(L)}\,)(x),\ [\![<]\!](\,\texttt{sort(N)}\,)(x)\,)$$
$$= [\![\mathcal{O}']\!](\,\lambda x.(\,\texttt{remove\_duplicates(L,}x\texttt{)},\ \texttt{sort(}x\texttt{,N)}\,)$$
$$= [\![\mathcal{O}]\!](\,\lambda x.(\,\texttt{remove\_duplicates(L,}x\texttt{)},\ \texttt{sort(}x\texttt{,N)}\,)\,).$$

The effect of the λ scoping in the operational semantics, as explained before,
leads to evaluating $[\![\mathcal{O}]\!](\,\texttt{remove\_duplicates(L,\_X)},\ \texttt{sort(\_X,N)}\,)$ in the environment augmented with a new variable _X.

One may think of A\B as expressing the "application" of B to the "result" of
A, but instead of functions and their evaluated results we mean procedures and
their multiple solutions. The notion of application is purely structural—it sets
up a "pipe" between A and B through a connecting extra variable, independently
of the operational semantics of the resulting expanded terms.

The pipe syntax, in the previous example, can be seen as syntactic sugar for
avoiding the explicit coding of intermediate variables, and as such is reminiscent
of the well-known syntactic device of definite clause grammars. What is important to realize is that the primary importance of pipe constructors, similarly to
all other structural operators, is that we can use them with *variable* arguments.
Contrary to DCG's, therefore, they are *dynamic* devices, affecting the operational semantics, and not just syntactic sugar amenable to static pre-processing.

The next thing that comes to mind is the ability to pipeline more than one
call, e.g. by writing things like `append(X,Y)~standardize~writeln`. Suppose
that '\' is defined as a left associative operator. Following the definitions,

$$[\![\mathcal{O}']\!](\,\texttt{append(X,Y)\~standardize\~writeln}\,)$$
$$= [\![\mathcal{O}']\!](\,\lambda x.(\,[\![>]\!](\,\texttt{append(X,Y)\~standardize}\,)(x),\ [\![<]\!](\,\texttt{writeln}\,)(x)\,)$$
$$= [\![\mathcal{O}']\!](\,\lambda x.(\,[\![>]\!](\,\texttt{append(X,Y)\~standardize}\,)(x),\ \texttt{writeln(}x\texttt{)}\,).$$

We come to the point where $[\![>]\!]$ must be applied to a term whose main constructor is a structural operator not meant as a regular predicate symbol. We
naturally do not wish to apply the term extension semantics directly to it, which
would result in a term with '\' as a ternary constructor. Instead we have to define
what it means to apply arguments to the start or end of pipe terms such as A\B.
The intuition seems to be clear: the start of A\B is the start of (the expansion
of) A and its end is the end of (the expansion of) B:

$$A\backslash B \overset{<}{\longmapsto} \lambda y.\lambda x.(\,[\![<]\!](\,[\![>]\!](A)(x)\,)(y),\ [\![<]\!](B)(x)\,),$$
$$A\backslash B \overset{>}{\longmapsto} \lambda y.\lambda x.(\,[\![>]\!](A)(x),\ [\![>]\!](\,[\![<]\!](B)(x)\,)(y)\,).$$

So, going back to the pipeline example,

$$[\![\mathcal{O}']\!](\ \lambda x.\ (\ [\![>]\!](\,\texttt{append(X,Y)}\,\tilde{}\,\texttt{standardize}\,)(x),\ \texttt{writeln}(x)\ )$$
$$=[\![\mathcal{O}']\!](\ \lambda x.\ (\ \lambda y.\,\lambda x.\ (\ [\![>]\!](\,\texttt{append(X,Y)}\,)(x),$$
$$[\![>]\!](\,[\![<]\!](\,\texttt{standardize}\,)(x)\,)(y)\ )(x),$$
$$\texttt{writeln}(x)\ )$$
$$=[\![\mathcal{O}']\!](\ \lambda x.\ (\ \lambda y.\,\lambda x.\ (\,\texttt{append(X,Y,}x\texttt{)},\ \texttt{standardize(}x\texttt{,}y\texttt{)}\ )(x),$$
$$\texttt{writeln}(x)\ )$$
$$=[\![\mathcal{O}']\!](\ \lambda x.\ (\ \lambda x'.\ (\,\texttt{append(X,Y,}x'\texttt{)},\ \texttt{standardize(}x'\texttt{,}x\texttt{)}\ ),\ \texttt{writeln}(x)\ )\ ),$$

and after successively expanding the environment with new variables _1 and _2 we end up executing (`append(X,Y,_1)`, `standardize(_1,_2)`, `writeln(_2)`), as expected.

The '\' operator implements the end-to-start type of pipe, which is the most practical case since in Prolog there is a justified practice of putting "output" arguments at the end and "input" arguments at the start. But this is not always so. Certain built-in predicates use the reverse convention, such as 'is', and others can be used in either fashion, such as 'name' or 'append'. So it becomes convenient to provide the other types of pipe connection, which we do with '/' for start-to-end, '\/' for end-to-end, and '/\' for start-to-start. As an example, admitting there is a predicate `prefix(L,P)` generating the prefix sublists P of L, we can define as follows a predicate for generating the "sub-atoms" whose names are prefixes of a given atom:

    sub_atom(A,S) :- name(A) /~prefix~name(S).

This is syntactic sugar for

    sub_atom(A,S) :- name(N,A), prefix(N,P), name(P,S).

The terms using the four pipe operators as main constructors are included (there are more to come) in the *pipe terms* $\mathcal{T}^P \subset \mathcal{T}^A$. The definitions of $[\![<]\!]$ and $[\![>]\!]$ given for '\' can be generalized to all pipe operators by introducing a semantic valuation $[\![\mathcal{P}]\!]$ of pipe terms as triples—the final constructor between the two component abstractions:

$$P \xmapsto{\ <\ } \lambda y.\,\lambda x.\ (\ A(x)(y)\ op\ B(x)\ ) \qquad \text{if}\quad P \xmapsto{\ \mathcal{P}\ } \langle A, op, B \rangle\,,$$
$$P \xmapsto{\ >\ } \lambda y.\,\lambda x.\ (\ A(x)\ op\ B(x)(y)\ ) \qquad \text{if}\quad P \xmapsto{\ \mathcal{P}\ } \langle A, op, B \rangle\,.$$

For this new definition the pipe variants are then formally defined as follows:

$$A\backslash B \xmapsto{\ \mathcal{P}\ } \langle\ [\![>]\!](A),\ (,),\ [\![<]\!](B)\ \rangle\,,$$
$$A/B \xmapsto{\ \mathcal{P}\ } \langle\ [\![<]\!](A),\ (,),\ [\![>]\!](B)\ \rangle\,,$$
$$A\backslash/B \xmapsto{\ \mathcal{P}\ } \langle\ [\![>]\!](A),\ (,),\ [\![>]\!](B)\ \rangle\,,$$
$$A/\backslash B \xmapsto{\ \mathcal{P}\ } \langle\ [\![<]\!](A),\ (,),\ [\![<]\!](B)\ \rangle\,.$$

The set of pipe operators at our disposal can be extended for other control constructors other than conjunction. In the variant of Prolog that we use in our motivating application [4], there is an iteration operator => with the meaning that a=>b executes b for each solution of a. It becomes very useful to define pipe syntax for =>, for example

$$A\backslash=>B \overset{\mathcal{P}}{\longmapsto} \langle \; [\![>]\!](A), \; (=>), \; [\![<]\!](B) \; \rangle \, .$$

5.3 Mode Switch

Although the introduced pipe constructors can handle cases of "non-natural" argument use in predicates, such as /\ for the first name in the last example, this is not always possible, typically when the involved predicate is used in the middle (rather than at an end-point) of a pipe. A related problem appears when we have to commit to a particular application mode in a generic piece of code, say Generate\:X, and want to pass into Generate a goal abstraction term whose missing "output" argument is at the start rather than at the end.

For increasing the usability of the operators, in such cases, we introduce a prefix operator # for switching the structural mode. Considering that all terms (# t) belong in $\mathcal{T}^{\mathcal{A}}$,

$$\# \, t \overset{\leq}{\longmapsto} [\![>]\!](t) \, ,$$
$$\# \, t \overset{\geq}{\longmapsto} [\![<]\!](t) \, .$$

For example, if we want to output an atom whose name results from stripping the last character of the name of another atom A we can invoke the pipe (name(A)~# append([_])~# name~writeln), that is syntactic sugar for (name(A,_N), append(_P,[_],_N), name(_A,_P), writeln(_A)). The structural syntax admittedly becomes messy and the advantage of conciseness is possibly outweighted by obscurity. However, one has to remember, yet again, that the true usefulness of the scheme lies in applying structural operators to variables, as in the other mismatching example above, where we can prefix the "wrong" term with # when passing it into Generate.

5.4 Meta Structures

The next subclass of $\mathcal{T}^{\mathcal{A}}$ that we consider is that of *meta* terms $\mathcal{T}^{\mathcal{M}}$, which includes those that are interpreted by $[\![\mathcal{O}]\!]$ as expressing control (and, or, if-then-else, etc.) over the execution of subterms. The practical demands of our application convinced us that the structural abstraction semantics should be lifted from atomic goals to control compositions thereof, the intuition being that $[\![\mathcal{A}]\!]$ should be pushed through the meta constructor envelope to some component subterm(s). But which? The answer depends on the meta constructor being considered.

Take the most common meta term, the conjunction (A, B), and the particular abstraction semantics $[\![<]\!]$. It is clear that $[\![<]\!]$, informally associated with "input", should be applied to A, but what about B? Our hesitation is between the asymmetrical operational reading of (,) as sequence, and its symmetrical declarative reading as conjunction. There are practical situations where each of the two readings is the most suitable. So we have not only to fine-tune the semantics to sub-classes of meta constructors, but also to provide a way to explore alternative views. The best solution appears to be to consider, by default, the largest number of subterms for which the abstraction might be meaningful, and devise an overriding mechanism for escaping application when needed.

For unary meta constructors $\mathcal{M}_1$ (assume them as prefix operators) there is clearly a unique definition:

$$op\ T \xmapsto{\mathcal{A}} \lambda m.\,\lambda x.\,(\,op\ [\![\mathcal{A}]\!](m)(T)(x)\,) \qquad \text{if} \quad op \in \mathcal{M}_1\ .$$

For the most common binary (assume infix) meta constructors we want $[\![<]\!]$ to apply to both sub-terms:

$$A\ op\ B \xmapsto{<} \lambda x.\,(\,[\![<]\!](A)(x)\ op\ [\![<]\!](B)(x)\,) \qquad \text{if} \quad op \in \mathcal{M}_2^< \ .$$

The exact extent of $\mathcal{M}_2^<$ is left open, but it includes (,), (;) and (->). If so, and assuming also that (not) $\in \mathcal{M}_1$, the invocation of the goal N:\Test with Test bound to (number, not integer), for example, will result in the execution of (number(N), not integer(N)).

We naturally envisage an analogous situation for $[\![>]\!]$,

$$A\ op\ B \xmapsto{>} \lambda x.\,(\,[\![>]\!](A)(x)\ op\ [\![>]\!](B)(x)\,) \qquad \text{if} \quad op \in \mathcal{M}_2^> \ ,$$

but the extents of $\mathcal{M}_2^>$ and $\mathcal{M}_2^<$ are different. We clearly have (;) $\in \mathcal{M}_2^>$, since the "output" solutions of the disjunction come from either branch, but for the conjunction it is unnatural to use a unified "output" of both conjuncts, so we consider that (,) $\notin \mathcal{M}_2^>$. The natural solution for (,) is to consider it included in another class $\mathcal{M}_r^>$ of binary meta constructors for which $[\![>]\!]$ works only on the right subterm:

$$A\ op\ B \xmapsto{>} \lambda x.\,(\,A\ op\ [\![>]\!](B)(x)\,) \qquad \text{if} \quad op \in \mathcal{M}_r^> \ .$$

As an example, if we call (answer(Q)\(list,sort)\display) we end up executing (answer(Q,_A),list(_A),sort(_A,_S),display(_S)).

As an example of the need for the classes $\mathcal{M}_l^<$ and $\mathcal{M}_l^>$ of left-applying binary (infix) meta constructors,

$$A\ op\ B \xmapsto{<} \lambda x.\,(\,[\![<]\!](A)(x)\ op\ B\,) \qquad \text{if} \quad op \in \mathcal{M}_l^< \ ,$$
$$A\ op\ B \xmapsto{>} \lambda x.\,(\,[\![>]\!](A)(x)\ op\ B\,) \qquad \text{if} \quad op \in \mathcal{M}_l^> \ ,$$

take the useful construction $(X\ \text{unless}\ C)$, whose solutions are those of X up to and excluding the first for which C succeeds. Indeed, for this to make sense, C has no "output" (when it succeeds, 'unless' fails) and its "input" is clearly X's "output" (the particular solutions), not its "input". Therefore, within the meta call, $[\![<]\!]$ or $[\![>]\!]$ should only be applied to X, i.e. (unless) $\in \mathcal{M}_l^< \cap \mathcal{M}_l^>$.

5.5 Escape from Application

As remarked earlier, the defined structural policies for meta constructors are sometimes in excess, and we need an overriding escape mechanism. To code this escape from application we include in $\mathcal{T}^A$ the terms $\{t\}$ (this is Prolog surface syntax for $\{\}(t)$), and define

$$\{t\} \overset{A}{\longmapsto} \lambda m.\lambda x.t\ .$$

As an example we can check that

$[\![\mathcal{O}']\!](\ \texttt{transform(X)\textasciitilde(\ \{write('Tr:\ ')\},\ writeln,\ save\ )\ )}$
$= [\![\mathcal{O}]\!](\ \texttt{transform(X,\_T),\ write('Tr:\ '),\ writeln(\_T),\ save(\_T)\ )}\ .$

5.6 Exploring the Framework with New Operators

The framework can be considered closed in the sense that the needed classes of application-specific terms $\mathcal{T}^A$ have been set, and $[\![<]\!]$ and $[\![>]\!]$ are completely defined relative to those classes. But the classes themselves can be left open, i.e. we can extend $[\![\mathcal{P}]\!]$ for new operators, or introduce them as new meta constructors in some of the corresponding classes, while extending $[\![\mathcal{R}]\!]$ for these new operators but typically through the use of old ones.

A very interesting example came up in our application that motivated this work [4]. There, we had to design a device for outputting HTML, and the desision was to use each tag either as a stand-alone atom or as a prefix operator for an attribute-specifying term, and use the colon (:) as an infix (right-associative) operator separating the (possibly attributed) tag from its (executable) argument. We can invoke, for example, the goal (`tr : td align center : X`) and thereby output something like (`<tr><td align="center">...</td></tr>`), where (...) stands for the output generated by executing `X`. For this to work, tags are defined as unary and binary predicates (to use respectively without and with attributes), and (:), when invoked as a goal, is but a syntactic variant of (\:), i.e. $[\![\mathcal{R}]\!](t{:}a) \equiv [\![\mathcal{R}]\!](t\backslash{:}a)$. But, interestingly, we want (:) to behave differently from (\:) under the abstraction semantics $[\![\mathcal{A}]\!]$, because it makes no sense to extend the binary tag calls with extra arguments. What we want is to force structural applications of extra arguments to $(t{:}a)$ to be directed to the inner subterm a. This is achieved by simply considering that $(:) \in \mathcal{M}_r^< \cap \mathcal{M}_r^>$. Thus we can have generic calls such as (`Format\:X`) and instantiate `Format` with e.g. (`center:h1:display`), resulting through the effect of (:) being in $\mathcal{M}_r^>$ in the call (`center:h1:display(X)`), which finally by virtue of $[\![\mathcal{R}]\!](t{:}a) \equiv [\![\mathcal{R}]\!](t\backslash{:}a)$ leads to calling (`center(h1(display(X)))`).

6 Implementation

The structural application and rewrite semantics can be implemented as a set of standard Prolog predicates. In fact we did so to produce the Prolog variant that is being used as the implementation platform for our large application [4].

The application of $[\![\mathcal{A}]\!]$ can be reified in the object language by the introduction of a predicate $\text{apply}(t,a,t')$ which unifies t' with the term denoted by $[\![<]\!](t)(x)$ or $[\![>]\!](t)(x)$ if a is respectively $(< x)$ or $(> x)$ with $(<)$ and $(>)$ defined as prefix operators.

The rewrite semantics is implemented with a predicate definition for each application operator, the body of the definition ultimately making use of apply. For example, we define thus the explicit application operators:[2]

```
A :~X  :-  apply_exec( X, <A ).
X \: A~:-  apply_exec( X, >A ).

apply_exec( X, A )  :-  apply( X, A )~call.
```

The main pipe operators are defined in a way that matches very closely their meta-level definitions:

```
A~B   :-  apply( A, >X, A_ ), apply( B, <X, _B ), ( A_, _B ).
A \/ B  :-  apply( A, >X, A_ ), apply( B, >X, B_ ), ( A_, B_ ).
A /~B  :-  apply( A, <X, _A ), apply( B, <X, _B ), ( _A, _B ).
A / B   :-  apply( A, <X, _A ), apply( B, >X, B_ ), ( _A, B_ ).
```

Notice that apply_exec is not used in this case for efficiency reasons: apply is deterministic whereas A_, _B, etc. may not be. Another crucial point to note is that the operational semantics of Prolog implicitly does for predicate definitions what was described as the scoping treatment of λ-terms. In fact we defined $A\backslash B \overset{\mathcal{R}}{\longmapsto} \lambda x.(\ [\![>]\!](A)(x),\ [\![<]\!](B)(x)\ )$ and said that such a λ-term is evaluated by applying it to a new variable with which the environment is extended. This is precisely what happens with the corresponding clause invocation, that uses a renamed version of the clause in the environment extended with fresh variables.

Other pipes are defined in the same vein, e.g.

```
A \=> B  :-  apply( A, >X, A_ ), apply( B, <X, _B ), ( A_ => _B ).
```

Let us now turn our attention to the definition of apply. We basically have to define clauses case by case, for each subclass of application-specific terms. To apply the last clauses (the default case) only to other terms, we have to guard each previous specific clause with a cut:[3]

```
apply( TX, _Y, TXY ) :- explicit( TX, T, X ),
                        !, apply2( _Y, T, X, TXY ).
apply( P , _Y, A_B ) :- pipe( P, A,B, A_,_B, A_B ),
                        !, apply_pipe( _Y, A,B, A_,_B ).
apply( #T, _X,  TX ) :- !, switch_apply( _X, T, TX ).
```

---

[2] Notice the use of pipe syntax in the last definition.

[3] In the actual Prolog variant that we designed and use there is a structural alternative to cut with compositional semantics, but this is a matter for describing in other forthcoming papers.

```
apply( M , _X,   MX )  :- meta( M, MX, L ),
                                !, meta_apply( L, X, _M ).
apply({T},  _,   T  )  :- !.   % escape
apply( T , <X, _T  )  :- start_arg( T, X, _P ).
apply( T , >X,   T_ )  :-    end_arg( T, X, P_ ).
```

The `explicit` predicate recognizes an explicit application term and splits it in two components.

```
explicit( T \: X, > T, X )  :- !.
explicit( X :~T, < T, X )  :- !.
```

In this case we use the < and > prefixes to pass the structural mode along with the term T to be expanded rather than with the argument X to be applied (contrary to `apply`), for use in `apply2`:

```
apply2( <Y, <T, X, __T )  :- apply(T,<X,_T), apply(_T,<Y,__T).
apply2( <Y, >T, X, _T_ )  :- apply(T,>X,T_), apply(T_,<Y,_T_).
apply2( >Y, <T, X, _T_ )  :- apply(T,<X,_T), apply(_T,>Y,_T_).
apply2( >Y, >T, X, T__ )  :- apply(T,<X,T_), apply(T_,>X,T__).
```

Notice that the external argument Y of the original `apply` is always applied after the internal X, as required.

The `pipe` predicate implements $[\![\mathcal{P}]\!]$. It recognizes and splits pipe terms into the pair of left and right components under the respective mode operator, and also returns a reification of the final λ-abstraction in the form of a pair of fresh variables (again the effect of clause renaming) and the constructed term where they occur. We factor the definitions according to the final constructor.

```
pipe( P, A,B, A_,_B, (A_, _B) )  :- sequence_pipe( P, A, B ), !.
pipe( P, A,B, A_,_B, (A_=>_B) )  :- iterator_pipe( P, A, B ), !.

sequence_pipe( A \B, >A, <B ).
sequence_pipe( A\/B, >A, >B ).
sequence_pipe( A/\B, <A, <B ).
sequence_pipe( A/ B, <A, >B ).

iterator_pipe( A \=>B, >A, <B ).
```

The predicate `apply_pipe` implements the generic definitions of $[\![<]\!]$ and $[\![>]\!]$ for pipes:

```
apply_pipe( <Y, A,B, A_,_B )  :- apply2(<Y,A,X,A_), apply1(B,X,_B).
apply_pipe( >Y, A,B, A_,_B )  :- apply2(>Y,B,X,_B), apply1(A,X,A_).
```

Notice yet again the effect of clause renaming on the local variable X to implement the λ-scoping of the meta-level definitions.

The predicate `apply1` is a version of `apply` with the mode coded along with the term to be expanded rather than with the argument:

```
apply1( <T, X, _T ) :- apply( T, <X, _T ).
apply1( >T, X, T_ ) :- apply( T, >X, T_ ).
```

The switching is as expected:

```
switch_apply( <X, T, T_ ) :- apply( T, >X, T_ ).
switch_apply( >X, T, _T ) :- apply( T, <X, _T ).
```

The **meta** predicate delivers, for each given meta term, an analogous skeleton term with variable components and a list of given-new component pairs:

```
meta( (A,B), (X,Y), [ A-X, B-Y ] ).
meta( (A:B), (X:Y), [ A-X, B-Y ] ).
meta( not A, not X, [ A-X      ] ).
```

Then **meta_apply** checks the meta constructor classes and performs the corresponding positional applications or else leaves the components unchanged:

```
meta_apply( [ T-TX      ], _X, _ ) :- apply( T, _X, TX ).
meta_apply( [ A-AX, B-BX ], _X, M ) :- ( meta_l( M, _X )
                                         -> apply( A, _X, AX )
                                         ;  A = AX ),
                                       ( meta_r( M, _X )
                                         -> apply( B, _X, BX )
                                         ;  B = BX ).
```

We define the meta constructor classes by specifying which ones have left and right application of which modes:

```
meta_l( (_,_), <_ ).

meta_r( (_,_), _ ).
meta_r( (_:_), _ ).
```

Finally, we have only to define the basic extension operations `start_arg` and `end_arg`. Although these are candidates for an efficient built-in implementation, we can easily define them through the built-in structural decomposition predicate:

```
start_arg( T, X, TX ) :- T  =.. [ F | A~], _A = [ X | A ],
                         TX =.. [ F | _A ].

  end_arg( T, X, TX ) :- T  =.. [ F | A~], append( A, [X], A_ ),
                         TX =.. [ F | A_ ].
```

7 Applicability — Final Remarks

The mechanisms described here are being used to good effect in a large application [4]. It was in fact the experience gained while developing the first prototype that convinced us of the need and usefulness of such a scheme. In this type of application there is a tremendous gain in being able to write very generic code, and one ends up devising a lot of implicit abstractions, coded as terms that are passed around and applied for both generation or wrapping of items. Examples are partial query expressions that are applied to specific parameters to get more restricted queries, that are then piped through appropriate constructors to get answers from the database, which are further piped into display procedures, and so on.

7.1 Generators

An ubiquitous feature of our generic code is the use of generators, i.e. terms that are later extended with an extra argument before being called as goals, the (free) argument being instantiated with the solutions. A typical example is the following procedure for filling HTML tables (we omit some extra parameter details):

```
fill_table(  C ) :- table : fill_rows( C ).
fill_rows(   C ) :- C \=> fill_row.
fill_row(    C ) :- tr : fill_colums( C ).
fill_colums( C ) :- C \=> fill_column.
fill_colum(  C ) :- td : C.
```

The second clause shows that the argument of `fill_table` is expected to be a generator, i.e. a term interpreted (by the pipe semantics) as the abstraction of a goal with an extra "output" argument, whose solutions are passed to `fill_row`. A typical use is the generation of answers for a database query. The basic binary predicate for doing this is (`<?`), so we may for example call (`<? Query`) `:~fill_table`, causing the term (`<? Query`) to be passed as the argument of `fill_rows`, whose body is (dynamically) rewritten into the goal (`Query <? Answer`) `=> fill_row( Answer )`. Each solution of this iterator instantiates `Answer`, which is also expected to be a generator, to be used in the definition of `fill_columns`. Now the practical representation of an answer tuple is a list of values, so we want a list to represent an implicit abstraction of a generator of its members. This is easily achieved. Since the list constructor is (`.`) we define a ternary predicate (`.`) "outputting" the list members:

```
.( X, _, X ).
.( _, L, X )  :-  X in L.
```

Now an answer such as e.g. `[1,2,3]` gives rise in the body of `fill_columns` to the goal `.(1,[2,3],X) => fill_column(X)`, triggering as wanted the calls `fill_column(1)`, `fill_column(2)` and `fill_column(3)`.

In short, we can use as generators either the abstractions of goals that will generate the solutions, or a ready-made solution list. This promotes the use of generators and gives us flexibility in deciding how and when to generate solutions. We can actually mix the two modes, due to the structural semantics of meta constructors, e.g. a generator ([1,2];g) will bind an "output" X successively with 1, 2 and the solutions of g(X).

7.2   Programmable Rewrite — Equating Abstractions

We have defined in this paper the structural semantics via program-independent meta-level functional definitions. But the fact that the implementation is done in Prolog offers the possibility of opening up the structural rewrite semantics to user-programmable definitions. This window of programmability must of course be restricted so as not to jeopardize the predefined semantics. The major need that we felt in our large application was the ability to code in atomic terms certain non-atomic structural abstractions, i.e. have the equivalent of predicate definitions for terms used as implicit structural abstractions.

The vehicle for carrying this out is the structural operator $(:)$. A goal $t{:}a$ applies an environment t (HTML tags are just examples) to some element a, and what is offered is the possibility of (recursively) equating environments through clauses for a binary predicate $(:=:)$, as patent in the definition below:

```
Env : X   :-  Env :=: E, !,   % equated
              E : X.
Env : X   :-  Env \: X.       % literal
```

Thus, for example, we can define

```
background( Pad, Color )   :=:   table(0,0,Pad,Color) : tr : td.
```

where the 4-argument table term is assumed to be also equated.

References

[1] Weidong Chen, Michael Kifer, and David S. Warren. HiLog: a foundation for higher-order logic programming. *The Journal of Logic Programming*, 15(3):187–230, 1993. 279

[2] Dale A. Miller and Gopalan Nadathur. Higher-order logic programming. In G. Goos and J. Hartmanis, editors, *Third International Conference on Logic Programming, Proceedings*, pages 448–462. Springer, 1986. 276, 277

[3] Gopalan Nadathur and Dale A. Miller. An overview of λPROLOG. In Robert A. Kowalski and Kenneth A. Bowen, editors, *Fifth International Conference on Logic Programming, Proceedings*, volume 2, pages 810–827. MIT Press, 1988. 276, 277

[4] António Porto. Towards fully integrated information services. In Lígia Maria Ribeiro and José Marques dos Santos, editors, *The Changing Universities: The Challenge of New Technologies, Eunis 2002, The 8th International Conference of European University Information Systems, Proceedings*, pages 319–324. FEUP edições, University of Porto, Portugal, 2002. 275, 276, 277, 282, 284, 288

[5] D. H. Warren. Higher-order extensions to PROLOG: are they needed? In J.E. Hayes, Donald Michie, and Y-H. Pao, editors, *Machine Intelligence 10*, pages 441–454. Ellis Horwood, 1982. 275, 276, 277

VMλ: A Functional Calculus for Scientific Discovery

Eijiro Sumii[1] and Hideo Bannai[2]

[1] Department of Computer Science
Graduate School of Information Science and Technology, University of Tokyo
sumii@yl.is.s.u-tokyo.ac.jp
[2] Laboratory of DNA Information Analysis, Human Genome Center
Institute of Medical Science, University of Tokyo
bannai@ims.u-tokyo.ac.jp

Abstract. We present VMλ, a formalization and implementation of the functional language VML.

VML is a programming language proposed by discovery scientists for the purpose of assisting the process of knowledge discovery. It is a non-trivial extension of ML with *hypothetical views*. Operationally, a hypothetical view is a value with a representation that indicates how the value was created. The notion of hypothetical views has already been successful in the domain of genome analysis, and known to be useful in the process of knowledge discovery. However, VML as a programming language was only informally defined in English prose, and indeed found problematic both in theory and in practice. Thus, a proper definition and implementation of VML with formal foundations would be of great help to discovery science and hence corresponding domain sciences.

This paper gives a solid foundation of VML by extending the standard simply typed call-by-value λ-calculus. Although this extension, VMλ, is simple and clear, its design required much care to find and fix problems of the original VML. We also present a real implementation of VMλ, written in Camlp4 as a conservative translator into OCaml. This implementation makes extensive use of labeled arguments and polymorphic variants – two advanced features of OCaml that originate in OLabl.

1 Introduction

Functional Programming for Scientific Discovery: Approaches and Problems. Higher-order functional programming languages are known to be good for complex applications such as theorem proving, artificial intelligence, program generation, database querying, and genome analysis [29, 13, 27, 23, 24, 12]. Given the success of functional languages in these domains, it is natural to consider the use of functional languages in the field of *discovery science* [1, 2, 3], an area of information science that aims to develop systematic methods of knowledge discovery. Indeed, the features of functional languages—in particular, first-class functions—seem to help much to create and evaluate scientific hypotheses.

Z. Hu and M. Rodríguez-Artalejo (Eds.): FLOPS 2002, LNCS 2441, pp. 290–304, 2002.
© Springer-Verlag Berlin Heidelberg 2002

For instance, suppose that we have the data of some people's heights and weights, and would like to find the relationship between each person's height and weight. The data can be represented by a list of pairs of two floating-point numbers, one for height in centimeters and the other for weight in kilograms. (For the sake of concreteness, we adopt OCaml-like syntax [16]. Readers who are familiar with other functional languages should not have much difficulty in understanding it.)

```
# let data =
    [(175.4, 73.9); (167.6, 66.1); (180.8, 81.2); ...] ;;
val data : (float * float) list =
    [(175.4, 73.9); (167.6, 66.1); (180.8, 81.2); ...]
```

A hypothesis for explaining this data can be modeled by a function that estimates each person's weight from the person's height, for example by subtracting 100. (The operator -. is the OCaml syntax of subtraction for floating-point numbers.)

```
# let simple_hypothesis h = h -. 100.0 ;;
val simple_hypothesis : float -> float = <fun>
```

Then, the appropriateness of this hypothesis can be evaluated by some statistical method implemented by a higher-order function that takes the hypothesis as an argument.

```
# (* fitness : (float -> float) ->
        (float * float) list -> float *)
  fitness simple_hypothesis data ;; (* 1.0 means a perfect fit *)
- : float = 0.81
```

Of course, there may well be other functions that fit the data better, for example:

```
# fitness (fun h -> h -. 101.0) data ;;
- : float = 0.83
```

Rather than trying the infinite possibilities of such functions one by one, it is nicer to have another higher-order function that returns the function (of a certain class) that fits the data best.

```
# let create_hypothesis data =
    let (a, b) = compute such a and b that f(x) = ax + b is
                  the affine function f that fits the data best in
    fun h -> a *. h +. b ;;
val create_hypothesis :
    (float * float) list -> float -> float = <fun>
```

Then, by using this hypothesis-creating function, we can automatically obtain a hypothesis that explains the data well.

```
# let good_hypothesis = create_hypothesis data ;;
val good_hypothesis : float -> float = <fun>
# fitness good_hypothesis data ;;
- : float = 0.95
```

Or can we? Not really – we cannot actually see what the function *is*, because we have access only to the *value* of the function. That is, we have no access to the *representation* of the hypothesis. Thus, there is no way for the user to interpret the meaning of this hypothesis and evaluate it under domain experience. This significant limitation makes the present system far less useful for knowledge discovery.

An obvious solution for this problem is to have the user modify the program and manipulate the representation by hand. For example, the hypothesis-creating function above can be rewritten as

```
# let create_hypothesis data =
    let (a, b) = ... in ((fun h -> a *. h +. b), (a, b)) ;;
val create_hypothesis : (float * float) list ->
    (float -> float) * (float * float) = <fun>
```

so that it returns the *pair* of the function and its parameters. In real programs, however, this approach is much more troublesome and error-prone than it may seem: the user must take care not to confuse the representations of a class of functions with those of another; furthermore, in typed languages, some trick (e.g., to use exceptions as an extensible data type) is necessary to unify the types of functions whose values have the same type but whose representations may have different types. These difficulties spoil the utility and simplicity of functional languages in this application.

Another naive solution is to remember or reconstruct the *source code* of a function, that is, taking the source code as the representation of a hypothesis. However, doing so is inefficient or even impossible (e.g., for preserving type abstraction) in many languages, though it is possible in a few situations (e.g., by *get-lambda-expression* in certain dialects of Lisp or by type-directed partial evaluation [7, 6]). Furthermore, the source code of functions can be rather complex and therefore is not very useful as representation of hypotheses. In addition, a similar problem arises in first-order values as well: in knowledge discovery, it is often necessary to know not only a value itself but also *how* the value was computed; however, remembering the history of computation is even more expensive than having the source code of a function.

VML: A Functional Language with Hypothetical Views. To address the issues above, a group of discovery scientists have recently proposed a functional language VML [4], an extension of ML with *hypothetical views* or just *views* in short. (Note that they are different from views for abstract data types [28].) Intuitively, a view is the pair of a value and its representation that remembers how the value was computed. Views are constructed by defining a *view constructor* via the keyword `view` and by applying the view constructor to an argument. A view thus constructed can then be destructed by pattern matching via the keyword `vmatch`.

For instance, in the example above, let us define the hypotheses as views rather than as ordinary functions. (For the sake of clarity, we use a little different syntax and semantics from the original VML.)

```
# view AffineFun(a, b) = fun h -> a *. h +. b ;;
view AffineFun of float * float : float -> float
```
The view constructor `AffineFun` takes a pair of two floating-point numbers a and b, and returns a function of type `float -> float` with the representation `AffineFun(a, b)` of the function.
```
# AffineFun(1.0, -100.0) ;;
- : (float -> float) view = <fun> as AffineFun(1.0, -100.0)
```
By using this view constructor, the hypothesis-creating function above can be rewritten as:
```
# let create_hypothesis data =
    let (a, b) = ... in AffineFun(a, b) ;;
val create_hypothesis :
  (float * float) list -> (float -> float) view = <fun>
```
Then, by applying this view-returning function and by pattern-matching the returned view, we can finally see what the automatically obtained good hypothesis is.
```
# let good_hypothesis = create_hypothesis data ;;
- : (float -> float) view = <fun> as AffineFun(1.03, -102.8)
# vmatch good_hypothesis with AffineFun(a, b) -> (a, b) ;;
- : float * float = (1.03, -102.8)
```
From the data, the hypothesis-creating function found the function $f(x) = 1.03x - 102.8$ to be the best affine function f that estimates each person's weight from his/her height. Of course, it is also possible to use the value part of the view (i.e., the function `fun h -> 1.03 *. h -. 102.8`) as well as its representation part.
```
# (valof good_hypothesis) 175.4 ;;
- : float = 77.862
```

Our Contributions. The notion of views itself has already been proved to be useful by several applications in the domain of genome analysis [5, 17, 18, 19]. However, the semantics and even the syntax of VML were only informally presented in English prose [4] and theoretically unclear as well as practically problematic. As a result, VML was never successfully implemented.

This paper formalizes the syntax, the type system, and the dynamic semantics of VML by extending the standard simply typed call-by-value λ-calculus. This formalization, VMλ, reveals and fixes problems in the original VML. Furthermore, we give a translation of VMλ into ordinary OCaml without views. The translation is fully implemented in Camlp4 [8] and is *conservative* – that is, features of the original OCaml are available for free.

2   Simple VMλ

First, we present the simplest version of VMλ, where every view constructor takes just one argument. Later in the next section, we will present a more sophisticated version of VMλ, where view constructors may take any number of arguments in any order, with partial application of view constructors supported as well as pattern matching against such partially applied view constructors.

2.1 Syntax and Informal Semantics

The syntax of VMλ is given as follows:

$$M ::= x \mid \lambda x.\, M \mid M_1 M_2 \mid \texttt{view } V\{x\} = M_1 \texttt{ in } M_2 \mid V \mid M_1\{M_2\}$$
$$\mid \texttt{vmatch } M_1 \texttt{ with } V\{x\} \Rightarrow M_2 \texttt{ else } M_3 \mid \texttt{valof } M$$

It assumes two countably infinite disjoint sets Var of variables x, y, z, ... and $Name$ of view constructors V, W, ... In addition to standard λ-terms, there are five kinds of terms involving views. Recall that a view is the pair of a value v_1 and its representation $V\{v_2\}$.

- A view definition $\texttt{view } V\{x\} = M_1 \texttt{ in } M_2$ first defines the view constructor V and then evaluates the body M_2, where the view constructor V takes an argument v, evaluates the term M_1 with the variable x bound to the value v, and returns the result with its representation $V\{v\}$. The name V is called *bound* in the term M_2 and can be implicitly renamed by α-conversion.
- A view constructor V refers to its own definition as above.
- A view application $M_1\{M_2\}$ first evaluates the term M_1 to a view constructor and the term M_2 to a value v, and then applies the view constructor to the argument v.
- A view matching $\texttt{vmatch } M_1 \texttt{ with } V\{x\} \Rightarrow M_2 \texttt{ else } M_3$ first evaluates the term M_1 to a view and then matches its representation part $W\{v\}$ against the pattern $V\{x\}$. If $V = W$, then the term M_2 is evaluated with the variable x bound to the value v. Otherwise, the term M_3 is evaluated.
- A view destruction $\texttt{valof } M$ evaluates the term M to a view and extracts its value part v.

For example, assuming primitives for integers and tuples, the term

$$\texttt{view } V\{x\} = x + 1 \texttt{ in let } v = V\{2\} \texttt{ in}$$
$$\langle \texttt{valof } v, \texttt{vmatch } v \texttt{ with } V\{y\} \Rightarrow y \texttt{ else } -1 \rangle$$

evaluates to the tuple $\langle 3, 2 \rangle$. Here, $\texttt{let } x = M_1 \texttt{ in } M_2$ is the syntax sugar of $(\lambda x.\, M_2) M_1$.

2.2 Operational Semantics

The semantics of VMλ is formalized by the *evaluation* relation $\mathcal{E} \vdash M \Downarrow v$, where v is a *value* denoting the result of evaluation and $\mathcal{E}$ is an *environment* mapping free variables (and free view constructors) of M to their values. Intuitively, the relation $\mathcal{E} \vdash M \Downarrow v$ means that the term M evaluates to the value v under the environment $\mathcal{E}$. Formally, $\mathcal{E} \vdash M \Downarrow v$ is the least relation over $\mathcal{E}$, M, and v that satisfies the rules in Figure 1.

A value v is either a closure $\langle \mathcal{E}; \lambda x.\, M \rangle$ of an ordinary function $\lambda x.\, M$, a closure $\langle \mathcal{E}; V\{x\} = M \rangle$ of a view constructor V defined as $V\{x\} = M$, or a view $V\{v_1\} = v_2$ of a value v_2 represented as $V\{v_1\}$.

The rules (E-Var), (E-Lam), and (E-FApp) are standard. The other rules formalize the intuitive semantics above of terms involving views. In rule (E-VDef),

$$v ::= \langle \mathcal{E}; \lambda x. M \rangle \mid \langle \mathcal{E}; V\{x\} = M \rangle \mid V\{v_1\} = v_2$$

$$\frac{V' \text{ fresh} \quad \mathcal{E}, V \mapsto \langle \mathcal{E}; V'\{x\} = M_1 \rangle \vdash M_2 \Downarrow v}{\mathcal{E} \vdash \text{view } V\{x\} = M_1 \text{ in } M_2 \Downarrow v} \text{(E-VDef)}$$

$$\frac{\mathcal{E} \vdash M_1 \Downarrow \langle \mathcal{E}'; V\{x\} = M' \rangle \quad \mathcal{E} \vdash M_2 \Downarrow v \quad \mathcal{E}', x \mapsto v \vdash M' \Downarrow v'}{\mathcal{E} \vdash M_1\{M_2\} \Downarrow V\{v\} = v'} \text{(E-VApp)}$$

$$\frac{\mathcal{E}(V) = \langle \_; V'\{\_\} = \_ \rangle \quad \mathcal{E} \vdash M_1 \Downarrow V'\{v'\} = \_ \quad \mathcal{E}, x \mapsto v' \vdash M_2 \Downarrow v}{\mathcal{E} \vdash \text{vmatch } M_1 \text{ with } V\{x\} \Rightarrow M_2 \text{ else } M_3 \Downarrow v} \text{(E-VMatch-Succ)}$$

$$\frac{\mathcal{E}(V) = \langle \_; V'\{\_\} = \_ \rangle \quad \mathcal{E} \vdash M_1 \Downarrow W\{\_\} = \_ \quad W \neq V' \quad \mathcal{E} \vdash M_3 \Downarrow v}{\mathcal{E} \vdash \text{vmatch } M_1 \text{ with } V\{x\} \Rightarrow M_2 \text{ else } M_3 \Downarrow v} \text{(E-VMatch-Fail)}$$

$$\frac{\mathcal{E}(V) = v}{\mathcal{E} \vdash V \Downarrow v} \text{(E-VCon)} \qquad \frac{\mathcal{E} \vdash M \Downarrow \_\{\_\} = v}{\mathcal{E} \vdash \text{valof } M \Downarrow v} \text{(E-ValOf)}$$

Fig. 1. Semantics of Simple VMλ (excerpt)

the premise that V is bound to a closure of fresh V' reflects the fact that view constructors are treated as *generative* because they are α-convertible but may escape their syntactic scopes. Accordingly, in the rules (E-VMatch-Succ) and (E-VMatch-Fail), this freshly generated V' is looked up in $\mathcal{E}$ by V and used for the pattern matching. Here, _ denotes the "don't-care" meta-variable.

For example, assuming primitives for integers and booleans, let M_1 be the term view $V\{x\} = $ if x then 1 else 0 in $V(\text{true})$. Then, under the empty environment, M_1 evaluates to the value $V'\{\text{true}\} = 1$ for a fresh view constructor V'. That is, $\vdash M_1 \Downarrow V'\{\text{true}\} = 1$. Let furthermore M_2 be the term view $V\{y\} = y + 1$ in vmatch M_1 with $V\{z\} \Rightarrow z - 2$ else -1. Since the V' above is fresh, the pattern matching in this term fails and M_2 evaluates to the integer -1 rather than causing the runtime type error $\text{true} - 2$.

2.3 Type System

The type system of VMλ, given in Figure 2, is an extension of the simple type system of the standard λ-calculus. In addition to standard types, there are two kinds of types involving views.

- A view constructor type $\text{view}\{\tau_1\}\tau_2$ denotes the type of a view constructor that takes an argument of type τ_1 and returns the view for a value of type τ_2.
- A view type $\text{view}\{\}\tau$ denotes the type of a view for a value of type τ.

Thus, in this version of VMλ, a view constructor type $\text{view}\{\tau_1\}\tau_2$ is actually equivalent to the function type $\tau_1 \rightarrow \text{view}\{\}\tau_2$. However, these types are distinguished for the sake of presentation consistent with the next section.

$$\tau ::= b \mid \tau_1 \rightarrow \tau_2 \mid \mathtt{view}\{\tau_1\}\tau_2 \mid \mathtt{view}\{\}\tau$$

$$\frac{\Gamma, x : \tau \vdash M_1 : \tau_1 \quad \Gamma, V : \mathtt{view}\{\tau\}\tau_1 \vdash M_2 : \tau_2}{\Gamma \vdash \mathtt{view}\ V\{x\} = M_1\ \mathtt{in}\ M_2 : \tau_2}\text{(T-VDef)} \qquad \frac{\Gamma(V) = \tau}{\Gamma \vdash V : \tau}\text{(T-VCon)}$$

$$\frac{\Gamma \vdash M_1 : \mathtt{view}\{\tau\}\tau' \quad \Gamma \vdash M_2 : \tau}{\Gamma \vdash M_1\{M_2\} : \mathtt{view}\{\}\tau'}\text{(T-VApp)} \qquad \frac{\Gamma \vdash M : \mathtt{view}\{\}\tau}{\Gamma \vdash \mathtt{valof}\ M : \tau}\text{(T-ValOf)}$$

$$\frac{\Gamma(V) = \mathtt{view}\{\tau\}\tau_1 \quad \Gamma \vdash M_1 : \mathtt{view}\{\}\tau_1 \quad \Gamma, x : \tau \vdash M_2 : \tau_2 \quad \Gamma \vdash M_3 : \tau_2}{\Gamma \vdash \mathtt{vmatch}\ M_1\ \mathtt{with}\ V\{x\} \Rightarrow M_2\ \mathtt{else}\ M_3 : \tau_2}\text{(T-VMatch)}$$

Fig. 2. Type System of Simple VMλ (excerpt)

The typing rules are straightforward, given the semantics of VMλ and the meanings of types above. Thanks to the generativity of view constructors, there is no worry about cases where two definitions of a syntactically identical view constructor expect different types of argument, as in the example above.

The soundness of this type system is formally proved as follows. First, the typing rules are naturally extended for values and environments. Next, the relation $\mathcal{E} \vdash M \Downarrow error$, denoting a runtime error in the evaluation of the term M under the environment $\mathcal{E}$, is defined. (In the present formalization, we could actually define $\mathcal{E} \vdash M \Downarrow error$ just as "there exists no such v that $e \vdash M \Downarrow v$." However, this approach does not scale to cases where evaluation may diverge, for example because of recursion.) Then, the type soundness is stated as follows.

Theorem 1 (Type Soundness). *If $\Gamma \vdash M : \tau$ and $\Gamma \vdash \mathcal{E}$, then $\mathcal{E} \vdash M \not\Downarrow$ error. Furthermore, if $\mathcal{E} \vdash M \Downarrow v$, then $\Gamma, \Gamma' \vdash v : \tau$ for some Γ' with $dom(\Gamma) \cap dom(\Gamma') = \emptyset$.*

Further details of the proof are found in the full version [25] of this paper.

3   VMλabl: An Extension of Simple VMλ with Labeled Arguments

In this section, we present VMλabl, a more sophisticated version of VMλ extended with *labeled arguments* [11].

Partial application of functions is a convenient feature of functional languages: it allows one to create a special function by fixing part of the arguments of a generic function, without having to name and define the special function explicitly and separately; furthermore, λ-abstraction enables giving any (rather than only the first) of the arguments of a function in advance, for example like $\lambda x.\ \lambda z.\ f(x, 123, z)$.

Unfortunately, however, in the simple VMλ in the previous section, this convenient feature is not available for views: even if $V\{(x, 123, z)\}$ is a view,

$\lambda x. \lambda z. V\{(x, 123, z)\}$ is not – it is a mere ordinary function that does not have a representation and cannot be pattern matched.

To overcome this limitation, the original VML allowed pattern matching over λ-abstracted views [4], like:

```
# vmatch (fun x -> fun z -> V(x, 123, z)) with V(_, y, _) -> y
  - : int = 123
```

However, it is rather problematic both theoretically and practically, because it requires evaluation inside functions and breaks the standard weak normalization strategy of most functional languages. For instance, pattern-matching $\lambda x. \lambda z. V\{(x, g(456), z)\}$ against $V(\_, y, \_)$ forces the quite unnatural evaluation of $g(456)$, which may diverge, have a side effect, or take a long time. (It may take more than an hour or even a week if the data is large.)

We solve the problems above by allowing partial and commutative application of view constructors via *labeled arguments* [11]. For this purpose, we define VMλabl, an extension of VMλ with labeled arguments of view constructors. With this extension, the example above can be rewritten like vmatch $V\{l_2 = g(456)\}$ with $V\{l_2 = y\} \Rightarrow y$, in which it is natural to evaluate $g(456)$.

3.1   Syntax

The syntax of VMλabl is given as follows:

$$M ::= \ldots \mid \texttt{view } V\{l^+ = x^+\} = M_1 \texttt{ in } M_2 \mid M_1\{l^+ = M_2^+\}$$
$$\mid \texttt{vmatch } M_1 \texttt{ with } V\{l^* = x^*\} \Rightarrow M_2 \texttt{ else } M_3$$

It is the same as VMλ except for three kinds of terms, namely, view definition, view application, and view matching, where the arguments of view constructors are *labeled*. We assume yet another countably infinite set *Lab* of labels $l, m, n, \ldots,$ distinct from variables and view constructors. The order of labeled arguments does not matter: for example, $\{l_1 = M_1, l_2 = M_2\}$ is the same as $\{l_2 = M_2, l_1 = M_1\}$.

For the sake of brevity, we use $+$ and $*$ to abbreviate sequences: X^+ denotes $X_1, \ldots, X_n$ where $n > 0$; X^* denotes $X_1, \ldots, X_n$ where $n \geq 0$ (i.e., the sequence may be empty). The notations X^+ *op* Y^+ and X^* *op* Y^* mean the sequence X_1 *op* $Y_1, \ldots, X_n$ *op* Y_n for any binary operator *op*. For example, $\{l^+ = M^+\}$ means $\{l_1 = M_1, \ldots, l_n = M_n\}$ where $n > 0$.

Also, for the sake of syntactic convenience, the view application $V\{l^+ = v^+\}$ can take more than one argument at a time. It is semantically equivalent to the sequence of view applications $V\{l_1 = v_1\} \ldots \{l_n = v_n\}$.

3.2   Semantics

The evaluation semantics of VMλabl is given in Figure 3. Its difference from the semantics of the simple VMλ is that view constructors may be partially applied, and also, that their arguments are labeled. The result of the partial application

$$v ::= \ldots \mid \langle \mathcal{E}; V\{l^* = v^*, m^+ = x^+\} = M \rangle \mid V\{l^+ = v^+\} = v$$

$$\frac{V' \text{ fresh} \quad \mathcal{E}, V \mapsto \langle \mathcal{E}; V'\{l^+ = x^+\} = M_1 \rangle \vdash M_2 \Downarrow v}{\mathcal{E} \vdash \texttt{view } V\{l^+ = x^+\} = M_1 \texttt{ in } M_2 \Downarrow v} \text{(E-VDef)}$$

$$\frac{\mathcal{E} \vdash M_1 \Downarrow \langle \mathcal{E}'; V\{l_1^* = v_1^*, l_2^+ = x^+, l_3^+ = y^+\} = M \rangle \quad \mathcal{E} \vdash M_2^+ \Downarrow v_2^+}{\begin{array}{c} \mathcal{E} \vdash M_1\{l_2^+ = M_2^+\} \Downarrow \\ \langle \mathcal{E}', x^+ \mapsto v_2^+; V\{l_1^* = v_1^*, l_2^+ = v_2^+, l_3^+ = y^+\} = M \rangle \end{array}} \text{(E-VApp-Part)}$$

$$\frac{\begin{array}{c} \mathcal{E} \vdash M_1 \Downarrow \langle \mathcal{E}'; V\{l_1^* = v_1^*, l_2^+ = x^+\} = M \rangle \\ \mathcal{E} \vdash M_2^+ \Downarrow v_2^+ \quad \mathcal{E}', x^+ \mapsto v_2^+ \vdash M \Downarrow v \end{array}}{\mathcal{E} \vdash M_1\{l_2^+ = M_2^+\} \Downarrow V\{l_1^* = v_1^*, l_2^+ = v_2^+\} = v} \text{(E-VApp-Full)}$$

$$\frac{\begin{array}{c} \mathcal{E} \vdash M_1 \Downarrow \langle \_; V'\{l^* = v^*, m^+ = y^+\} = \_ \rangle \\ \mathcal{E}(V) = \langle \_; V'\{\ldots\} = \_ \rangle \quad \mathcal{E}, x^* \mapsto v^* \vdash M_2 \Downarrow v \end{array}}{\mathcal{E} \vdash \texttt{vmatch } M_1 \texttt{ with } V\{l^* = x^*\} \Rightarrow M_2 \texttt{ else } M_3 \Downarrow v} \text{(E-VMatch-Succ-Part)}$$

$$\frac{\begin{array}{c} \mathcal{E} \vdash M_1 \Downarrow \langle \_; V'\{\ldots\} = \_ \rangle \quad \mathcal{E}(V) = \langle \_; W\{\ldots\} = \_ \rangle \\ W \neq V' \quad \mathcal{E} \vdash M_3 \Downarrow v \end{array}}{\mathcal{E} \vdash \texttt{vmatch } M_1 \texttt{ with } V\{l^* = x^*\} \Rightarrow M_2 \texttt{ else } M_3 \Downarrow v} \text{(E-VMatch-Fail-Part)}$$

$$\frac{\begin{array}{c} \mathcal{E} \vdash M_1 \Downarrow V'\{l^+ = v^+\} = \_ \quad \mathcal{E}(V) = \langle \_; V'\{\ldots\} = \_ \rangle \\ \mathcal{E}, x^+ \mapsto v^+ \vdash M_2 \Downarrow v \end{array}}{\mathcal{E} \vdash \texttt{vmatch } M_1 \texttt{ with } V\{l^+ = x^+\} \Rightarrow M_2 \texttt{ else } M_3 \Downarrow v} \text{(E-VMatch-Succ-Full)}$$

$$\frac{\begin{array}{c} \mathcal{E} \vdash M_1 \Downarrow V'\{\ldots\} = \_ \quad \mathcal{E}(V) = \langle \_; W\{\ldots\} = \_ \rangle \\ W \neq V' \quad \mathcal{E} \vdash M_3 \Downarrow v \end{array}}{\mathcal{E} \vdash \texttt{vmatch } M_1 \texttt{ with } V\{l^+ = x^+\} \Rightarrow M_2 \texttt{ else } M_3 \Downarrow v} \text{(E-VMatch-Fail-Full)}$$

Fig. 3. Semantics of VMλabl

$V\{l^+ = v^+\}$ of a view constructor defined as $V\{l^+ = y^+, m^+ = x^+\} = M$ is written $V\{l^+ = v^+, m^+ = x^+\} = M$. Note that the labels m^+ of the yet unknown arguments x^+ are non-empty, which makes this application partial. The body M is evaluated when all of the arguments are given, that is, when the view constructor V is fully applied. Thus, the rules (E-VApp), (E-VMatch-Succ) and (E-VMatch-Fail) are divided into two cases (...-Part) and (...-Full) each, according to whether the view constructor of concern is partially applied (or not applied at all) or fully applied.

3.3   Type System

Having introduced partial application of view constructors, types in VMλabl are actually *simpler* than those in the simple VMλ, because the type $\texttt{view}\{\}\tau$ of views are integrated into the type $\texttt{view}\{l^* : \tau^*\}\tau$ of view constructors that are

$$\tau ::= \dots \mid \text{view}\{l^* : \tau^*\}\tau$$

$$\frac{\Gamma, x^+ : \tau^+ \vdash M_1 : \tau_1 \quad \Gamma, V : \text{view}\{l^+ : \tau^+\}\tau_1 \vdash M_2 : \tau_2}{\Gamma \vdash \text{view } V\{l^+ = x^+\} = M_1 \text{ in } M_2 : \tau_2}(\text{T-VDef})$$

$$\frac{\Gamma \vdash M_1 : \text{view}\{l^+ : \tau^+, l_0^* : \tau_0^*\}\tau \quad \Gamma \vdash M_2^+ : \tau^+}{\Gamma \vdash M_1\{l^+ = M_2^+\} : \text{view}\{l_0^* : \tau_0^*\}\tau}(\text{T-VApp})$$

$$\frac{\begin{array}{c}\Gamma(V) = \text{view}\{l^* : \tau^*, l_0^* : \tau_0^*\}\tau \quad \Gamma \vdash M_1 : \text{view}\{l_0^* : \tau_0^*\}\tau \\ \Gamma, x^* : \tau^* \vdash M_2 : \tau' \quad \Gamma \vdash M_3 : \tau'\end{array}}{\Gamma \vdash \text{vmatch } M_1 \text{ with } V\{l^* = x^*\} \Rightarrow M_2 \text{ else } M_3 : \tau'}(\text{T-VMatch})$$

Fig. 4. Type System of VMλabl

possibly partially applied, as a special case where the yet unknown arguments l^* are empty. The typing rules of VMλabl, given in Figure 4, are straightforward adaptation of those of the simple VMλ. The type soundness proof is omitted since it is also similar.

4   Translation of VMλabl into OCaml

This section explains an implementation of VMλabl, specifically, its translation into OCaml [16]. The translation itself is implemented by using Camlp4 [8], a pre-processor (and pretty printer) for OCaml. The translated code uses labeled arguments and polymorphic variants [10] (so the target language may well be called OLabl [9] rather than OCaml). Although we have adopted OCaml as the actual target language, observations in this section would also apply to other typed languages extended with labeled arguments and polymorphic variants. (We are interested in typed languages because views are originally typed [5, 17, 18, 19].)

The main ideas of the translation are as follows. A possibly partially applied view $V\{l^* = v^*, m^* = x^*\} = M$, including a non-applied view $V\{m^+ = x^+\} = M$ and a fully applied view $V\{l^+ = v^+\} = v$, is represented as a record with three fields `valu`, `repr`, and `addargs`. The field `valu` holds a function `fun` $m_1 : x_1$ `-> ... -> fun` $m_n : x_n$ `-> ` M with its arguments x^* labeled as m^*. The field `repr` keeps the polymorphic variant `'V ['`$l_1(v_1)$`; ...; '`$l_n(v_n)$`]` of a list of polymorphic variants `'`$l^*(v^*)$. The field `addargs` is an auxiliary function for allowing the translation of a view application to apply the view constructor without knowing its label.

Why do we use polymorphic variants? The reason is twofold: one is to unify the types of two views whose values have the same type but whose representations have different types (this demand precludes encodings using tuples, records, or objects); the other is to avoid unnecessary type declaration (this demand precludes encodings using exceptions or modules). The types of the arguments of polymorphic variants need not be declared, and the types [> 'V_1 of τ_1] and [> 'V_2 of τ_2] of different polymorphic variants V_1 and V_2 can naturally be unified to [> 'V_1 of τ_1 | 'V_2 of τ_2], which is indeed the main point of polymorphic variants.

One drawback of this approach is that labels of polymorphic variants are not generative, so view constructors are not actually generative either; rather, they are *applicative* [14] in the present implementation. Fortunately, however, this problem is not so significant: since view constructors can be renamed by α-conversion at compile time, the conflict of view types occurs only in subtle cases involving polymorphic functions, for example as below, and incurs only static (rather than dynamic) type errors. (As for pattern matching between different instances of the same view constructor, it may actually be even *better* to have applicativity rather than generativity.)

```
# let f x = (view V{1 = _} = 123 in V{1 = x}) ;;
val f : 'a -> int view = <fun>
# if true then f 4.56 else f "abc" ;;
  (* causes mysterious static type error *)
Characters 25-32:
This expression has type
    [> 'V_1 of [> '1 of string] list]
but is here used with type
    [> 'V_1 of [> '1 of float] list]
```

A simple way of avoiding such unfortunate cases is to apply view constructors to monomorphic values only. (This restriction would be compulsory in encodings using exceptions, since they cannot carry polymorphic values.)

Another drawback is that the notorious *value restriction* interferes with separate compilation of modules that export (possibly partially) applied view constructors, since their representations have non-generalizable types such as _[> 'V of _[> '1 of int | 'm of bool] list]. This problem is solved if a weaker restriction on polymorphism ([20], for instance) is adopted.

On the bases of the ideas above, generic rules of the translation are given in Figure 5. Further details of the implementation are omitted.

5   Related Work and Future Work

ML-Like Exceptions. The representation part of a view is similar to ML-like exceptions in that they carry arguments, have generative constructors, and can be pattern matched. Indeed, representations of views can be implemented by exceptions. (In the implementation above, we did not take this approach because of the lack of type information in Camlp4: in OCaml, exception definitions require explicit type annotations.) However, views are different from ML-like exceptions in that a view has its own value part in addition to the representation part. Nevertheless, techniques developed for exceptions, such as static detection of uncaught exceptions [15, 30, 31], can perhaps be adapted for views, for example to analyze the flow of view constructors and check the exhaustiveness (or redundancy) of pattern matching.

```
exception VMatchFailure
type ('v, 'r, 'a) view =
 {valu : 'v; repr : 'r; addargs : 'r -> 'a list -> 'r}
```

$[\![\text{view } V\{l^+ = x^+\} = M_1 \text{ in } M_2]\!] =$
```
 let W_i = generate_fresh_name_from V in
 let vml_V =
   {valu = fun ~l_1:x_1 -> ... -> fun ~l_n:x_n -> [M_1];
    repr = `W_i [];
    addargs = fun newargs ->
                (function `W_i oldargs -> `W_i (oldargs @ newargs)
                       | _ -> failwith "a bug in VMλ")} in
 let vml_V_getargs = (function `W_i args -> args
                             | _ -> raise VMatchFailure) in [M_2]
```

$[\![V]\!] = \text{vml\_}V$

$[\![M_1\{l^+ = M_2^+\}]\!] =$
```
 let {valu = vml_valu; repr = vml_repr; addargs = vml_addargs} = [M_1] in
 let vml_arg_l_1 = [M_{21}] in
 ...
 let vml_arg_l_n = [M_{2n}] in
 {valu = vml_valu ~l_1:vml_arg_l_1 ... ~l_n:vml_arg_l_n;
   repr = vml_addargs vml_repr [`l_1(vml_arg_l_1); ...; `l_n(vml_arg_l_n)];
   addargs = vml_addargs}
```

$[\![\text{vmatch } M_1 \text{ with } V\{l^* = x^*\} \Rightarrow M_2 \text{ else } M_3]\!] =$
```
 let {valu = vml_valu; repr = vml_repr; addargs = vml_addargs} = [M_1] in
 let _ = fun () -> TypeCheck in
 try let vml_repr' = vml_V_getargs vml_repr in
     let x_1 = search_l_1 vml_repr' in
     ...
     let x_n = search_l_n vml_repr' in [M_2]
 with VMatchFailure -> [M_3]
where
 let rec search_l_i = (function [] -> failwith "a bug in VMλ"
                              | [`l_i(x) :: _] -> x
                              | [_ :: r] -> search_l_i r)
 TypeCheck = fun ~l_1:vml_arg_l_1 -> ... -> ~l_n:vml_arg_l_n ->
               vml_valu == vml_V.valu ~l_1:vml_arg_l_1 ... ~l_n:vml_arg_l_n
```

$[\![\text{valof } M]\!] = [\![M]\!].\text{valu}$

Fig. 5. Translation of VMλabl into OCaml with Labeled Arguments and Polymorphic Variants

Views for Abstract Data Types. Originally, hypothetical views had nothing to do with views for abstract data types [28]. Taking a hindsight, however, it would be interesting to consider implementing hypothetical views by using views for abstract data types, because they might enable hiding the type of the representation part of a view, yet allowing pattern matching over this representation.

Generative Names. As stated before, view constructors in (the formalization of) VMλ are generative. In our formal semantics, however, fresh generation of view constructors is assumed *a priori* and left implicit. More rigorous treatment of generative names is already studied in the literature [22, 21, 26, etc.].

Extensions of Hypothetical Views. Since a view is just a pair of a value and its representation, it is straightforward to introduce *recursive views* on the basis of standard recursive types and recursive functions.

It is also straightforward to extend VMλ for remembering and pattern-matching the values of the free variables of a view definition, for example like:

```
# let x = 3 ;;
val x : int = 3
# view V{y = y} = x + y ;; (* x is free in the definition of V *)
view V of { _x : int = 3; y : int } : int
# let v = V{y = 7} ;;
val v : int view = 10 as V{_x = 3; y = 7} ;;
# vmatch v with V{_x = x; y = y} -> (x, y) ;;
- : int * int = (3, 7)
```

Views for views deserve more consideration. For example, suppose that we define a view constructor W applying another view constructor V as follows.

```
# view V{x = x; y = y} = x + y ;;
view V of { x : int; y : int } : int
# view W{z = z} = V{x = 1; y = z + 2} ;;
view W of { z : int } : int view
```

Currently, applying W yields a view whose *value* is another view.

```
# let v = W{z = 3} ;;
val v : int view view = (6 as V{x = 1; y = 5}) as W{z = 3} ;;
# vmatch v with W{z = z} -> z ;;
- : int = 3
# vmatch v with V{x = x; y = y} -> (x, y) ;;
Uncaught exception: VMatchFailure.
# vmatch (valof v) with V{x = x; y = y} -> (x, y) ;;
- : int * int = (1, 5)
```

However, it may be useful if one can pattern match this view *both* with V and with W, for example as follows.

```
# let v = W{z = 3} ;;
val v : int view = 6 as V{x = 1; y = 5} and W{z = 3} ;;
# vmatch v with W{z = z} -> z ;;
```

```
- : int = 3
# vmatch v with V{x = x; y = y} -> (x, y) ;;
- : int * int = (1, 5)
```
As for fully applied views, this extension is straightforwardly realizable by re-membering a *list* of representations. As for partially applied views, however, the extension is more subtle for the same reason as pattern matching over λ-abstracted views was problematic in the original VML (cf. Section 3).

Other Directions. Real examples[1] of scientific knowledge discovery using the notion of views can be found in previous work [4, 5, 17, 18, 19]. Using VMλ, we also plan to attempt other novel knowledge discovery tasks with different data sets. A more user-friendly interface to the language for non-programmers is a future topic of research interest as well.

References

[1] Setsuo Arikawa and Koichi Furukawa, editors. *Proceedings of the Second Interna-tional Conference on Discovery Science*, volume 1721 of *Lecture Notes in Artificial Intelligence*. Springer-Verlag, 1999. 290, 304

[2] Setsuo Arikawa and Shinichi Morishita, editors. *Proceedings of the Third Interna-tional Conference on Discovery Science*, volume 1967 of *Lecture Notes in Artificial Intelligence*. Springer-Verlag, 2000. 290

[3] Setsuo Arikawa and Hiroshi Motoda, editors. *Proceedings of the First Interna-tional Conference on Discovery Science*, volume 1532 of *Lecture Notes in Artificial Intelligence*. Springer-Verlag, 1998. 290, 304

[4] Hideo Bannai, Yoshinori Tamada, Osamu Maruyama, and Satoru Miyano. VML: A view modeling language for computational knowledge discovery. In *Proceed-ings of the Fourth International Conference on Discovery Science*, volume 2226 of *Lecture Notes in Artificial Intelligence*, pages 30–44, 2001. 292, 293, 297, 303

[5] Hideo Bannai, Yoshinori Tamada, Osamu Maruyama, Kenta Nakai, and Satoru Miyano. Views: Fundamental building blocks in the process of knowledge discov-ery. In *Proceedings of the 14th International FLAIRS Conference*, pages 233–238. AAAI Press, 2001. 293, 299, 303

[6] Olivier Danvy. Type-directed partial evaluation. In *Proceedings of the 23rd ACM SIGPLAN-SIGACT Symposium on Principles of Programming Languages*, pages 242–257, 1996. 292

[7] Olivier Danvy. Type-directed partial evaluation. In *Partial Evaluation – Practice and Theory*, volume 1706 of *Lecture Notes in Computer Science*, pages 367–411. Springer-Verlag, 1999. 292

[8] Daniel de Rauglaudre. Camlp4. http://caml.inria.fr/camlp4/. 293, 299

[9] Jacques Garrigue. OLabl. http://wwwfun.kurims.kyoto-u.ac.jp/soft/olabl/. 299

[10] Jacques Garrigue. Programming with polymorphic variants. In *Proceedings of the 1998 ACM SIGPLAN Workshop on ML*, 1998. 299

[11] Jacques Garrigue and Hassan Aït-Kaci. The typed polymorphic label-selective lambda-calculus. In *Proceedings of the 21st ACM SIGPLAN-SIGACT Symposium on Principles of Programming Languages*, pages 35–47, 1994. 296, 297

---

[1] which could not be presented in this paper because of the limited space

[12] Haskell in practice (applications written in Haskell). http://www.haskell.org/practice.html. 290

[13] John Hughes. Why functional programming matters. *Computer Journal*, 32(2):98–107, 1989. 290

[14] Xavier Leroy. Applicative functors and fully transparent higher-order modules. In *Proceedings of the 22th ACM SIGPLAN-SIGACT Symposium on Principles of Programming Languages*, 1995. 300

[15] Xavier Leroy and Francois Pessaux. Type-based analysis of uncaught exceptions. *ACM Transactions on Programming Languages and Systems*, 22(2):340–377, 2000. An extended abstract appeared in *Proceedings of the 26th ACM SIGPLAN-SIGACT Symposium on Principles of Programming Languages*, 1999, pages 276–290. 300

[16] Xavier Leroy et al. Objective Caml. http://caml.inria.fr/ocaml/. 291, 299

[17] Osamu Maruyama and Satoru Miyano. Design aspects of discovery systems. *IEICE Transactions in Information and Systems*, E83-D(1):61–70, 2000. 293, 299, 303

[18] Osamu Maruyama, Tomoyuki Uchida, Takayoshi Shoudai, and Satoru Miyano. Toward genomic hypothesis creator: View designer for discovery. In Arikawa and Motoda [3], pages 105–116. 293, 299, 303

[19] Osamu Maruyama, Tomoyuki Uchida, Kim Lan Sim, and Satoru Miyano. Designing views in hypothesiscreator: System for assisting in discovery. In Arikawa and Furukawa [1], pages 115–127. 293, 299, 303

[20] Atsushi Ohori and Nobuaki Yoshida. Type inference with rank 1 polymorphism for type-directed compilation of ML. In *Proceedings of the Fourth ACM SIGPLAN International Conference on Functional Programming*, pages 160–171, 1999. 300

[21] Claudio V. Russo. *Types For Modules*. PhD thesis, University of Edinburgh, 1998. http://www.dcs.ed.ac.uk/home/cvr/ECS-LFCS-98-389.html. 302

[22] Ian Stark. *Names and Higher-Order Functions*. PhD thesis, University of Cambridge, 1994. http://www.dcs.ed.ac.uk/home/stark/publications/thesis.html. 302

[23] Basile Starynkevitch et al. Our users' achievements (significant applications written in Caml). http://caml.inria.fr/users_programs-eng.html. 290

[24] Gerd Stolpmann. The O'Caml link database. http://www.npc.de/ocaml/linkdb. 290

[25] Eijiro Sumii and Hideo Bannai. VMλ: A functional calculus for scientific discovery. http://www.yl.is.s.u-tokyo.ac.jp/ sumii/pub/vml.ps.gz, 2001. 296

[26] Eijiro Sumii and Benjamin Pierce. Logical relations for encryption. In *14th IEEE Computer Security Foundations Workshop*, pages 256–269, 2001. 302

[27] Philip Wadler. Functional programming in the real world. http://cm.bell-labs.com/cm/cs/who/wadler/realworld/. 290

[28] Philip Wadler. Views: a way for pattern matching to cohabit with data abstraction. In *Proceedings of the 14th ACM SIGPLAN-SIGACT Symposium on Principles of Programming Languages*, pages 307–313, 1987. 292, 302

[29] Philip Wadler. Functional programming: An angry half-dozen. *SIGPLAN Notices*, 33(2):25–30, 1998. 290

[30] Kwangkeun Yi. An abstract interpretation for estimating uncaught exceptions in Standard ML programs. *Science of Computer Programming*, 31(1):147–173, 1998. 300

[31] Kwangkeun Yi and Sukyoung Ryu. A cost-effective estimation of uncaught exceptions in SML programs. *Theoretical Computer Science*. To appear. 300

Author Index

Lecture Notes in Computer Science

For information about Vols. 1–2387
please contact your bookseller or Springer-Verlag